THE WISDOM OF CONSERVATISM

/\

THE

WISDOM OF

CONSERVATISM

EDITED BY
PETER WITONSKI

Volume III

ARLINGTON HOUSE   New Rochelle, N.Y.

Library of Congress Catalog Card Number 71-157758

ISBN 0-87000-118-3

MANUFACTURED IN THE UNITED STATES OF AMERICA BY HADDON CRAFTSMEN, INC., SCRANTON, PA.

ALEXIS CHARLES HENRI CLÉREL DE TOCQUEVILLE

That Among the European Nations of our Time the Power of Governments is Increasing, Although the Persons who Govern are Less Stable.

On reflecting upon what has already been said, the reader will be startled and alarmed to find that in Europe everything seems to conduce to the indefinite extension of the prerogatives of government, and to render all that enjoyed the rights of private independence more weak, more subordinate, and more precarious.

The democratic nations of Europe have all the general and permanent tendencies which urge the Americans to the centralization of government, and they are moreover exposed to a number of secondary and incidental causes with which the Americans are unacquainted. It would seem as if every step they make toward equality brings them nearer to despotism.

And indeed if we do but cast our looks around, we shall be convinced that such is the fact. During the aristocratic ages which preceded the present time, the sovereigns of Europe had been deprived of, or had relinquished, many of the rights inherent in their power. Not a hundred years ago, among the greater part of European nations, numerous private persons and corporations were sufficiently independent to administer justice, to raise and maintain troops, to levy taxes, and frequently even to make or interpret the law. The State has everywhere resumed to itself alone these natural attributes of sovereign power; in all matters of government the State tolerates no intermediate agent between itself and the people, and in general business it directs the people by its own immediate influence. I am far from blaming this concentration of power, I simply point it out.

At the same period a great number of secondary powers existed in Europe, which represented local interests and administered local affairs. Most of these local authorities have already disappeared; all are speedily tending to disappear, or to fall into the most complete dependance. From one end of Europe to the other the privileges of the nobility, the liberties of cities, and the powers of provincial bodies, are either destroyed or upon the verge of destruction.

Europe has endured, in the course of the last half century, many revolutions and counter-revolutions which have agitated it in opposite directions: but all these perturbations resemble each other in one respect—they have all shaken or destroyed the secondary powers of government. The local privileges which the French did not abolish in the countries they conquered, have finally succumbed to the policy of the princes who conquered the French. Those princes rejected all the innovations of the French revolution except centralization: that is the only principle they consented to receive from such a source.

My object is to remark, that all these various rights, which have been successively wrested, in our time, from classes, corporations, and individuals, have not served to raise new secondary powers on a more democratic basis, but have uniformly been concentrated in the hands of the sovereign. Everywhere the State acquires more and more direct control over the humblest members of the community, and a more exclusive power of governing each of them in his smallest concerns.*

---

*This gradual weakening of individuals in relation to society at large may be traced in a thousand ways. I shall select from among these examples one derived from the law of wills.

Almost all the charitable establishments of Europe were formerly in the hands of private persons or of corporations; they are now almost all dependant on the supreme government, and in many countries are actually administered by that power. The State almost exclusively undertakes to supply bread to the hungry, assistance and shelter to the sick, work to the idle, and to act as the sole reliever of all kind of misery.

Education, as well as charity, is become in most countries at the present day a national concern. The State receives, and often takes the child from the arms of the mother, to hand it over to official agents: the State undertakes to train the heart and to instruct the mind of each generation. Uniformity prevails in the courses of public instruction as in everything else; diversity, as well as freedom, are disappearing day by day.

Nor do I hesitate to affirm, that among almost all the Christian nations of our days, Catholic as well as Protestant, religion is in danger of falling into the hands of the government. Not that rulers are over-jealous of the right of settling points of doctrine, but they get more and more hold upon the will of those by whom doctrines are expounded; they deprive the clergy of their property, and pay them by salaries;

In aristocracies it is common to profess the greatest reverence for the last testamentary dispositions of a man; this feeling sometimes even became superstitious among the elder nations of Europe: the power of the State, far from interfering with the caprices of a dying man, gave full force to the very least of them, and insured to him a perpetual power.

When all living men are enfeebled, the will of the dead is less respected: it is circumscribed within a narrow range, beyond which it is annulled or checked by the supreme power of the laws. In the middle ages, testamentary power had, so to speak, no limits: among the French at the present day, a man cannot distribute his fortune among his children without the interference of the State: after having domineered over a whole life, the law insists upon regulating the very last act of it.

they divert to their own use the influence of the priesthood, they make them their own ministers—often their own servants—and by this alliance with religion they reach the inner depths of the soul of man.*

But this is as yet only one side of the picture. The authority of government has not only spread, as we have just seen, throughout the sphere of all existing powers, till that sphere can no longer contain it, but it goes further, and invades the domain heretofore reserved to private independence. A multitude of actions, which were formerly entirely beyond the control of the public administration, have been subjected to that control in our time, and the number of them is constantly increasing.

Among aristocratic nations the supreme government usually contented itself with managing and superintending the community in whatever directly and ostensibly concerned the national honour; but in all other respects the people were left to work out their own free will. Among these nations the government often seemed to forget that there is a point at which the faults and the sufferings of private persons involve the general prosperity, and that to prevent the ruin of a private individual must sometimes be a matter of public importance.

The democratic nations of our time lean to the opposite extreme. It is evident that most of our rulers will not content themselves with governing the people collectively; it would seem as if they thought

---

*In proportion as the duties of the central power are augmented, the number of public officers by whom that power is represented must increase also. They form a nation in each nation; and as they share the stability of the government, they more and more fill up the place of an aristocracy.

In almost every part of Europe the government rules in two ways; it rules one portion of the community by the fear which they entertain of its agents, and the other by the hope they have of becoming its agents.

themselves responsible for the actions and private condition of their subjects—as if they had undertaken to guide and to instruct each of them in the various incidents of life, and to secure their happiness quite independently of their own consent. On the other hand private individuals grow more and more apt to look upon the supreme power in the same light; they invoke its assistance in all their necessities, and they fix their eyes upon the administration as their mentor or their guide.

I assert that there is no country in Europe in which the public administration has not become, not only more centralized, but more inquisitive and more minute: it everywhere interferes in private concerns more than it did; it regulates more undertakings, and undertakings of a lesser kind; and it gains a firmer footing every day about, above, and around all private persons, to assist, to advise, and to coerce them.

Formerly a sovereign lived upon the income of his lands, or the revenue of his taxes; this is no longer the case now that his wants have increased as well as his power. Under the same circumstances which formerly compelled a prince to put on a new tax, he now has recourse to a loan. Thus the State gradually becomes the debtor of most of the wealthier members of the community, and centralizes the largest amounts of capital in its own hands.

Small capital is drawn into its keeping by another method. As men are intermingled and conditions become more equal, the poor have more resources, more education, and more desires; they conceive the notion of bettering their condition, and this teaches them to save. These savings are daily producing an infinite number of small capitals, the slow and gradual produce of labour, which are always increasing. But the greater part of this money would be unproductive if it remained scattered in the hands of its owners. This circumstance has given rise to a philanthropic institution, which will soon become, if I am not mistaken, one of our most important political institutions. Some charitable persons conceived the notion of collecting the savings of the poor and placing them out at interest. In some countries these benevolent associations are still completely distinct from the state; but in almost all they manifestly tend to identify themselves with the government; and in some of them the government has superseded them, taking upon itself the enormous task of centralizing in one place, and putting out at interest on its own responsibility, the daily savings of many millions of the working classes.

Thus the State draws to itself the wealth of the rich by loans, and has the poor man's mite at its disposal in the savings' banks. The wealth of the country is perpetually flowing around the government and passing through its hands; the accumulation increases in the same proportion as the equality of conditions; for in a democratic country the State alone inspires private individuals with confidence, because the State alone appears to be endowed with strength and durability.*

Thus the sovereign does not confine himself to the management of the public treasury; he interferes in private money-matters; he is the superior, and often

---

*On the one hand the taste for worldly welfare is perpetually increasing, and on the other the government gets more and more complete possession of the sources of that welfare.

Thus men are following two separate roads to servitude: the taste for their own welfare withholds them from taking a part in the government, and their love of that welfare places them in closer dependance upon those who govern.

the master, of all the members of the community; and, in addition to this, he assumes the part of their steward and paymaster.

The central power not only fulfils of itself the whole of the duties formerly discharged by various authorities—extending those duties, and surpassing those authorities—but it performs them with more alertness, strength, and independence than it displayed before. All the governments of Europe have in our time singularly improved the science of administration: they do more things, and they do everything with more order, more celerity, and at less expense; they seem to be constantly enriched by all the experience of which they have stripped private persons. From day to day the princes of Europe hold their subordinate officers under stricter control, and they invent new methods for guiding them more closely, and inspecting them with less trouble. Not content with managing everything by their agents, they undertake to manage the conduct of their agents in everything: so that the public administration not only depends upon one and the same power, but it is more and more confined to one spot and concentrated in the same hands. The government centralizes its agency while it increases its prerogative—hence a two-fold increase of strength.

In examining the ancient constitution of the judicial power, among most European nations, two things strike the mind—the independence of that power, and the extent of its functions. Not only did the courts of justice decide almost all differences between private persons, but in very many cases they acted as arbiters between private persons and the State.

I do not here allude to the political and administrative offices which courts of judicature had in some countries usurped, but to the judicial office common to them all. In most of the countries of Europe, there were, and there still are, many private rights, connected for the most part with the general right of property, which stood under the protection of the courts of justice, and which the State could not violate without their sanction. It was this semi-political power which mainly distinguished the European courts of judicature from all others; for all nations have had judges, but all have not invested their judges with the same privileges.

Upon examining what is now occurring among the democratic nations of Europe which are called free, as well as among the others, it will be observed that new and more dependant courts are everywhere springing up by the side of the old ones, for the express purpose of deciding, by an extraordinary jurisdiction, such litigated matters as may arise between the government and private persons. The elder judicial power retains its independence, but its jurisdiction is narrowed; and there is a growing tendency to reduce it to be exclusively the arbiter between private interests.

The number of these special courts of justice is continually increasing, and their functions increase likewise. Thus the government is more and more absolved from the necessity of subjecting its policy and its rights to the sanction of another power. As judges cannot be dispensed with, at least the State is to select them, and always to hold them under its control; so that, between the government and private individuals, they place the effigy of justice rather than justice itself. The State is not satisfied with drawing all concerns to itself, but it acquires an ever-increasing power of deciding on them all without restriction and without appeal.*

There exists among the modern nations of Europe one great cause, independent of all those which have already been pointed out, which perpetually contributes to extend the agency or to strengthen the prerogative of the supreme power, though it has not been sufficiently attended to: I mean the growth of manufactures, which is fostered by the progress of social equality. Manufactures generally collect a multitude of men on the same spot, among whom new and complex relations spring up. These men are exposed by their calling to great and sudden alternations of plenty and want, during which public tranquillity is endangered. It may also happen that these employments sacrifice the health, and even the life, of those who gain by them, or of those who live by them. Thus the manufacturing classes require more regulation, superintendence, and restraint than the other classes of society, and it is natural that the powers of government should increase in the same proportion as those classes.

This is a truth of general application; what follows more especially concerns the nations of Europe. In the centuries which preceded that in which we live, the aristocracy was in possession of the soil, and was competent to defend it: landed property was therefore surrounded by ample securities, and its possessors enjoyed great independence. This gave rise to

---

*A strange sophism has been made on this head in France. When a suit arises between the government and a private person, it is not to be tried before an ordinary judge—in order, they say, not to mix the administrative and the judicial powers: as if it were not to mix those powers, and to mix them in the most dangerous and oppressive manner, to invest the government with the office of judging and administering at the same time.

laws and customs which have been perpetuated, notwithstanding the subdivision of lands and the ruin of the nobility; and, at the present time, land-owners and agriculturists are still those among the community who most easily escape from the control of the supreme power.

In these same aristocratic ages, in which all the sources of our history are to be traced, personal property was of small importance, and those who possessed it were despised and weak: the manufacturing class formed an exception in the midst of those aristocratic communities; as it had no certain patronage, it was not outwardly protected, and was often unable to protect itself. Hence a habit sprung up of considering manufacturing property as something of a peculiar nature, not entitled to the same deference, and not worthy of the same securities as property in general; and manufacturers were looked upon as a small class in the bulk of the people, whose independence was of small importance, and who might with propriety be abandoned to the disciplinary passions of princes. On glancing over the codes of the middle ages, one is surprised to see, in those periods of personal independence, with what incessant royal regulations manufactures were hampered, even in their smallest details: on this point centralization was as active and as minute as it can ever be.

Since that time a great revolution has taken place in the world: manufacturing property, which was then only in the germ, has spread till it covers Europe: the manufacturing class has been multiplied and enriched by the remnants of all other ranks; it has grown and is still perpetually growing in number, in importance, in wealth. Almost all those who do not belong to it are connected with it at least on some one point: after having been an exception in society, it threatens to become the chief, if not the only, class; nevertheless the notions and political precedents engendered by it of old still cling about it. These notions and these precedents remain unchanged, because they are old, and also because they happen to be in perfect accordance with the new notions and general habits of our contemporaries.

Manufacturing property then does not extend its rights in the same ratio as its importance. The manufacturing classes do not become less dependant, while they become more numerous; but, on the contrary, it would seem as if despotism lurked within them, and naturally grew with their growth.*

As a nation becomes more engaged in manufactures, the want of roads, canals, harbours and other works of a semi-public nature, which facilitate the acquisition of wealth, is more strongly felt; and as a nation becomes more democratic, private individuals are less able, and the State more able, to execute works of such magnitude. I do not hesitate to assert

---

*I shall quote a few facts in corroboration of this remark:—

Mines are the natural sources of manufacturing wealth: as manufactures have grown up in Europe, as the produce of mines has become of more general importance, and good mining more difficult from the subdivision of property, which is a consequence of the equality of conditions, most governments have asserted a right of owning the soil in which the mines lie, and of inspecting the works; which has never been the case with any other kind of property.

Thus mines, which were private property, liable to the same obligations and sheltered by the same guarantees as all other landed property, have fallen under the control of the State. The State either works them or farms them; the owners of them are mere tenants, deriving their rights from the State; and, moreover, the State almost everywhere claims the power of directing their operations; it lays down rules, enforces the adoption of particular methods, subjects the mining adventurers to constant superintendence, and, if refractory, they are ousted by a government-court of justice, and the government transfers their contract to other hands; so that the government not only possesses the mines, but has all the adventurers in its power. Nevertheless, as manufactures increase, the working of old mines increases also; new ones are opened; the mining population extends and grows up; day by day governments augment their subterranean dominions, and people them with their agents.

that the manifest tendency of all governments at the present time is to take upon themselves alone the execution of these undertakings; by which means they daily hold in closer dependance the population which they govern.

On the other hand, in proportion as the power of a state increases, and its necessities are augmented, the state consumption of manufactured produce is always growing larger, and these commodities are generally made in the arsenals or establishments of the government. Thus, in every kingdom, the ruler becomes the principal manufacturer: he collects and retains in his service a vast number of engineers, architects, mechanics, and handicraftsmen.

Not only is he the principal manufacturer, but he tends more and more to become the chief, or rather the master of all other manufacturers. As private persons become more powerless by becoming more equal, they can effect nothing in manufactures without combination; but the government naturally seeks to place these combinations under its own control.

It must be admitted that these collective beings, which are called combinations, are stronger and more formidable than a private individual can ever be, and that they have less of the responsibility of their own actions; whence it seems reasonable that they should not be allowed to retain so great an independence of the supreme government as might be conceded to a private individual.

Rulers are the more apt to follow this line of policy, as their own inclinations invite them to it. Among democratic nations it is only by association that the resistance of the people to the government can ever display itself: hence the latter always looks with ill-favour on those associations which are not in its own power; and it is well worthy of remark, that among democratic nations, the people themselves often entertain a secret feeling of fear and jealousy against these very associations, which prevents the citizens from defending the institutions of which they stand so much in need. The power and the duration of these small private bodies, in the midst of the weakness and instability of the whole community, astonish and alarm the people; and the free use which each association makes of its natural powers is almost regarded as a dangerous privilege. All the associations which spring up in our age are, moreover, new corporate powers, whose rights have not been sanctioned by time; they come into existence at a time when the notion of private rights is weak, and when the power of government is unbounded; hence it is not surprising that they lose their freedom at their birth.

Among all European nations there are some kinds of associations which cannot be formed until the State has examined their by-laws and authorized their existence. In several others, attempts are made to extend this rule to all associations; the consequences of such a policy, if it were successful, may easily be foreseen.

If once the sovereign had a general right of authorizing associations of all kinds upon certain conditions, he would not be long without claiming the right of superintending and managing them, in order to prevent them from departing from the rules laid down by himself. In this manner, the State, after having reduced all who are desirous of forming associations into dependance, would proceed to reduce into the same condition all who belong to associations already formed—that is to say almost all the men who are now in existence.

Governments thus appropriate to themselves, and convert to their own purposes, the greater part of this new power which manufacturing interests have in our time brought into the world. Manufactures govern us—they govern manufactures.

I attach so much importance to all that I have just been saying, that I am tormented by the fear of having impaired my meaning in seeking to render it more clear. If the reader thinks that the examples I have adduced to support my observations are insufficient or ill-chosen—if he imagines that I have anywhere exaggerated the encroachments of the supreme power, and, on the other hand, that I have underrated the extent of the sphere which still remains open to the exertions of individual independence, I entreat him to lay down the book for a moment, and to turn his mind to reflect for himself upon the subjects I have attempted to explain. Let him attentively examine what is taking place in France and in other countries—let him inquire of those about him—let him search himself, and I am much mistaken if he does not arrive, without my guidance, and by other paths, at the point to which I have sought to lead him.

He will perceive that for the last half century, centralization has everywhere been growing up in a thousand different ways. Wars, revolutions, conquests, have served to promote it; all men have laboured to increase it. In the course of the same period, during which men have succeeded each other with singular rapidity at the head of affairs, their notions, interests, and passions have been infinitely diversified; but all have by some means or other sought to centralize. This instinctive centralization has been the only settled point amidst the extreme mutability of their lives and of their thoughts.

If the reader, after having investigated these details of human affairs, will seek to survey the wide prospect as a whole, he will be struck by the result. On the one hand the most settled dynasties shaken or overthrown;—the people everywhere escaping by violence from the sway of their laws—abolishing or limiting the authority of their rulers or their princes; —the nations, which are not in open revolution, restless at least, and excited—all of them animated by the same spirit of revolt: and on the other hand, at this very period of anarchy, and among these untractable nations, the incessant increase of the prerogative of the supreme government, becoming more centralized, more adventurous, more absolute, more extensive:—the people perpetually falling under the control of the public administration—led insensibly to surrender to it some further portion of their individual independence, till the very men, who from time to time upset a throne and trample on a race of kings, bend more and more obsequiously to the slightest dictate of a clerk. Thus, two contrary revolutions appear, in our days, to be going on; the one continually weakening the supreme power, the other as continually strengthening it: at no other period in our history has it appeared so weak or so strong.

But upon a more attentive examination of the state of the world, it appears that these two revolutions are intimately connected together, that they originate in the same source, and that after having followed a separate course, they lead men at last to the same result.

I may venture once more to repeat what I have already said or implied in several parts of this book: great care must be taken not to confound the principle of equality itself, with the revolution which finally establishes that principle in the social condition and the laws of a nation: here lies the reason of almost all the phenomena which occasion our astonishment.

All the old political powers of Europe, the greatest as well as the least, were founded in ages of aristocracy, and they more or less represented or defended the principles of inequality and of privilege. To make the novel wants and interests, which the growing principle of equality introduced, preponderate in government, our contemporaries had to overturn or to coerce the established powers. This led them to make revolutions, and breathed into many of them, that fierce love of disturbance and independence, which all revolutions, whatever be their object, always engender.

I do not believe that there is a single country in Europe in which the progress of equality has not been preceded or followed by some violent changes in the state of property and persons; and almost all these changes have been attended with much anarchy and license, because they have been made by the least civilized portion of the nation against that which is most civilized.

Hence proceeded the twofold contrary tendencies which I have just pointed out. As long as the democratic revolution was glowing with heat, the men who were bent upon the destruction of old aristocratic powers hostile to that revolution, displayed a strong spirit of independence; but as the victory of the principle of equality became more complete, they gradually surrendered themselves to the propensities natural to that condition of equality, and they strengthened and centralized their governments. They had sought to be free in order to make themselves equal; but in proportion as equality was more established by the aid of freedom, freedom itself was thereby rendered of more difficult attainment.

These two states of a nation have sometimes been contemporaneous: the last generation in France showed how a people might organise a stupendous tyranny in the community, at the very time when they were baffling the authority of the nobility and braving the power of all kings—at once teaching the world the way to win freedom, and the way to lose it.

In our days men see that constituted powers are dilapidated on every side—they see all ancient authority gasping away, all ancient barriers tottering to their fall, and the judgement of the wisest is troubled at the sight: they attend only to the amazing revolution which is taking place before their eyes, and they imagine that mankind is about to fall into perpetual anarchy: if they looked to the final consequences of this revolution, their fears would perhaps assume a different shape. For myself, I confess that I put no trust in the spirit of freedom which appears to animate my contemporaries: I see well enough that the nations of this age are turbulent, but I do not clearly perceive that they are liberal; and I fear lest, at the close of those perturbations which rock the base of thrones, the domination of sovereigns may prove more powerful than it ever was before.

ALEXIS CHARLES HENRI CLÉREL DE TOCQUEVILLE

What Sort of Despotism Democratic Nations Have to Fear.

I had remarked during my stay in the United States, that a democratic state of society, similar to that of the Americans, might offer singular facilities for the establishment of despotism; and I perceived, upon my return to Europe, how much use had already been made by most of our rulers, of the notions, the sentiments, and the wants engendered by this same social condition, for the purpose of extending the circle of their power. This led me to think that the nations of Christendom would perhaps eventually undergo some sort of oppression like that which hung over several of the nations of the ancient world.

A more accurate examination of the subject, and five years of further meditations, have not diminished my apprehensions, but they have changed the object of them.

No sovereign ever lived in former ages so absolute or so powerful as to undertake to administer by his own agency, and without the assistance of intermediate powers, all the parts of a great empire: none ever attempted to subject all his subjects indiscriminately to strict uniformity of regulation, and personally to tutor and direct every member of the community. The notion of such an undertaking never occurred to the human mind; and if any man had conceived it, the want of information, the imperfection of the administrative system, and above all, the natural obstacles caused by the inequality of conditions, would speedily have checked the execution of so vast a design.

When the Roman emperors were at the height of their power, the different nations of the empire still preserved manners and customs of great diversity; although they were subject to the same monarch, most of the provinces were separately administered; they abounded in powerful and active municipalities; and although the whole government of the empire was centered in the hands of the emperor alone, and he always remained, upon occasions, the supreme arbiter in all matters, yet the details of social life and private occupations lay for the most part beyond his control. The emperors possessed, it is true, an immense and unchecked power, which allowed them to gratify all their whimsical tastes, and to employ for that purpose the whole strength of the State. They frequently abused that power arbitrarily to deprive their subjects of property or of life: their tyranny was extremely onerous to the few, but it did not reach the greater number; it was fixed to some few main objects, and neglected the rest; it was violent, but its range was limited.

But it would seem that if despotism were to be established among the democratic nations of our days, it might assume a different character; it would be more extensive and more mild; it would degrade men without tormenting them. I do not question, that in an age of instruction and equality like our own, sovereigns might more easily succeed in collecting all political power into their own hands, and might interfere more habitually and decidedly within the circle of private interests, than any sovereign of antiquity could ever do. But this same principle of equality which facilitates despotism, tempers its rigour. We have seen how the manners of society become more humane and gentle in proportion as men become more equal and alike. When no member of the community has much power or much wealth, tyranny is, as it were, without opportunities and a field of action. As all fortunes are scanty, the passions of men are naturally circumscribed—their imagination limited, their pleasures simple. This universal moderation moderates the sovereign himself, and checks within certain limits the inordinate stretch of his desires.

Independently of these reasons drawn from the nature of the state of society itself, I might add many others arising from causes beyond my subject; but I shall keep within the limits I have laid down to myself.

Democratic governments may become violent and even cruel at certain periods of extreme effervescence or of great danger; but these crises will be rare and brief. When I consider the petty passions of our contemporaries, the mildness of their manners, the extent of their education, the purity of their religion, the gentleness of their morality, their regular and industrious habits, and the restraint which they almost all observe in their vices no less than in their virtues, I have no fear that they will meet with tyrants in their rulers, but rather guardians.*

I think then that the species of oppression by which democratic nations are menaced is unlike

---

*I have often asked myself what would happen if, amid the relaxation of democratic manners, and as a consequence of the restless spirit of the army, a military government were ever to be founded among any of the nations of the present age. I think that even such a government would not differ very much from the outline I have drawn, and that it would retain none of the fierce characteristics of a military oligarchy. I am persuaded that, in such a case, a sort of fusion would take place between the habits of official men, and those of the military service. The administration would assume something of a military character, and the army some of the usages of the civil administration. The result would be a regular, clear, exact, and absolute system of government: the people would become the reflection of the army, and the community be drilled like a garrison.

anything which ever before existed in the world: our contemporaries will find no prototype of it in their memories. I am trying myself to choose an expression which will accurately convey the whole of the idea I have formed of it, but in vain; the old words despotism and tyranny are inappropriate: the thing itself is new; and since I cannot name it, I must attempt to define it.

I seek to trace the novel features under which despotism may appear in the world. The first thing that strikes the observation is an innumerable multitude of men all equal and alike, incessantly endeavouring to procure the petty and paltry pleasures with which they glut their lives. Each of them, living apart, is as a stranger to the fate of all the rest—his children and his private friends constitute to him the whole of mankind; as for the rest of his fellow-citizens, he is close to them, but he sees them not;—he touches them, but he feels them not; he exists but in himself and for himself alone; and if his kindred still remain to him, he may be said at any rate to have lost his country.

Above this race of men stands an immense and tutelary power, which takes upon itself alone to secure their gratifications, and to watch over their fate. That power is absolute, minute, regular, provident, and mild. It would be like the authority of a parent, if, like that authority, its object was to prepare men for manhood; but it seeks on the contrary to keep them in perpetual childhood: it is well content that the people should rejoice, provided they think of nothing but rejoicing. For their happiness such a government willingly labours, but it chooses to be the sole agent and the only arbiter of that happiness: it provides for their security, foresees and supplies their necessities, facilitates their pleasures, manages their principal concerns, directs their industry, regulates the descent of property, and subdivides their inheritances—what remains, but to spare them all the care of thinking and all the trouble of living?

Thus it every day renders the exercise of the free agency of man less useful and less frequent; it circumscribes the will within a narrower range, and gradually robs a man of all the uses of himself. The principle of equality has prepared men for these things: it has predisposed men to endure them, and oftentimes to look on them as benefits.

After having thus successively taken each member of the community in its powerful grasp, and fashioned them at will, the supreme power then extends its arm over the whole community. It covers the surface of society with a net-work of small complicated rules, minute and uniform, through which the most original minds and the most energetic characters cannot penetrate, to rise above the crowd. The will of man is not shattered, but softened, bent, and guided: men are seldom forced by it to act, but they are constantly restrained from acting: such a power does not destroy, but it prevents existence; it does not tyrannize, but it compresses, enervates, extinguishes, and stupifies a people, till each nation is reduced to be nothing better than a flock of timid and industrious animals, of which the government is the shepherd.

I have always thought that servitude of the regular, quiet, and gentle kind which I have just described, might be combined more easily than is commonly believed with some of the outward forms of freedom; and that it might even establish itself under the wing of the sovereignty of the people.

Our contemporaries are constantly excited by two conflicting passions; they want to be led, and they wish to remain free: as they cannot destroy either one or the other of these contrary propensities, they strive to satisfy them both at once. They devise a sole, tutelary, and all-powerful form of government, but elected by the people. They combine the principle of centralization and that of popular sovereignty; this gives them a respite: they console themselves for being in tutelage by the reflection that they have chosen their own guardians. Every man allows himself to be put in leading-strings, because he sees that it is not a person or a class of persons, but the people at large that holds the end of his chain.

By this system the people shake off their state of dependence just long enough to select their master, and then relapse into it again. A great many persons at the present day are quite contented with this sort of compromise between administrative despotism and the sovereignty of the people; and they think they have done enough for the protection of individual freedom when they have surrendered it to the power of the nation at large. This does not satisfy me: the nature of him I am to obey signifies less to me than the fact of extorted obedience.

I do not however deny that a constitution of this kind appears to me to be infinitely preferable to one, which, after having concentrated all the powers of government, should vest them in the hands of an irresponsible person or body of persons. Of all the forms which democratic despotism could assume, the latter would assuredly be the worst.

When the sovereign is elective, or narrowly watched by a legislature which is really elective and independent, the oppression which he exercises over individuals is sometimes greater, but it is always less degrading; because every man, when he is oppressed and disarmed, may still imagine, that while he yields obedience it is to himself he yields it, and that it is to one of his own inclinations that all the rest give way. In like manner I can understand that when the sovereign represents the nation, and is dependent upon the people, the rights and the power of which every citizen is deprived, not only serve the head of the state, but the state itself; and that private persons derive some return from the sacrifice of their independence which they have made to the public. To create a representation of the people in a very centralized country is, therefore, to diminish the evil which extreme centralization may produce, but not to get rid of it.

I admit that by this means room is left for the intervention of individuals in the more important affairs; but it is not the less suppressed in the smaller and more private ones. It must not be forgotten that it is especially dangerous to enslave men in the minor details of life. For my own part, I should be inclined to think freedom less necessary in great things than in little ones, if it were possible to be secure of the one without possessing the other.

Subjection in minor affairs breaks out every day, and is felt by the whole community indiscriminately. It does not drive men to resistance, but it crosses them at every turn, till they are led to surrender the exercise of their will. Thus their spirit is gradually broken and their character enervated; whereas that obedience, which is exacted on a few important but rare occasions, only exhibits servitude at certain intervals, and throws the burden of it upon a small number of men. It is vain to summon a people, which has been rendered so dependent on the central power, to choose from time to time the representatives of that power; this rare and brief exercise of their free choice, however important it may be, will not prevent them from gradually losing the faculties of thinking, feeling, and acting for themselves, and thus gradually falling below the level of humanity.*

I add that they will soon become incapable of exercising the great and only privilege which remains to them. The democratic nations which have introduced freedom into their political constitution, at the very time when they were augmenting the despotism of their administrative constitution, have been led into strange paradoxes. To manage those minor affairs in which good sense is all that is wanted—the people are held to be unequal to the task; but when the government of the country is at stake, the people are invested with immense powers; they are alternately made the playthings of their ruler, and his masters—more than kings, and less than men. After having exhausted all the different modes of election, without finding one to suit their purpose, they are still amazed, and still bent on seeking further; as if the evil they remark did not origi-

---

*It cannot be absolutely or generally affirmed that the greatest danger of the present age is license or tyranny, anarchy or despotism. Both are equally to be feared; and the one may as easily proceed as the other from the self-same cause, namely, that *general apathy,* which is the consequence of what I have termed Individualism: it is because this apathy exists, that the executive government, having mustered a few troops, is able to commit acts of oppression one day, and the next day a party, which has mustered some thirty men in its ranks, can also commit acts of oppression. Neither one nor the other can found anything to last; and the causes which enable them to succeed easily, prevent them from succeeding long: they rise because nothing opposes them, and they sink because nothing supports them. The proper object therefore of our most strenuous resistance, is far less either anarchy or despotism, than that apathy which may almost indifferently beget either the one or the other.

nate in the constitution of the country far more than in that of the electoral body.

It is, indeed, difficult to conceive how men who have entirely given up the habit of self-government should succeed in making a proper choice of those by whom they are to be governed; and no one will ever believe that a liberal, wise, and energetic government can spring from the suffrages of a subservient people.

A constitution, which should be republican in its head and ultramonarchical in all its other parts, has ever appeared to me to be a short-lived monster. The vices of rulers and the ineptitude of the people would speedily bring about its ruin; and the nation, weary of its representatives and of itself, would create freer institutions, or soon return to stretch itself at the feet of a single master.

ALEXIS CHARLES HENRI
CLÉREL DE TOCQUEVILLE

Continuation of the Preceding Chapters.

I believe that it is easier to establish an absolute and despotic government among a people in which the conditions of society are equal, than among any other; and I think that if such a government were once established among such a people, it would not only oppress men, but would eventually strip each of them of several of the highest qualities of humanity. Despotism therefore appears to me peculiarly to be dreaded in democratic ages. I should have loved freedom, I believe, at all times, but in the time in which we live I am ready to worship it.

On the other hand, I am persuaded that all who shall attempt, in the ages upon which we are entering, to base freedom upon aristocratic privilege, will fail;—that all who shall attempt to draw and to retain authority within a single class, will fail. At the present day no ruler is skilful or strong enough to found a despotism, by re-establishing permanent distinctions of rank among his subjects: no legislator is wise or powerful enough to preserve free institutions, if he does not take equality for his first principle and his watchword. All those of our contemporaries who would establish or secure the independence and the dignity of their fellow-men, must show themselves the friends of equality; and the only worthy means of showing themselves as such, is to be so: upon this depends the success of their holy enterprise. Thus the question is not how to reconstruct aristocratic society, but how to make liberty proceed out of that democratic state of society in which God has placed us.

These two truths appear to me simple, clear, and fertile in consequences; and they naturally lead me to consider what kind of free government can be established among a people in which social conditions are equal.

It results from the very constitution of democratic nations and from their necessities, that the power of government among them must be more uniform, more centralized, more extensive, more searching, and more efficient than in other countries. Society at large is naturally stronger and more active, individuals more subordinate and weak; the former does more, the latter less; and this is inevitably the case.

It is not therefore to be expected that the range of private independence will ever be as extensive in democratic as in aristocratic countries;—nor is this to be desired; for, among aristocratic nations, the mass is often sacrificed to the individual, and the prosperity of the greater number to the greatness of the few. It is both necessary and desirable that the government of a democratic people should be active and powerful: and our object should not be to render it weak or indolent, but solely to prevent it from abusing its aptitude and its strength.

The circumstance which most contributed to secure the independence of private persons in aristocratic ages, was, that the supreme power did not affect to take upon itself alone the government and administration of the community; those functions were necessarily partially left to the members of the aristocracy: so that as the supreme power was always divided, it never weighed with its whole weight and in the same manner on each individual.

Not only did the government not perform everything by its immediate agency; but as most of the agents who discharged its duties derived their power not from the State, but from the circumstance of their birth, they were not perpetually under its control. The government could not make or unmake them in an instant, at pleasure, nor bend them in strict uniformity to its slightest caprice—this was an additional guarantee of private independence.

I readily admit that recourse cannot be had to the same means at the present time; but I discover certain democratic expedients which may be substituted for them. Instead of vesting in the government alone all the administrative powers of which corporations and nobles have been deprived, a portion of them may be entrusted to secondary public bodies, temporarily composed of private citizens: thus the liberty of private persons will be more secure, and their equality will not be diminished.

The Americans, who care less for words than the French, still designate by the name of County the largest of their administrative districts: but the duties of the count or lord-lieutenant are in part performed by a provincial assembly.

At a period of equality like our own it would be unjust and unreasonable to institute hereditary officers; but there is nothing to prevent us from substituting elective public officers to a certain extent. Election is a democratic expedient which ensures the independence of the public officer in relation to the government, as much and even more than hereditary rank can ensure it among aristocratic nations.

Aristocratic countries abound in wealthy and influential persons who are competent to provide for themselves, and who cannot be easily or secretly oppressed: such persons restrain a government within general habits of moderation and reserve. I am very well aware that democratic countries contain no such persons naturally; but something analogous to them may be created by artificial means. I firmly believe that an aristocracy cannot again be founded in the world; but I think that private citizens, by combining together, may constitute bodies of great wealth, influence, and strength, corresponding to the persons of an aristocracy. By this means many of the greatest political advantages of aristocracy would be obtained without its injustice or its dangers. An association for political, commercial, or manufacturing purposes, or even for those of science and literature, is a powerful and enlightened member of the community, which cannot be disposed of at pleasure or oppressed without remonstrance; and which, by defending its own rights against the encroachments of the government, saves the common liberties of the country.

In periods of aristocracy every man is always bound so closely to many of his fellow-citizens, that he cannot be assailed without their coming to his assistance. In ages of equality every man naturally stands alone; he has no hereditary friends whose cooperation he may demand—no class upon whose sympathies he may rely: he is easily got rid of, and he is trampled on with impunity. At the present time, an oppressed member of the community has therefore only one method of self-defence—he may appeal to the whole nation; and if the whole nation is deaf to his complaint, he may appeal to mankind: the only means he has of making this appeal is by the press. Thus the liberty of the press is infinitely more valuable among democratic nations than among all others; it is the only cure for the evils which equality may produce. Equality sets men apart and weakens them; but the press places a powerful weapon within every man's reach, which the weakest and loneliest of them all may use. Equality deprives a man of the support of his connexions; but the press enables him to summon all his fellow-countrymen and all his fellow-men to his assistance. Printing has accelerated the progress of equality, and it is also one of its best correctives.

I think that men living in aristocracies may, strictly speaking, do without the liberty of the press: but such is not the case with those who live in democratic countries. To protect their personal independence I trust not to great political assemblies, to parliamentary privilege, nor to the assertion of popular sovereignty. All these things may, to a certain extent, be reconciled with personal servitude—but that servitude cannot be complete if the press is free: the press is the chiefest democratic instrument of freedom.

Something analogous may be said of the judicial power. It is a part of the essence of judicial power to attend to private interests, and to fix itself with predilection on minute objects submitted to its observation: another essential quality of judicial power is never to volunteer its assistance to the oppressed, but always to be at the disposal of the humblest of those who solicit it; their complaint, however feeble they may themselves be, will force itself upon the ear of justice and claim redress, for this is inherent in the very constitution of the courts of justice.

A power of this kind is therefore peculiarly adapted to the wants of freedom, at a time when the eye and finger of the government are constantly intruding into the minutest details of human actions, and when private persons are at once too weak to protect themselves, and too much isolated for them to reckon upon the assistance of their fellows. The strength of the courts of law has ever been the greatest security which can be offered to personal independence; but this is more especially the case in democratic ages: private rights and interests are in constant danger, if the judicial power does not grow more extensive and more strong to keep pace with the growing equality of conditions.

Equality awakens in men several propensities extremely dangerous to freedom, to which the attention of the legislator ought constantly to be directed. I shall only remind the reader of the most important among them.

Men living in democratic ages do not readily comprehend the utility of forms: they feel an instinctive contempt for them—I have elsewhere shown for what reasons. Forms excite their contempt and often their hatred; as they commonly aspire to none but easy and present gratifications, they rush onward to the object of their desires, and the slightest delay exasperates them. This same temper, carried with them into political life, renders them hostile to forms, which perpetually retard or arrest them in some of their projects.

Yet this objection which the men of democracies make to forms is the very thing which renders forms so useful to freedom; for their chief merit is to serve as a barrier between the strong and the weak, the ruler and the people, to retard the one, and to give the other time to look about him. Forms become more necessary in proportion as the government becomes more active and more powerful, while private persons are becoming more indolent and more feeble. Thus democratic nations naturally stand more in need of forms than other nations, and they naturally respect them less. This deserves most serious attention.

Nothing is more pitiful than the arrogant disdain of most of our contemporaries for questions of form; for the smallest questions of form have acquired in our time an importance which they never had before: many of the greatest interests of mankind depend upon them. I think that if the statesmen of aristocratic ages could sometimes contemn forms with impunity, and frequently rise above them, the statesmen to whom the government of nations is now confided ought to treat the very least among them with respect, and not neglect them without imperious necessity. In aristocracies the observance of forms was superstitious; among us they ought to be kept with a deliberate and enlightened deference.

Another tendency, which is extremely natural to democratic nations and extremely dangerous, is that which leads them to despise and undervalue the rights of private persons. The attachment which men feel to a right, and the respect which they display for it, is generally proportioned to its importance, or to the length of time during which they have enjoyed it. The rights of private persons among democratic nations are commonly of small importance, of recent growth, and extremely precarious— the consequence is that they are often sacrificed without regret, and almost always violated without remorse.

But it happens that at the same period and among the same nations in which men conceive a natural contempt for the rights of private persons, the rights of society at large are naturally extended and consolidated: in other words, men become less attached to private rights at the very time at which it would be most necessary to retain and to defend what little remains of them. It is therefore most especially in the present democratic ages, that the true friends of the liberty and the greatness of man ought constantly to be on the alert to prevent the power of government from lightly sacrificing the private rights of individuals to the general execution of its designs. At such times no citizen is so obscure that it is not very dangerous to allow him to be oppressed—no private rights are so unimportant that they can be surrendered with impunity to the caprices of a government. The reason is plain:—if the private right of an individual is violated at a time when the human mind is fully impressed with the importance and the sanctity of such rights, the injury done is confined to the individual whose right is infringed; but to violate such a right, at the present day, is deeply to corrupt the manners of the nation and to put the whole community in jeopardy, because the very notion of this kind of right constantly tends among us to be impaired and lost.

There are certain habits, certain notions, and certain vices which are peculiar to a state of revolution, and which a protracted revolution cannot fail to engender and to propagate, whatever be, in other respects, its character, its purpose, and the scene on which it takes place. When any nation has, within a short space of time, repeatedly varied its rulers, its opinions, and its laws, the men of whom it is composed eventually contract a taste for change, and grow accustomed to see all changes effected by sudden violence. Thus they naturally conceive a contempt for forms which daily prove ineffectual; and they do not support without impatience the dominion of rules which they have so often seen infringed.

As the ordinary notions of equity and morality no longer suffice to explain and justify all the innovations daily begotten by a revolution, the principle of public utility is called in, the doctrine of political necessity is conjured up, and men accustom themselves to sacrifice private interests without scruple, and to trample on the rights of individuals in order more speedily to accomplish any public purpose.

These habits and notions, which I shall call revolutionary, because all revolutions produce them, occur in aristocracies just as much as among democratic nations; but among the former they are often less powerful and always less lasting, because there they meet with habits, notions, defects, and impediments, which counteract them: they consequently disappear as soon as the revolution is terminated, and the nation reverts to its former political courses. This is not always the case in democratic countries, in which it is ever to be feared that revolutionary tendencies, becoming more gentle and more regular, without entirely disappearing from society, will be gradually transformed into habits of subjection to the administrative authority of the government. I know of no countries in which revolutions are more dangerous than in democratic countries; because, independently of the accidental and transient evils which must always attend them, they may always create some evils which are permanent and unending.

I believe that there are such things as justifiable resistance and legitimate rebellion: I do not therefore assert, as an absolute proposition, that the men of democratic ages ought never to make revolutions; but I think that they have especial reason to hesitate before they embark in them, and that it is far better to endure many grievances in their present condition than to have recourse to so perilous a remedy.

I shall conclude by one general idea, which comprises not only all the particular ideas which have been expressed in the present chapter, but also most of those which it is the object of this book to treat of. In the ages of aristocracy which preceded our own, there were private persons of great power, and a social authority of extreme weakness. The outline of society itself was not easily discernible, and constantly confounded with the different powers by which the community was ruled. The principal efforts of the men of those times were required to strengthen, aggrandize, and secure the supreme power; and on the other hand, to circumscribe individual independence within narrower limits, and to subject private interests to the interests of the public. Other perils and other cares await the men of our age. Among the greater part of modern nations, the government, whatever may be its origin, its constitution, or its name, has become almost omnipotent, and private persons are falling, more and more, into the lowest stage of weakness and dependance.

In olden society everything was different: unity and uniformity were nowhere to be met with. In modern society everything threatens to become so much alike, that the peculiar characteristics of each individual will soon be entirely lost in the general aspect of the world. Our forefathers were ever prone to make an improper use of the notion, that private rights ought to be respected; and we are naturally prone on the other hand to exaggerate the idea that the interest of a private individual ought always to bend to the interest of the many.

The political world is metamorphosed: new remedies must henceforth be sought for new disorders. To lay down extensive, but distinct and settled limits, to the action of the government; to confer certain rights on private persons, and to secure to them the undisputed enjoyment of those rights; to enable individual man to maintain whatever independence, strength, and original power he still possesses; to raise him by the side of society at large, and uphold him in that position—these appear to me the main objects of legislators in the ages upon which we are now entering.

It would seem as if the rulers of our time sought only to use men in order to make things great; I wish that they would try a little more to make great men; that they would set less value on the work, and more upon the workman; that they would never forget that a nation cannot long remain strong when every man belonging to it is individually weak, and that no form or combination of social polity has yet been devised, to make an energetic people out of a community of pusillanimous and enfeebled citizens.

I trace among our contemporaries two contrary notions which are equally injurious. One set of men can perceive nothing in the principle of equality but the anarchical tendencies which it engenders: they dread their own free agency—they fear themselves. Other thinkers, less numerous but more enlightened, take a different view: beside that track which starts from the principle of equality to terminate in anarchy, they have at last discovered the road which seems to lead men to inevitable servitude. They shape their souls beforehand to this necessary condition; and, despairing of remaining free, they already do obeisance in their hearts to the master who is soon to appear. The former abandon freedom, because they think it dangerous; the latter, because they hold it to be impossible.

If I had entertained the latter conviction, I should not have written this book, but I should have confined myself to deploring in secret the destiny of mankind. I have sought to point out the dangers to which the principle of equality exposes the independence of man, because I firmly believe that these dangers are the most formidable, as well as the least foreseen, of all those which futurity holds in store; but I do think that they are insurmountable.

The men who live in the democratic ages upon which we are entering have naturally a taste for independence: they are naturally impatient of regulation, and they are wearied by the permanence even of the condition they themselves prefer. They are fond of power; but they are prone to despise and hate those who wield it, and they easily elude its grasp by their own mobility and insignificance.

These propensities will always manifest themselves, because they originate in the groundwork of society, which will undergo no change: for a long time they will prevent the establishment of any despotism, and they will furnish fresh weapons to each succeeding generation which shall struggle in favour of the liberty of mankind. Let us then look forward to the future with that salutary fear which makes men keep watch and ward for freedom, not with that faint and idle terror which depresses and enervates the heart.

SIR JAMES FITZJAMES STEPHEN

In his youth J. F. Stephen (1829–1894) had been a Utilitarian. He was to become one of the greatest opponents of Utilitarianism, and one of the most eloquent British conservatives of the 19th century. Rousseau, Mill, and Bentham were his special enemies, and he attacked them and their ideology with great enthusiasm in his *Liberty, Equality, Fraternity.* No extremist, he could neither accept the Rousseauistic anthropology or the pessimistic anthropology of de Maistre. "I believe that many men are bad, a vast majority of men indifferent, and many good, and that the great mass of indifferent people sway this way or that according to circumstances. . . ." He had no desire to be ruled by such people. "I believe," he explained, "that wise and good men ought to rule those who are foolish and bad." As to liberty, equality, fraternity: men are not free in most matters, they are essentially unequal, and they are not brothers.

From *Liberty, Equality, Fraternity* (London, 1874).

SIR JAMES FITZJAMES STEPHEN

1. The whole management and direction of human life depends upon the question whether or not there is a God and a future state of human existence. If there is a God, but no future state, God is nothing to us. If there is a future state, but no God, we can form no rational guess about the future state.

2. If there is no God and no future state, reasonable men will regulate their conduct either by inclination or by common utilitarianism.

3. If there is a God and a future state, reasonable men will regulate their conduct by a wider kind of utilitarianism.

4. By whatever rule they regulate their conduct, no room is left for any rational enthusiasm for the order of ideas hinted at by the phrase 'Liberty, Equality, and Fraternity;' for, whichever rule is applied, there are a vast number of matters in respect of which men ought not to be free; they are fundamentally unequal, and they are not brothers at all, or only under qualifications which make the assertion of their fraternity unimportant.

It is impossible to carry on speculations which lead to such results without being led to ask oneself the question whether they are or can be of any sort of importance? The questions which I have been discussing have been debated in various forms for thousands of years. Is this consistent with the possibility that they can ever be solved, and, if not, why should they be debated by any one who has no taste for a conflict never ending, still beginning, fighting still, and still destroying?

The answer is, that though these speculations may be expected to be endless, and though their results are mainly destructive, they are nevertheless of great use, and, indeed, are absolutely necessary. They can show that particular sets of opinions are incoherent, and so, properly speaking, not opinions at all. They can cut down to their proper proportions exaggerated estimates of the probability of particular systems and expose their pretensions to attain to something more than probability. Lastly, they can show how particular opinions are related to each other. And this is a wide field. As long as men have any mental activity at all, they will speculate, as they always have speculated, about themselves, their destiny, and their nature. They will ask in different dialects the questions What? Whence? Whither? And their answers to these questions will be bold and copious, whatever else they may be. It seems to me improbable in the highest degree that any answer will ever be devised to any one of these questions which will be accepted by all mankind in all ages as final and conclusive. The facts of life are ambiguous. Different inferences may be drawn from them, and they do not present by any means the same general appearance to people who look at them from different points of view. To a scientific man society has a totally different appearance, it is, as far as he is concerned, quite a different thing, from which it is to a man whose business lies with men.

Again, the largest and by far the most important part of all our speculations about mankind is based upon our experience of ourselves, and proceeds upon the supposition that the motives and principles of action of others are substantially the same as our own. The degree to which tastes of all sorts differ is a standing proof of the truth that this assumption includes an allowance of error, though it is error of a kind from which it is impossible for any human creature to free himself. It would be easy to accumulate other observations of the same sort. It is enough for my purpose to observe in general that mankind appear to me to be in the following difficulty, from which I see no means of extrication. Either they must confine their conclusions to matters which can be verified by actual experience, in which case the questions which principally interest them must be dismissed from consideration as insoluble riddles; or they must be satisfied with probable solutions of them, in which case their solutions will always contain a certain degree of error and will require reconstruction from age to age as circumstances change. Moreover, more solutions than one will always be possible, and there will be no means of deciding conclusively which is right. Experience appears to me to show that the second branch of the alternative is the one which will be accepted by mankind, and I think it is the one which reasonable people ought to accept. I think they should accept it openly and with a distinct appreciation of its nature and consequences.

As a matter of fact this conclusion has been and is accepted, though in a strangely inverted form, by many persons whom it would startle. The whole doctrine of faith involves an admission that doubt is the proper attitude of mind about religion, if the subject is regarded from the intellectual side alone. No human creature ever yet preached upon the virtue of faith in Euclid's demonstrations. They, and many other propositions far less cogently supported, speak for themselves. People naturally believe them on the evidence, and do not require to be exhorted to believe them as a matter of religious duty. If a man actually did rise from the dead and find himself in a different world, he would no longer be told to believe in a future state; he would know it. When St. Paul contrasts seeing in a glass darkly with seeing face to face—when he says that now we know in part and believe in part—he admits that belief is not knowledge; and he would have found it impossible to distinguish (at least no one has ever yet established an intelligible distinction) between faith and acting on a probability—in other words, between faith and a kind of doubt. The difference between the two states of mind is moral, not intellectual. Faith says, Yes, I will, *though* I am not sure. Doubt says, No, I will not, *because* I am not sure; but they agree in not being sure. Both faith and doubt would be swallowed up in actual knowledge and direct experience.

It is easy to understand why men passionately eager about the propagation of their creed should persistently deny the force of this argument, and should try by every means in their power to prove that in regard to religious subjects insufficient evidence may and ought to produce an unnatural effect. Their object is obvious. If an act is to be done, it is done equally, whatever may be the motive for doing it, and a probable opinion may be an adequate motive as well as demonstration. Perfect certainty of the approach of death, or a doubt whether death may not be approaching, are states of mind either of which may cause a man to make his will, and when he dies it will be equally valid whether his death was foreseen with confidence or indistinctly apprehended. But it is otherwise with feeling. A general knowledge of the uncertainty of life produces very different feelings from an immediate and confident expectation of death. In the same way the apprehension that the leading doctrines of religion may be true may be a motive to much the same line of conduct as the most certain conviction that they are true, but it will produce a very different state of mind and feeling. It will give life a very different colour.

This does not justify the attempt to give evidence a weight which does not belong to it. Our feelings ought to be regulated by the facts which excite them. It is a great mistake, and the source of half the errors which exist in the world, to yield to the temptation to allow our feelings to govern our estimate of facts. Rational religious feeling is that feeling, whatever it may be, which is excited in the mind by a true estimate of the facts known to us which bear upon religion. If we do not know enough to feel warmly, let us by all means feel calmly; but it is dishonest to try to convert excited feeling into evidence of facts which would justify it. To say, 'There must be a God because I love him,' is just like saying, 'That man must be a rogue because I hate him,' which many people do say, but not wisely. There are in these days many speculations by very able men, or men reputed to be of great ability, which can all be resolved into attempts to increase the bulk and the weight of evidence by heating it with love. Dr. Newman's 'Grammar of Assent,' with all its hair-splitting about the degrees of assent, and the changes which it rings upon certainty and certitude, is a good illustration of this, but it is like the wriggling of a worm on a hook, or like the efforts which children sometimes make to draw two straight lines so as to enclose a space, or to make a cross on a piece of paper with a single stroke of a pencil, not passing twice over any part of the cross. Turn and twist as you will, you can never really get out of the proposition that the Christian history is just as probable as the evidence makes it, and no more; and that to give a greater degree of assent to it, or, if the expression is preferred, to give an unreserved assent to the proposition that it has a greater degree of probability than the evidence warrants, is to give up its character as an historical event altogether.

There is, indeed, no great difficulty in showing that we cannot get beyond probability at all in any department of human knowledge. One short proof of this is as follows: The present is a mere film melting as we look at it. Our knowledge of the past depends on memory, our knowledge of the future on anticipation, and both memory and anticipation are fallible. The firmest of all conclusions and judgments are dependent upon facts which, for aught we know, may have been otherwise in the past, may be otherwise in the future, and may at this moment present a totally different appearance to other intelligent beings from that which they present to ourselves. It is possible to suggest hypotheses which would refute what appear to us self-evident truths, even truths which transcend thought and logic. The proposition tacitly assumed by the use of the word 'I' may be false to a superior intelligence seeing in each of us, not individuals, but parts of some greater whole. The multiplication table assumes a world which will stay to be counted. 'One and one are two' is either a mere definition of the word two, or an assertion that each one is, and for some time continues to be, one. The proposition would never have occurred to a person who lived in a world where everything was in a state of constant flux. It may be doubted whether it would appear true to a being so constituted as to regard the universe as a single connected whole.

But leaving these fancies, for they are little more,

it is surely obvious that all physical science is only a probability, and, what is more, one which we have no means whatever of measuring. The whole process of induction and deduction rests on the tacit assumption that the course of nature has been, is, and will continue to be uniform. Such, no doubt, is the impression which it makes on us. It is the very highest probability to which we can reach. It is the basis of all systematic thought. It has been verified with wonderful minuteness in every conceivable way, and yet no one has ever been able to give any answer at all to the question, What proof have you that the uniformities which you call laws will not cease or alter to-morrow? In regard to this, our very highest probability, we are like a man rowing one way and looking another, and steering his boat by keeping her stern in a line with an object behind him. I do not say this to undervalue science, but to show the conditions of human knowledge. Nothing can be more certain than a conclusion scientifically established. It is far more certain than an isolated present sensation or an isolated recollection of a past sensation, and yet it is but a probability. In acting upon scientific conclusions we are exposed to a risk of error which we have no means of avoiding and of which we cannot calculate the value. If our conclusions about matters of sense which we can weigh, measure, and handle are only probable, how can speculations, which refer to matters transcending sense, and which are expressed in words assuming sense, be more than probable?

If upon this it is asked whether there is no such thing as certainty? I reply that certainty or certitude (for I do not care to distinguish between words between which common usage makes no distinction) is in propriety of speech the name of a state of mind, and not the name of a quality of propositions. Certainty is the state of mind in which, as a fact, a man does not doubt. Reasonable certainty is the state of mind in which it is prudent not to doubt. It may be produced in many different ways and may relate to every sort of subject. The important thing to remember is the truism that it does not follow that a man is right because he is positive; though it may be prudent that he should be positive, and take the chance of being wrong. The conditions which make certainty reasonable or prudent in regard to particular matters are known with sufficient accuracy for most purposes, though they do not admit of being stated with complete precision; but the certainty which they warrant is in all cases contingent and liable to be disturbed, and it differs in the degree of its stability indefinitely according to circumstances. There are many matters of which we are certain upon grounds which are, and which we know to be of the most precarious kind. In these cases our certainty might be overthrown as readily as it was established. There are other cases in which our certainty is based upon foundations so broad that, though it is no doubt imaginable that it might be overthrown, no rational man would attach the smallest practical importance to the possibility. No one really doubts of a scientific conclusion if he once really understands what science means. No jury would doubt a probable story affirmed by credible witnesses whose evidence was duly tested. No reasonable man in common life doubts either his own senses or immediate inferences from them, or the grave assertions of persons well known to him to be truthful upon matters within their personal knowledge, and not in themselves improbable. Yet in each case, a modest and rational man would be ready, if he saw cause, to admit that he might be wrong. There is probably no proposition whatever which under no imaginable change of circumstances could ever appear false, or at least doubtful, to any reasonable being at any time or any place.

There is, perhaps, hardly any subject about which so many webs of sophistry have been woven as about this. I cannot notice more than one of them by way of illustration. It assumes every sort of form, and is exemplified in a thousand shapes in the writings of modern Roman Catholics and of some mystical Protestants. It may be thus stated. Whereas certainty is often produced by probable evidence, and whereas the propositions of which people are rendered certain by probable evidence are frequently true, therefore the weight of the evidence ought not to be taken as a measure of the mental effect which it ought to produce. The fallacy is exactly like the superstition of gamblers—I betted three times running on the red. I felt sure I should win, and I did win, therefore the pretence to calculate chances is idle. What more could any such calculation give any one than a certitude? I got my certitude by an easier process, and the event justified it. To guess is often necessary. To guess right is always fortunate, but no number of lucky guesses alters the true character of the operation or decreases the insecurity of the foundation on which the person who guesses proceeds.

It may be objected to all this that I have myself referred to some subjects as lying beyond the reach both of language and even of thought, and yet as being matters with which we are intimately concerned—more intimately and more enduringly indeed than with any other matters whatever. How, it may be asked, can you admit that there are matters which transcend all language and all thought, and yet declare that we cannot get beyond probability?

I am, of course, well aware of the fact that a belief in what are sometimes called transcendental facts— facts, that is, of which sensation does not inform us —is frequently coupled with a belief that a certain set of verbal propositions about these facts are not only true, but are perceived to be true by some special faculty which takes notice of them. This has always seemed to be illogical. If there are facts of which we are conscious, and of which sensation does not inform us, and if all our language is derived from and addressed to our senses, it would seem to follow that language can only describe in a very inadequate manner, that it can only hint at and seek to express by metaphors taken from sense things which lie beyond sense. That to which the word 'I' points can neither be seen, touched, nor heard. It is an inscrutable mystery; but the image which the word 'I' raises in our minds is the image of a particular human body. Indeed, the opinion that the facts with which we are most intimately concerned transcend both language and thought, and the opinion that words, whether spoken or unspoken, can never reach to those facts, or convey anything more than sensible images of them, more or less incorrect, inadequate, and conjectural, are the opposite sides of one and the same opinion. The true inference from the inadequacy of human language to the expression of truths of this class is expressed in the words, 'He is in heaven and thou art on earth, therefore let thy words be few.' As upon these great subjects we have to express ourselves in a very imperfect way, and under great disadvantages, we shall do well to say as little as we can, and to abstain as far as possible from the process of piling inference upon inference, each inference becoming more improbable in a geometrical ratio as it becomes more remote from actual observation. As we must guess, let us make our conjectures as modest and as simple as we can. A probability upon a probability closely resembles an improbability.

It must never be forgotten that it is one thing to doubt of the possibility of exactly adjusting words to facts, and quite another to doubt of the reality and the permanence of the facts themselves. Though, as I have said, the facts which we see around us suggest several explanations, it is equally true that of those explanations one only can be true. When the oracle said to Pyrrhus, 'Aio te, Æacida, Romanos vincere posse,' it meant, not that he could conquer the Romans, but that the Romans could conquer him, though to Pyrrhus the words would convey either meaning; and, however fully we may admit that the question whether men are spirits or funguses is one which cannot be conclusively determined by mere force of argument, it is perfectly clear that, if the one opinion is true, the other is false. In nearly all the important transactions of life, indeed in all transactions whatever which have relation to the future, we have to take a leap in the dark. Though life is proverbially uncertain, our whole course of life assumes that our lives will continue for a considerable, though for an indefinite period. When we are to take any important resolution, to adopt a profession, to make an offer of marriage, to enter upon a speculation, to write a book—to do anything, in a word, which involves important consequences—we have to act for the best, and in nearly every case to act upon very imperfect evidence.

The one talent which is worth all other talents put together in all human affairs is the talent of judging right upon imperfect materials, the talent if you please of guessing right. It is a talent which no rules will ever teach and which even experience does not always give. It often coexists with a good deal of slowness and dulness and with a very slight power of expression. All that can be said about it is, that to see things as they are, without exaggeration or passion, is essential to it; but how can we see things as they are? Simply by opening our eyes and looking with whatever power we may have. All really important matters are decided, not by a process of argument worked out from adequate premisses to a necessary conclusion, but by making a wise choice between several possible views.

I believe it to be the same with religious belief. Several coherent views of the matter are possible, and, as they are suggested by actual facts, may be called probable. Reason, in the ordinary sense of the word, can show how many such views there are, and can throw light upon their comparative probability, by discussing the different questions of fact which they involve, and by tracing out their connection with other speculations. It is by no means improbable that the ultimate result of this process may be to reduce the views of life which are at once coherent and suggested by facts to a very small number, but when all has been done that can be done, these questions will remain—What do you think of yourself? What do you think of the world? Are you a mere machine, and is your consciousness, as has been said, a mere resultant? Is the world a mere fact suggesting nothing beyond itself worth thinking about? These are questions with which all must deal as it seems good to them. They are riddles of the Sphinx, and in some way or other we must deal with them. If we decide to leave them unanswered, that is a choice. If we waver in our answer, that too is a choice; but whatever choice we make, we make it at our peril. If a man chooses to turn his back altogether on God and the future, no one can prevent him. No one can show beyond all reasonable doubt that he is mistaken. If a man thinks otherwise, and acts as he thinks, I do not see how any one can prove that *he* is mistaken. Each must act as he thinks best, and if he is wrong so much the worse for him. We stand on a mountain pass in the midst of whirling snow and blinding mist, through which we get glimpses now and then of paths which may be deceptive. If we stand still, we shall be frozen to death. If we take the wrong road, we shall be dashed to pieces. We do not certainly know whether there is any right one. What must we do? 'Be strong and of a good courage.'* Act for the best, hope for the best, and take what comes. Above all, let us dream no dreams, and tell no lies, but go our way, wherever it may lead, with our eyes open and our heads erect. If death ends all, we cannot meet it better. If not, let us enter whatever may be the next scene like honest men, with no sophistry in our mouths and no masks on our faces.

*Deuteronomy, xxxi. 6 and 7. 'Be strong and of a good courage, fear not nor be afraid of them.' It is the charge of Moses to Joshua.

SIR HENRY JAMES SUMNER MAINE

Sir Henry Sumner Maine (1822–1888), along with J. F. Stephen, was one of the leading Tory theorists of the latter part of the 19th century. As a legal scholar he had no equal, and was to have a wide influence in Europe and America, as well as in Britain. His *Ancient Law,* in particular, was widely read and commented upon in France and Germany. His classic treatise *On Popular Government* (1886) carries on the traditional conservative concern over the relationship between liberty and equality, as well as a masterly account of the American Constitution. An open-minded and undogmatic writer, Maine has never been more meaningful than he is today.

From *On Popular Government* (London, 1886).

SIR HENRY JAMES SUMNER MAINE

Liberty and Equality

Political liberty, said Hobbes, is political power.
When a man burns to be free, he is not longing for the
"desolate freedom of the wild ass"; what he wants is
a share of political government. But, in wide democracies, political power is minced into morsels, and
each man's portion of it is almost infinitesimally
small. One of the first results of this political commi-
nution is described by Mr. Justice Stephen in a work[7]
of earlier date than that which I have quoted above.
It is that two of the historical watchwords of Democracy exclude one another, and that, where there is
political Liberty, there can be no Equality.

> The man who can sweep the greatest number of frag-
> ments of political power into one heap will govern the rest.
> The strongest man in one form or another will always
> rule. If the government is a military one, the qualities
> which make a man a great soldier will make him a ruler.
> If the government is a monarchy, the qualities which
> kings value in counsellors, in administrators, in generals,
> will give power. In a pure democracy, the ruling men will
> be the Wire-pullers and their friends; but they will be no
> more on an equality with the people than soldiers or Minis-
> ters of State are on an equality with the subjects of a
> Monarchy. . . . In some ages, a powerful character, in oth-
> ers cunning, in others power of transacting business, in
> others eloquence, in others a good hold upon common-
> places and a facility in applying them to practical pur-
> poses, will enable a man to climb on his neighbours'
> shoulders and direct them this way or that; but under all
> circumstances the rank and file are directed by leaders of
> one kind or another who get the command of their collec-
> tive force.

[7] *Liberty, Fraternity, and Equality.* By Sir James Stephen. 1873. P. 239.

There is no doubt that, in popular governments resting on a wide suffrage, either without an army or having little reason to fear it, the leader, whether or not he be cunning, or eloquent, or well provided with commonplaces, will be the Wire-puller.* The process of cutting up political power into petty fragments has in him its most remarkable product. The morsels of power are so small that men, if left to themselves, would not care to employ them. In England, they would be largely sold, if the law permitted it; in the United States they are extensively sold in spite of the law; and in France, and to a less extent in England, the number of "abstentions" shows the small value attributed to votes. But the political *chiffonnier* who collects and utilises the fragments is the Wire-puller. I think, however, that it is too much the habit in this country to describe him as a mere organiser, contriver, and manager. The particular mechanism which he constructs is no doubt of much importance. The form of this mechanism recently erected in this country has a close resemblance to the system of the Wesleyan Methodists; one system, however, exists for the purpose of keeping the spirit of Grace a-flame, the other for maintaining the spirit of Party at a white heat. The Wire-puller is not intelligible unless we take into account one of the strongest forces acting on human nature—Party feeling. Party feeling is probably far more a survival of the primitive combativeness of mankind than a consequence of conscious intellectual differences between man and man. It is essentially the same sentiment which in certain states of society leads to civil, intertribal, or international war; and it is as universal as

*Politician.

humanity. It is better studied in its more irrational manifestations than in those to which we are accustomed. It is said that Australian savages will travel half over the Australian continent to take in a fight the side of combatants who wear the same Totem as themselves. Two Irish factions who broke one another's heads over the whole island are said to have originated in a quarrel about the colour of a cow. In Southern India, a series of dangerous riots are constantly arising through the rivalry of parties who know no more of one another than that some of them belong to the party of the right hand and others to that of the left hand. Once a year, large numbers of English ladies and gentlemen, who have no serious reason for preferring one University to the other, wear dark or light blue colours to signify good wishes for the success of Oxford or Cambridge in a cricket-match or boat-race. Party differences, properly so called, are supposed to indicate intellectual, or moral, or historical preferences; but these go a very little way down into the population, and by the bulk of partisans they are hardly understood and soon forgotten. "Guelf" and "Ghibelline" had once a meaning, but men were under perpetual banishment from their native land for belonging to one or other of these parties long after nobody knew in what the difference consisted. Some men are Tories or Whigs by conviction; but thousands upon thousands of electors vote simply for yellow, blue, or purple, caught at most by the appeals of some popular orator.

It is through this great natural tendency to take sides that the Wire-puller works. Without it he would be powerless. His business is to fan its flame; to keep it constantly acting upon the man who has once declared himself a partisan; to make escape from it difficult and distasteful. His art is that of the Non-conformist preacher, who gave importance to a body of commonplace religionists by persuading them to wear a uniform and take a military title, or of the man who made the success of a Temperance Society by prevailing on its members to wear always and openly a blue ribbon. In the long-run, these contrivances cannot be confined to any one party, and their effects on all parties and their leaders, and on the whole ruling democracy, must be in the highest degree serious and lasting. The first of these effects will be, I think, to make all parties very like one another, and indeed in the end almost indistinguishable, however leaders may quarrel and partisan hate partisan. In the next place, each party will probably become more and more homogeneous; and the opinions it professes, and the policy which is the outcome of those opinions, will less and less reflect the individual mind of any leader, but only the ideas which seem to that mind to be most likely to win favour with the greatest number of supporters. Lastly, the wire-pulling system, when fully developed, will infallibly lead to the constant enlargement of the area of suffrage. What is called universal suffrage has greatly declined in the estimation, not only of philosophers who follow Bentham, but of the *a priori* theorists who assumed that it was the inseparable accompaniment of a Republic, but who found that in practice it was the natural basis of a tyranny. But extensions of the suffrage, though no longer believed to be good in themselves, have now a permanent place in the armoury of parties, and are sure to be a favourite weapon of the Wire-puller. The Athenian statesmen who, worsted in a quarrel of aristocratic cliques, "took the people into partnership," have a

close parallel in the modern politicians who introduce household suffrage into towns to "dish" one
side, and into counties to "dish" the other.

Let us now suppose the competition of Parties,
stimulated to the utmost by the modern contrivances
of the Wire-puller, to have produced an electoral system under which every adult male has a vote, and
perhaps every adult female. Let us assume that the
new machinery has extracted a vote from every one
of these electors. How is the result to be expressed?
It is, that the average opinion of a great multitude
has been obtained, and that this average opinion
becomes the basis and standard of all government
and law. There is hardly any experience of the way
in which such a system would work, except in the
eyes of those who believe that history began since
their own birth. The universal suffrage of white
males in the United States is about fifty years old;
that of white and black is less than twenty. The
French threw away universal suffrage after the
Reign of Terror; it was twice revived in France, that
the Napoleonic tyranny might be founded on it; and
it was introduced into Germany, that the personal
power of Prince Bismarck might be confirmed. But
one of the strangest of vulgar ideas is that a very
wide suffrage could or would promote progress, new
ideas, new discoveries and inventions, new arts of
life. Such a suffrage is commonly associated with
Radicalism; and no doubt amid its most certain
effects would be the extensive destruction of existing institutions . . . For to what end, towards what
ideal state, is the process of stamping upon law the
average opinion of an entire community directed?
The end arrived at is identical with that of the Roman Catholic Church, which attributes a similar sa-

credness to the average opinion of the Christian world. "Quod semper, quod ubique, quod ab omnibus," was the canon of Vincent of Lerins. "Securus judicat orbis terrarum," were the words which rang in the ears of Newman and produced such marvellous effects on him. But did any one in his senses ever suppose that these were maxims of progress? . . .

It is perfectly possible, I think, as Mr. Herbert Spencer has shown in a recent admirable volume,* to revive even in our day the fiscal tyranny which once left even European populations in doubt whether it was worth while preserving life by thrift and toil. You have only to tempt a portion of the population into temporary idleness by promising them a share in a fictitious hoard lying (as Mill puts it) in an imaginary strong-box which is supposed to contain all human wealth. You have only to take the heart out of those who would willingly labour and save, by taxing them *ad misericordiam* for the most laudable philanthropic objects. For it makes not the smallest difference to the motives of the thrifty and industrious part of mankind whether their fiscal oppressor be an Eastern despot, or a feudal baron, or a democratic legislature, and whether they are taxed for the benefit of a Corporation called Society, or for the advantage of an individual styled King or Lord. Here then is the great question about democratic legislation, when carried to more than a moderate length. How will it affect human motives? What motives will it substitute for those now acting on men? The motives, which at present impel mankind to the labour and pain which produce the resuscitation of wealth in ever-increasing quantities, are such as in-

---

*The Man versus the State, by Herbert Spencer. London, 1884.

fallibly to entail inequality in the distribution of wealth. They are the springs of action called into activity by the strenuous and never-ending struggle for existence, the beneficent private war which makes one man strive to climb on the shoulders of another and remain there through the law of the survival of the fittest.

These truths are best exemplified in the part of the world to which the superficial thinker would perhaps look for the triumph of the opposite principle. The United States have justly been called the home of the disinherited of the earth; but, if those vanquished under one sky in the struggle for existence had not continued under another the same battle in which they had been once worsted, there would have been no such exploit performed as the cultivation of the vast American territory from end to end and from side to side. There could be no grosser delusion than to suppose this result to have been attained by democratic legislation. It has really been obtained through the sifting out of the strongest by natural selection. The Government of the United States . . . now rests on universal suffrage, but then it is only a political government. It is a government under which coercive restraint, except in politics, is reduced to a minimum. There has hardly ever before been a community in which the weak have been pushed so pitilessly to the wall, in which those who have succeeded have so uniformly been the strong, and in which in so short a time there has arisen so great an inequality of private fortune and domestic luxury. And at the same time, there has never been a country in which, on the whole, the persons distanced in the race have suffered so little from their ill-success. All this beneficent prosperity is the fruit of recognising the principle of population, and the one remedy for its excess in perpetual emigration. It all reposes on the sacredness of contract and the stability of private property, the first the implement, and the last the reward, of success in the universal competition. These, however, are all principles and institutions which the British friends of the 'artisan' and 'agricultural labourer' seem not a little inclined to treat as their ancestors did agricultural and industrial machinery. The Americans are still of opinion that more is to be got for human happiness by private energy than by public legislation. The Irish, however, even in the United States, are of another opinion, and the Irish opinion is manifestly rising into favour here. But on the question, whether future democratic legislation will follow the new opinion, the prospects of popular government to a great extent depend. There are two sets of motives, and two only, by which the great bulk of the materials of human subsistence and comfort have hitherto been produced and reproduced. One has led to the cultivation of the territory of the Northern States of the American Union, from the Atlantic to the Pacific. The other had a considerable share in bringing about the industrial and agricultural progress of the Southern States, and in old days it produced the wonderful prosperity of Peru under the Incas. One system is economical competition; the other consists in the daily task, perhaps fairly and kindly allotted, but enforced by the prison or the scourge. So far as we have any experience to teach us, we are driven to the conclusion, that every society of men must adopt one system or the other, or it will pass through penury to starvation.

I have thus shown that popular governments of the

modern type have not hitherto proved stable as compared with other forms of political rule, and that
they include certain sources of weakness which do
not promise security for them in the near or remote
future. My chief conclusion can only be stated nega-
tively. There is not at present sufficient evidence to
warrant the common belief that these governments
are likely to be of indefinitely long duration. There is,
however, one positive conclusion from which no one
can escape who bases a forecast of the prospects of
popular government, not on moral preference or *a
priori* assumption, but on actual experience as witnessed to by history. If there be any reason for thinking that constitutional freedom will last, it is a
reason furnished by a particular set of facts, with
which Englishmen ought to be familiar, but of which
many of them, under the empire of prevailing ideas,
are exceedingly apt to miss the significance. The
British Constitution has existed for a considerable
length of time, and therefore free institutions generally may continue to exist. I am quite aware that this
will seem to some a commonplace conclusion, perhaps as commonplace as the conclusion of M. Taine,
who, after describing the conquest of all France by
the Jacobin Club, declares that his inference is so
simple, that he hardly ventures to state it. "Jusqu'à
présent, je n'ai guère trouvé qu'un (principe) si simple qu'il semblera puéril et que j'ose à peine l'é-
noncer. Il consiste tout entier dans cette remarque,
qu'une société humaine, surtout une société mo-
derne, est une chose vaste et compliquée." This observation, that "a human society, and particularly a
modern society, is a vast and complicated thing," is
in fact the very proposition which Burke enforced
with all the splendour of his eloquence and all the

power of his argument; but, as M. Taine says, it may now seem to some too simple and commonplace to be worth putting into words. In the same way, many persons in whom familiarity has bred contempt, may think it a trivial observation that the British Constitution, if not (as some call it) a holy thing, is a thing unique and remarkable. A series of undesigned changes brought it to such a condition, that satisfaction and impatience, the two great sources of political conduct, were both reasonably gratified under it. In this condition it became, not metaphorically but literally, the envy of the world, and the world took on all sides to copying it. The imitations have not been generally happy. One nation alone, consisting of Englishmen, has practised a modification of it successfully, amidst abounding material plenty. It is not too much to say, that the only evidence worth mentioning for the duration of popular government is to be found in the success of the British Constitution during two centuries under special conditions, and in the success of the American Constitution during one century under conditions still more peculiar and more unlikely to recur. Yet, so far as our own Constitution is concerned, that nice balance of attractions, which caused it to move evenly on its stately path, is perhaps destined to be disturbed. One of the forces governing it may gain dangerously at the expense of the other; and the British political system, with the national greatness and material prosperity attendant on it, may yet be launched into space and find its last affinities in silence and cold.

SIR HENRY JAMES SUMNER MAINE

On The American Constitution

It was not to be expected that all the hopes of the founders of the American Constitution would be fulfilled. They do not seem to have been prepared for the rapid development of party, chiefly under the influence of Thomas Jefferson, nor for the thorough organisation with which the American parties before long provided themselves. They may have expected the House of Representatives, which is directly elected by the people, to fall under the dominion of faction, but the failure of their mechanism for the choice of a President was a serious disappointment. I need hardly say that the body intended to be a true Electoral College has come to consist of mere deputies of the two great contending parties, and that a Presidential Elector has no more active part in choosing a President than has a balloting paper. The miscarriage has told upon the qualities of American Presidents. An Electoral College may commit a blunder, but a candidate for the Presidency, nominated for election by the whole people, will, as a rule, be a man selected because he is not open to obvious criticism, and will therefore in all probability be a mediocrity. But, although the President of the United States has not been all which Washington and Hamilton, Madison and Jay, intended him to be, nothing has occurred in America to be compared with the distortion which the Presidency has suffered at the hands of its copyists on the European Continent. It is probable that no foreigner but an Englishman can fully understand the Constitution of the United States, though even an Englishman is apt to assume it to have been much more of a new political departure than it really was, and to forget to compare it with the English institutions of a century since. But, while it has made the deepest possible impression on Continental European opinion, it has been hardly ever comprehended. Its imitators have sometimes made the historical mistake of confounding the later working of some of its parts with that originally intended by its founders. And sometimes they have fallen into the practical error of attempting to combine its characteristics with some of the modern characteristics of the British Constitution. The President of the Second French Republic was directly elected by the French people in conformity with the modern practice of the Americans, and the result was that, confident in the personal authority witnessed to by the number of his supporters, he overthrew the Republic and established a military despotism. The President of the Third French Republic is elected in a different and a safer way; but the Ministers whom he appoints have seats in the French Legislature, mix in its debates, and are responsible to the Lower House, just as are the members of an English Cabinet. The effect is, that there is no living functionary who occupies a more pitiable position than a French President. The old Kings of France reigned and governed. The Constitutional King, according to M. Thiers, reigns, but does not govern. The President of the United States governs, but he does not reign. It has been reserved for the President of the French Republic neither to reign nor yet to govern.

The Senate has proved a most successful institution except in one particular. Congress includes many honourable as well as very many able men, but it would be affectation to claim for the American

Federal Legislature as a whole that its hands are quite clean. It is unnecessary to appeal on this point to satire or fiction; the truth is, that too many Englishmen have been of late years concerned with Congressional business for there to be any want of evidence that much money is spent in forwarding it which is not legitimately expended. One provision of the Constitution has here defeated another. One portion of the 6th section of the First Article provides securities against corruption on the part of Senators and Representatives, but the portion immediately preceding provides that "Senators and Representatives shall have a compensation for their services, to be ascertained by law and paid out of the Treasury of the United States." This system of payment for legislative services, which prevails throughout the whole of the Union, has produced a class of professional politicians, whose probity in some cases has proved unequal to the strain put upon it by the power of dealing with the public money and the public possessions of what will soon be the wealthiest community in the world. It is a point of marked inferiority to the British political system, even in its decline.

It may be thought that a great American institution failed on one occasion conspicuously and disastrously. The Supreme Court of the United States did not succeed in preventing by its mediation the War of Secession. But the inference is not just. The framers of the Constitution of the United States, like succeeding generations of American statesmen, deliberately thrust the subject of Slavery as far as they could out of their own sight. It barely discloses itself in the method of counting population for the purpose of fixing the electoral basis of the House of Representatives, and in the subsequently famous provision of the Fourth Article, that persons "bound to service or labour in one State" shall be delivered up if they escape into another. But, on the whole, the makers of the Constitution pass by on the other side. They have not the courage of their opinions, whatever they were. They neither guarantee Slavery on the one hand, nor attempt to regulate it on the other, or to provide for its gradual extinction. When then, about seventy years afterwards, the Supreme Court was asked to decide whether the owner of slaves taking them into one of the territories of the Union, not yet organised as a State, retained his right of ownership, it had not in reality sufficient materials for a decision. The grounds of its judgment in the *Dred Scott* case may have been perhaps satisfactory to lawyers, but in themselves they satisfied nobody else. It is extremely significant that, in the one instance in which the authors of the Constitution declined of set purpose to apply their political wisdom to a subject which they knew to be all-important, the result was the bloodiest and costliest war of modern times.

Let me repeat the points which I trust I have done something towards establishing. The Constitution of the United States is a modified version of the British Constitution; but the British Constitution which served as its original was that which was in existence between 1760 and 1787. The modifications introduced were those, and those only, which were suggested by the new circumstances of the American Colonies, now become independent. These circumstances excluded an hereditary king, and virtually excluded an hereditary nobility. When the American Constitution was framed, there was no such sacredness to be expected for it as before 1789 was supposed to attach to all parts of the British Constitution. There was every prospect of political mobility, if not of political disorder. The signal success of the Constitution of the United States in stemming these tendencies is, no doubt, owing in part to the great portion of the British institutions which were preserved in it; but it is also attributable to the sagacity with which the American statesmen filled up the interstices left by the inapplicability of certain of the then existing British institutions to the emancipated colonies. The sagacity stands out in every part of the "Federalist," and it may be tracked in every page of subsequent American history. It may well fill the Englishmen who now live *in fæce Romuli* with wonder and envy.

WILLIAM HARTPOLE LECKY

Conservatives have always been suspicious of novelty. William Lecky's (1804–1881) views on woman's suffrage are typical of a conservative response to a new concept. A spokesman for the landed gentry and upper-middle classes, Lecky opposed the democratization of Britain, which he viewed as a movement towards the enslavement of society. In the end he was extremely pessimistic for the future of the West, and, as Russell Kirk has noted, "Six decades later, the observer of life in Marxist states would envy Lecky's optimism."

From *Democracy and Liberty* (London, 1869).

WILLIAM HARTPOLE LECKY

The Dangers of Female Suffrage

The strong and growing interest, however, of women in political affairs, and the increased clearness with which the injustices I have enumerated were brought into relief, prepared the way for a movement in favour of female suffrage which has for many years been increasing. Its prominence has been more due to John Stuart Mill than to any other single man. He brought it before the House of Commons as an amendment to the Reform Bill of 1867, and he advocated it powerfully in his treatise on the subjection of women, and incidentally in several other works. The case has been much strengthened by many subsequent measures, which have thrown open the doors of public life to women by giving them votes in a multitude of spheres which are very closely associated with politics. The Municipal Reform Act of 1869 gave them votes in all municipal elections. The Act of 1870 gave them votes for school boards. The Act of 1888 made them voters for the county councils. The Act of 1894, which transformed the whole system of local government and vastly extended the system of local representation, abolished in all its departments the qualification of sex.

A ratepaying woman is thus constantly voting at elections, and often at contested elections, conducted for the most part in much the same way as elections for members of parliament. She votes for parish and district councils, for country councils, for school boards, and poor-law guardians. In nearly all these elections she may be a candidate as well as a voter. Large numbers of women have stood and large numbers have been chosen for such posts. Many of these elections are fought on purely political and party lines; and a vast proportion of the taxation of the country is now levied by bodies which women's votes contribute to elect, and of which women are frequently members. It is surely not too much to say that under such circumstances the *onus probandi* rests upon those who refuse to go one step further and admit them to elections for members of Parliament.

Of the reasons that have been alleged against it, several may be dismissed at once as manifestly absurd. It is said that the faculties of women are, on the whole, inferior to those of men; that there has never been a female Shakespeare, or female Handel, or female Raphael. It will hardly, however, be seriously contended that the exercise of such exalted powers is required for the average British voter, or that women have not, both in the past and in the present, shown themselves to be largely endowed with capacities that are very useful in political life. . . .

Another argument, which appears to me to deserve very little attention or respect, is that derived from the inferiority of women to men in physical force, and from the fact that they are not expected to defend their country in the battle-field. . . . Even if a possible participation in warfare were required as a qualification for voters, this would be no argument against female suffrage. Women, like men, pay increased taxes at every declaration of war, and although they do not, like the German women described by Tacitus, or like the Irish women of the seventh century, accompany their husbands into the battle-field, they have borne in all modern wars a distinct and most valuable part.

But, in truth, war and its concerns form but one of the numerous interests of national life, and there is no real reason why it should have any special connection with the right of voting. It has been said that votes represent force, as a bank-note represents gold, and that it is a dangerous thing if preponderant voting power in the nation should be dissociated from preponderant physical force. The argument is a strange one in a country where the great majority of adult men have been for generations excluded from the franchise; and it has no real bearing on the question of female suffrage, for the women whose enfranchisement is asked would form only a small fraction in the electorate, and would certainly be dispersed, divided, and absorbed in existing parties.

It has also been gravely alleged that the whole character of the female sex would be revolutionised, or at least seriously impaired, if they were brought by the suffrage into public life. There is perhaps no subject in which exaggerations so enormous and so grotesque may be found in the writings of considerable men. Considered in itself, the process of voting is now merely that of marking once in five or six years a ballot-paper in a quiet room, and it may be easily accomplished in five minutes. And can it reasonably be said that the time or thought which an average male elector bestows on the formation of his political opinions is such as to interfere in any appreciable degree with the currents of his thoughts, with the tendencies of his character or life? Men write on this subject as if public life and interests formed the main occupation of an ordinary voter. It is said that domestic life should be the one sphere of women. Very many women—especially those to whom the vote would be conceded—have no domestic, or but few domestic, duties to attend to, and are compelled, if they are not wholly frivolous or wholly apathetic, to seek spheres of useful activity beyond their homes. Even a full domestic life is scarcely more absorbing to a woman than professional life to a man. Scarcely any woman is so engrossed in it that she cannot bestow on public affairs an amount of time and intelligence equal to that which is bestowed on them by thousands of masculine voters. Nothing can be more fantastic than to argue as if electors in England were a select body, mainly occupied with political studies and public interests.

It is possible, indeed, to contend that it is unbecoming for women to take any part or interest in political matters; and it is certainly not unreasonable to contend that it is very desirable, for their own sakes, that they should be kept altogether out of the arena. This . . . was the opinion of ancient Greece; it is still the opinion of several Continental nations. It has prevailed widely in Great Britain up to the present century, and it is by no means extinct. It is, however, surely too late to oppose such an argument to female suffrage in England. No single feature of our political history during the closing years of the nineteenth century is more conspicuous than the vast and ever-increasing part which women are playing in politics. Very few political organisations in the history of the world have attained in a few years to the dimensions of the Primrose League, and the example set by Conservative women is being ardently followed in the other political parties. Women now frequently appear on the platform, and scarcely an election occurs in which they are not active and successful canvassers. It is idle to contend with accomplished and irrevocable facts. The interest of women in politics, and the participation of women in politics, already exist. The concession of a vote is not needed to make them politicians, though it might make their politics more serious and less irresponsible. Can anyone suppose that voting for members of Parliament is a more unfeminine thing than canvassing for them, more fatal to the beauty of the female character than voting for a county councillor, or a poor-law guardian, or a member of a school board?

The introduction of the ballot has also largely affected this question. It has almost taken away from elections their old turbulence, and has thus destroyed a powerful argument against female suffrage. It must, however, be added that this and some other influences have gone far to destroy the force of one argument on the other side. It used to be said, with truth, that the widows of farmers or of small householders were often removed from their homes, or were seriously impeded in their attempt to secure houses, on account of their political incapacity, the landlords and proprietors desiring the influence which the command of many votes could give them. This state of things grew out of a relation and dependency of classes which has now passed away; there are, I imagine, few cases in which it can occur.

Metaphysical arguments about supposed natural rights and about innate, universal, and unchangeable laws of nature, may, I think, on both sides be cast away. The inalienable right which, according to the school of Rousseau, every man possesses to a share of political power, and the irreversible law of nature which pronounces women to be the dependents of men, and unfit for any share in the ruling power, are equally baseless. It may, however, be truly said that where in political institutions great inequalities and anomalies are found, they may at least be expected to justify their existence by some proved utility. It is surely an anomaly that the purchase of a house or a piece of land should confer the right of voting if the purchaser is a male, but not if she is a female; that women who are landed proprietors or heads of great industrial undertakings should be surrounded by dependents and tenants who possess the right of voting through their favour, while the proprietor herself is denuded of all political power; that, in a land where the inseparable connection of taxation and representation has been preached as a cardinal principle of freedom, female taxpayers should have no voice in the disposal of imperial taxation; that women should vote for all the great public interests I have enumerated, but not for the highest public interest of all—a representative in the House of Commons. For such inequalities there are only two possible defences. One is, that women do not desire a vote. The other is, that if they possessed it they would employ it in a way which would be plainly injurious to the nation. . . .

Female suffrage in matters of education and in municipal elections has spread very widely through the whole English-speaking world; it has also been adopted by the Scandinavian countries, and several other countries allow women to vote, either directly or by proxy, in rural or communal elections. Their voice in the control of communal property is very ancient, and extends far into the Middle Ages. In the Austrian Empire this system is considerably developed, and it is remarkable that when Lombardy was annexed to Italy, many women lost a franchise which they had possessed in what was deemed the period of servitude.[1] Of purely political female suf-

---

[1] Giraud, *La Condition des Femmes,* pp. 165–66.

frage, however, there are as yet but few examples. There are, indeed, some traces in the English history of the sixteenth and seventeenth century of members of Parliament returned by female electors, and the case has often been cited of Dorothy Packington, who, in the reign of Elizabeth, nominated two burgesses for the borough of Aylesbury in her quality of lady of the manor.[2] During the Middle Ages feudal tenures were often inherited by women, and those tenures carried with them no small share of political power. Bentham has noticed the curious fact that, at a time when women were excluded from every other kind of political influence, they voted equally with men in the election of the directors of that East India Company which governed despotically one of the most populous empires in the world.[3]

In England the probable influence, either for good or evil, of a limited female suffrage based on a property qualification seems to me to be greatly exaggerated. It is not likely that it would be dominant and decisive in any field, and the tendencies it would strengthen would not be in the same direction. There can, I think, be little doubt that women are on the whole more conscientious than men—at least where the obligation of performing some definite duty is clearly set before them, and gives a serious character to their words and actions. At a time when there are many signs that the standard of morality in political life is declining, the infusion into the electorate of a large number of voters who act under some real sense of duty could scarcely fail to be beneficial. It would raise the standard of private morality required in public men, and increase the importance of

[2]See Stubbs's *Const. Hist.* iii. 454; Ostrogorski, pp. 40–41.
[3]Bentham's *Works,* ix. 109.

character in public life. It would probably be a conservative influence, very hostile to revolutionary and predatory change. It would also probably tend somewhat, though not in any overwhelming degree, to strengthen ecclesiastical influence, especially in questions relating to religious education. The wide personal experience which large numbers of women possess of the circumstances, wants and temptations of the poor would give questions connected with the social condition of the masses of the people an increased prominence in legislation, and make it the interest of members of Parliament to give them an increased share of their attention.

At the same time it can hardly, I think, be doubted that female influence in politics would tend to accentuate some tendencies which are already dangerously powerful in English legislation. Women, and especially unmarried women, are on the whole more impulsive and emotional than men; more easily induced to gratify an undisciplined or misplaced compassion, to the neglect of the larger and more permanent interests of society; more apt to dwell upon the proximate than the more distant results; more subject to fanaticisms, which often acquire almost the intensity of monomania. We have had a melancholy example of this in the attitude assumed of late years by a large class of educated Englishwomen on the subject of vivisection. That a practice which may be and has been gravely abused is properly subject to legislative control will probably be very generally admitted. But it would be difficult to conceive an act of greater folly or wickedness than to prohibit absolutely the most efficient of all methods of tracing the origin, course, and filiation of disease, the only safe way of testing the efficacy of possible preventives and remedies which may either prove fatal or be of inestimable benefit to mankind. What tyrant could inflict a greater curse upon his kind than deliberately to shut it out from the best chance of preventing, alleviating, or curing masses of human suffering, the magnitude and poignancy of which it is impossible for any imagination adequately to conceive? What folly could be greater than to do this in a country where experiments on animals are so guarded and limited by law that they undoubtedly inflict far less suffering in the space of a year than field sports in the space of a day?

The spectacle of great numbers of most humane and excellent women taking up such a cause with a passion that would undoubtedly lead them, if they possessed political power, to subordinate to it all the great interests of party or national welfare, has probably done as much as any other single thing to shake the confidence of cool observers in the political capacities of women. It is true that they are not alone in their crusade; but it is only necessary to look down any annual list of subscriptions in such societies to perceive how enormously the female element preponderates. In the administration of justice; in measures relating to distress and poverty that may be mainly due to improvidence or vice; in all questions of peace and war, such a spirit would prove most dangerous. There have been ages in which insensibility to suffering was the prevailing vice of public opinion. In our own there is, perhaps, more to be feared from wild gusts of unreasoning, uncalculating, hysterical emotion. 'Les races,' as Buffon said, 'se féminisent.' A due sense of the proportion of things; an adequate subordination of impulse to reason; an habitual regard to the ultimate and distant consequences of political measures; a sound, sober and unexaggerated judgment, are elements which already are lamentably wanting in political life, and female influence would certainly not tend to increase them.

Nor is it likely that it would be in the direction of liberty. With women, even more than men, there is a strong disposition to overrate the curative powers of legislation, to attempt to mould the lives of men in all their details by meddlesome or restraining laws; and an increase of female influence could hardly fail to increase that habit of excessive legislation which is one of the great evils of the time.

Different minds will form different estimates of the balance of good and evil in the tendencies which I have endeavoured faithfully to enumerate. It must, however, again be said that English legislation has now fully adopted the principle of conferring the suffrage on almost the largest scale without any attempt to discriminate capacity or to estimate the manner in which it is likely to be exercised, and the distinctive evils to be feared from female influence in politics are, at least partly, due to the want of political experience, and would therefore, probably, be gradually mitigated. It may be added, too, that when it is argued that it is for the benefit of the nation that a new class of voters should be brought into the Constitution, this usually merely means that the special interests of that portion of the nation are likely to be more fully attended to and represented. Women form a great section of the community, and, as we have seen, they have many special interests. The opening to them of employments, professions and endowments; the regulation of their labour; questions of women's property and succession; the punishment of crimes against women; female education; laws relating to marriage, guardianship, and divorce, may all be cited; and in the great drink question they are even more interested than men, for though they are the more sober sex, they are also, it is to be feared, the sex which suffers most from the consequences of intemperance. With such a catalogue of special interests it is impossible to say that they have not a claim to representation if they desire it.

They would probably find that, like other classes, they had greatly overestimated the value of a vote. The chief danger that befalls the interests of an unrepresented class is that those interests are simply forgotten, or at least postponed till more pressing claims are attended to. But, whatever may have been the case in the past, a review of the measures which have been carried of late years relating to women seems clearly to show that modern Parliaments are quite ready to deal with such questions. The great majority of the serious grievances under which women laboured in England have been redressed, and the practice of basing important legislation upon the reports of parliamentary commissions, before which representatives of all the interests concerned give full evidence, has secured them a certain representation. To a large number of women the concession of female suffrage would, I believe, still be extremely distasteful, as bringing with it duties and entanglements they would gladly avoid. But with the rapidly increasing prominence of women in English public life this feeling is manifestly declining, and if the demand for a parliamentary suffrage should prove growing and persistent, it is scarcely possible to doubt that it must ultimately triumph.

WILLIAM HURRELL MALLOCK

Of W. H. Mallock (1848–1923), Saintsbury wrote, "He might have seemed . . . to have in him the making of an Aristophanes or a Swift. . . . And yet after the scandalous success of [his book] the NEW REPUBLIC he never came off." Of his 27 published volumes the *New Republic,* written while he was an undergraduate at Oxford, was to remain his most famous work, and a major contribution to ultra-conservatism. Russell Kirk has rightly described Mallock as "a country gentleman . . . by inclination a poet . . . [he] turned himself into a pamphleteer and statistician . . . all for the sake of the old English life . . . —the splendid houses, the good talk, the wines and dinners, the tranquility of immemorial ways." His criticism of socialism, reveals a far greater understanding of "the enemy" than the writings of other conservatives do.

From *Aristocracy and Evolution* (London, 1892).

WILLIAM HURRELL MALLOCK

On Socialism

Socialists contend that the source of all power is in the multitude. It is impossible to imagine a greater or more abject error. The multitude, or the mass of average men—the men undistinguished by any exceptional faculties—are the source of certain powers, or rather they possess certain powers. That is true; but what may these powers be? Their most striking characteristic is their limitation. In the domain of industry the many, if left to themselves, could produce only a very small amount, which would have, moreover, no appreciable tendency to increase. In the domain of government they could initiate the simplest movements only, and carry out only the simplest measures. The powers which they actually possess under existing circumstances are as much greater than these as the man is greater than the child; but these added powers acquired by the average men, or by the many, do not depend upon average men alone. They are developed only with the development of another set of powers altogether —the powers belonging to the exceptional men or to the few; and if these latter powers were impaired, the former would be impaired also. In the domain of production and the domain of government alike, not all, but nearly all, the powers of a democracy presuppose the powers of a *de facto* aristocracy, and although they modify them, they depend upon them. Here are the two factors or forces which we can never get rid of unless we get rid of civilisation altogether—the force represented by the mass of ordinary men, and the force represented by those who in various ways are more than ordinary. Let us destroy society a hundred times over, and attempt to reconstruct it in what way we will, these two forces will inevitably reassert themselves, and reveal their existence in the form which society takes, as surely as a man's figure will give its shape to whatever kind of cloak we hang on it. These two forces at the present time attract our attention principally by their activity in the domain of industry, where they show themselves under the forms of employer and employed. In order that any satisfactory solution of our industrial difficulties may be arrived at it is necessary that employers and employed alike should each recognise the importance of the part played by the other, the nature and the extent of the other's strength, and the permanent need each has of the other's strenuous co-operation. It is hardly to be expected that between these two, serious disputes and difficulties will ever completely cease. In the interest of social progress it is not necessary that they should. What is necessary is that whatever disputes between these two parties may arise, and however unreasonable or excessive on any given occasion the claims of the few may seem to the many, or the claims of the many to the few, neither party shall regard the other as its opponent, excepting with reference to the particular points at issue; that the few shall not deal with the many as though the many, in asserting themselves, were rebels, nor the many attack the few, as though the powers of the few were usurpations. What is necessary is that each should recognise its own position and its own functions, and the position and the functions of the other, as being, in a general sense, all equally unalterable, and although admitting of indefinitely improved adjustment, not admitting of any fundamental change.

And what is true of the social forces that are in-

volved in the production of wealth, is true of those
that are involved in political government. In political government, just as in the production of wealth,
the power of the few has a root in the nature of
things as indestructible as has that of the many; and
though the few can produce progress only when the
many can co-operate with them, it is not from the
many that their power is primarily derived. In the
domain of speculative knowledge this is self-evident. The ordinary brains are pensioners of the few
brains that are superior to them; and yet the superior
brains are powerless to produce social results, except
in so far as the ordinary brains respond to what their
superiors teach them. So it is in economic production, so it is in political government. The power of
democracy is not only an actual power; it is a power
from which no society can ever wholly escape; but
never—not even when nominally it reaches its extreme development—does it, or can it, or does it ever
tend to be, a power which is self-existent. It always
implies and rests upon the corresponding power of
the few, as one half of an arch implies and rests upon
the other. The whole object of the democratic formulas popular to-day is to deny or to obscure this
fundamental truth; and no greater obstacle to general progress exists than the prevalence of the spirit
which the acceptance of these formulas engenders.
If there is anything sacred in the rights of the poorest wage-earners, there is something equally sacred
in those of the greatest millionaires; and if the latter
are capable of abusing their power, so also are the
former; but nothing will tend to prevent their abuse
of it so much as the recognition that such an abuse
on either side is possible. If there is any wisdom and
power in the cumulative opinions of ordinary men,
there is another kind of wisdom and another kind of

power in the ideas, the insight, the imagination, and strength of will which belong to exceptional men; and these last, though they may give effect to what the many wish, do so only because they represent what the many do not possess. What is required to bring our political philosophy—and not only our political philosophy but our political temper—into correspondence with facts is not to deny the power that has been claimed during this century for the many, but to recognise that this power does not stand alone, and that those other powers represented by the wealthy few are not only essential to the wealth of the few themselves, but also to the prosperity, and most emphatically to the progress, of all.

The progress of all, instead of being incompatible with the fact that the positions of all have no tendency to become equal, assumes, on the contrary, a more and more practicable aspect in proportion to the accuracy with which this fact is recognised; and that such is the case shall, in conclusion, be briefly shown by reference to the theory of progress which at present deceives the socialists. This theory, which was formulated by Karl Marx, bases itself on the fact, which is indubitable, that the industrial systems of the civilised races of the world have undergone great changes in the past, and may therefore be expected to undergo changes as great in the future. The three most marked stages in the sequence of change referred to are slavery, feudalism, and capitalism; and the practical conclusion drawn from them by the socialists is that as feudalism arose out of slavery, and capitalism arose out of feudalism, so will socialism arise out of capitalism. This argument is merely another example of those self-confusions by which the socialists are distinguished as reasoners. It is an argument which depends for its whole apparent point on the defective manner in which these various systems—socialism included—have been analysed. For, though slavery, feudalism, and capitalism differ from one another in many most important points, they happen not to differ at all in respect of that one particular point in respect of which socialism will have to differ from all three of them. That is to say, in whatever way these three systems differ from one another, they all agree with one another in being systems under which the few, the strongest, the most intellectual, the most energetic, not only controlled the actions of the average many, but received for their exceptional action a correspondingly exceptional recompense. The few who occupied this commanding position differed, at different times, in the nature of the powers which gave them the command. Sometimes it was the great fighters who were paramount, sometimes the great legislators, sometimes the great industrialists. But into whatever mould human society has been cast, with whatever circumstances it has been surrounded, and whatever kind of talent or strength has been most essential to it at given periods, the few who have possessed this kind of talent and strength to the highest degree have, as a whole, and with them their families, invariably occupied a position of exceptional wealth and power. We may deplore this fact or no, but the fact still remains, and consequently the argument of the socialists from the facts of social evolution, when reduced to its true terms, merely amounts to this—that because many social changes have taken place already, but one particular change in spite of these has never taken place, yet this particular change which has refused to take place in the past is perfectly certain to take place in the future.

The historical evolution of society, however, and the social changes that have taken place, do indeed convey to us a very important moral; but this moral which the changes convey to us is curiously different from that which the socialists draw from them. They draw from them the moral that because social arrangements have been greatly changed, therefore they can be fundamentally changed. The true moral is that, although they may be changed greatly, they can never be changed fundamentally; and from this there follows another as its yet more important corollary—that although social arrangements can never be changed fundamentally, they can, nevertheless, be progressively and indefinitely improved, but that real reforms can be accomplished only by those who abandon altogether every dream of fundamental revolution. Many reforms which socialists eagerly recommend, and many wishes which socialists entertain, may meet with the approval and sympathy of the most determined conservatives; but the error of the socialists is sufficiently indicated by the fact, already remarked upon in the course of this work, that the changes which they advocate, and whose advent they delight to prophesy, leave the possible and approach the absolutely impossible, in precise proportion as these visionaries set value upon them.

Nowhere is the impossibility of such changes more clearly indicated than in the phrases now most frequently used to indicate their specific nature—such phrases as *"the emancipation"* and *"the economic freedom"* of the labourer. These phrases, if they have any meaning at all, can mean one thing only—

the emancipation of the average man, endowed with average capacities, from the control, from the guidance, or, in other words, from the help, of any man or men whose capacities are above the average—whose speculative abilities are exceptionally keen, whose inventive abilities are exceptionally great, whose judgments are exceptionally sound, and whose powers of will, enterprise, and initiative are exceptionally strong. That is to say, these phrases, if they have any meaning at all, mean the deliberate loss and rejection, by the less efficient majority of mankind, of any advantage that might come to it from the powers of the more efficient minority. *"Economic freedom,"* in fact, would mean economic poverty; and the *"emancipation"* of the average man would merely be the emancipation which a blind man achieves when he breaks away from his guide. The human race progresses because and when the strongest human powers and the highest human faculties lead it; such powers and faculties are embodied in and monopolised by a minority of exceptional men; these men enable the majority to progress, only on condition that the majority submit themselves to their control; and if all the ruling classes of to-day could be disposed of in a single massacre, and nobody left but those who at present call themselves the workers, these workers would be as helpless as a flock of shepherdless sheep, until out of themselves a new minority had been evolved, to whose order the majority would have to submit themselves, precisely as they submit themselves to the orders of the ruling classes now, and whose rule, like the rule of all new masters, would be harder, and more arbitrary, and less humane than the rule of the old.

MATTHEW ARNOLD

In his masterpiece, *Culture and Anarchy,* Matthew Arnold (1822–1888) introduced the term *philistinism* into the modern English vocabulary. A poet of great genius, Arnold recoiled against the degradation of culture and education in 19th-century England. The philistines that Arnold railed against were the same men that Irving Babbitt blasted when he mused, "A few more Harrimans and we are undone." The spawn of 19th-century plutocratic culture, rootless, without true civilization, was Arnold's target. He had little truck with the aristocratic barbarians, children of the same sick plutocracy, or the ignorant masses. His solution: a return to conservatizing values, the classics in education, a renaissance of religion, Hebraism, and Hellenism.

From *Culture and Anarchy* (New York, 1883). Numerous editions of this work are available.

MATTHEW ARNOLD

Barbarians, Philistines, Populace

From a man without a philosophy no one can expect philosophical completeness. Therefore I may observe without shame, that in trying to get a distinct notion of our aristocratic, our middle, and our working class, with a view of testing the claims of each of these classes to become a centre of authority, I have omitted, I find, to complete the old-fashioned analysis which I had the fancy of applying, and have not shown in these classes, as well as the virtuous mean and the excess, the defect also. I do not know that the omission very much matters. Still, as clearness is the one merit which a plain, unsystematic writer, without a philosophy, can hope to have, and as our notion of the three great English classes may perhaps be made clearer if we see their distinctive qualities in the defect, as well as in the excess and in the mean, let us try, before proceeding further, to remedy this omission.

It is manifest, if the perfect and virtuous mean of that fine spirit which is the distinctive quality of aristocracies, is to be found in a high, chivalrous style, and its excess in a fierce turn for resistance, that its defect must lie in a spirit not bold and high enough, and in an excessive and pusillanimous unaptness for resistance. If, again, the perfect and virtuous mean of that force by which our middle class has done its great works, and of that self-reliance with which it contemplates itself and them, is to be seen in the performances and speeches of our commercial member of Parliament, and the excess of that force and of that self-reliance in the performances and speeches of our fanatical Dissenting minister, then it is manifest that their defect must lie in a helpless inaptitude for the great works of the middle class, and in a poor and despicable lack of its self-satisfaction.

To be chosen to exemplify the happy mean of a good quality, or set of good qualities, is evidently a praise to a man; nay, to be chosen to exemplify even their excess, is a kind of praise. Therefore I could have no hesitation in taking actual personages to exemplify, respectively, the mean and the excess of aristocratic and middle-class qualities. But perhaps there might be a want of urbanity in singling out this or that personage as the representative of defect. Therefore I shall leave the defect of aristocracy unillustrated by any representative man. But with oneself one may always, without impropriety, deal quite freely; and, indeed, this sort of plain-dealing with oneself has in it, as all the moralists tell us, something very wholesome. So I will venture to humbly offer myself as an illustration of defect in those forces and qualities which make our middle class what it is. The too well-founded reproaches of my opponents declare how little I have lent a hand to the great works of the middle class; for it is evidently these works, and my slackness at them, which are meant, when I am said to "refuse to lend a hand to the humble operation of uprooting certain definite evils" (such as church-rates and others), and that therefore "the believers in action grow impatient" with me. The line, again, of a still unsatisfied seeker which I have followed, the idea of self-transformation, of growing towards some measure of sweetness and light not yet reached, is evidently at clean variance with the perfect self-satisfaction current in my class, the middle class, and may serve to indicate in me, therefore, the extreme defect of this feeling. But these confessions, though salutary, are bitter and unpleasant.

To pass, then, to the working class. The defect of this class would be the falling short in what Mr. Frederic Harrison calls those "bright powers of sympathy and ready powers of action," of which we saw in Mr. Odger the virtuous mean, and in Mr. Bradlaugh the excess. The working class is so fast growing and rising at the present time, that instances of this defect cannot well be now very common. Perhaps Canning's "Needy Knife-Grinder" (who is dead, and therefore cannot be pained at my taking him for an illustration) may serve to give us the notion of defect in the essential quality of a working class; or I might even cite (since, though he is alive in the flesh, he is dead to all heed of criticism) my poor old poaching friend, Zephaniah Diggs, who, between his hare-snaring and his gin-drinking, has got his powers of sympathy quite dulled and his powers of action in any great movement of his class hopelessly impaired. But examples of this defect belong, as I have said, to a bygone age rather than to the present.

The same desire for clearness, which has led me thus to extend a little my first analysis of the three great classes of English society, prompts me also to improve my nomenclature for them a little, with a view to making it thereby more manageable. It is awkward and tiresome to be always saying the aristocratic class, the middle class, the working class. For the middle class, for that great body which, as we know, "has done all the great things that have been done in all departments," and which is to be conceived as moving between its two cardinal points of our commercial member of Parliament and our fanatical Protestant Dissenter,—for this class we have a designation which now has become pretty well known, and which we may as well still keep for them, the designation of Philistines. What this term means I have so often explained that I need not repeat it here. For the aristocratic class, conceived mainly as a body moving between the two cardinal points of our chivalrous lord and our defiant baronet, we have as yet got no special designation. Almost all my attention has naturally been concentrated on my own class, the middle class, with which I am in closest sympathy, and which has been, besides, the great power of our day, and has had its praises sung by all speakers and newspapers.

Still the aristocratic class is so important in itself, and the weighty functions which Mr. Carlyle proposes at the present critical time to commit to it, must add so much to its importance, that it seems neglectful, and a strong instance of that want of coherent philosophic method for which Mr. Frederic Harrison blames me, to leave the aristocratic class so much without notice and denomination. It may be thought that the characteristic which I have occasionally mentioned as proper to aristocracies,—their natural inaccessibility, as children of the established fact, to ideas,—points to our extending to this class also the designation of Philistines; the Philistine being, as is well known, the enemy of the children of light or servants of the idea. Nevertheless, there seems to be an inconvenience in thus giving one and the same designation to two very different classes; and besides, if we look into the thing closely, we shall find that the term Philistine conveys a sense which makes it more peculiarly appropriate to our middle class than to our aristocratic. For *Philistine* gives the notion of something particularly stiff-necked and perverse in the resistance to light and its children; and therein it specially suits our middle class, who not only do not pursue sweetness and light, but who even prefer to them that sort of machinery of business, chapels, tea-meetings, and addresses from Mr. Murphy, which makes up the dismal and illiberal life on which I have so often touched. But the aristocratic class has actually, as we have seen, in its well-known politeness, a kind of image or shadow of sweetness; and as for light, if it does not pursue light, it is not that it perversely cherishes some dismal and illiberal existence in preference to light, but it is lured off from following light by those mighty and eternal seducers of our race which weave for this class their most irresistible charms,—by worldly splendour, security, power, and pleasure. These seducers are exterior goods, but in a way they are goods; and he who is hindered by them from caring for light and ideas, is not so much doing what is perverse as what is too natural.

Keeping this in view, I have in my own mind often indulged myself with the fancy of employing, in order to designate our aristocratic class, the name of *The Barbarians.* The Barbarians, to whom we all owe so much, and who reinvigorated and renewed our worn-out Europe, had, as is well known, eminent merits; and in this country, where we are for the most part sprung from the Barbarians, we have never had the prejudice against them which prevails among the races of Latin origin. The Barbarians brought with them that staunch individualism, as the modern phrase is, and that passion for doing as one likes, for the assertion of personal liberty, which appears to Mr. Bright the central idea of English life, and of which we have, at any rate, a very rich supply. The stronghold and natural seat of this passion was in the nobles of whom our aristocratic class are the inheritors; and this class, accordingly, have signally manifested it, and have done much by their example to recommend it to the body of the nation, who already, indeed, had it in their blood. The Barbarians, again, had the passion for field-sports; and they have handed it on to our aristocratic class, who of this passion too, as of the passion for asserting one's personal liberty, are the great natural stronghold. The care of the Barbarians for the body, and for all manly exercises; the vigour, good looks, and fine complexion which they acquired and perpetuated in their families by these means,—all this may be observed still in our aristocratic class. The chivalry of the Barbarians, with its characteristics of high spirit, choice manners, and distinguished bearing,—what is this but the attractive commencement of the politeness of our aristocratic class? In some Barbarian noble, no doubt, one would have admired, if one could have been then alive to see it, the rudiments of our politest peer. Only, all this culture (to call it by that name) of the Barbarians was an exterior culture mainly. It consisted principally in outward gifts and graces, in looks, manners, accomplishments, prowess. The chief inward gifts which had part in it were the most exterior, so to speak, of inward gifts, those which come nearest to outward ones; they were courage, a high spirit, self-confidence. Far within, and unawakened, lay a whole range of powers of thought and feeling, to which these interesting productions of nature had, from the circumstances of their life, no access. Making allowances for the difference of the times, surely we can observe precisely the same thing now in our aristocratic class. In general its culture is exterior chiefly; all the exterior graces and accomplishments, and the more external of the inward virtues, seem to be principally its portion. It now, of course, cannot but be often in contact with those studies by which, from the world of thought and feeling, true culture teaches us to fetch sweetness and light; but its hold upon these very studies appears remarkably external, and unable to exert any deep power upon its spirit. Therefore the one insufficiency which we noted in the perfect mean of this class was an insufficiency of light. And owing to the same causes, does not a subtle criticism lead us to make, even on the good looks and politeness of our aristocratic class, and of even the most fascinating half of that class, the feminine half, the one qualifying remark, that in these charming gifts there should perhaps be, for ideal perfection, a shade more *soul?*

I often, therefore, when I want to distinguish clearly the aristocratic class from the Philistines proper, or middle class, name the former, in my own mind, *the Barbarians.* And when I go through the country, and see this and that beautiful and imposing seat of theirs crowning the landscape, "There," I say to myself, "is a great fortified post of the Barbarians."

It is obvious that that part of the working class which, working diligently by the light of Mrs. Gooch's Golden Rule, looks forward to the happy day when it will sit on thrones with commercial members of Parliament and other middle-class potentates, to survey, as Mr. Bright beautifully says, "the cities it has built, the railroads it has made, the manufactures it has produced, the cargoes which freight the ships of the greatest mercantile navy the world has ever seen,"—it is obvious, I say, that this part of the working class is, or is in a fair way to be, one in spirit with the industrial middle class. It is notorious that our middle-class Liberals have long looked forward to this consummation, when the working class shall join forces with them, aid them heartily to carry forward their great works, go in a body to their tea-meetings, and, in short, enable them to bring about their millennium. That part of the working class, therefore, which does really seem to lend itself to these great aims, may, with propriety, be numbered by us among the Philistines. That part of it, again, which so much occupies the attention of philanthropists at present,—the part which gives all its energies to organising itself, through trades' unions and other means, so as to constitute, first, a great working-class power independent of the middle and aristocratic classes, and then, by dint of numbers, give the law to them and itself reign absolutely,—this lively and promising part must also, according to our definition, go with the Philistines; because it is its class and its class instinct which it seeks to affirm—its ordinary self, not its best self; and it is a machinery, an industrial machinery, and power and pre-eminence and other external goods, which fill its thoughts, and not an inward perfection. It is wholly occupied, according to Plato's subtle expression, with the things of itself and not its real self, with the things of the State and not the real State. But that vast portion, lastly, of the working class which, raw and half-developed, has long lain half-hidden amidst its poverty and squalor, and is now issuing from its hiding-place to assert an Englishman's heaven-born privilege of doing as he likes, and is beginning to perplex us by marching where it likes, meeting where it likes, bawling what it likes, breaking what it likes,—to this vast residuum we may with great propriety give the name of *Populace.*

Thus we have got three distinct terms, *Barbarians, Philistines, Populace,* to denote roughly the three great classes into which our society is divided; and though this humble attempt at a scientific nomenclature falls, no doubt, very far short in precision of what might be required from a writer equipped with a complete and coherent philosophy, yet, from a notoriously unsystematic and unpretending writer, it will, I trust, be accepted as sufficient.

But in using this new, and, I hope, convenient division of English society, two things are to be borne in mind. The first is, that since, under all our class divisions, there is a common basis of human nature, therefore, in every one of us, whether we be properly Barbarians, Philistines, or Populace, there exists, sometimes only in germ and potentially, sometimes more or less developed, the same tendencies, sometimes more or less developed, the same tendencies and passions which have made our fellow-citizens of other classes what they are. This consideration is very important, because it has great influence in begetting that spirit of indulgence which is a necessary part of sweetness, and which, indeed, when our culture is complete, is, as I have said, inexhaustible. Thus, an English Barbarian who examines himself will, in general, find himself to be not so entirely a Barbarian but that he has in him, also, something of the Philistine, and even something of the Populace as well. And the same with Englishmen of the two other classes.

This is an experience which we may all verify every day. For instance, I myself (I again take myself as a sort of *corpus vile* to serve for illustration in a matter where serving for illustration may not by every one be thought agreeable), I myself am properly a Philistine,—Mr. Swinburne would add, the son of a Philistine. And although, through circumstances which will perhaps one day be known if ever the affecting history of my conversion comes to be written, I have, for the most part, broken with the ideas and the tea-meetings of my own class, yet I have not, on that account, been brought much the nearer to the ideas and works of the Barbarians or of the Populace. Nevertheless, I never take a gun or a fishing-rod in my hands without feeling that I have in the ground of my nature the self-same seeds which, fostered by circumstances, do so much to make the Barbarian; and that, with the Barbarian's advantages, I might have rivalled him. Place me in one of his great fortified posts, with these seeds of a love for field-sports sown in my nature, with all the means of developing them, with all pleasures at my command, with most whom I met deferring to me, every one I met smiling on me, and with every appearance of permanence and security before me and behind me,—then I too might have grown, I feel, into a very passable child of the established fact, of commendable spirit and politeness, and, at the same time, a little inaccessible to ideas and light; not, of course, with either the eminent fine spirit of our type of aristocratic perfection, or the eminent turn for resistance of our type of aristocratic excess, but, according to the measure of the common run of mankind, something between the two. And as to the Populace, who, whether he be Barbarian or Philistine, can look at them without sympathy, when he remembers how often,—every time that we snatch up a vehement opinion in ignorance and passion, every time that we long to crush an adversary by sheer violence, every time that we are envious, every time that we are brutal, every time that we adore mere power or success, every time that we add our voice to swell a blind clamour against some unpopular personage, every time that we trample savagely on the fallen,—he has found in his own bosom the eternal spirit of the Populace, and that there needs only a little help from circumstances to make it triumph in him untamably.

The second thing to be borne in mind I have indicated several times already. It is this. All of us, so far as we are Barbarians, Philistines, or Populace, imagine happiness to consist in doing what one's ordinary self likes. What one's ordinary self likes differs according to the class to which one belongs, and has its severer and its lighter side; always, however, remaining machinery, and nothing more. The graver self of the Barbarian likes honours and consideration; his more relaxed self, field-sports and pleasure. The graver self of one kind of Philistine likes fanaticism, business, and money-making; his more relaxed self, comfort and tea-meetings. Of another kind of Philistine, the graver self likes rattening; the relaxed self, deputations, or hearing Mr. Odger speak. The sterner self of the Populace likes bawling, hustling, and smashing; the lighter self, beer. But in each class there are born a certain number of natures with a curiosity about their best self, with a bent for seeing things as they are, for disentangling themselves from machinery, for simply concerning themselves with reason and the will of God, and doing their best to make these prevail;—for the pursuit, in a word, of perfection. To certain manifestations of this love for perfection mankind have accustomed themselves to give the name of genius; implying, by this name, something original and heaven-bestowed in the passion. But the passion is to be found far beyond those manifestations of it to which the world usually gives the name of genius, and in which there is, for the most part, a *talent* of some kind or other, a special and striking faculty of execution, informed by the heaven-bestowed ardour, or genius. It is to be found in many manifestations besides these, and may best be called, as we have called it, the love and pursuit of perfection; culture being the true nurse of the pursuing love, and sweetness and light the true character of the pursued perfection. Natures with this bent emerge in all classes,—among the Barbarians, among the Philistines, among the Populace. And this bent always tends to take them out of their class, and to make their distinguishing characteristic not their Barbarianism or their Philistinism, but their *humanity.* They have, in general, a rough time of it in their lives; but they are sown more abundantly than one might think, they appear where and when one least expects it, they set up a fire which enfilades, so to speak, the class with which they are ranked; and, in general, by the extrication of their best self as the self to develop, and by the simplicity of the ends fixed by them as paramount, they hinder the unchecked predominance of that class-life which is the affirmation of our ordinary self, and seasonably disconcert mankind in their worship of machinery.

Therefore, when we speak of ourselves as divided into Barbarians, Philistines, and Populace, we must be understood always to imply that within each of these classes there are a certain number of *aliens,* if we may so call them,—persons who are mainly led, not by their class spirit, but by a general *humane* spirit, by the love of human perfection; and that this number is capable of being diminished or augmented. I mean, the number of those who will succeed in developing this happy instinct will be greater or smaller, in proportion both to the force of the original instinct within them, and to the hindrance or encouragement which it meets with from without. In almost all who have it, it is mixed with some infusion of the spirit of an ordinary self, some quantity of class-instinct, and even, as has been shown, of more than one class-instinct at the same time; so that, in general, the extrication of the best self, the predominance of the *humane* instinct, will very much depend upon its meeting, or not, with what is fitted to help and elicit it. At a moment, therefore, when it is agreed that we want a source of authority, and when it seems probable that the right source is our best self, it becomes of vast importance to see whether or not the things around us are, in general, such as to help and elicit our best self, and if they are not, to see why they are not, and the most promising way of mending them.

Now, it is clear that the very absence of any powerful authority amongst us, and the prevalent doctrine of the duty and happiness of doing as one likes, and asserting our personal liberty, must tend to prevent the erection of any very strict standard of excellence, the belief in any very paramount authority of right reason, the recognition of our best self as anything very recondite and hard to come at. It may be, as I have said, a proof of our honesty that we do not attempt to give to our ordinary self, as we have it in

action, predominant authority, and to impose its rule
upon other people. But it is evident also, that it is not
easy, with our style of proceeding, to get beyond the
notion of an ordinary self at all, or to get the paramount authority of a commanding best self, or right
reason, recognised. The learned Martinus Scriblerus
well says:—"the taste of the bathos is implanted by
nature itself in the soul of man; till, perverted by
custom or example, he is taught, or rather compelled, to relish the sublime." But with us everything
seems directed to prevent any such perversion of us
by custom or example as might compel us to relish
the sublime; by all means we are encouraged to keep
our natural taste for the bathos unimpaired.

I have formerly pointed out how in literature the
absence of any authoritative centre, like an Academy, tends to do this. Each section of the public has
its own literary organ, and the mass of the public is
without any suspicion that the value of these organs
is relative to their being nearer a certain ideal centre
of correct information, taste, and intelligence, or
farther away from it. I have said that within certain
limits, which any one who is likely to read this will
have no difficulty in drawing for himself, my old
adversary, the *Saturday Review,* may, on matters of
literature and taste, be fairly enough regarded, relatively to the mass of newspapers which treat these
matters, as a kind of organ of reason. But I remember
once conversing with a company of Nonconformist
admirers of some lecturer who had let off a great
firework, which the *Saturday Review* said was all
noise and false lights, and feeling my way as ten-
derly as I could about the effect of this unfavourable
judgment upon those with whom I was conversing.
"Oh," said one who was their spokesman, with the

most tranquil air of conviction, "It is true the *Saturday Review* abuses the lecture, but the *British Banner*" (I am not quite sure it was the *British Banner,* but it was some newspaper of that stamp) "says that the *Saturday Review* is quite wrong." The speaker had evidently no notion that there was a scale of value for judgments on these topics, and that the judgments of the *Saturday Review* ranked high on this scale, and those of the *British Banner* low; the taste of the bathos implanted by nature in the literary judgments of man had never, in my friend's case, encountered any let or hindrance.

Just the same in religion as in literature. We have most of us little idea of a high standard to choose our guides by, of a great and profound spirit which is an authority while inferior spirits are none. It is enough to give importance to things that this or that person says them decisively, and has a large following of some strong kind when he says them. This habit of ours is very well shown in that able and interesting work of Mr. Hepworth Dixon's, which we were all reading lately, *The Mormons, by One of Themselves.* Here, again, I am not quite sure that my memory serves me as to the exact title, but I mean the well-known book in which Mr. Hepworth Dixon described the Mormons, and other similar religious bodies in America, with so much detail and such warm sympathy. In this work it seems enough for Mr. Dixon that this or that doctrine has its Rabbi, who talks big to him, has a staunch body of disciples, and, above all, has plenty of rifles. That there are any further stricter tests to be applied to a doctrine, before it is pronounced important, never seems to occur to him. "It is easy to say," he writes of the Mormons, "that these saints are dupes and fanatics, to laugh at Joe

Smith and his church, but what then? *The great facts remain.* Young and his people are at Utah; a church of 200,000 souls; an army of 20,000 rifles." But if the followers of a doctrine are really dupes, or worse, and its promulgators are really fanatics, or worse, it gives the doctrine no seriousness or authority the more that there should be found 200,000 souls,—200,-000 of the innumerable multitude with a natural taste for the bathos,—to hold it, and 20,000 rifles to defend it. And again, of another religious organisation in America: "A fair and open field is not to be refused when hosts so mighty throw down wager of battle on behalf of what they hold to be true, however strange their faith may seem." A fair and open field is not to be refused to any speaker; but this solemn way of heralding him is quite out of place, unless he has, for the best reason and spirit of man, some significance. "Well, but," says Mr. Hepworth Dixon, "a theory which has been accepted by men like Judge Edmonds, Dr. Hare, Elder Frederick, and Professor Bush!" And again: "Such are, in brief, the bases of what Newman Weeks, Sarah Horton, Deborah Butler, and the associated brethren, proclaimed in Rolt's Hall as the new covenant!" If he was summing up an account of the doctrine of Plato, or of St. Paul, and of its followers, Mr. Hepworth Dixon could not be more earnestly reverential. But the question is, Have personages like Judge Edmonds, and Newman Weeks, and Elderess Polly, and Elderess Antoinette, and the rest of Mr. Hepworth Dixon's heroes and heroines, anything of the weight and significance for the best reason and spirit of man that Plato and St. Paul have? Evidently they, at present, have not; and a very small taste of them and their doctrines ought to have convinced Mr. Hepworth

Dixon that they never could have. "But," says he,
"the magnetic power which Shakerism is exercising
on American thought would of itself compel us,"—
and so on. Now, so far as real thought is concerned,
—thought which affects the best reason and spirit of
man, the scientific or the imaginative thought of the
world, the only thought which deserves speaking of
in this solemn way,—America has up to the present
time been hardly more than a province of England,
and even now would not herself claim to be more
than abreast of England; and of this only real human
thought, English thought itself is not just now, as we
must all admit, the most significant factor. Neither,
then, can American thought be; and the magnetic
power which Shakerism exercises on American
thought is about as important, for the best reason
and spirit of man, as the magnetic power which Mr.
Murphy exercises on Birmingham Protestantism.
And as we shall never get rid of our natural taste for
the bathos in religion,—never get access to a best self
and right reason which may stand as a serious authority,—by treating Mr. Murphy as his own disciples treat him, seriously, and as if he was as much an
authority as any one else: so we shall never get rid of
it while our able and popular writers treat their Joe
Smiths and Deborah Butlers, with their so many
thousands souls and so many thousand rifles, in the
like exaggerated and misleading manner, and so do
their best to confirm us in a bad mental habit to
which we are already too prone.

If our habits make it hard for us to come at the idea
of a high best self, of a paramount authority, in literature or religion, how much more do they make this
hard in the sphere of politics! In other countries the
governors, not depending so immediately on the fa-

vour of the governed, have everything to urge them, if they know anything of right reason (and it is at least supposed that governors should know more of this than the mass of the governed), to set it authoritatively before the community. But our whole scheme of government being representative, every one of our governors has all possible temptation, instead of setting up before the governed who elect him, and on whose favour he depends, a high standard of right reason, to accommodate himself as much as possible to their natural taste for the bathos; and even if he tries to go counter to it, to proceed in this with so much flattering and coaxing, that they shall not suspect their ignorance and prejudices to be anything very unlike right reason, or their natural taste for the bathos to differ much from a relish for the sublime. Every one is thus in every possible way encouraged to trust in his own heart; but, "he that trusteth in his own heart," says the Wise Man, "is a fool;" and at any rate this, which Bishop Wilson says, is undeniably true: "The number of those who need to be awakened is far greater than that of those who need comfort."

But in our political system everybody is comforted. Our guides and governors who have to be elected by the influence of the barbarians, and who depend on their favour, sing the praises of the Barbarians, and say all the smooth things that can be said of them. With Mr. Tennyson, they celebrate "the great broad-shouldered genial Englishman," with his "sense of duty," his "reverence for the laws," and his "patient force," who saves us from the "revolts, republics, revolutions, most no graver than a schoolboy's barring out," which upset other and less broad-shouldered nations. Our guides who are chosen by the

Philistines and who have to look to their favour, tell the Philistines how "all the world knows that the great middle class of this country supplies the mind, the will, and the power requisite for all the great and good things that have to be done," and congratulate them on their "earnest good sense, which penetrates through sophisms, ignores commonplaces, and gives to conventional illusions their true value." Our guides who look to the favour of the Populace, tell them that "theirs are the brightest powers of sympathy, and the readiest powers of action."

Harsh things are said too, no doubt, against all the great classes of the community; but these things so evidently come from a hostile class, and are so manifestly dictated by the passions and prepossessions of a hostile class, and not by right reason, that they make no serious impression on those at whom they are launched, but slide easily off their minds. For instance, when the Reform League orators inveigh against our cruel and bloated aristocracy, these invectives so evidently show the passions and point of view of the Populace, that they do not sink into the minds of those at whom they are addressed, or awaken any thought or self-examination in them. Again, when our aristocratical baronet describes the Philistines and the Populace as influenced with a kind of hideous mania for emasculating the aristocracy, that reproach so clearly comes from the wrath and excited imagination of the Barbarians, that it does not much set the Philistines and the Populace thinking. Or when Mr. Lowe calls the Populace drunken and venal, he so evidently calls them this in an agony of apprehension for his Philistine or middle-class Parliament, which has done so many great and heroic works, and is now threatened with mixture and debasement, that the populace do not lay his words seriously to heart.

So the voice which makes a permanent impression on each of our classes is the voice of its friends, and this is from the nature of things, as I have said, a comforting voice. The Barbarians remain in the belief that the great broad-shouldered genial Englishman may be well satisfied with himself; the Philistines remain in the belief that the great middle class of this country, with its earnest common-sense penetrating through sophisms and ignoring commonplaces, may be well satisfied with itself; the Populace, that the working man with his bright powers of sympathy and ready powers of action, may be well satisfied with himself. What hope, at this rate, of extinguishing the taste of the bathos implanted by nature itself in the soul of man, or of inculcating the belief that excellence dwells among high and steep rocks, and can only be reached by those who sweat blood to reach her?

But it will be said, perhaps, that candidates for political influence and leadership, who thus caress the self-love of those whose suffrages they desire, know quite well that they are not saying the sheer truth as reason sees it, but that they are using a sort of conventional language, or what we call clap-trap, which is essential to the working of representative institutions. And therefore, I suppose, we ought rather to say with Figaro: *Qui est-ce qu'on trompe ici?* Now, I admit that often, but not always, when our governors say smooth things to the self-love of the class whose political support they want, they know very well that they are overstepping, by a long stride, the bounds of truth and soberness; and while they talk, they in a manner, no doubt, put their tongue in their cheek. Not always; because, when a Barbarian appeals to his own class to make him their representative and give him political power, he, when he pleases their self-love by extolling broad-shouldered genial Englishmen with their sense of duty, reverence for the laws, and patient force, pleases his own self-love and extols himself, and is, therefore, himself ensnared by his own smooth words. And so, too, when a Philistine wants to be sent to Parliament by his brother Philistines, and extols the earnest good sense which characterises Manchester and supplies the mind, the will, and the power, as the *Daily News* eloquently says, requisite for all the great and good things that have to be done, he intoxicates and deludes himself as well as his brother Philistines who hear him.

But it is true that a Barbarian often wants the political support of the Philistines; and he unquestionably, when he flatters the self-love of Philistinism, and extols, in the approved fashion, its energy, enterprise, and self-reliance, knows that he is talking clap-trap, and so to say, puts his tongue in his cheek. On all matters where Nonconformity and its catchwords are concerned, this insincerity of Barbarians needing Nonconformist support, and, therefore, flattering the self-love of Nonconformity and repeating its catchwords without the least real belief in them, is very noticeable. When the Nonconformists, in a transport of blind zeal, threw out Sir James Graham's useful Education Clauses in 1843, one-half of their Parliamentary advocates, no doubt, who cried aloud against "trampling on the religious liberty of the Dissenters by taking the money of Dissenters to teach the tenets of the Church of England," put their tongue in their cheek while they so cried out. And perhaps there is even a sort of motion of Mr. Frederic Harrison's tongue towards his cheek when he talks of "the shriek of superstition," and tells the working class that "theirs are the brightest powers of sympathy and the readiest powers of action." But the point on which I would insist is, that this involuntary tribute to truth and soberness on the part of certain of our governors and guides never reaches at all the mass of us governed, to serve as a lesson to us, to abate our self-love, and to awaken in us a suspicion that our favourite prejudices may be, to a higher reason, all nonsense. Whatever by-play goes on among the more intelligent of our leaders, we do not see it; and we are left to believe that, not only in our own eyes, but in the eyes of our representative and ruling men, there is nothing more admirable than our ordinary self, whatever our ordinary self happens to be, Barbarian, Philistine, or Populace.

Thus everything in our political life tends to hide from us that there is anything wiser than our ordinary selves, and to prevent our getting the notion of a paramount right reason. Royalty itself, in its idea the expression of the collective nation, and a sort of constituted witness to its best mind, we try to turn into a kind of grand advertising van, meant to give publicity and credit to the inventions, sound or unsound, of the ordinary self of individuals.

I remember, when I was in North Germany, having this very strongly brought to my mind in the matter of schools and their institution. In Prussia, the best schools are Crown patronage schools, as they are called; schools which have been established and endowed (and new ones are to this day being established and endowed) by the Sovereign himself out of his own revenues, to be under the direct con-

trol and management of him or of those representing him, and to serve as types of what schools should
be. The Sovereign, as his position raises him above
many prejudices and littlenesses, and as he can always have at his disposal the best advice, has evident
advantages over private founders in well planning
and directing a school; while at the same time his
great means and his great influence secure, to a well-
planned school of his, credit and authority. This is
what, in North Germany, the governors do in the
matter of education for the governed; and one may
say that they thus give the governed a lesson, and
draw out in them the idea of a right reason higher
than the suggestions of an ordinary man's ordinary
self.

But in England how different is the part which in
this matter our governors are accustomed to play!
The Licensed Victuallers or the Commercial Travellers propose to make a school for their children;
and I suppose, in the matter of schools, one may call
the Licensed Victuallers or the Commercial Travellers ordinary men, with their natural taste for the
bathos still strong; and a Sovereign with the advice
of men like Wilhelm von Humboldt or Schleier-
macher may, in this matter, be a better judge, and
nearer to right reason. And it will be allowed, probably, that right reason would suggest that, to have a
sheer school of Licensed Victuallers' children, or a
sheer school of Commercial Travellers' children,
and to bring them all up, not only at home but at
school too, in a kind of odour of licensed victualism
or of bagmanism, is not a wise training to give to
these children. And in Germany, I have said, the action of the national guides or governors is to suggest
and provide a better. But, in England, the action of

the national guides or governors is, for a Royal Prince or a great Minister to go down to the opening of the Licensed Victuallers' or of the Commercial Travellers' school, to take the chair, to extol the energy and self-reliance of the Licensed Victuallers or the Commercial Travellers, to be all of their way of thinking, to predict full success to their schools, and never so much as to hint to them that they are probably doing a very foolish thing, and that the right way to go to work with their children's education is quite different. And it is the same in almost every department of affairs. While, on the Continent, the idea prevails that it is the business of the heads and representatives of the nation, by virtue of their superior means, power, and information, to set an example and to provide suggestions of right reason, among us the idea is that the business of the heads and representatives of the nation is to do nothing of the kind, but to applaud the natural taste for the bathos showing itself vigorously in any part of the community, and to encourage its works.

Now I do not say that the political system of foreign countries has not inconveniences which may outweigh the inconveniences of our own political system; nor am I the least proposing to get rid of our own political system and to adopt theirs. But a sound centre of authority being what, in this disquisition, we have been led to seek, and right reason, or our best self, appearing alone to offer such a sound centre of authority, it is necessary to take note of the chief impediments which hinder, in this country, the extrication or recognition of this right reason as a paramount authority, with a view to afterwards trying in what way they can best be removed.

This being borne in mind, I proceed to remark how

not only do we get no suggestions of right reason, and no rebukes of our ordinary self, from our governors, but a kind of philosophical theory is widely spread among us to the effect that there is no such thing at all as a best self and a right reason having claim to paramount authority, or, at any rate, no such thing ascertainable and capable of being made use of; and that there is nothing but an infinite number of ideas and works of our ordinary selves, and suggestions of our natural taste for the bathos, pretty nearly equal in value, which are doomed either to an irreconcilable conflict, or *else to a perpetual give and take;* and that wisdom consists in choosing the give and take rather than the conflict, and in sticking to our choice with patience and good humour.

And, on the other hand, we have another philosophical theory rife among us, to the effect that without the labour of perverting ourselves by custom or example to relish right reason, but by continuing all of us to follow freely our natural taste for the bathos, we shall, by the mercy of Providence, and by a kind of natural tendency of things, come in due time to relish and follow right reason.

The great promoters of these philosophical theories are our newspapers, which, no less than our Parliamentary representatives, may be said to act the part of guides and governors to us; and these favourite doctrines of theirs I call,—or should call, if the doctrines were not preached by authorities I so much respect,—the first, a peculiarly British form of Atheism, the second, a peculiarly British form of Quietism. The first-named melancholy doctrine is preached in the *Times* with great clearness and force of style; indeed, it is well known, from the example of the poet Lucretius and others, what great masters of style the atheistic doctrine has always counted among its promulgators. "It is of no use," says the *Times,* "for us to attempt to force upon our neighbours our several likings and dislikings. We must take things as they are. Everybody has his own little vision of religious or civil perfection. Under the evident impossibility of satisfying everybody, we agree to take our stand on equal laws and on a system as open and liberal as is possible. The result is that everybody has more liberty of action and of speaking here than anywhere else in the Old World." We come again here upon Mr. Roebuck's celebrated definition of happiness, on which I have so often commented: "I look around me and ask what is the state of England? Is not every man able to say what he likes? I ask you whether the world over, or in past history, there is anything like it? Nothing. I pray that our unrivalled happiness may last." This is the old story of our system of checks and every Englishman doing as he likes, which we have already seen to have been convenient enough so long as there were only the Barbarians and the Philistines to do what they liked, but to be getting inconvenient, and productive of anarchy, now that the Populace wants to do what it likes too.

But for all that, I will not at once dismiss this famous doctrine, but will first quote another passage from the *Times,* applying the doctrine to a matter of which we have just been speaking,—education. "The difficulty here" (in providing a national system of education), says the *Times,* "does not reside in any removable arrangements. It is inherent and native in the actual and inveterate state of things in this country. All these powers and personages, all these conflicting influences and varieties of character, exist, and have long existed among us; they are fighting it out, and will long continue to fight it out, without coming to that happy consummation when some one element of the British character is to destroy or to absorb all the rest." There it is! the various promptings of the natural taste for the bathos in this man and that amongst us are fighting it out; and the day will never come (and, indeed, why should we wish it to come?) when one man's particular sort of taste for the bathos shall tyrannise over another man's; nor when right reason (if that may be called an element of the British character) shall absorb and rule them all. "The whole system of this country, like the constitution we boast to inherit, and are glad to uphold, is made up of established facts, prescriptive authorities, existing usages, powers that be, persons in possession, and communities or classes that have won dominion for themselves, and will hold it against all comers." Every force in the world, evidently, except the one reconciling force, right reason! Barbarian here, Philistine there, Mr. Bradlaugh and Populace striking in!—pull devil, pull baker! Really, presented with the mastery of style of our leading journal, the sad picture, as one gazes upon it, assumes the iron and inexorable solemnity of tragic Destiny.

After this, the milder doctrine of our other philosophical teacher, the *Daily News,* has, at first, something very attractive and assuaging. The *Daily News* begins, indeed, in appearance, to weave the iron web of necessity round us like the *Times.* "The alternative is between a man's doing what he likes and his doing what some one else, probably not one whit wiser than himself, likes." This points to the tacit compact, mentioned in my last paper, between the

Barbarians and the Philistines, and into which it is hoped that the Populace will one day enter; the compact, so creditable to English honesty, that since each class has only the ideas and aims of its ordinary self to give effect to, none of them shall, if it exercise power, treat its ordinary self too seriously, or attempt to impose it on others; but shall let these others,—the fanatical Protestant, for instance, in his Papist-baiting, and the popular tribune in his Hyde Park anarchy-mongering,—have their fling. But then the *Daily News* suddenly lights up the gloom of necessitarianism with bright beams of hope. "No doubt," it says, "the common reason of society ought to check the aberrations of individual eccentricity." This common reason of society looks very like our best self or right reason, to which we want to give authority, by making the action of the *State,* or nation in its collective character, the expression of it. But of this project of ours, the *Daily News,* with its subtle dialectics, makes havoc. "Make the State the organ of the common reason?"—it says. "You make it the organ of something or other, but how can you be certain that reason will be the quality which will be embodied in it?" You cannot be certain of it, undoubtedly, if you never try to bring the thing about; but the question is, the action of the State being the action of the collective nation, and the action of the collective nation carrying naturally great publicity, weight, and force of example with it, whether we should not try to put into the action of the State as much as possible of right reason or our best self, which may, in this manner, come back to us with new force and authority; may have visibility, form, and influence; and help to confirm us, in the many moments when we are tempted to be our ordinary selves merely, in resisting our natural taste of the bathos rather than in giving way to it?

But no! says our teacher: "It is better there should be an infinite variety of experiments in human action; the common reason of society will in the main check the aberrations of individual eccentricity well enough, if left to its natural operation." This is what I call the specially British form of Quietism, or a devout, but excessive reliance on an over-ruling Providence. Providence, as the moralists are careful to tell us, generally works in human affairs by human means; so, when we want to make right reason act on individual inclination, our best self on our ordinary self, we seek to give it more power of doing so by giving it public recognition and authority, and embodying it, so far as we can, in the State. It seems too much to ask of Providence, that while we, on our part, leave our congenital taste for the bathos to its natural operation and its infinite variety of experiments, Providence should mysteriously guide it into the true track, and compel it to relish the sublime. At any rate, great men and great institutions have hitherto seemed necessary for producing any considerable effect of this kind. No doubt we have an infinite variety of experiments and an ever-multiplying multitude of explorers. Even in these few chapters I have enumerated many: the *British Banner,* Judge Edmonds, Newman Weeks, Deborah Butler, Elderess Polly, Brother Noyes, Mr. Murphy, the Licensed Victuallers, the Commercial Travellers, and I know not how many more; and the members of the noble army are swelling every day. But what a depth of Quietism, or rather, what an over-bold call on the direct interposition of Providence, to believe that these interesting explorers will discover the true track, or at any rate, "will do so in the main well enough" (whatever that may mean) if left to their natural operation; that is, by going on as they are! Philosophers say, indeed, that we learn virtue by performing acts of virtue; but to say that we shall learn virtue by performing any acts to which our natural taste for the bathos carries us, that the fanatical Protestant comes at his best self by Papist-baiting, or Newman Weeks and Deborah Butler at right reason by following their noses, this certainly does appear over-sanguine.

It is true, what we want is to make right reason act on individual reason, the reason of individuals; all our search for authority has that for its end and aim. The *Daily News* says, I observe, that all my argument for authority "has a non-intellectual root;" and from what I know of my own mind and its poverty I think this so probable, that I should be inclined easily to admit it, if it were not that, in the first place, nothing of this kind, perhaps, should be admitted without examination; and, in the second, a way of accounting for the charge being made, in this particular instance, without good grounds, appears to present itself. What seems to me to account here, perhaps, for the charge, is the want of flexibility of our race, on which I have so often remarked. I mean, it being admitted that the conformity of the individual reason of the fanatical Protestant or the popular rioter with right reason is our true object, and not the mere restraining them, by the strong arm of the State, from Papist-baiting, or railing-breaking,—admitting this, we English have so little flexibility that we cannot readily perceive that the State's restraining them from these indulgences may yet fix clearly in their minds that, to the collective nation, these indulgences appear irrational and unallowable, may make them pause and reflect, and may contribute to bringing, with time, their individual reason into harmony with right reason. But in no country, owing to the want of intellectual flexibility above mentioned, is the leaning which is our natural one, and, therefore, needs no recommending to us, so sedulously recommended, and the leaning which is not our natural one, and, therefore, does not need dispraising to us, so sedulously dispraised, as in ours. To rely on the individual being, with us, the natural leaning, we will hear of nothing but the good of relying on the individual; to act through the collective nation on the individual being not our natural leaning, we will hear nothing in recommendation of it. But the wise know that we often need to hear most of that to which we are least inclined, and even to learn to employ, in certain circumstances, that which is capable, if employed amiss, of being a danger to us.

Elsewhere this is certainly better understood than here. In a recent number of the *Westminster Review,* an able writer, but with precisely our national want of flexibility of which I have been speaking, has unearthed, I see, for our present needs, an English translation, published some years ago, of Wilhelm von Humboldt's book, *The Sphere and Duties of Government.* Humboldt's object in this book is to show that the operation of government ought to be severely limited to what directly and immediately relates to the security of person and property. Wilhelm von Humboldt, one of the most beautiful souls that have ever existed, used to say that one's business in life was first to perfect one's self by all the means in one's power, and secondly, to try and create in the world around one an aristocracy, the most numerous that one possibly could, of talents and characters. He saw, of course, that, in the end, everything comes to this,—that the individual must act for himself, and must be perfect in himself; and he lived in a country, Germany, where people were disposed to act too little for themselves, and to rely too much on the Government. But even thus, such was his flexibility, so little was he in bondage to a mere abstract maxim, that he saw very well that for his purpose itself, of enabling the individual to stand perfect on his own foundations and to do without the State, the action of the State would for long, long years be necessary. And soon after he wrote his book on *The Sphere and Duties of Government,* Wilhelm von Humboldt became Minister of Education in Prussia; and from his ministry all the great reforms which give the control of Prussian education to the State,— the transference of the management of public schools from their old boards of trustees to the State, the obligatory State-examination for schoolmasters, and the foundation of the great State-University of Berlin,—take their origin. This his English reviewer says not a word of. But, writing for a people whose dangers lie, as we have seen, on the side of their unchecked and unguided individual action, whose dangers none of them lie on the side of an over-reliance on the State, he quotes just so much of Wilhelm von Humboldt's example as can flatter them in their propensities, and do them no good; and just what might make them think, and be of use to them, he leaves on one side. This precisely recalls the manner, it will be observed, in which we have seen that our royal and noble personages proceed with the Licensed Victuallers.

In France the action of the State on individuals is

yet more preponderant than in Germany; and the
need which friends of human perfection feel for
what may enable the individual to stand perfect on
his own foundations is all the stronger. But what
says one of the staunchest of these friends, M. Renan, on State action; and even State action in that
very sphere where in France it is most excessive, the
sphere of education? Here are his words:—"A Liberal
believes in liberty, and liberty signifies the non-
intervention of the State. *But such an ideal is still a
long way off from us, and the very means to remove
it to an indefinite distance would be precisely the
State's withdrawing its action too soon."* And this,
he adds, is even truer of education than of any other
department of public affairs.

BENJAMIN DISRAELI

Benjamin Disraeli (1804–1881) was the founder of the British Conservative Party. A man of genius and wit, Disraeli dominated Parliamentary debate and helped to shape British Conservatism as an effective political movement. A fragment of his speech on Toryism, and his speech on the Berlin Treaty of 1878 follow.

From *Selected Speeches of the Late Right Honorable the Earl of Beaconsfield,* ed. T. E. Kebbel, 12 vols. (London, 1882).

BENJAMIN DISRAELI

Disraeli on Toryism

Ever since that period of disaster and dismay, when my friends and myself were asked for the first time to sit upon these benches, it has ever been our habit, in counselling the Tory party, to recur gradually but most sincerely to the original elements of that great political connection. To build up a community, not upon Liberal opinions, which anyone may fashion to his fancy, but upon popular principles, which assert equal rights, civil and religious; to uphold the institutions of the country because they are the embodiments of the wants and wishes of the nation, and protect us alike from individual tyranny and popular outrage; equally to resist democracy and obligarchy, and favour that principle of free aristocracy which is the only basis and security for constitutional government; to be vigilant to guard and prompt to vindicate the honour of the country, but to hold aloof from the turbulent diplomacy which only distracts the mind of a people from internal improvement; to lighten taxation; frugally but wisely to administer the public treasure; to favour popular education, because it is the best guarantee for public order; to defend local government, and to be as jealous of the rights of the working man as of the prerogative of the Crown and the privileges of the senate—these were once the principles which regulated Tory statesmen, and I for one have no wish that the Tory party should ever be in power unless they practise them.

The Tory party is only in its proper position when it represents popular principles. Then it is truly irresistible. Then it can uphold the throne and the altar, the majesty of the empire, the liberty of the nation, and the rights of the multitude. There is nothing mean, petty, or exclusive, about the real character of Toryism. It necessarily depends upon enlarged sympathies and noble aspirations, because it is essentially national.

BENJAMIN DISRAELI

The Berlin Treaty

My lords, in laying on the table of your lordships' House, as I am about to do, the protocols of the Congress of Berlin, I have thought I should be only doing my duty to your lordships' House, to Parliament generally, and to the country, if I made some remarks on the policy which was supported by the representatives of Her Majesty at the Congress, and which is embodied in the Treaty of Berlin and in the convention which was placed on your lordships' table during my absence.

My lords, you are aware that the treaty of San Stefano was looked on with much distrust and alarm by Her Majesty's Government—that they believed it was calculated to bring about a state of affairs dangerous to European independence and injurious to the interests of the British Empire. Our impeachment of that policy is before your lordships and the country, and is contained in the circular of my noble friend the Secretary of State for Foreign Affairs in April last. Our present contention is, that we can show that, by the changes and modifications which have been made in the treaty of San Stefano by the Congress of Berlin and the Convention of Constantinople, the menace to European independence has been removed, and the threatened injury to the British Empire has been averted. Your lordships will recollect that by the treaty of San Stefano about one half of Turkey in Europe was formed into a State called Bulgaria—a State consisting of upwards of 50,000 geographical square miles, and containing a population of 4,000,000, with harbours on either sea —both on the shores of the Euxine and of the Archipelago. That disposition of territory severed Constantinople and the limited district which was still spared to the possessors of that city—severed it from the provinces of Macedonia and Thrace by Bulgaria descending to the very shores of the Ægean; and, altogether, a State was formed, which, both from its natural resources and its peculiarly favourable geographical position, must necessarily have exercised a predominant influence over the political and commercial interests of that part of the world. The remaining portion of Turkey in Europe was reduced also to a considerable degree by affording what was called compensation to previous rebellious tributary principalities, which have now become independent States—so that the general result of the treaty of San Stefano was, that while it spared the authority of the Sultan so far as his capital and its immediate vicinity, it reduced him to a state of subjection to the great Power which had defeated his armies, and which was present at the gates of his capital. Accordingly, though it might be said that he still seemed to be invested with one of the highest functions of public duty—the protection and custody of the Straits— it was apparent that his authority in that respect could be exercised by him in deference only to the superior Power which had vanquished him, and to whom the proposed arrangements would have kept him in subjection.

My lords, in these matters, the Congress of Berlin have made great changes. They have restored to the Sultan two-thirds of the territory which was to have formed the great Bulgarian State. They have restored to him upwards of 30,000 geographical square miles, and 2,500,000 of population—that territory being the richest in the Balkans, where most of the land is rich, and the population one of the wealthiest, most ingenious, and most loyal of his subjects. The frontiers of his State have been pushed forward from the mere environs of Salonica and Adrianople to the lines of the Balkans and Trajan's pass; the new principality, which was to exercise such an influence, and produce a revolution in the disposition of the territory and policy of that part of the globe, is now merely a State in the Valley of the Danube, and both in its extent and its population is reduced to one-third of what was contemplated by the treaty of San Stefano. . . .

My lords, in consequence of that arrangement cries have been raised against our "partition of Turkey." My lords, our object has been directly the reverse, our object has been to prevent partition. The question of partition is one upon which, it appears to me, very erroneous ideas are in circulation. Some two years ago—before, I think, the war had commenced, but when the disquietude and dangers of the situation were very generally felt—there was a school of statesmen who were highly in favour of what they believed to be the only remedy, what they called the partition of Turkey. Those who did not agree with them were those who thought we should, on the whole, attempt the restoration of Turkey. Her Majesty's Government at all times have resisted the partition of Turkey. They have done so because, exclusive of the high moral considerations that are mixed up with the subject, they believed an attempt, on a great scale, to accomplish the partition of Turkey, would inevitably lead to a long, a sanguinary, and often recurring struggle, and that Europe and Asia would both be involved in a series of troubles and sources of disaster and danger of which no adequate idea could be formed.

These professors of partition—quite secure, no doubt, in their own views—have freely spoken to us on this subject. We have been taken up to a high mountain and shown all the kingdoms of the earth, and they have said, "All these shall be yours if you will worship Partition." But we have declined to do so for the reasons I have shortly given. And it is a remarkable circumstance that after the great war, and after the prolonged diplomatic negotiations, which lasted during nearly a period of three years, on this matter, the whole Powers of Europe, including Russia, have strictly, and as completely as ever, come to the unanimous conclusion that the best chance for the tranquility and order of the world is to retain the Sultan as part of the acknowledged political system of Europe. My lords, unquestionably after a great war—and I call the late war a great war, because the greatness of a war now must not be calculated by its duration, but by the amount of the forces brought into the field, and where a million of men have struggled for supremacy, as has been the case recently, I call that a great war—but, I say, after a great war like this, it is utterly impossible that you can have a settlement of any permanent character without a redistribution of territory and considerable changes. But that is not partition. My lords, a country may have lost provinces, but that is not partition. We know that not very long ago a great country—one of the foremost countries of the world—lost provinces; yet is not France one of the great Powers of the world, and with a future—a commanding future?

Austria herself has lost provinces—more provinces even than Turkey, perhaps; even England has lost provinces—the most precious possessions—the loss of which every Englishman must deplore to this moment. We lost them from bad government. Had the principles which now obtain between the metropolis and her dependencies prevailed then, we should not, perhaps, have lost those provinces, and the power of this Empire would have been proportionally increased. It is perfectly true that the Sultan of Turkey has lost provinces; it is true that his armies have been defeated; it is true that his enemy is even now at his gates; but all that has happened to other Powers. But a sovereign who has not yet forfeited his capital, whose capital has not yet been occupied by his enemy—and that capital one of the strongest in the world—who has armies and fleets at his disposal, and who still rules over 20,000,000 of inhabitants, cannot be described as a Power whose dominions have been partitioned. My lords, it has been said that no limit has been fixed to the occupation of Bosnia by Austria. Well, I think that was a very wise step. The moment you limit an occupation you deprive it of half its virtue. All those opposed to the principles which occupation was devised to foster and strengthen, feel that they have only to hold their breath and wait a certain time, and the opportunity for their interference would again present itself. Therefore, I cannot agree with the objection which is made to the arrangement with regard to the occupation of Bosnia by Austria on the question of its duration. . . .

Now, my lords, I have touched upon most of the points connected with Turkey in Europe. My summary is that at this moment—of course, no longer counting Servia or Roumania, once tributary principalities, as part of Turkey; not counting even the New Bulgaria, though it is a tributary principality, as part of Turkey; and that I may not be taunted with taking an element which I am hardly entitled to place in the calculation, omitting even Bosnia—European Turkey still remains a dominion of 60,000 geographical square miles, with a population of 6,-000,000, and that population in a very great degree concentrated and condensed in the provinces contiguous to the capital. My lords, it was said, when the line of the Balkans was carried—and it was not carried until after long and agitating discussions—it was said by that illustrious statesman who presided over our labours, that "Turkey in Europe once more exists." My lords, I do not think that, so far as European Turkey is concerned, this country has any right to complain of the decisions of the Congress, or, I would hope, of the labours of the plenipotentiaries. You cannot look at the map of Turkey as it had been left by the treaty of San Stefano, and as it has been rearranged by the Treaty of Berlin, without seeing that great results have accrued. If these results had been the consequences of a long war—if they had been the results of a struggle like that we underwent in the Crimea—I do not think they would have been even then unsubstantial or unsatisfactory. My lords, I hope that you and the country will not forget that these results have been obtained without shedding the blood of a single Englishman; and if there has been some expenditure, it has been an expenditure which, at least, has shown the resources and determination of this country. Had you entered into that war—for which you were prepared—and well prepared—probably in a month you would have exceeded the whole expenditure you have now incurred.

My lords, I now ask you for a short time to quit Europe and to visit Asia, and consider the labours of

the Congress in another quarter of the world. My
lords, you well know that the Russian arms met with
great success in Asia, and that in the treaty of San
Stefano considerable territories were yielded by Turkey to Russia. . . . The Congress have so far approved
the treaty of San Stefano that they have sanctioned
the retention by Russia of Kars and Batoum. . . . Now
is that a question for which England would be justified in going to war with Russia? My lords, we have,
therefore, thought it advisable not to grudge Russia
those conquests which have been made—especially
after obtaining the restoration of the town of Baya-
zid and its important district. . . .

But I must make this observation to your lordships.
We have a substantial interest in the East; it is a
commanding interest, and its behest must be obeyed.
But the interest of France in Egypt, and her interest
in Syria, are, as she acknowledges, sentimental and
traditionary interests; and, although I respect them,
and although I wish to see in the Lebanon and Egypt
the influence of France fairly and justly maintained,
and although her officers and ours in that part of the
world—and especially in Egypt—are acting together
with confidence and trust, we must remember that
our connection with the East is not merely an affair
of sentiment and tradition, but that we have urgent
and substantial and enormous interests which we
must guard and keep. Therefore, when we find that
the progress of Russia is a progress which, whatever
may be the intentions of Russia, necessarily in that
part of the world produces such a state of disorgani-
sation and want of confidence in the Porte, it comes
to this—that if we do not interfere in vindication of
our own interests, that part of Asia must become the
victim of anarchy, and ultimately become part of the
possessions of Russia.

Now, my lords, I have ventured to review the chief points connected with the subject on which I wished to address you—namely, what was the policy pursued by us, both at the Congress of Berlin and in the Convention of Constantinople? I am told, indeed, that we have incurred an awful responsibility by the Convention into which we have entered. My lords, a prudent minister certainly would not recklessly enter into any responsibility; but a minister who is afraid to enter into any responsibility is, to my mind, not a prudent minister. We do not, my lords, wish to enter into any unnecessary responsibility; but there is one responsibility from which we certainly shrink; we shrink from the responsibility of handing to our successors a weakened or a diminished Empire. Our opinion is, that the course we have taken will arrest the great evils which are destroying Asia Minor and the equally rich countries beyond. We see in the present state of affairs the Porte losing its influence over its subjects; we see a certainty, in our opinion, of increasing anarchy, of the dissolution of all those ties which, though feeble, yet still exist and which have kept society together in those countries. We see the inevitable result of such a state of things, and we cannot blame Russia for availing herself of it. But, yielding to Russia what she has obtained, we say to her—"Thus far, and no farther." Asia is large enough for both of us. There is no reason for these constant wars, or fears of wars, between Russia and England. Before the circumstances which led to the recent disastrous war, when none of those events which we have seen agitating the world had occurred, and when we were speaking in "another place" of the conduct of Russia in Central Asia, I vindicated that conduct, which I thought was unjustly attacked, and

I said then—what I repeat now—there is room enough for Russia and England in Asia.

But the room that we require we must secure. We have, therefore, entered into an alliance—a defensive alliance—with Turkey, to guard her against any further attack from Russia. We believe that the result of this Convention will be order and tranquility. And then it will be for Europe—for we ask no exclusive privileges or commercial advantages—it will then be for Europe to assist England in availing ourselves of the wealth which has been so long neglected and undeveloped in regions once so fertile and so favoured. We are told, as I have said before, that we are undertaking great responsibilities. From those responsibilities we do not shrink. We think that, with prudence and discretion, we shall bring about a state of affairs as advantageous for Europe as for ourselves; and in that conviction we cannot bring ourselves to believe that the act which we have recommended is one that leads to trouble and to warfare. No, my lords, I am sure there will be no jealousy between England and France upon this subject. In taking Cyprus the movement is not Mediterranean, it is Indian. We have taken a step there which we think necessary for the maintenance of our Empire and for its preservation in peace. . . .

My lords, I have now laid before you the general decline of the policy we have pursued, both in the Congress of Berlin and at Constantinople. They are intimately connected with each other, and they must be considered together. I only hope that the House will not misunderstand—and I think the country will not misunderstand—our motives in occupying Cyprus, and in encouraging those intimate relations between ourselves and the Government and the population of Turkey. They are not movements of war; they are operations of peace and civilisation. We have no reason to fear war. Her Majesty has fleets and armies which are second to none. England must have seen with pride the Mediterrean covered with her ships; she must have seen with pride the discipline and devotion which have been shown to her and her Government by all her troops, drawn from every part of her Empire. I leave it to the illustrious duke, in whose presence I speak, to bear witness to the spirit of imperial patriotism which has been exhibited by the troops from India, which he recently reviewed at Malta. But it is not on our fleets and armies, however necessary they may be for the maintenance of our imperial strength, that I alone or mainly depend in that enterprise on which this country is about to enter. It is on what I most highly value —the consciousness that in the Eastern nations there is confidence in this country, and that, while they know we can enforce our policy, at the same time they know that our Empire is an Empire of liberty, of truth, and of justice.

LORD RANDOLPH CHURCHILL

One of the great might-have-beens of history, Lord Randolph Churchill (1849–1895) was the prophet of modern British Conservatism. His "Tory democracy," and his cry, "Trust the people"—although rejected in his own lifetime—have become accepted Tory policy. His was, in Sir Shane Leslie's phrase, "the freest lance" among late 19th-century conservatives, and his voice was one of the most eloquent. Here from two of his most famous speeches is his philosophy of conservatism, a philosophy that was to influence his son, Sir Winston Churchill.

From "Tory Democracy," a speech given at Manchester, Nov. 6, 1885; "Trust the People," a speech delivered in Birmingham on April 16. Reprinted in *Speeches of the Rt. Hon. Lord Randolph Churchill, M.P.,* ed. Louis J. Hennings (London, 1889).

LORD RANDOLPH CHURCHILL

Tory Democracy

What is the Tory democracy that the Whigs should deride it and hold it to the execration of the people? It has been called a contradiction in terms; it has been described as a nonsensical appellation. I believe it to be the most simple and the most easily understood political denomination ever assumed. The Tory democracy is a democracy which has embraced the principles of the Tory party. It is a democracy which believes that an hereditary monarchy and hereditary House of Lords are the strongest fortifications which the wisdom of man, illuminated by the experience of centuries, can possibly devise for the protection, not of Whig privilege, but of democratic freedom. The Tory democracy is a democracy which adheres to and will defend the Established Church, because it believes that Establishment is a guarantee of State morality, and that the connection between Church and State imparts to the ordinary functions of executive and law something of a divine sanction. The Tory democracy is a democracy which, under the shadow and under the protection of those great and ancient institutions, will resolutely follow the path of administrative reform.

LORD RANDOLPH CHURCHILL

Trust the People

What is the great and wide difference which distinguishes the two great political parties who endeavour to attract the support of the English people? It has been well and wisely said—but I do not think it can be too often repeated—that the Tory party clings with veneration and affection to the institutions of our country. The Radicals regard them with aversion and distrust and will always give multitudinous and specious reasons for their destruction. But how can we, the Tory party, give no good convincing reasons to the people for the faith which is in us? We do not defend the Constitution from mere sentiment for the past, or from any infatuated superstition about Divine right or hereditary excellence. We defend the Constitution solely on the ground of its utility to the people. It is on the ground of utility alone that we go forth to meet our foes, and if we fail to make good our ground with utilitarian arguments and for utilitarian ends, then let the present combination of Throne, Lords and Commons be for ever swept away.

An hereditary throne is the surest device that has ever been imagined or invented for the perpetuation of civil order and for that first necessity of civilised society—continuity of government . . . it would be impossible to devise a form of governmental summit as effectual, and yet cheaper and more simple. . . .

I maintain that the House of Lords should be preserved solely on the ground of its utility to the people. I do not put forward as an argument for its preservation its long history, in order to show you that it possesses great merit as an institution. I do not argue, as some do, that it has acquired stability from the circumstance that by its composition it is rooted in the soil. I content myself with the fact of its existence at the present moment, and I find in it not only a powerful check on popular impulses arising from imperfect information, not only an aggregate of political wisdom and experience such as no other country can produce, but, above all, because I find it literally the only effectual barrier against that most fatal foe to freedom, the one-man power. . . . From a national and imperial point of view, you need never be alarmed at the dangers of one-man power so long as the House of Lords endures. Be he minister, be he capitalist, be he demagogue . . . against that bulwark of popular liberty and civil order, he will dash himself in vain. The House of Lords may, perhaps, move slowly; they may, perhaps, be over-cautious about accepting the merits of the legislation of the House of Commons; they may, perhaps, at times regard with some exaggeration of sentiment the extreme rights of property. That is the price you have to pay —and a small price it is for so valuable a possession —which guards you against so great a danger. They are essentially of the people. Year by year they are recruited from the people. Every privilege, every franchise, every liberty which is gained by the people, is treasured up and guarded by those who, animated by tradition and custom, by long descent and lofty name, fear neither monarchs, nor ministers, nor men, but only the people, whose trustees they are. . . .

I cannot pass from this subject of the House of Lords without alluding to that other bugbear of the Radical party, the Church of England, and its connection with the State. . . . Again I adhere to my utilitarian line of defence, and I would urge upon you not to lend yourselves too hastily to any project for the demolition of the Established Church. But I would also, in dealing with this question, mingle a little of the wine of sentiment with the cold clear spring water of utilitarianism.

... I see in the Church of England an immense and omnipresent ramification of machinery working without cost to the people—and daily and hourly lifting the masses of the people, rich and poor alike, from the dead and dreary level of the lowest and most material cares of life, up to the comfortable contemplation of higher and serener forms of existence and of destiny. I see in the Church of England a centre and a source and a guide of charitable effort, mitigating by its mendicant importunity the violence of human misery. . . . And I urge upon you not to throw that source of charity upon the haphazard almsgiving of a busy and a selfish world. I view the Church of England eagerly co-operating in the work of national education, not only benefiting your children but saving your pockets; and I remember that it has been the work of the Church to pour forth floods of knowledge, purely secular and scientific, even from the days when knowledge was not; and I warn you against hindering the diffusion of knowledge, inspired by religion, amongst those who will have devolved upon them the responsibility for the government of this wide Empire.

But I own that my chief reason for supporting the Church of England I find in the fact that, when compared with other creeds and other sects, it is essentially the Church of religious liberty. Whether in one direction or another, it is continually possessed by the ambition, not of excluding, but of including, all shades of religious thought, all sorts and conditions of men. . . . I cannot, and will not, allow myself to believe that the English people, who are not only naturally religious, but also eminently practical . . . will ever consent to deprive themselves of so abundant a fountain of aid and consolation, or acquiesce in the demolition of an institution which elevates the life of the nation and consecrates the acts of State. . . .

Last, but not least—no; rather first—in the scheme of Tory politics come the Commons of England. . . . The social progress of the Commons by means of legislative reform under the lines and carried on under the protection of the institutions whose utility I have endeavoured to describe to you—that must be the policy of the Tory party. . . . No class interests should be allowed to stand in the way of this mighty movement, and with this movement, the Tory party not only sympathise, but identify themselves. Social reform, producing direct and immediate benefit to the Commons—that must be our cry, as opposed to the Radicals, who foolishly scream for organic change, and waste their energies and their time in attacking institutions whose destruction would not only endanger popular freedom, but would leave the social condition of the people precisely where it was . . .

"Trust the people"—I have long tried to make that my motto; but I know, and will not conceal, that there are still a few in our party who have that lesson yet to learn and have yet to understand that the Tory party of to-day is no longer identified with that small and narrow class which is connected with the ownership of land; but that its great strength can be found, and must be developed, in our large towns as well as in our country districts. Yes, trust the people. You, who are ambitious, and rightly ambitious, of being the guardians of the British Constitution, trust the people, and they will trust you—and they will follow you and join you in the defence of that Constitution against any and every foe. I have no fear of democracy. . . . Modern checks and securities are not worth a brass farthing. Give me a fair arrangement of the constituencies, and one part of England will correct and balance the other.

I do not think that electoral reform is a matter of national emergency. . . . But you may be sure that the English Constitution will endure and thrive, whether you add two millions of electors or two hundred to the electoral roll, so long as the Tory party is true to its past, mindful of its history, faithful to the policy that was bequeathed to it by Lord Beaconsfield. The future of the Constitution, the destinies of the Empire, are in the hands of the Tory party; and if only the leaders of the party in Parliament will have the courage of their convictions, grasp their responsibilities, and adapt their policy to those responsibilities, and if they are supported and stimulated by you who are here to-night, and by others like you in our large towns, that future and those destinies are great and assured. To rally the people round the Throne, to unite the Throne with the people, a loyal Throne and a patriotic people, that is our policy and that is our faith.

ANTHONY MARIO LUDOVICI

Anthony Ludovici (1882–   ), soldier, writer, politician, has written the standard 20th-century *apologia*
for aristocratic government. Aristocracy, he argued,
was the essence of Toryism, which, in turn, was the
best party to rule Britain. His little-read *A Defence of
Aristocracy*, from which the following is taken,
represents the thinking of the extreme monarchist
wing of the British Conservative Party.

From *A Defence of Aristocracy: A Text for Tories* (London, 1915).

ANTHONY MARIO LUDOVICI

The principle of aristocracy is, that seeing that human life, like any other kind of life, produces some flourishing and some less flourishing, some fortunate and some less fortunate specimens; in order that flourishing, full and fortunate life may be prolonged, multiplied and, if possible, enhanced on earth, the wants of flourishing life, its optimum of conditions, must be made known and authoritatively imposed upon men by its representatives. Who are its representatives? The fanatics and followers of Science are not its representatives, for their taste is too indefinite; it is often pronounced too late to be of any good and it is not reached by an instinctive bodily impulse, but by long empirical research which often comes to many wrong conclusions before attaining to the right one. It must be clear that the true representatives of flourishing and fortunate life are the artists,[1] the men of taste. The artist, the man of taste—the successful number, so to speak, in the many blanks that human life produces in every generation—is in himself a chip of flourishing life. His own body is a small synopsis, a diminutive digest of full, flourishing and fortunate life. What he wants, therefore, life wants; what he knows is good, the best kind of life knows is good. His voice is the very voice of full, flourishing and fortunate life. No number of committees or deliberative assemblies, consisting of men less fortunately constituted than he, can possibly form an adequate substitute for him in this. For

[1] I do not use the word artist here to mean a painter or a musician or an actor. The word artist has been hopelessly vulgarised by the fact that a legion of inartistic painters, musicians and actors have used it as a designation of their ignoble class. By artist I mean a man of taste, a man who unhesitatingly knows what is right and what is wrong. Nowadays there are perhaps only two or three such men in every generation of painters, sculptors, musicians, writers, poets, legislators and actors.

the voice one has, and the desires and wants it expresses, are not a question of chance or of upbringing, they are a question of the body with which one's ancestors have endowed one. All science, all the known laws of heredity, prove this conclusively.

If one's choice of ways and means, if one's taste, if one's wants, therefore, are such that when they become general wants and general tastes they lead to an ascent in the line of human life, then unconsciously one's body, which is a specimen of flourishing and fortunate life, is uttering the credo of flourishing and fortunate life. If, on the other hand, one's choice of ways and means, if one's tastes and wants are such that when they become general tastes and general wants they lead to a descent in the line of human life, then unconsciously one's body, which is a specimen of mediocre or impoverished life, is pronouncing the doctrine of decline and of Nemesis.

Now, if all this is true—and to us who uphold the aristocratic principle it is the only Divine Truth on earth, and one which Science is bound ultimately to confirm and to prove—then it is obvious that only where the voice of flourishing life is raised to authority can there be any hope of an ascent in the line of life, or even of a level of health and beauty in the line of life.

What do those maintain who stand for the aristocratic principle? They simply hold a finger of warning up to their opponents and say, "Your foolish ideals will have a term; their end will come! You cannot with impunity turn a deaf ear to the voice of flourishing life. You must follow the men who know, the men of taste. If you do not your days are numbered. And the men who know, the men of taste, are simply those examples of flourishing life, those lucky strokes of nature's dice, who, when in authority, lead to the multiplication of flourishing life and an ascent in the line of life. No number of the mediocre or of the botched can hope to fill the place of one or of a few men of taste. Disbelieve in this principle and die. Believe in this principle and live to triumph over all those who do not believe in it!"[1]

This is not a "matter of opinion," it is not a matter concerning which every futile *flâneur* in Fleet Street can have his futile opinion. It is the Divine Truth of life. And the democrat who dares to deny it is not only a blind imbecile, he is not only a corrupt and sickly specimen of manhood, he is a rank blasphemer, whose hands are stained with the blood of his people's future.

*   *   *   *   *

If a race, or a nation, or a people be blessed with a few such rulers, then its security, comfort and heart will be in safe keeping. And not only will the industry of the people reward the ruler and make him great and powerful, but their character, which is the most important of all, by becoming an approximation to the type dictated by the voice of flourishing life, will constitute a sound and stable basis upon which an almost *permanent creation may be built by the aristocrat if he chooses.*

And the converse of this condition gives the exact

---

[1]The Chinaman, Ku Hung-Ming, in his wonderful little book, *The Story of a Chinese Oxford Movement* (Shanghai, 1910), knew this to be so when, speaking of what the Englishman would discover if he studied the Chinese more carefully, he wrote (p. 60): "In the Chinaman, he (the Englishman) would find Confucianism with 'its way of the superior man' which, little as the Englishman suspects, will one day change the social order and break up the civilisation of Europe." Why? Because the civilisation of Europe is *not* based upon "the way of the superior man."

formula of decadence and degeneration. For what are decadence and degeneration? Decadence and degeneration are states in a nation's career in which it has forgotten the precepts and values of flourishing life, and in which the voice of flourishing life can no longer make itself heard in its midst. Why, then, are England, France, Germany and almost the whole of Europe decadent to-day? Because for many hundreds of years now the precepts and principles of flourishing life have been neglected, forgotten and even scorned in the Western world. Decadence means practically that the voice of flourishing life has been silenced, that the true aristocrat is dethroned or no longer bred.

You must not, however, suppose that in a decadent or degenerate State the people, the masses, are guided by no taste, by no values. Because nothing could be more plain to-day than the fact that they are so guided or prompted. But the taste which guides them is confused, uncertain, independent of any higher or wise authority; it is self-made, reared on insufficient knowledge, culture and health. And, therefore, the promptings of their heart, instead of leading them to an ascent in life, lead them to further degeneration. It is bad taste which reigns to-day. All taste which is not the precept of flourishing life must be bad or dangerous taste.

With Guicciardini, Disraeli also realised the importance of this matter of the heart and character of a nation, and in *Coningsby* we read: "A political institution is a machine; the motive power is in the national character—with that it rests whether the machine will benefit society, or destroy it."[1]

[1]Langdon Davies Edition, p. 290.

Thus all attempts at ruling a people on purely materialistic lines, all attempts at exploiting their industry without tending their heart, their imagination and their character, must and do invariably fail. A people that is going to flourish must be taught a certain fastidiousness in the manner in which it works and spends the fruit of its labour;[1] it must be given a sound taste for discerning good from bad, that which is beneficial from that which is harmful, and healthy, vital conduct from sick, degenerate conduct. I do not mean that they must have that spontaneous and unerring taste which is the possession of nature's "lucky strokes"—the incarnations of full and flourishing life—who are the true aristocrats; but I mean that they should have a taste founded on likes and dislikes, points of view and opinions, acquired from a higher, guiding and discriminating authority. "For," as Hobbes says, "the actions of men proceed from their opinions, and in the well-governing of opinions consisteth the well-governing of men's actions."[2]

It is for this reason that I believe that the factor which has largely contributed to the downfall of the European aristocracies has been the relegation of the care of the people's character to a body distinct from and often hostile to the actual governors.[3] For apart from the fact that the credo of this indepen-

[1]See Ku Hung-Ming, *The Story of a Chinese Oxford Movement*, pp. 13 and 14: "When the power of industry of a people in a community or nation is nobly directed and not wasted, then the community or nation is truly rich, not in money or possession of big ugly houses, but rich in the health of the body and beauty of the soul of the people.... For without these things which Goethe calls the beautiful, there is no nobility of character, and without nobility of character, as we have seen, the power of industry of the people in a nation will be wasted in ignoble and wasteful consumption."

[2]*Leviathan,* Chapter XVIII.

[3]See Palgrave's *History of the Anglo-Saxons,* where the Church is shown to have been "the corner-stone of English liberty."

dent body, the Church, happens to be hostile to sharp distinctions between man and man, and irrespective of the undoubted truth that to it all men, whether aristocrats or plebeians, have always appeared more or less as equals, or at least as subordinates who, when the interests of the Church were at stake, might, if necessary, be treated as a mass without distinctions of rank, there is this feature in the influence of the Church which should not be forgotten: it robbed the rulers of that active exercise of the "tutorship" of governing by which the people, as we have seen, lay such great store, and which is the most potent medium for binding a people and their rulers together. Because, as Hobbes says, "Benefits oblige, and obligation is thraldom, and unrequitable obligation perpetual thraldom."[1] And no benefit is more unrequitable than that gift to the heart which makes a man conscious of a higher purpose and aim in life than the mere material round of everyday existence. The idea of an ecclesiastical body ministering to the spiritual wants of the people is not, however, necessarily anti-aristocratic in itself, for the Church might have been conducted and controlled absolutely by the aristocracy, as it was in Venice in the hey-day of her power. It is the fact that it was not so controlled by the majority of aristocracies that proved harmful to them, and Machiavelli is among the most distinguished politicians who understood this.[2]

But the relation of the ecclesiastical body to the people in Europe had another and perhaps still more deleterious influence, though, maybe, it was more indirect than the first. For by undertaking indepen-

---

[1]*Leviathan,* Chapter XI.
[2]See his reply to Cardinal Rouen in Chapter III of *The Prince.*

dently to minister to the hearts of the people, not for a national or racial purpose, but for a purpose that lay beyond races and nations, it not only undermined the jealous love of race and nationality which we find so constructive a force in the Greeks of the seventh and sixth centuries B.C., but also gradually divorced the very idea of aristocracy from that noble duty of caring for the hearts of the masses, which was the very task that gave all the gravity and higher responsibility to the calling of the ruler-aristocrat. By doing this, it destroyed in part his conscientiousness and his earnestness, and left him only the "craft" or business of governing, which, as I have pointed out, is much more often taken for granted by a people, even when it is done with the most consummate skill, than that more delicate and artistic duty of firing their imaginations and filling their hearts, which constitutes the divine element of rulership.

"I say it seems to me," says Bolingbroke,[1] "that the Author of nature has thought fit to mingle from time to time, among the societies of men, a few, and but a few of those, on whom He is graciously pleased to bestow a larger proportion of the ethereal spirit than is given in the ordinary course of His providence to the sons of men. These are they who engross almost the whole reason of the species, who are born to instruct, to guide and to preserve; who are designed to be the tutors and the guardians of human kind. When they prove such, they exhibit to us example of the highest virtue and the truest piety; and they deserve to have their festivals kept, instead of the pack of *Anachorites and Enthusiasts* with whose names the calendar is crowded and disgraced. When these men

---

[1] *On the Spirit of Patriotism* (Davies, 1775), p. 2.

apply their talents to other purposes, when they strive to be great and despise being good, they commit a most sacrilegious breach of trust; they pervert the means, they defeat as far as in them lies the designs of Providence, and disturb in some sort the system of Infinite Wisdom. To misapply these talents is the most diffused, and therefore the greatest, of crimes in its nature and consequences, but to keep them unexerted and unemployed is a crime too."

And now, apart from the broad and general advantages to which I have already referred, what other real and lasting benefits does human society derive from these divine missionaries sent direct from flourishing life who occasionally descend among us, as Bolingbroke says, and who are much more deserving of a place in the Calendar than all the neurotic, exasperated and bitter saints who now figure there?

By the order and stability they establish, by their instinctive avoidance of those by-paths which lead to degeneration, and their deliberate choice of those highways leading to the ascent of their fellows, they give rise to everything which is of value on earth and which makes life a boon instead of a bane.

Beauty, Art, Will, Conscience and Spiritual Strength to face and to endure even the inevitable pangs and pains of a full life—nay, the very willingness to embrace them, because they are known to have a vital purpose—these are some of the things that can be reared by long tradition and careful discipline alone, and these are some of the things that depend for their existence on the aristocratic rule. For real Beauty is impossible without regular and stable living, lasting over generations; real Art is impossible without surplus health and energy, the outcome of generations of careful storing and garnering of vital forces, and without that direction and purpose which the supreme artist—the tasteful legislator—alone can give to the minor artists, be they painters, architects or musicians, within his realm. Will is impossible without sound instincts getting the mastery of a family or a tribe through generations spent in the rearing of those instincts, and causing that family or tribe passionately to desire one thing more than another; while Conscience and Spiritual Strength depend for their degree of development simply upon the length of the line of ancestors who have systematically built them up for an individual. For what I call conscience is nothing more than the voice of a man's ancestors speaking in him, saying this is right and that is wrong, and uttering this accompanying comment to his deeds, either feebly or powerfully in proportion to the length of the time during which unbroken traditions have lasted in his family. And Spiritual Strength in facing or assailing difficulties or pain is the outcome of the consciousness of being right, which arises from the fact that the comment of one's ancestors in one's breast is heard to be on one's side and with one's cause.

For all these things to be reared, even for the unbroken tradition, on which these things depend, to be established, there must, however, be great stability and permanence in the institutions of a race or a people, and it is the direction of flourishing life, alone, speaking through her representatives, that can reveal the good taste and the good judgment necessary for the preservation of such stability and permanence. For stability and permanence are desired only when beauty is present. When, therefore, we see things constantly changing, as they are to-day, when every day brings a new custom and a new curse, we may feel sure not only that the voice of the real ruler is silent in our midst, but that life is growing conscious of her ugliness. For, like a beautiful woman looking into a mirror, a people who have once achieved beauty, real beauty, and caught a glimpse of this beauty in all the departments of their social life, *must* cry for permanence rather than change, stability rather than flux. It is only then that change is the most dreaded catastrophe of all; for change threatens to rob the beauty from the face, the limbs and trunk of their civilisation, and their pride and love of its beauty is outraged by the very thought of such vandalism. The permanence and stability of a people's institutions are called by the ugly name of "stagnation" only when these institutions have little or no beauty.

But there is one more problem, and a very important one, which finds its best solution in the rule, not of all men by their equals, but of the mass of men by the aristocrat as I have attempted to sketch him in the preceding pages.

In all civilised human communities there have been and always will be a certain number of menial offices that some have to perform for others—offices which do not necessarily debase, but which may on occasion humiliate. It is, therefore, clear that in order that even the menial office may seem to have a sheen of gold upon it, the personality for whom it is performed must be such as to glorify it and transfigure it in the eyes of the servant. It is not only foolish, it is actually brutal to lose sight of this fact. Look into yourselves and inquire when it is that you feel humiliated by the performance of menial offices. You know perfectly well that for some people you perform them quite cheerfully, willingly; for others you resolutely decline to do so. What makes the difference in your attitude? It is useless to point to the menial office itself, for we can imagine that as remaining the same for all cases. What is it, then, that effects the change in your attitude? Obviously it is the quality of the person for whom the menial office is performed.

When men exist, therefore, whose characters and achievements shed a glamour upon everything that surrounds them, no duty they can impose upon their immediate entourage, no effort they can demand of it, whether it be the bearing of children or the building of a pyramid, can be felt as a humiliation or as an act of oppression. And it is only in such conditions that menial offices are performed daily, year in, year out, century after century, without a suggestion of that rankling spirit of detestation and loathing which, when it ultimately finds a vent, rises up in the form of the black cloud of revolution and revolt, and thunders out the cry of Liberty and Emancipation!

JACOB BURCKHARDT

The great Swiss historian Jacob Burckhardt (1818–1897) was inspired by fear; he feared for the future of civilization; he feared for the future of man. Like his great contemporary, Tocqueville, he was regarded as something of a crank in his own time. Like Tocqueville, he is regarded as a great prophet by our time; his voice speaks with a special meaning to a generation that has witnessed the horrors of Nazism and Communism. He feared democracy, oriented as it is to the caprices of mass man, and predicted the rise of the *terribles simplificateurs,* Adam Müller's *gewaltmenschen,* who would introduce rule by naked force. "In the twentieth century," he lamented, "authoritarianism will raise its head . . . and a terrifying head it will be." To a German official he wrote, "I have a presentiment that may now seem completely mad, but yet will not leave me. The military state must become a large scale industrialist . . . the development of a crafty and enduring tyranny is still in its infancy: it is in Germany that it will probably first grow to maturity." Among those to accept this chilling prophecy was Burckhardt's colleague at Basle University, Nietzsche. But Burckhardt was not a mere prophet; he was a historian of immense genius. We still view the Italian Renaissance as he did in his masterpiece, *The Civilization of the Renaissance in Italy* (1860). His other great works, *The Age of Constantine the Great* (1852) and *Cicerone* (1853) are still avidly studied by historians. "If Burckhardt's conservatism was inspired by fear," H. R. Trevor-Roper has written, "at least it was not fear of material loss: it was fear of a renewal of barbarism through social discontinuity; and who can say . . . his . . . prophesies, which were to be so soon and so shockingly fulfilled, [were] wrong? Or who can afford to disregard his warning that when a civilization loses interest in its history, viewed as a continuous, living culture, it is in danger of decay?"[1]

From *Force and Freedom: Reflections on History*, ed. James Hasting Nichols (New York: Pantheon Books, 1943). Reprinted with permission of the publisher.

JACOB BURCKHARDT

Notes on the Origin and Nature of the Present Crisis

The long peace dating from 1815 had created an optical illusion, namely that a permanent balance of power had been established. In any case, from the very outset too little account was taken of the mutability of national temperaments.

The Restoration and its ostensible principle of Legitimacy, which was in effect a reaction against the spirit of the French Revolution, restored in most unequal fashion a number of former modes of life and law and a series of national frontiers; on the other hand, it was impossible to banish from the world the continuing after-effects of the French Revolution, namely, the actual and far-reaching equality before the law (in taxation, qualification for office, the division of inheritances), the transferability of landed property, the placing of all property at the disposal of industry, and religious parity in a number of countries whose populations were now very mixed.

The State itself, moreover, was determined not to relinquish one of the results of the Revolution, namely the great expansion in the idea of its power which had come about in the interim and was due, among other things, to the Napoleonic Caesarism which had been imitated everywhere. The Power State of its very nature postulated equality, even where it abandoned places at Court and in the army as spoils to its aristocracy.

Opposing this, there stood the spirit of those peoples who had waged the wars of 1812–1815 in a state of extreme national fervor. A spirit of criticism had awakened which, however much men needed rest, could no longer lie still, and henceforth applied a new standard to life as a whole.

When the July Revolution broke out in 1830, its general significance as a European crisis far outweighed its specific political significance. Austria, Prussia and Russia remained to all appearances where they were. Everywhere else the constitution was hailed as a panacea, where any serious efforts were made in that direction.

Constitutions, however, were as powerless as anything else on earth to satisfy the greed that had been aroused. Firstly, the French constitution itself was a very unsatisfactory structure. The suffrage was so restricted that the Chamber was later powerless to come to the help of the government in its impasse, because it was itself representative only of a small minority. At the same time, the government's programme, *la paix à tout prix,* was artificially charged with hatred. Louis Philippe would have been able to bequeath his peace programme to the Chamber had it been on a much broader basis, namely that of universal suffrage.

In Western Europe, during the Thirties, politics developed into a general radicalism, namely that way of thinking which attributed all evils to existing political conditions and their representatives, and thought to find salvation in demolishing and rebuilding the whole structure from the foundations with the help of abstract principles which already revealed a much closer kinship with North America.

With the Forties there set in a development of Socialistic and Communistic theories, in part the product of conditions in the great English and French industrial towns; they embraced the whole social edifice, an inevitable result of untrammelled traffic. The freedom actually existing was ample for such ideas to spread unchecked, so that, according to Renan, after 1840 a deterioration of their quality was distinctly perceptible. At the same time, nobody had any idea of what and how strong the opposing forces might be. How far the right of defence was misunderstood became evident in February 1848.

This state of affairs was reflected in the literature and poetry of the time. Derision, loud snarling and *Weltschmerz* characterized its new, post-Byronic attitude.

Then came the February Revolution of 1848. In the midst of the general upheaval, it caused a sudden clearing of the horizon. By far its most important, though only ephemeral, result was the proclamation of union in Germany and Italy. Socialism proved far less powerful than people had imagined, for the June days in Paris almost at once restored the monarchist and constitutional party to power, and the sense of property and money-making was more intense than ever.

The climax of the movement in the first battle of Custozza was followed, it is true, for the time being by a general reaction, the forms and frontiers previously existing being for the most part restored. The reaction, however, was in most countries far from complete, and cross-currents set in everywhere.

With dynasties, bureaucracies and militarisms continuing to exist, the *inward* crisis in men's minds had to be left almost entirely out of account. Public opinion, the press, the swiftly rising tide of traffic, won the day everywhere and were already so intrinsic a part of money-making that any check on the one meant damage to the other. Everywhere industry was striving for a place in world industry.

At the same time, the events of 1848 had given the ruling classes a deeper insight into the people. Louis Napoleon had risked universal suffrage for the elections, and others followed his lead. The conservative strain in the rural populations had been recognized, though no attempt had been made to assess precisely how far it might be extended from the elections to everything and everybody (institutions, taxes, etc.).

With all business swelling into big business, the views of the business man took the following line: on the one hand, the State should be no more than the protective guarantor of his interests and of his type of intelligence, henceforth assumed to be the main purpose of the world. Indeed, it was his desire that his type of intelligence should obtain possession of the State by means of constitutional adjustments. On the other hand, there prevailed a profound distrust of constitutional liberty in practice, since it was more likely to be used by destructive forces.

For at the same time the ideas of the French Revolution and the reform principles of modern times were both finding active expression in democracy, so-called, a doctrine nourished by a thousand springs, and varying greatly with the social status of its adherents. Only in one respect was it consistent, namely, in the insatiability of its demand for State control of the individual. Thus it effaces the boundaries between State and Society, and looks to the State for the things that Society will most likely refuse to do, while maintaining a permanent condition of argument and change and ultimately vindicating the right to work and subsistence for certain castes.

Meanwhile, the general menace of the political situation was deepening. All positions had been radically changed, and many profoundly unsettled, by the events of 1848. The governments of the greatest powers could not but welcome some foreign diversion.

Only complete unanimity among all the governments could have preserved existing frontiers and the so-called balance of power.

March 1873. The first great phenomenon to follow the war of 1870–1871 was a further extraordinary intensification of money-making, which went far beyond the mere making good of gaps and losses, and was combined with the exploitation and activation of an infinite number of sources of wealth and the inevitable fraudulent schemes connected with them (big business).

The spiritual results, however, of which some are already visible, and some about to become so, are that the so-called "best minds" are going into business or are actually being educated to that end by their parents. Bureaucracy, like the army in France and other countries, is no longer a career. In Prussia the most strenuous efforts are necessary in order to keep it as such.

Art and science have the greatest difficulty in preventing themselves from sinking into a mere branch of urban money-making and from being carried away on the stream of general unrest. The utmost effort and self-denial will be necessary if they are to remain creatively independent in view of the relation in which they stand to the daily press, to cosmopolitan traffic, to world exhibitions. A further menace is the decay of local patriotism, with its advantages and disadvantages, and a great decrease even in national patriotism.

What classes and strata of society will now become the real representatives of culture, will give us our scholars, artists and poets, our creative personalities?

Or is everything to turn into big business, as in America?

Now for the political results. Two great nations, Germany and Italy, have been founded, partly with the help of public opinion, long since in a state of extreme agitation, partly by means of great wars. A further factor is the spectacle of rapid demolition and reconstruction in countries whose established polity had long been regarded as immutable. Hence political adventure has become a matter of daily occurrence among the nations, and the opposing convictions, which tended to defend any existing institutions, grow steadily weaker. Statesmen no longer seek to combat "democracy," but in some way or other to reckon with it, to eliminate risks as far as possible from the transition to what is now regarded as inevitable. The form of a State is to all intents and purposes no longer defended, but only its area and power, democracy for the time being lending a helping hand. The sense of power and democratic feeling are for the most part indistinguishable. The Socialist systems have been the first to abandon the quest for power and to place their specific aims before anything else.

The republics of France and Spain may very well subsist as republics by sheer force of habit and from fear of the terrible moment of change, and if, from time to time, they take on some other form, it will tend to be a Caesarian rather than a dynastic monarchy.

One wonders how soon the other countries will follow suit.

These ferments, however, conflict with the money-making current, and ultimately the latter proves the stronger. The masses want their peace and their pay. If they get them from a republic or a monarchy, they will cling to either. If not, without much ado they will support the first constitution to promise them what they want. A decision of the kind, of course, is never taken directly, but is always influenced by passion, personalities and the lingering effects of former situations.

The most complete programme is contained in Grant's last speech, which postulates one State and one language as the necessary goal of a purely money-making world.

And finally, the question of the Church. In the whole of Western Europe the philosophy issuing from the French Revolution is in conflict with the Church, particularly the Catholic Church, a conflict ultimately springing from the optimism of the former and the pessimism of the latter.

Of late, that pessimism has been deepened by the Syllabus, the *Concilium* and the doctrine of infallibility, the Church, for obscure reasons, having decided to offer a conscious opposition to modern ideas on a wide front.

Italy profited by the occasion to take Rome. Otherwise Italy, France and Spain, etc., have left theoretical questions alone, while Germany and Switzerland are attempting to force Catholicism into perfect obedience to the State, not only depriving it of any exemption from the common law, but reducing it to permanent impotence.

The great decision can only come from the mind of men. Will optimism, under the guise of power and money, continue to survive, and how long? Or, as the pessimist philosophy of today might seem to suggest, will there be a general change in thought such as took place in the third and fourth centuries?

FRIEDRICH NIETZSCHE

Nietzsche (1844–1900) has been called Rousseau in reverse. The traditional conservative hatred of Rousseau came to a head in Nietzsche's thought. To Nietzsche, Rousseau was an "idealist and canaille," his egalitarianism was a perversion of man's nature, putting the herd in control of society. In the democratic society, he argued, "the center of gravity belongs among the mediocre: mediocrity, as the surety and vehicle of the future, consolidates its position against the rule of the mob and the eccentrics (both usually in league). . . ." In the end, "mediocrity acquires spirit, genius, it becomes entertaining, it seduces. . . ." To Nietzsche, a Hitler or some similar degraded type must inevitably come to the head of the herd. His prophecy of this coming tyranny is one of the most chilling testaments of the 19th century. A man of immense philosophical genius, he held the chair of philology at Basle while still in his twenties. His books are among the most beautifully written philosophical works in the German language but have not always been successfully translated. He has been accused of all sorts of things—such as anti-Semitism and proto-Nazism—which appear no place in his writings, and which he himself would have bitterly opposed. The recent scholarship of Professor Walter Kauffman and others has greatly helped in revaluating Nietzsche as a thinker, and in refuting the charges made by his ideological critics.

From *Beyond Good and Evil,* trans. Helen Zimmern (London, 1909).

FRIEDRICH NIETZSCHE

Europe in the Age of Democracy

We "good Europeans," we also have hours when we allow ourselves a warm-hearted patriotism, a plunge and relapse into old loves and narrow views—I have just given an example of it—hours of national excitement, of patriotic anguish, and all other sorts of old-fashioned floods of sentiment. Duller spirits than we, may only get done with what confines its operations in us to hours and plays itself out in hours—in a considerable time: some in half a year, others in half a lifetime, according to the speed and strength with which they digest and "change their material." Indeed, I could think of sluggish, hesitating races, which, even in our rapidly moving Europe, would require half a century ere they could surmount such atavistic attacks of patriotism and soil-attachment, and return once more to reason, that is to say, to "good Europeanism." And while digressing on this possibility, I happen to become an ear-witness of a conversation between two old patriots—they were evidently both hard of hearing and consequently spoke all the louder. "*He* has as much, and knows as much, philosophy as a peasant or a corps-student," said the one—"he is still innocent. But what does that matter nowadays! It is the age of the masses: they lie on their belly before everything that is massive. And so also *in politicis*. A statesman who rears up for them a new Tower of Babel, some monstrosity of empire and power, they call 'great'—what does it matter that we more prudent and conservative ones do not meanwhile give up the old belief that it is only the great thought that gives greatness to an action or affair. Supposing a statesman were to bring his people into the position of being obliged henceforth to practise 'high politics,' for which they were by nature badly endowed and prepared, so that they would have to sacrifice their old and reliable virtues, out of love to a new and doubtful mediocrity;—supposing a statesman were to condemn his people generally to 'practise politics,' when they have hitherto had something better to do and think about, and when in the depths of their souls they have been unable to free themselves from a prudent loathing of the restlessness, emptiness, and noisy wranglings of the essentially politics-practising nations;—supposing such a statesman were to stimulate the slumbering passions and avidities of his people, were to make a stigma out of their former diffidence and delight in aloofness, an offence out of their exoticism and hidden permanency, were to depreciate their most radical proclivities, subvert their consciences, make their minds narrow, and their tastes 'national'— what! a statesman who should do all this, which his people would have to do penance for throughout their whole future, if they had a future, such a statesman would be *great*, would he?"—"Undoubtedly!" replied the other old patriot vehemently; "otherwise he *could not* have done it! It was mad perhaps to wish such a thing! But perhaps everything great has just been mad at its commencement!"— "Misuse of words!" cried his interlocutor, contradictorily—"strong! strong! Strong and mad! *Not* great!" —The old men had obviously become heated as they thus shouted their "truths" in each other's faces; but I, in my happiness and apartness, considered how soon a stronger one will become master of the strong; and also that there is a compensation for the intellectual superficialising of a nation—namely, in the deepening of another.

Whether we call it "civilisation," or "humanising," or "progress," which now distinguishes the European; whether we call it simply, without praise or blame, by the political formula: the *democratic* movement in Europe—behind all the moral and political foregrounds pointed to by such formulas, an immense *physiological* process goes on, which is ever extending: the process of the assimilation of Europeans; their increasing detachment from the conditions under which, climatically and hereditarily, united races originate; their increasing independence of every definite *milieu,* that for centuries would fain inscribe itself with equal demands on soul and body;—that is to say, the slow emergence of an essentially *super-national* and nomadic species of man, who possesses, physiologically speaking, a maximum of the art and power of adaptation as his typical distinction. This process of the *evolving European,* which can be retarded in its *tempo* by great relapses, but will perhaps just gain and grow thereby in vehemence and depth—the still raging storm and stress of "national sentiment" pertains to it, and also the anarchism which is appearing at present—this process will probably arrive at results on which its naïve propagators and panegyrists, the apostles of "modern ideas," would least care to reckon. The same new conditions under which on an average a levelling and mediocrising of man will take place—a useful, industrious, variously serviceable and clever herd-animal-like man—are in the highest degree suitable to give rise to exceptional men of the most dangerous and attractive qualities. For, while the capacity for adaptation, which is ever trying changing conditions, and begins a new work with every generation, almost with every decade, makes the *powerfulness* of the type impossible; while the collective impression of such future Europeans will probably be that of numerous, talkative, weak-willed, and very handy workmen who *require* a master, a commander, as they require their daily bread; while, therefore, the democratising of Europe will tend to the production of a type prepared for *slavery* in the most subtle sense of the term: the *strong* man will necessarily in individual and exceptional cases, become stronger and richer than he has perhaps ever been before—owing to the unprejudicedness of his schooling, owing to the immense variety of practice, art, and disguise. I meant to say that the democratising of Europe is at the same time an involuntary arrangement for the rearing of *tyrants* —taking the word in all its meanings, even in its most spiritual sense.

Part VI

The Conservators of Liberty

Liberty plays a central role in the thinking of most post–French Revolutionary conservative thinkers. And to conserve liberty has been one of their highest goals. The intellectual armor of the libertarians is impressive, both philosophically and politically. Theirs is a tradition that includes philosophers (Adam Smith and Adam Ferguson), historians (Lord Acton and Walter Bagehot), as well as economists and sociologists in the modern sense of those disciplines. In recent years this wing of conservative thought—largely because of its intellectual importance—has gained a wide following within the academy. And in the realm of practical politics, the two most controversial English-speaking politicians of the 1960s, Barry Goldwater and Enoch Powell, have been libertarians. In an age that has witnessed the rise of collectivist ideologies, the philosophers and politicians of freedom are more important sources of truth than ever before.

ADAM SMITH

The name of Adam Smith (1723–1790) is known even to people who have never bothered to read any of his works. His *Inquiry into the Nature and Causes of the Wealth of Nations* (1776) is more often referred to than read. His *Theory of Moral Sentiments,* one of the greatest examples of Scottish philosophy, is virtually ignored. Like his friend David Hume, he was regarded in his own time primarily as a philosopher and not an economist. Numerous strains appear in his thought: the French Physiocrats play as important a role in his approach to economic analysis as do the mercantilists whom he criticized. Smith, as his biographer E. G. West has reminded us, was not the doctrinaire apostle of any single school of thought. Like any sound economic thinker, he was prepared to make concessions to his own rules. [1]

From *The Wealth of Nations* (London, 1932). This work is available in numerous editions.

[1]E. G. West, *Adam Smith: The Man and His Works* (New Rochelle, N. Y.: Arlington House, 1969), p. 24.

ADAM SMITH

Of the Causes of Improvement in the Productive Powers of Labour, and of the Order According to Which its Produce is Naturally Distributed Among the Different Ranks of the People

OF THE DIVISION OF LABOUR

The greatest improvement in the productive powers of labour, and the greater part of the skill, dexterity, and judgment with which it is anywhere directed, or applied, seem to have been the effects of the division of labour.

The effects of the division of labour, in the general business of society, will be more easily understood by considering in what manner it operates in some particular manufactures. It is commonly supposed to be carried furthest in some very trifling ones; not perhaps that it really is carried further in them than in others of more importance: but in those trifling manufactures which are destined to supply the small wants of but a small number of people, the whole number of workmen must necessarily be small; and those employed in every different branch of the work can often be collected into the same workhouse, and placed at once under the view of the spectator. In those great manufactures, on the contrary, which are destined to supply the great wants of the great body of the people, every different branch of the work employs so great a number of workmen that it is impossible to collect them all into the same workhouse. We can seldom see more, at one time, than those employed in one single branch. Though in such manufactures, therefore, the work may really be divided into a much greater number of parts than in those of a more trifling nature, the division is not near so obvious, and has accordingly been much less observed.

To take an example, therefore, from a very trifling manufacture; but one in which the division of labour has been very often taken notice of, the trade of the pin-maker; a workman not educated to this business (which the division of labour has rendered a distinct trade), nor acquainted with the use of the machinery employed in it (to the invention of which the same division of labour has probably given occasion), could scarce, perhaps, with his utmost industry, make one pin in a day, and certainly could not make twenty. But in the way in which this business is now carried on, not only the whole work is a peculiar trade, but it is divided into a number of branches, of which the greater part are likewise peculiar trades. One man draws out the wire, another straights it, a third cuts it, a fourth points it, a fifth grinds it at the top for receiving the head; to make the head requires two or three distinct operations; to put it on is·a peculiar business, to whiten the pins is another; it is even a trade by itself to put them into the paper; and the important business of making a pin is, in this manner, divided into about eighteen distinct operations, which, in some manufactories, are all performed by distinct hands, though in others the same man will sometimes perform two or three of them. I have seen a small manufactory of this kind where ten men only were employed, and where some of them consequently performed two or three distinct operations. But though they were very poor, and therefore but indifferently accommodated with the necessary machinery, they could, when they exerted themselves, make among them about twelve pounds of pins in a day. There are in a pound upwards of four thousand pins of a middling size. Those ten persons, therefore, could make among them upwards of forty-eight thousand pins in a day. Each person, therefore, making a tenth part of forty-eight thousand pins, might be considered as making four thousand eight hundred pins in a day. But if they had all wrought separately and independently, and without any of them having been educated to this peculiar business, they certainly could not each of them have made twenty, perhaps not one pin in a day; that is, certainly, not the two hundred and fortieth, perhaps not the four thousand eight hundredth part of what they are at present capable of performing, in consequence of a proper division and combination of their different operations.

In every other art and manufacture, the effects of the division of labour are similar to what they are in this very trifling one; though, in many of them, the labour can neither be so much subdivided, nor reduced to so great a simplicity of operation. The division of labour, however, so far as it can be introduced, occasions, in every art, a proportionable increase of the productive powers of labour. The separation of different trades and employments from one another seems to have taken place in consequence of this advantage. This separation, too, is generally carried furthest in those countries which enjoy the highest degree of industry and improvement; what is the work of one man in a rude state of society being generally that of several in an improved one. In every improved society, the farmer is generally nothing but a farmer; the manufacturer, nothing but a manufacturer. The labour, too, which is necessary to produce any one complete manufacture is almost always divided among a great number of hands. How many different trades are employed in each branch of the linen and woollen manufactures from the growers of the flax and the wool, to the bleachers and smoothers of the linen, or to the dyers and dressers of the cloth! The nature of agriculture, indeed, does not admit of so many subdivisions of labour, nor of so complete a separation of one business from another, as manufactures. It is impossible to separate so entirely the business of the grazier from that of the corn-farmer as the trade of the carpenter is commonly separated from that of the smith. The spinner is almost always a distinct person from the weaver; but the ploughman, the harrower, the sower of the seed, and the reaper of the corn, are often the same. The occasions for those different sorts of labour returning with the different seasons of the year, it is impossible that one man should be constantly employed in any one of them. This impossibility of making so complete and entire a separation of all the different branches of labour employed in agriculture is perhaps the reason why the improvement of the productive powers of labour in this art does not always keep pace with their improvement in manufactures. The most opulent nations, indeed, generally excel all their neighbours in agriculture as well as in manufactures; but they are commonly more distinguished by their superiority in the latter than in the former. Their lands are in general better cultivated, and having more labour and expense bestowed upon them, produce more in proportion to the extent and natural fertility of the ground. But this superiority of produce is seldom much more than in proportion to the superiority of labour and expense. In agriculture, the labour of the rich country is not always much more productive than that of the poor; or, at least, it is never so much more productive as it commonly is in manufactures. The corn of the rich country, therefore, will not always, in the same degree of goodness, come cheaper to market than that of the poor. The corn of Poland, in the same degree of goodness, is as cheap as that of France, notwithstanding the superior opulence and improvement of the latter country. The corn of France is, in the corn provinces, fully as good, and in most years nearly about the same price with the corn of England, though, in opulence and improvement, France is perhaps inferior to England. The corn-lands of England, however, are better cultivated than those of France, and the corn-lands of France are said to be much better cultivated than those of Poland. But though the poor country, notwithstanding the inferiority of its cultivation, can, in some measure, rival the rich in the cheapness and goodness of its corn, it can pretend to no such competition in its manufactures; at least if those manufactures suit the soil, climate, and situation of the rich country. The silks of France are better and cheaper than those of England, because the silk manufacture, at least under the present high duties upon the importation of raw silk, does not so well suit the climate of England as that of France. But the hardware and the coarse woollens of England are beyond all comparison superior to those of France, and much cheaper too in the same degree of goodness. In Poland there are said to be scarce any manufactures of any kind, a few of those coarser household manufactures excepted, without which no country can well subsist.

This great increase of the quantity of work which, in consequence of the division of labour, the same number of people are capable of performing, is owing to three different circumstances; first, to the increase of dexterity in every particular workman; secondly, to the saving of the time which is commonly lost in passing from one species of work to another; and lastly, to the invention of a great number of machines which facilitate and abridge labour, and enable one man to do the work of many.

First, the improvement of the dexterity of the workman necessarily increases the quantity of the work he can perform; and the division of labour, by reducing every man's business to some one simple operation, and by making this operation the sole employment of his life, necessarily increases very much the dexterity of the workman. A common smith, who, though accustomed to handle the hammer, has never been used to make nails, if upon some particular occasion he is obliged to attempt it, will scarce, I am assured, be able to make above two or three hundred nails in a day, and those too very bad ones. A smith who has been accustomed to make nails, but whose sole or principal business has not been that of a nailer, can seldom with his utmost diligence make more than eight hundred or a thousand nails in a day. I have seen several boys under twenty years of age who had never exercised any other trade but that of making nails, and who, when they exerted themselves, could make, each of them, upwards of two thousand three hundred nails in a day. The making of a nail, however, is by no means one of the simplest operations. The same person blows the bellows, stirs or mends the fire as there is occasion, heats the iron, and forges every part of the nail: in forging the head too he is obliged to change his tools. The different operations into which the making of a pin, or of a metal button, is subdivided, are all of them much more simple, and the dexterity of the person, of whose life it has been the sole business to perform them, is usually much greater. The rapidity with which some of the operations of those manufactures are performed, exceeds what the human hand could, by those who had never seen them, be supposed capable of acquiring.

Secondly, the advantage which is gained by saving the time commonly lost in passing from one sort of work to another is much greater than we should at first view be apt to imagine it. It is impossible to pass very quickly from one kind of work to another that is carried on in a different place and with quite different tools. A country weaver, who cultivates a small farm, must lose a good deal of time in passing from his loom to the field, and from the field to his loom. When the two trades can be carried on in the same workhouse, the loss of time is no doubt much less. It is even in this case, however, very considerable. A man commonly saunters a little in turning his hand from one sort of employment to another. When he first begins the new work he is seldom very keen and hearty; his mind, as they say, does not go to it, and for some time he rather trifles than applies to good purpose. The habit of sauntering and of indolent careless application, which is naturally, or rather necessarily acquired by every country workman who is obliged to change his work and his tools every half hour, and to apply his hand in twenty different ways almost every day of his life, renders him almost always slothful and lazy, and incapable of any vigorous application even on the most pressing occasions. Independent, therefore, of his deficiency in point of dexterity, this cause alone must always reduce considerably the qualtity of work which he is capable of performing.

Thirdly, and lastly, everybody must be sensible how much labour is facilitated and abridged by the application of proper machinery. It is unnecessary to give any example. I shall only observe, therefore, that the invention of all those machines by which labour is so much facilitated and abridged seems to have been originally owing to the division of labour. Men are much more likely to discover easier and readier methods of attaining any object when the whole attention of their minds is directed towards that single object than when it is dissipated among a great variety of things. But in consequence of the division of labour, the whole of every man's attention comes naturally to be directed towards some one very simple object. It is naturally to be expected, therefore, that some one or other of those who are employed in each particular branch of labour should soon find out easier and readier methods of performing their own particular work, wherever the nature of it admits of such improvement. A great part of the machines made use of in those manufactures in which labour is most subdivided, were originally the inventions of common workmen, who, being each of them employed in some very simple operation, naturally turned their thoughts towards finding out easier and readier methods of performing it. Whoever has been much accustomed to visit such manufactures must frequently have been shown very pretty machines, which were the inventions of such workmen in order to facilitate and quicken their own particular part of the work. In the first fire-engines, a boy was constantly employed to open and shut alternately the communication between the boiler and the cylinder, according as the piston either ascended or descended. One of those boys, who loved to play with his companions, observed that, by tying a string from the handle of the valve which opened this communication to another part of the machine, the valve would open and shut without his assistance, and leave him at liberty to divert himself with his play-fellows. One of the greatest improvements that has been made upon this machine, since it was first invented, was in this manner the discovery of a boy who wanted to save his own labour.

All the improvements in machinery, however, have by no means been the inventions of those who had occasion to use the machines. Many improvements have been made by the ingenuity of the makers of the machines, when to make them became the business of a peculiar trade; and some by that of those who are called philosophers or men of speculation, whose trade it is not to do anything, but to observe everything; and who, upon that account, are often capable of combining together the powers of the most distant and dissimilar objects. In the progress of society, philosophy or speculation becomes, like every other employment, the principal or sole trade and occupation of a particular class of citizens. Like every other employment too, it is subdivided into a great number of different branches, each of which affords occupation to a peculiar tribe or class of philosophers; and this subdivision of employment in philosophy, as well as in every other business, improves dexterity, and saves time. Each individual becomes more expert in his own peculiar branch, more work is done upon the whole, and the quantity of science is considerably increased by it.

It is the great multiplication of the productions of all the different arts, in consequence of the division of labour, which occasions, in a well-governed society, that universal opulence which extends itself to the lowest ranks of the people. Every workman has a great quantity of his own work to dispose of beyond what he himself has occasion for; and every other workman being exactly in the same situation, he is enabled to exchange a great quantity of his own goods for a great quantity, or, what comes to the same thing, for the price of a great quantity of theirs. He supplies them abundantly with what they have occasion for, and they accommodate him as amply with what he has occasion for, and a general plenty diffuses itself through all the different ranks of the society.

Observe the accommodation of the most common artificer or day-labourer in a civilised and thriving country, and you will perceive that the number of people of whose industry a part, though but a small part, has been employed in procuring him this accommodation, exceeds all computation. The woollen coat, for example, which covers the day-labourer, as coarse and rough as it may appear, is the produce of the joint labour of a great multitude of workmen. The shepherd, the sorter of the wool, the wool-comber or carder, the dyer, the scribbler, the spinner, the weaver, the fuller, the dresser, with many others, must all join their different arts in order to complete even this homely production. How many merchants and carriers, besides, must have been employed in transporting the materials from some of those workmen to others who often live in a very distant part of the country! how much commerce and navigation in particular, how many ship-builders, sailors, sailmakers, rope-makers, must have been employed in order to bring together the different drugs made use of by the dyer, which often come from the remotest corners of the world! What a variety of labour, too, is necessary in order to produce the tools of the meanest of those workmen! To say nothing of such complicated machines as the ship of the sailor, the mill of the fuller, or even the loom of the weaver, let us consider only what a variety of labour is requisite in order to form that very simple machine, the shears with which the shepherd clips the wool. The miner, the builder of the furnace for smelting the ore, the seller of the timber, the burner of the charcoal to be made use of in the smelting-house, the brick-maker, the brick-layer, the workmen who attend the furnace, the mill-wright, the forger, the smith, must all of them join their different arts in order to produce them. Were we to examine, in the same manner, all the different parts of his dress and household furniture, the coarse linen shirt which he wears next his skin, the shoes which cover his feet, the bed which he lies on, and all the different parts which compose it, the kitchen-grate at which he prepares his victuals, the coals which he makes use of for that purpose, dug from the bowels of the earth, and brought to him perhaps by a long sea and a long land carriage, all the other utensils of his kitchen, all the furniture of his table, the knives and forks, the earthen or pewter plates upon which he serves up and divides his victuals, the different hands employed in preparing his bread and his beer, the glass window which lets in the heat and the light, and keeps out the wind and the rain, with all the knowledge and art requisite for preparing that beautiful and happy invention, without which these northern parts of the world could scarce have afforded a very comfortable habitation, together with the tools of all the different workmen employed in producing those different conveniences; if we examine, I say, all these things, and consider what a variety of labour is employed about each of them, we shall be sensible that, without the assistance and co-operation of many thousands, the very meanest person in a civilised country could not be provided, even according to what we very falsely imagine the easy and simple manner in which he is commonly accommodated. Compared, indeed, with the more extravagant luxury of the great, his accommodation must no doubt appear extremely simple and easy; and yet it may be true, perhaps, that the accommodation of a European prince does not always so much exceed that of an industrious and frugal peasant as the accommodation of the latter exceeds that of many an African king, the absolute master of the lives and liberties of ten thousand naked savages.

OF THE PRINCIPLE WHICH GIVES OCCASION TO THE DIVISION OF LABOUR

This division of labour, from which so many advantages are derived, is not originally the effect of any human wisdom, which foresees and intends that general opulence to which it gives occasion. It is the necessary, though very slow and gradual consequence of a certain propensity in human nature which has in view no such extensive utility; the propensity to truck, barter, and exchange one thing for another.

Whether this propensity be one of those original principles in human nature of which no further account can be given; or whether, as seems more proba-

ble, it be the necessary consequence of the faculties
of reason and speech, it belongs not to our present
subject to inquire. It is common to all men, and to be
found in no other race of animals, which seem to
know neither this nor any other species of contracts.
Two greyhounds, in running down the same hare,
have sometimes the appearance of acting in some
sort of concert. Each turns her towards his compan-
ion, or endeavours to intercept her when his com-
panion turns her towards himself. This, however, is
not the effect of any contract, but of the accidental
concurrence of their passions in the same object at
that particular time. Nobody ever saw a dog make a
fair and deliberate exchange of one bone for another
with another dog. Nobody ever saw one animal by its
gestures and natural cries signify to another, this is
mine, that yours; I am willing to give this for that.
When an animal wants to obtain something either of
a man or of another animal, it has no other means of
persuasion but to gain the favour of those whose
service it requires. A puppy fawns upon its dam, and
a spaniel endeavours by a thousand attractions to
engage the attention of its master who is at dinner,
when it wants to be fed by him. Man sometimes uses
the same arts with his brethren, and when he has no
other means of engaging them to act according to his
inclinations, endeavours by every servile and fawn-
ing attention to obtain their good will. He has not
time, however, to do this upon every occasion. In
civilised society he stands at all times in need of the
cooperation and assistance of great multitudes,
while his whole life is scarce sufficient to gain the
friendship of a few persons. In almost every other
race of animals each individual, when it is grown up
to maturity, is entirely independent, and in its natu-

ral state has occasion for the assistance of no other living creature. But man has almost constant occasion for the help of his brethren, and it is in vain for him to expect it from their benevolence only. He will be more likely to prevail if he can interest their self-love in his favour, and show them that it is for their own advantage to do for him what he requires of them. Whoever offers to another a bargain of any kind, proposes to do this. Give me that which I want, and you shall have this which you want, is the meaning of every such offer; and it is in this manner that we obtain from one another the far greater part of those good offices which we stand in need of. It is not from the benevolence of the butcher, the brewer, or the baker that we expect our dinner, but from their regard to their own interest. We address ourselves, not to their humanity but to their self-love, and never talk to them of our own necessities but of their advantages. Nobody but a beggar chooses to depend chiefly upon the benevolence of his fellow-citizens. Even a beggar does not depend upon it entirely. The charity of well-disposed people, indeed, supplies him with the whole fund of his subsistence. But though this principle ultimately provides him with all the necessaries of life which he has occasion for, it neither does nor can provide him with them as he has occasion for them. The greater part of his occasional wants are supplied in the same manner as those of other people, by treaty, by barter, and by purchase. With the money which one man gives him he purchases food. The old clothes which another bestows upon him he exchanges for other old clothes which suit him better, or for lodging, or for food, or for money, with which he can buy either food, clothes, or lodging, as he has occasion.

As it is by treaty, by barter, and by purchase that we obtain from one another the greater part of those mutual good offices which we stand in need of, so it is this same trucking disposition which originally gives occasion to the division of labour. In a tribe of hunters or shepherds a particular person makes bows and arrows, for example, with more readiness and dexterity than any other. He frequently exchanges them for cattle or for venison with his companions; and he finds at last that he can in this manner get more cattle and venison than if he himself went to the field to catch them. From a regard to his own interest, therefore, the making of bows and arrows grows to be his chief business, and he becomes a sort of armourer. Another excels in making the frames and covers of their little huts or movable houses. He is accustomed to be of use in this way to his neighbours, who reward him in the same manner with cattle and with venison, till at last he finds it his interest to dedicate himself entirely to this employment, and to become a sort of house-carpenter. In the same manner a third becomes a smith or a brazier, a fourth a tanner or dresser of hides or skins, the principal part of the clothing of savages. And thus the certainty of being able to exchange all that surplus part of the produce of his own labour, which is over and above his own consumption, for such parts of the produce of other men's labour as he may have occasion for, encourages every man to apply himself to a particular occupation, and to cultivate and bring to perfection whatever talent or genius he may possess for that particular species of business.

The difference of natural talents in different men is, in reality, much less than we are aware of; and the very different genius which appears to distinguish men of different professions, when grown up to maturity, is not upon many occasions so much the cause as the effect of the division of labour. The difference between the most dissimilar characters, between a philosopher and a common street porter, for example, seems to arise not so much from nature as from habit, custom, and education. When they came into the world, and for the first six or eight years of their existence, they were perhaps very much alike, and neither their parents nor play-fellows could perceive any remarkable difference. About that age, or soon after, they come to be employed in very different occupations. The difference of talents comes then to be taken notice of, and widens by degrees, till at last the vanity of the philosopher is willing to acknowledge scarce any resemblance. But without the disposition to truck, barter, and exchange, every man must have procured to himself every necessary and conveniency of life which he wanted. All must have had the same duties to perform, and the same work to do, and there could have been no such difference of employment as could alone give occasion to any great difference of talents.

As it is this disposition which forms that difference of talents, so remarkable among men of different professions, so it is this same disposition which renders that difference useful. Many tribes of animals acknowledged to be all of the same species derive from nature a much more remarkable distinction of genius, than what, antecedent to custom and education, appears to take place among men. By nature a philosopher is not in genius and disposition half so different from a street porter, as a mastiff is from a greyhound, or a greyhound from a spaniel, or this last from a shepherd's dog. Those different tribes of animals, however, though all of the same species, are of scarce any use to one another. The strength of the mastiff is not, in the least, supported either by the swiftness of the greyhound, or by the sagacity of the spaniel, or by the docility of the shepherd's dog. The effects of those different geniuses and talents, for want of the power or disposition to barter and exchange, cannot be brought into a common stock, and do not in the least contribute to the better accommodation and conveniency of the species. Each animal is still obliged to support and defend itself, separately and independently, and derives no sort of advantage from that variety of talents with which nature has distinguished its fellows. Among men, on the contrary, the more dissimilar geniuses are of use to one another; the different produces of their respective talents, by the general disposition to truck, barter, and exchange, being brought, as it were, into a common stock, where every man may purchase whatever part of the produce of other men's talents he has occasion for.

THAT THE DIVISION OF LABOUR IS LIMITED BY THE EXTENT OF THE MARKET

As it is the power of exchanging that gives occasion to the division of labour, so the extent of this division must always be limited by the extent of that power, or, in other words, by the extent of the market. When the market is very small, no person can have any encouragement to dedicate himself entirely to one employment, for want of the power to exchange all that surplus part of the produce of his own labour, which is over and above his own consumption, for such parts of the produce of other men's labour as he has occasion for.

There are some sorts of industry, even of the lowest kind, which can be carried on nowhere but in a great town. A porter, for example, can find employment and subsistence in no other place. A village is by much too narrow a sphere for him; even an ordinary market town is scarce large enough to afford him constant occupation. In the lone houses and very small villages which are scattered about in so desert a country as the Highlands of Scotland, every farmer must be butcher, baker and brewer for his own family. In such situations we can scarce expect to find even a smith, a carpenter, or a mason, within less than twenty miles of another of the same trade. The scattered families that live at eight or ten miles distance from the nearest of them must learn to perform themselves a great number of little pieces of work, for which, in more populous countries, they would call in the assistance of those workmen. Country workmen are almost everywhere obliged to apply themselves to all the different branches of industry that have so much affinity to one another as to be employed about the same sort of materials. A country carpenter deals in every sort of work that is made of wood: a country smith in every sort of work that is made of iron. The former is not only a carpenter, but a joiner, a cabinet-maker, and even a carver in wood, as well as a wheel-wright, a plough-wright, a cart and waggon maker. The employments of the latter are still more various. It is impossible there should be such a trade as even that of a nailer in the remote and inland parts of the Highlands of Scotland. Such a workman at the rate of a thousand nails a day, and three hundred working days in the year, will make three hundred thousand nails in the year. But in such a situation it would be impossible to dispose of one thousand, that is, of one day's work in the year. As by means of water-carriage a more extensive market is opened to every sort of industry than what land-carriage alone can afford, it, so it is upon the sea-coast, and along the banks of navigable rivers, that industry of every kind naturally begins to subdivide and improve itself, and it is frequently not till a long time after that those improvements extend themselves to the inland parts of the country. A broad-wheeled waggon, attended by two men, and drawn by eight horses, in about six weeks' time carries and brings back between London and Edinburgh near four ton weight of goods. In about the same time a ship navigated by six or eight men, and sailing between the ports of London and Leith, frequently carries and brings back two hundred ton weight of goods. Six or eight men, therefore, by the help of water-carriage, can carry and bring back in the same time the same quantity of goods between London and Edinburgh, as fifty broad-wheeled waggons, attended by a hundred men, and drawn by four hundred horses. Upon two hundred tons of goods, therefore, carried by the cheapest land-carriage from London to Edinburgh, there must be charged the maintenance of a hundred men for three weeks and both the maintenance, and, what is nearly equal to the maintenance, the wear and tear of four hundred horses as well as of fifty great waggons. Whereas, upon the same quantity of goods carried by water, there is to be charged only the maintenance of six or eight men, and the wear and tear of a ship of two hundred tons burden, together with the value of the superior risk, or the difference of the insurance between land and water-carriage. Were there no other communication between those two places, therefore, but by land-carriage, as no goods could be transported from the one to the other, except such whose price was very considerable in proportion to their weight, they could carry on but a small part of that commerce which at present subsists between them, and consequently could give but a small part of that encouragement which they at present mutually afford to each other's industry. There could be little or no commerce of any kind between the distant parts of the world. What goods could bear the expense of land-carriage between London and Calcutta? Or if there were any so precious as to be able to support this expense, with what safety could they be transported through the territories of so many barbarous nations? Those two cities, however, at present carry on a very considerable commerce with each other, and by mutually affording a market, give a good deal of encouragement to each other's industry.

Since such, therefore, are the advantages of water-carriage, it is natural that the first improvements of art and industry should be made where this conveniency opens the whole world for a market to the produce of every sort of labour, and that they should always be much later in extending themselves into the inland parts of the country. The inland parts of the country can for a long time have no other market for the greater part of their goods, but the country which lies round about them, and separates them from the sea-coast, and the great navigable rivers. The extent of their market, therefore, must for a long time be in proportion to the riches and populousness of that country, and consequently their improvement must always be posterior to the improvement of that country. In our North American colonies the plantations have constantly followed either the sea-coast or the banks of the navigable rivers, and have scarce anywhere extended themselves to any considerable distance from both.

The nations that, according to the best authenticated history, appear to have been first civilised, were those that dwelt round the coast of the Mediterranean Sea. That sea, by far the greatest inlet that is known in the world, having no tides, nor consequently any waves except such as are caused by the wind only, was, by the smoothness of its surface, as well as by the multitude of its islands, and the proximity of its neighbouring shores, extremely favourable to the infant navigation of the world; when, from their ignorance of the compass, men were afraid to quit the view of the coast, and from the imperfection of the art of ship-building, to abandon themselves to the boisterous waves of the ocean. To pass beyond the pillars of Hercules, that is, to sail out of the Straits of Gibraltar, was, in the ancient world, long considered as a most wonderful and dangerous exploit of navigation. It was late before even the Phœnicians and Carthaginians, the most skilful navigators and ship-builders of those old times, attempted it, and they were for a long time the only nations that did attempt it.

Of all the countries on the coast of the Mediterranean Sea, Egypt seems to have been the first in which either agriculture or manufactures were cultivated and improved to any considerable degree. Upper Egypt extends itself nowhere above a few miles from the Nile, and in Lower Egypt that great river breaks itself into many different canals, which, with the assistance of a little art, seem to have afforded a communication by water-carriage, not only between all the great towns, but between all the considerable villages, and even to many farm-houses in the country; nearly in the same manner as the Rhine and the Maese do in Holland at present. The extent and easiness of this inland navigation was probably one of the principal causes of the early improvement of Egypt.

The improvements in agriculture and manufactures seem likewise to have been of very great antiquity in the provinces of Bengal, in the East Indies, and in some of the eastern provinces of China; though the great extent of this antiquity is not authenticated by any histories of whose authority we, in this part of the world, are well assured. In Bengal the Ganges and several other great rivers form a great number of navigable canals in the same manner as the Nile does in Egypt. In the Eastern provinces of China too, several great rivers form, by their different branches, a multitude of canals, and by communicating with one another afford an inland navigation much more extensive than that either of the Nile or the Ganges, or perhaps than both of them put together. It is remarkable that neither the ancient Egyptians, nor the Indians, nor the Chinese, encouraged foreign commerce, but seem all to have derived their great opulence from this inland navigation.

All the inland parts of Africa, and all that part of Asia which lies any considerable way north of the Euxine and Caspian seas, the ancient Scythia, the modern Tartary and Siberia, seem in all ages of the world to have been in the same barbarous and uncivilised state in which we find them at present. The Sea of Tartary is the frozen ocean which admits of no navigation, and though some of the greatest rivers in the world run through that country, they are at too great a distance from one another to carry commerce and communication through the greater part of it. There are in Africa none of those great inlets, such as the Baltic and Adriatic seas in Europe, the Mediterranean and Euxine seas in both Europe and Asia, and the gulfs of Arabia, Persia, India, Bengal, and Siam, in Asia, to carry maritime commerce into the interior parts of that great continent: and the great rivers of Africa are at too great a distance from one another to give occasion to any considerable inland navigation. The commerce besides which any nation can carry on by means of a river which does not break itself into any great number of branches or canals, and which runs into another territory before it reaches the sea, can never be very considerable; because it is always in the power of the nations who possess that other territory to obstruct the communication between the upper country and the sea. The navigation of the Danube is of very little use to the different states of Bavaria, Austria and Hungary, in comparison of what it would be if any of them possessed the whole of its course till it falls into the Black Sea.

ADAM FERGUSON

The most brilliant of a brilliant generation of Scottish philosophers, Adam Ferguson (1723–1816), is today virtually ignored, save by a handful of professional pedagogues. Along with his friend Adam Smith, he was a defender of individual freedom. A pioneer in sociology, anthropology, political theory, and moral philosophy, Ferguson mustered a vast knowledge of history and philosophy to make his points. His thoughts on liberty, equality, public safety, population, and wealth, reprinted below, display a unique genius and understanding. Friedrich von Hayek, among contemporary conservative thinkers, owes a great deal of his philosophy to Ferguson.

From *Moral Philosophy* (Edinburgh, 1786); and *History of Civil Society* (London, 1823).

ADAM FERGUSON

Of the Safety of the People.

By *the people* is to be understood, not any separate class, but all the members of the community, the magistrate as well as the subject.

The safety of the people consists in the secure enjoyment of their rights.

That the rights of men may be secure, it is necessary, either that there should be no one to invade, or that there should be a sufficient power to defend.

The first is not to be expected in human affairs; the second is the principal object of political establishments.

It has been the object, or the fortune, of some communities, to possess members who might be intrusted with any powers.

It has been the object of other communities, to grant such powers only as might be intrusted with any men.

These several cases, real or supposed, may be intitled, The government of *Innocence,* of *Virtue,* and of *Law.*

Under the government of innocence, or of virtue, matters of form are easily adjusted.

Under the government of law, it is necessary, that the rights and obligations of men should be clearly expressed.

This is the object of conventional law.

In every convention is supposed the consent of parties given in person, or by others properly authorised.

The sovereign is authorised to enact laws.

Laws relate to the constitution, to civil rights, or to crimes.

The most perfect laws relating to the constitution, are such as confer on the magistrate power to restrain crimes, and to defend the community; but under limitations sufficient to prevent the abuse of this power.

The most perfect laws relating to civil rights, are such as effectually secure every person in his state.

It is the maxim of civil law, That every person should remain in his possession, until a better title be undoubtedly proved.

Laws relating to crimes, prescribe the form of trials, and point out the overt acts for which certain punishments are appointed.

The following are maxims of natural law relating to prosecutions.

1. That every person is to be deemed innocent until he is proved to be guilty.

2. That no one shall be obliged to give evidence that may affect himself.

3. That no one shall be coerced into confessions or discoveries of any sort.

4. That no one shall be punished, unless he shall have committed some action in itself pernicious, or specially declared by the law to be criminal.

5. That it is better the guilty escape, than that the innocent suffer.

6. That the object of punishment be to correct the guilty, and to deter others.

7. That the punishment be not such as would shock humanity, or disorder society more than the crime.

To secure legal rights, it is necessary that the laws should be strictly interpreted and applied.

Under the government of law, discretionary powers are not safely intrusted, except to judges named by the parties; or to juries purged by the challenge of parties, and interested equally to protect the innocent and to punish the guilty.

In the security of rights consists civil and political liberty.

Liberty is opposed to injustice, not to restraint; for liberty cannot subsist without the supposition of every just restraint.

Natural liberty is not impaired, as sometimes supposed, by political institutions; but owes its existence to political institutions, and is impaired only by usurpations and wrongs.

The laws of different communities bestow unequal privileges on their members; but liberty consists in the secure possession of what the law bestows.

Those are the most salutary laws which distribute the benefits and the burdens of civil society in the most equitable manner to all its members.

ADAM FERGUSON

Of National Felicity.

MAN is, by nature, the member of a community; and when considered in this capacity, the individual appears to be no longer made for himself. He must forego his happiness and his freedom, where these interfere with the good of society. He is only part of a whole; and the praise we think due to his virtue, is but a branch of that more general commendation we bestow on the member of a body, on the part of a fabric or engine, for being well fitted to occupy its place, and to produce its effect.

IF this follow from the relation of a part to its whole, and if the public good be the principal object with individuals, it is likeways true, that the happiness of individuals is the great end of civil society: For, in what sense can a public enjoy any good, if its members, considered apart, be unhappy?

THE interests, of society, however, and of its members, are easily reconciled. If the individual owe every degree of consideration to the public, he receives, in paying that very consideration, the greatest happiness of which his nature is capable; and the greatest blessing the public can bestow on its members, is to keep them attached to itself. That is the most happy state, which is most beloved by its subjects; and they are the most happy men, whose hearts are engaged to a community, in which they find every object of generosity and zeal, and a scope to the exercise of every talent, and of every virtuous disposition.

AFTER we have thus found general maxims, the greater part of our trouble remains, their just application to particular cases. Nations are different in respect to their extent, numbers of people, and wealth; in respect to the arts they practice, and the accommodations they have procured. These circumstances may not only affect the manners of men; they even, in our esteem, come into competition with the article of manners itself; are supposed to constitute a national felicity, independent of virtue; and give a title, upon which we indulge our own vanity, and that of other nations, as we do that of private men, on the score of their fortunes and honours.

BUT if this way of measuring happiness, when applied to private men, be ruinous and false, it is so no less when applied to nations. Wealth, commerce, extent of territory, and the knowledge of arts, are, when properly employed, the means of preservation, and the foundations of power. If they fail in part, the nation is weakened; if they were entirely with-held, the race would perish: Their tendency is to maintain numbers of men, but not to constitute happiness. They will accordingly maintain the wretched, as well as the happy. They answer one purpose, but are not therefore sufficient for all; and are of little significance, when only employed to maintain a timid, dejected, and servile people.

GREAT and powerful states are able to overcome and subdue the weak; polished and commercial nations have more wealth, and practise a greater variety of arts, than the rude: But the happiness of men, in all cases alike, consists in the blessings of a candid, an active, and strenuous mind. And if we consider the state of society merely as that into which mankind are led by their propensities, as a state to be valued from its effect in preserving the species, in ripening their talents, and exciting their virtues, we need not enlarge our communities, in order to enjoy these advantages. We frequently obtain them in the most remarkable degree, where nations remain independent, and are of a small extent.

TO increase the numbers of mankind, may be admitted, as a great and important object: But to extend the limits of any particular state, is not, perhaps, the way to obtain it; while we desire that our fellow-creatures should multiply, it does not follow, that the whole should, if possible, be united under one head. We are apt to admire the empire of the Romans, as a model of national greatness and splendour: But the greatness we admire in this case, was ruinous to the virtue and the happiness of mankind; it was found to be inconsistent with all the advantages which that conquering people had formerly enjoyed in the articles of government and manners.

THE emulation of nations proceeds from their division. A cluster of states, like a company of men, find the exercise of their reason, and the test of their virtues, in the affairs they transact, upon a foot of equality, and of separate interest. The measures taken for safety, including great part of the national policy, are relative in every state to what is apprehended from abroad. Athens was necessary to Sparta, in the exercise of her virtue, as steel is to flint in the production of fire; and if the cities of Greece had been united under one head, we should never have heard of Epaminondas or Thrasybulus, or Lycurgus or Solon.

WHEN we reason in behalf of our species, therefore, although we may lament the abuses which sometimes arise from independence, and opposition of interest; yet, whilst any degrees of virtue remain with mankind, we cannot wish to croud, under one establishment, numbers of men who may serve to constitute several; or to commit affairs to the conduct of one senate, one legislative or executive power, which, upon a distinct and separate footing, might furnish an exercise of ability, and a theatre of glory to many.

THIS may be a subject upon which no determinate rule can be given, but the admiration of boundless dominion is a ruinous error; and in no instance, perhaps, is the real interest of mankind more entirely mistaken.

THE measure of enlargement to be wished for any particular state, is often to be taken from the condition of its neighbours. Where a number of states are contiguous, they should be near an equality, in order that they may be mutually objects of respect and consideration, and in order that they may possess that independence in which the political life of a nation consists.

WHEN the kingdoms of Spain were united, when the great fiefs in France were annexed to the crown, it was no longer expedient for the nations of Great Britain to continue disjoined.

THE small republics of Greece, indeed, by their subdivisions, and the balance of their power, found almost in every village the object of nations. Every little district was a nursery of excellent men, and what is now the wretched corner of a great empire, was the field on which mankind have reaped their principal honours. But in modern Europe, republics of a similar extent, are like shrubs, under the shade of a taller wood, choked by the neighbourhood of more powerful states. In their case, a certain disproportion of force frustrates, in a great measure, the advantage of separation. They are like the trader in Poland, who is the more despicable, and the less secure, that he is neither master nor slave.

INDEPENDENT communities, in the mean time, however weak, are averse to a coalition, not only where it comes with an air of imposition, or unequal treaty, but even where it implies no more than the admission of new members to an equal share of consideration with the old. The citizen has no interest in the annexation of kingdoms; he must find his importance diminished, as the state is enlarged: But ambitious men, under the enlargement of territory, find a more plentiful harvest of power, and of wealth, while government itself is an easier task. Hence the ruinous progress of empire; and hence free nations, under the shew of acquiring dominion, suffer themselves, in the end, to be yoked with the slaves they had conquered.

OUR desire to augment the force of a nation is the only pretext for enlarging its territory; but this measure, when pursued to extremes, seldom fails to frustrate itself.

NOTWITHSTANDING the advantage of numbers, and superior resources in war, the strength of a nation is derived from the character, not from the wealth, nor

from the multitude of its people. If the treasure of a
state can hire numbers of men, erect ramparts, and
furnish the implements of war; the possessions of
the fearful are easily seized; a timorous multitude
falls into rout of itself; ramparts may be scaled
where they are not defended by valour; and arms are
of consequence only in the hands of the brave. The
band to which Agesilaus pointed as the wall of his
city, made a defence for their country more permanent, and more effectual, than the rock and the cement with which other cities were fortified.

WE should owe little to that statesman who were to
contrive a defence that might supersede the external
uses of virtue. It is wisely ordered for man, as a rational being, that the employment of reason is necessary to his preservation; it is fortunate for him, in the
pursuit of distinction, that his personal consideration depends on his character; and it is fortunate for
nations, that, in order to be powerful and safe, they
must strive to maintain the courage, and cultivate
the virtues, of their people. By the use of such means,
they at once gain their external ends, and are happy.

PEACE and unanimity are commonly considered as
the principal foundations of public felicity; yet the
rivalship of separate communities, and the agita-
tions of a free people, are the principles of political
life, and the school of men. How shall we reconcile
these jarring and opposite tenets? It is, perhaps, not
necessary to reconcile them. The pacific may do
what they can to allay the animosities, and to reconcile the opinions, of men; and it will be happy if they
can succeed in repressing their crimes, and in calm-
ing the worst of their passions. Nothing in the mean

time, but corruption or slavery can suppress the debates that subsist among men of integrity, who bear an equal part in the administration of state.

A perfect agreement in matters of opinion is not to be obtained in the most select company; and if it were, what would become of society? "The Spartan legislator," says Plutarch, "appears to have sown the seeds of variance and dissension among his countrymen: he meant that good citizens should be led to dispute; he considered emulation as the brand by which their virtues were kindled; and seemed to apprehend, that a complaisance, by which men submit their opinions without examination, is a principal source of corruption."

FORMS of government are supposed to decide of the happiness or misery of mankind. But forms of government must be varied, in order to suit the extent, the way of subsistence, the character, and the manners of different nations. In some cases, the multitude may be suffered to govern themselves; in others they must be severely restrained. The inhabitants of a village, in some primitive age, may have been safely intrusted to the conduct of reason, and to the suggestion of their innocent views; but the tenants of Newgate can scarcely be trusted, with chains locked to their bodies, and bars of iron fixed to their legs. How is it possible, therefore, to find any single form of government that would suit mankind in every condition?

WE proceed, however, in the following section, to point out the distinctions, and to explain the language which occurs in this place, on the head of different models for subordination and government.

ADAM FERGUSON

The same subject continued.

IT is a common observation, That mankind were originally equal. They have indeed by nature equal rights to their preservation, and to the use of their talents; but they are fitted for different stations; and when they are classed by a rule taken from this circumstance, they suffer no injustice on the side of their natural rights. It is obvious, that some mode of subordination is as necessary to men as society itself; and this, not only to attain the ends of government, but to comply with an order established by nature.

PRIOR to any political institution whatever, men are qualified by a great diversity of talents, by a different tone of the soul, and ardour of the passions, to act a variety of parts. Bring them together, each will find his place. They censure or applaud in a body; they consult and deliberate in more select parties; they take or give an ascendant as individuals; and numbers are by this means fitted to act in company, and to preserve their communities, before any formal distribution of office is made.

WE are formed to act in this manner; and if we have any doubts with relation to the rights of government in general, we owe our perplexity more to the subtilties of the speculative, than to any uncertainty in the feelings of the heart. Involved in the resolutions of our company, we move with the croud before we have determined the rule by which its will is collected. We follow a leader, before we have settled the ground of his pretensions, or adjusted the form of his election: and it is not till after mankind have committed many errors in the capacities of magistrate and subject, that they think of making government itself a subject of rules.

IF therefore, in considering the variety of forms under which societies subsist, the casuist is pleased to inquire, What title one man, or any number of men, have to controul his actions? he may be answered, None at all, provided that his actions have no effect to the prejudice of his fellow-creatures; but if they have, the rights of defence, and the obligation to repress the commission of wrongs, belong to collective bodies, as well as to individuals. Many rude nations, having no formal tribunals for the judgment of crimes, assemble, when alarmed by any flagrant offence, and take their measures with the criminal as they would with an enemy.

BUT will this consideration, which confirms the title to sovereignty, where it is exercised by the society in its collective capacity, or by those to whom the powers of the whole are committed, likewise support the claim to dominion, where-ever it is casually lodged, or even where it is only maintained by force?

THIS question may be sufficiently answered, by observing, that a right to do justice, and to do good, is competent to every individual, or order of men; and that the exercise of this right has no limits but in the defect of power. Whoever, therefore, has power, may employ it to this extent; and no previous convention is required to justify his conduct. But a right to do wrong, or to commit injustice, is an abuse of language, and a contradiction in terms. It is no more competent to the collective body of a people, than it is to any single usurper. When we admit such a prerogative in the case of any sovereign, we can only mean to express the extent of his power, and the force with which he is enabled to execute his pleasure. Such a prerogative is assumed by the leader of banditti at the head of his gang, or by a despotic prince at the head of his troops. When the sword is presented by either, the traveller or the inhabitant may submit from a sense of necessity or fear; but he lyes under no obligation from a motive of duty or justice.

THE multiplicity of forms, in the mean time, which different societies offer to our view, is almost infinite. The classes into which they distribute their members, the manner in which they establish the legislative and executive powers, the imperceptible circumstances by which they are led to have different customs, and to confer on their governors unequal measures of power and authority, give rise to perpetual distinctions between constitutions the most nearly resembling each other, and give to human affairs a variety in detail, which, in its full extent, no understanding can comprehend, and no memory retain.

IN order to have a general and comprehensive knowledge of the whole, we must be determined on this, as on every other subject, to overlook many particulars and singularities, distinguishing different governments; to fix our attention on certain points, in which many agree; and thereby establish a few general heads, under which the subject may be distinctly considered. When we have marked the characteristics which form the general points of coincidence; when we have pursued them to their consequences in the several modes of legislation, execution, and judicature, in the establishments which relate to police, commerce, religion, or domestic life; we have made an acquisition of knowledge, which, though it does not supersede the necessity of experience, may serve to direct our inquiries, and, in the midst of affairs, give an order and a method for the arrangement of particulars that occur to our observation.

WHEN I recollect what the President Montesquieu has written, I am at a loss to tell, why I should treat of human affairs: But I too am instigated by my reflections, and my sentiments; and I may utter them more to the comprehension of ordinary capacities, because I am more on the level of ordinary men. If it be necessary to pave the way for what follows on the general history of nations, by giving some account of the heads under which various forms of government may be conveniently ranged, the reader should perhaps be referred to what has been already delivered on the subject by this profound politician and amiable moralist. In his writings will be found, not only the original of what I am now, for the sake of order, to copy from him, but likewise probably the source of many observations, which, in different places, I may, under the belief of invention, have repeated, without quoting their author.

THE ancient philosophers treated of government commonly under three heads; the Democratic, the Aristocratic, and the Despotic. Their attention was chiefly occupied with the varieties of republican government; and they paid little regard to a very important distinction, which Mr. Montesquieu has made, between despotism and monarchy. He too has considered government as reducible to three general forms; and, "to understand the nature of each," he observes, "it is sufficient to recall ideas which are familiar with men of the least reflection, who admit three definitions, or rather three facts: That a republic is a state in which the people in a collective body, or a part of the people, possess the sovereign power: That monarchy is that in which one man governs, according to fixed and determinate laws: And a despotism is that in which one man, without law, or rule of administration, by the mere impulse of will or caprice, decides, and carries every thing before him."

REPUBLICS admit of a very material distinction, which is pointed out in the general definition; that between democracy and aristocracy. In the first, supreme power remains in the hands of the collective body. Every office of magistracy, at the nomination of this sovereign, is open to every citizen; who, in the discharge of his duty, becomes the minister of the people, and accountable to them for every object of his trust.

IN the second, the sovereignty is lodged in a particular class, or order of men; who, being once named, continue for life; or by the hereditary distinctions of birth and fortune, are advanced to a station of permanent superiority. From this order, and by their nomination, all the offices of magistracy are filled; and in the different assemblies which they constitute, whatever relates to the legislation, the execution, or jurisdiction, is finally determined.

MR Montesquieu has pointed out the sentiments or maxims from which men must be supposed to act under these different governments.

IN democracy, they must love equality; they must respect the rights of their fellow-citizens; they must unite by the common ties of affection to the state. In forming personal pretensions, they must be satisfied with that degree of consideration they can procure by their abilities fairly measured with those of an opponent; they must labour for the public without hope of profit; they must reject every attempt to create a personal dependence. Candour, force, and elevation of mind, in short, are the props of democracy; and virtue is the principle of conduct required to its preservation.

HOW beautiful a pre-eminence on the side of popular government? and how ardently should mankind wish for the form, if it tended to establish the principle, or were, in every instance, a sure indication of its presence!

BUT perhaps we must have possessed the principle, in order, with any hopes of advantage, to receive the form; and where the first is entirely extinguished, the other may be fraught with evil, if any additional evil deserves to be shunned where men are already unhappy.

AT Constantinople or Algiers, it is a miserable spectacle when men pretend to act on a foot of equality: They only mean to shake off the restraints of government, and to seize as much as they can of that spoil, which, in ordinary times, is ingrossed by the master they serve.

IT is one advantage of democracy, that the principal ground of distinction being personal qualities, men are classed according to their abilities, and to the merit of their actions. Though all have equal pretensions to power, yet the state is actually governed by a few. The majority of the people, even in their capacity of sovereign, only pretend to employ their senses; to feel, when pressed by national inconveniences, or threatened by public dangers; and with the ardour which is apt to arise in crouded assemblies, to urge the pursuits in which they are engaged, or to repel the attacks with which they are menaced.

THE most perfect equality of rights can never exclude the ascendant of superior minds, nor the assemblies of a collective body govern without the direction of select councils. On this account, popular government may be confounded with aristocracy. But this alone does not constitute the character of aristocratical government. Here the members of the state are divided, at least, into two classes; of which one is destined to command, the other to obey. No merits or defects can raise or sink a person from one class to the other. The only effect of personal character is, to procure to the individual a suitable degree of consideration with his own order, not to vary his rank. In one situation he is taught to assume, in another to yield the preeminence. He occupies the station of patron or client, and is either the sovereign or the subject of his country. The whole citizens may unite in executing the plans of state, but never in deliberating on its measures, or enacting its laws. What belongs to the whole people under democracy, is here confined to a part. Members of the superior order, are among themselves, possibly, classed according to their abilities, but retain a perpetual ascendant over those of inferior station. They are at once the servants and the masters of the state, and pay with their personal attendance and with their blood, for the civil or military honours they enjoy.

TO maintain for himself, and to admit in his fellow-citizen, a perfect equality of privilege and station, is no longer the leading maxim of the member of such a community. The rights of men are modified by their condition. One order claims more than it is willing to yield; the other must be ready to yield what it does not assume to itself: and it is with good reason that Mr Montesquieu gives to the principle of such governments the name of *moderation* not of *virtue.*

THE elevation of one class is a moderated arrogance; the submission of the other a limited deference. The first must be careful, by concealing the invidious part of their distinction, to palliate what is grievous in the public arrangement, and by their education, their cultivated manners, and improved talents, to appear qualified for the stations they occupy. The other must be taught to yield, from respect and personal attachment, what could not otherwise be extorted by force. When this moderation fails on either side, the constitution totters. A populace enraged to mutiny, may claim the right of equality to which they are admitted in democratical states; or a nobility bent on dominion, may chuse among themselves, or find already pointed out to them, a sovereign, who, by advantages of fortune, popularity, or abilities, is ready to seize for his own family, that envied power, which has already carried his order beyond the limits of moderation, and infected particular men with a boundless ambition.

MONARCHIES have accordingly been found with the recent marks of aristocracy. There, however, the monarch is only the first among the nobles; he must be satisfied with a limited power; his subjects are ranged into classes; he finds on every quarter a pretence to privilege, that circumscribes his authority; and he finds a force sufficient to confine his administration within certain bounds of equity, and determinate laws.

UNDER such governments, however, the love of equality is preposterous, and moderation itself is unnecessary. The object of every rank is precedency, and every order may display its advantages to their full extent. The sovereign himself owes great part of his authority to the founding titles and the dazzling equipage which he exhibits in public. The subordinate ranks lay claim to importance by a like exhibition, and for that purpose carry in every instant the ensigns of their birth, or the ornaments of their fortune. What else could mark out to the individual the relation in which he stands to his fellow-subjects, or distinguish the numberless ranks that fill up the interval between the state of the sovereign and that of the peasant? Or what else could, in states of a great extent, preserve any appearance of order, among members disunited by ambition and interest, and destined to form a community, without the sense of any common concern?

MONARCHIES are generally found, where the state is enlarged in population and in territory, beyond the numbers and dimensions that are consistent with republican government. Together with these circumstances, great inequalities arise in the distribution of property; and the desire of pre-eminence becomes the predominant passion. Every rank would exercise its prerogative, and the sovereign is perpetually tempted to enlarge his own; if subjects, who despair of precedence, plead for equality, he is willing to favour their claims, and to aid them in reducing pretensions, with which he himself is, on many occasions, obliged to contend. In the event of such a policy, many invidious distinctions and grievances peculiar to monarchical government, may, in appearance, be removed; but the state of equality to which the subjects approach, is that of slaves, equally dependent on the will of a master, not that of freemen in a condition to maintain their own.

THE principle of monarchy, according to Montesquieu, is honour. Men may possess good qualities, elevation of mind, and fortitude; but the sense of equality, that will bear no incroachment on the personal rights of the meanest citizen; the indignant spirit, that will not court a protection, nor accept as a favour, what is due as a right; the public affection, which is founded on the neglect of personal considerations, are neither consistent with the preservation of the constitution, nor agreeable to the habits acquired in any station assigned to its members.

EVERY condition is possessed of peculiar dignity, and points out a propriety of conduct, which men of station are obliged to maintain. In the commerce of superiors and inferiors, it is the object of ambition, and of vanity, to refine on the advantages of rank; while, to facilitate the intercourse of polite society, it is the aim of good breeding to disguise, or reject them.

THOUGH the objects of consideration are rather the dignities of station than personal qualities; though friendship cannot be formed by mere inclination, nor alliances by the mere choice of the heart; yet men so united, and even without changing their order, are highly susceptible of moral excellence, or liable to many different degrees of corruption. They may act a vigorous part as members of the state, an amiable one in the commerce of private society; or they may yield up their dignity as citizens, even while they raise their arrogance and presumption as private parties.

IN monarchy, all orders of men derive their honours from the crown; but they continue to hold them as a right, and they exercise a subordinate power in the state, founded on the permanent rank they enjoy, and on the attachment of those whom they are appointed to lead and protect. Though they do not force themselves into national councils, and public assemblies, and though the name of senate is unknown; yet the sentiments they adopt must have weight with the sovereign; and every individual, in his separate capacity, in some measure, deliberates for his country. In whatever does not derogate from his rank, he has an arm ready to serve the community; in whatever alarms his sense of honour, he has aversions and dislikes, which amount to a negative on the will of his prince.

INTANGLED together by the reciprocal ties of dependence and protection, though not combined by the sense of a common interest, the subjects of monarchy, like those of republics, find themselves occupied as the members of an active society, and engaged to treat with their fellow-creatures on a liberal footing. If those principles of honour which save the individual from servility in his own person, or from becoming an engine of oppression in the hands of another, should fail; if they should give way to the maxims of commerce, to the refinements of a supposed philosophy, or to the misplaced ardours of a republican spirit; if they are betrayed by the cowardice of subjects, or subdued by the ambition of princes; what must become of the nations of Europe?

DESPOTISM is monarchy corrupted, in which a court and a prince in appearance remain, but in which every subordinate rank is destroyed; in which the subject is told, that he has no rights; that he cannot possess any property, nor fill any station, independent of the momentary will of his prince. These doctrines are founded on the maxims of conquest; they must be inculcated with the whip and the sword; and are best received under the terror of chains and imprisonment. Fear, therefore, is the principle which qualifies the subject to occupy his station: and the sovereign, who holds out the ensigns of terror so freely to others, has abundant reason to give this passion a principal place with himself. That tenure which he has devised for the rights of others, is soon applied to his own; and from his eager desire to secure, or to extend his power, he finds it become, like the fortunes of his people, a creature of mere imagination and unsettled caprice.

WHILST we thus, with so much accuracy, can assign the ideal limits that may distinguish constitutions of government, we find them, in reality, both in respect to the principle and the form, variously blended together. In what society are not men classed by external distinctions, as well as personal qualities? In what state are they not actuated by a variety of principles; justice, honour, moderation, and fear? It is the purpose of science, not to disguise this confusion in its object, but, in the multiplicity and combination of particulars, to find the principal points which deserve our attention; and which, being well understood, save us from the embarassment which the varieties of singular cases might otherwise create. In the same degree in which governments require men to act from principles of virtue, of honour, or of fear, they are more or less fully comprised under the heads of republic, monarchy, or despotism, and the general theory is more or less applicable to their particular case.

FORMS of government, in fact, mutually approach or recede by many, and often insensible gradations. Democracy, by admitting certain inequalities of rank, approaches to aristocracy. In popular, as well as aristocratical governments, particular men, by their personal authority, and sometimes by the credit of their family, have maintained a species of monarchical power. The monarch is limited in different degrees: Even the despotic prince is only that monarch whose subjects claim the fewest privileges, or who is himself best prepared to subdue them by force. All these varieties are but steps in the history of mankind, and mark the fleeting and transient situations through which they have passed, while supported by virtue, or depressed by vice.

PERFECT democracy and despotism appear to be the opposite extremes at which constitutions of government farthest recede from each other. Under the first, a perfect virtue is required; under the second, a total corruption is supposed: Yet in point of mere form, there being nothing fixed in the ranks and distinctions of men, beyond the casual and temporary possession of power, societies easily pass from a condition in which every individual has an equal title to reign, into one in which they are equally destined to serve. The same qualities in both, courage, popularity, address, and military conduct, raise the ambitious to eminence. With these qualities, the citizen or the slave easily passes from the ranks to the command of an army, from an obscure to an illustrious station. In either, a single person may rule with unlimited sway; and in both, the populace may break down every barrier of order, and restraint of law.

IF we suppose that the equality established among the subjects of a despotic state, has inspired its members with confidence, intrepidity, and the love of justice; the despotic prince, having ceased to be an object of fear, must sink among the croud. If, on the contrary, the personal equality which is enjoyed by the members of a democratical state, should be valued merely as an equal pretension to the objects of avarice and ambition, the monarch may start up anew, and be supported by those who mean to share in his profits. When the rapacious and mercenary assemble in parties, it is of no consequence under what leader they inlist, whether Cæsar or Pompey; the hopes of rapine or pay are the only motives from which they become attached to either.

IN the disorder of corrupted societies, the scene has been frequently changed from democracy to despotism, and from the last too, in its turn, to the first. From amidst the democracy of corrupt men, and from a scene of lawless confusion, the tyrant ascends a throne with arms reeking in blood. But his abuses, or his weaknesses, in the station he has gained, in their turn awaken and give way to the spirit of mutiny and revenge. The cries of murder and desolation, which in the ordinary course of military government terrified the subject in his private retreat, sound through the vaults, and pierce the grates and iron doors of the seraglio. Democracy seems to revive in a scene of wild disorder and tumult: But both the extremes are but the transient fits of paroxysm or languor in a distempered state.

IF men be any where arrived at this measure of depravity, there appears no immediate hope of redress. Neither the ascendancy of the multitude, nor that of the tyrant, will secure the administration of justice: Neither the license of mere tumult, nor the calm of dejection and servitude, will teach the citizen that he was born for candour and affection to his fellow-creatures. And if the speculative would find that habitual state of war which they are sometimes pleased to honour with the name of *the state of nature,* they will find it in the contest that subsists between the despotical prince and his subjects, not in the first approaches of a rude and simple tribe to the condition and the domestic arrangement of nations.

ADAM FERGUSON

Of Population and Wealth.

WHEN we imagine what the Romans must have felt when the tidings came that the flower of their city had perished at Cannæ; when we think of what the orator had in his mind when he said, "That the youth among the people was like the spring among the seasons;" when we hear of the joy with which the huntsman and the warrior is adopted, in America, to sustain the honours of the family and the nation; we are made to feel the most powerful motives to regard the increases and preservation of our fellow citizens. Interest, affection, and views of policy, combine to recommend this object; and it is treated with entire neglect only by the tyrant who mistakes his own advantage, by the statesman who trifles with the charge committed to his care, or by the people who are become corrupted, and who consider their fellow-subjects as rivals in interest, and competitors in their lucrative pursuits.

AMONG rude societies, and among small communities in general, who are engaged in frequent struggles and difficulties, the preservation and increase of their members is a most important object. The American rates his defeat from the numbers of men he has lost, or he estimates his victory from the prisoners he has made; not from his having remained the master of a field, or being driven from a ground on which he encountered his enemy. A man with whom he can associate in all his pursuits, whom he can embrace as his friend; in whom he finds an object to his affections, and an aid in his struggles, is to him the most precious accession of fortune.

EVEN where the friendship of particular men is out of the question, the society, being occupied in forming a party that may defend itself, or annoy its enemy, finds no object of greater moment than the increase of its numbers. Captives who may be adopted, or children of either sex who may be reared for the public, are accordingly considered as the richest spoil of an enemy. The practice of the Romans in admitting the vanquished to share in the privileges of their city, the rape of the Sabines, and the subsequent coalition with that people, were not singular or uncommon examples in the history of mankind. The same policy has been followed, and was natural and obvious where-ever the strength of a state consisted in the arms of a few, and where men were valued in themselves, without regard to estate or fortune.

IN rude ages, therefore, while mankind subsist in small divisions, it should appear, that if the earth be thinly peopled, this defect does not arise from the negligence of those who ought to repair it. It is even probable, that the most effectual course that could be taken to increase the species, would be, to prevent the coalition of nations, and to oblige mankind to act in such small bodies as would make the preservation of their numbers a principal object of their care. This alone, it is true, would not be sufficient: we must probably add the encouragement for rearing families, which mankind enjoy under a favourable policy, and the means of subsistence which they owe to the practice of arts.

THE mother is unwilling to increase her offspring, and is ill provided to rear them, where she herself is obliged to undergo great hardships in the search of her food. In North America, we are told, that she joins to the reserves of a cold or a moderate temperament, the abstinencies to which she submits from the consideration of this difficulty. In her apprehension, it is a matter of prudence, and of conscience to bring one child to the condition of feeding on venison, and of following on foot, before she will hazard a new burden in travelling the woods.

IN warmer latitudes, by the different temperament, perhaps, which the climate bestows, and by a greater facility in procuring subsistence, the numbers of mankind increase, while the object itself is neglected; and the commerce of the sexes, without any concern for population, is made a subject of mere debauch. In some places, we are told, it is even made the object of a barbarous policy, to defeat or to restrain the intentions of nature. In the island of Formosa, the males are prohibited to marry before the age of forty; and females, if pregnant before the age of thirty six, have an abortion procured by order of the magistrate, who employs a violence that endangers the life of the mother, together with that of the child*.

IN China, the permission given to parents to kill or to expose their children, was probably meant as a relief from the burden of a numerous offspring. But notwithstanding what we hear of a practice so repugnant to the human heart, it has not, probably, the effects in restraining population, which it seems to threaten; but, like many other institutions, has an

*Collection of Dutch voyages.

influence the reverse of what it seemed to portend. The parents marry with this means of relief in their view, and the children are saved.

HOWEVER important the object of population may be held by mankind, it will be difficult to find, in the history of civil policy, any wise or effectual establishments solely calculated to obtain it. The practice of rude or feeble nations is inadequate, or cannot surmount the obstacles which are found in their manner of life. The growth of industry, the endeavours of men to improve their arts, to extend their commerce, to secure their possessions, and to establish their rights, are indeed the most effectual means to promote population: but they arise from a different motive; they arise from regards to interest and personal safety. They are intended for the benefit of those who exist, not to procure the increase of their numbers.

IT is, in the mean time, of importance to know, that where a people are fortunate in their political establishments, and successful in the pursuits of industry, their population is likely to grow in proportion. Most of the other devices thought of for this purpose, only serve to frustrate the expectations of mankind, or to mislead their attention.

IN planting a colony, in striving to repair the occasional wastes of pestilence or war, the immediate contrivance of statesmen may be useful; but if in reasoning on the increase of mankind in general, we overlook their freedom, and their happiness, our aids to population become weak and ineffectual. They only lead us to work on the surface, or to pursue a shadow, while we neglect the substantial concern; and in a decaying state, make us tamper with palliatives, while the roots of an evil are suffered to remain. Octavius revived or inforced the laws that related to population at Rome: But it may be said of him, and of many sovereigns in a similar situation, that they administer the poison, while they are devising the remedy; and bring a damp and a palsy on the principles of life, while they endeavour, by external applications to the skin, to restore the bloom of a decayed and sickly body.

IT is indeed happy for mankind, that this important object is not always dependent on the wisdom of sovereigns, or the policy of single men. A people intent on freedom, find for themselves a condition in which they may follow the propensities of nature with a more signal effect, than any which the councils of state could devise. When sovereigns, or projectors, are the supposed masters of this subject, the best they can do, is to be cautious of hurting an interest they cannot greatly promote, and of making breaches they cannot repair.

"WHEN nations were divided into small territories, and petty commonwealths, where each man had his house and his field to himself, and each county had its capital free and independent; what a happy situation for mankind," says Mr Hume, "how favourable to industry and agriculture, to marriage and to population!" Yet here were probably no schemes of the statesman for rewarding the married, or for punishing the single; for inviting foreigners to settle, or for prohibiting the departure of natives. Every citizen finding a possession secure, and a provision for his heirs, was not discouraged by the gloomy fears of oppression or want: and where every other function of nature was free, that which furnished the nursery could not be restrained. Nature has required the powerful to be just; but she has not otherwise intrusted the preservation of her works to their visionary plans. What fewel can the statesman add to the fires of youth? Let him only not smother it, and the effect is secure. Where we oppress or degrade mankind with one hand, it is vain, like Octavius, to hold out in the other, the baits of marriage, or the whip to barrenness. It is vain to invite new inhabitants from abroad, while those we already possess are made to hold their tenure with uncertainty; and to tremble, not only under the prospect of a numerous family, but even under that of a precarious and doubtful subsistence for themselves. The arbitrary sovereign, who has made this the condition of his subjects, owes the remains of his people to the powerful instincts of nature, not to any device of his own.

MEN will croud where the situation is tempting, and, in a few generations, will people every country to the measure of its means of subsistence. They will even increase under circumstances that portend a decay. The frequent wars of the Romans, and of many a thriving community; even the pestilence, and the market for slaves, find their supply, if, without destroying the source, the drain become regular; and if an issue is made for the offspring, without unsettling the families from which they arise. Where a happier provision is made for mankind, the statesman, who by premiums to marriage, by allurements to foreigners, or by confining the natives at home, apprehends, that he has made the numbers of his people to grow, is often like the fly in the fable, who admired its success, in turning the wheel, and in moving the carriage: he has only accompanied what was already in motion; he has dashed with his oar, to hasten the cataract; and waved with his fan, to give speed to the winds.

PROJECTS of mighty settlement, and of sudden population, however successful in the end, are always expensive to mankind. Above a hundred thousand peasants, we are told, were yearly driven, like so many cattle, to Petersburgh, in the first attempts to replenish that settlement, and yearly perished for want of subsistence*. The Indian only attempts to settle in the neighbourhood of the plantain†, and while his family increases, he adds a tree to the walk.

IF the plantain, the cocoa, or the palm, were sufficient to maintain an inhabitant, the race of men in the warmer climates might become as numerous as the trees of the forest. But in many parts of the earth, from the nature of the climate, and the soil, the spontaneous produce being next to nothing, the means of subsistence are the fruits only of labour and skill. If a people, while they retain their frugality, increase their industry, and improve their arts, their numbers must grow in proportion. Hence it is, that the cultivated fields of Europe are more peopled than the wilds of America, or the plains of Tartary.

BUT even the increase of mankind which attends the accumulation of wealth, has its limits. The

*Strachlenberg.
†Dampier.

necessary of life is a vague and a relative term: It is one thing in the opinion of the savage; another in that of the polished citizen: It has a reference to the fancy, and to the habits of living. While arts improve, and riches increase; while the possessions of individuals, or their prospects of gain, come up to their opinion of what is required to settle a family, they enter on its cares with alacrity. But when the possession, however redundant, falls short of the standard, and a fortune supposed sufficient for marriage is attained with difficulty, population is checked, or begins to decline. The citizen, in his own apprehension, returns to the state of the savage; his children, he thinks, must perish for want; and he quits a scene overflowing with plenty, because he has not the fortune which his supposed rank, or his wishes, require. No ultimate remedy is applied to this evil, by merely accumulating wealth; for rare and costly materials, whatever these are, continue to be sought; and if silks and pearl are made common, men will begin to covet some new decorations, which the wealthy alone can procure. If they are indulged in their humour, their demands are repeated: For it is the continual increase of riches, not any measure attained, that keeps the craving imagination at ease.

MEN are tempted to labour, and to practice lucrative arts, by motives of interest. Secure to the workman the fruit of his labour, give him the prospects of independence or freedom, the public has found a faithful minister in the acquisition of wealth, and a faithful steward in hoarding what he has gained. The statesman, in this, as in the case of population itself, can do little more than avoid doing mischief. It is well, if, in the beginnings of commerce, he knows how to repress the frauds to which it is subject. Commerce, if continued, is the branch in which men, committed to the effects of their own experience, are least apt to go wrong.

THE trader, in rude ages, is short-sighted, fraudulent, and mercenary; but in the progress, and advanced state of his art, his views are enlarged, his maxims are established: He becomes punctual, liberal, faithful, and enterprising; and in the period of general corruption, he alone has every virtue, except the force to defend his acquisitions. He needs no aid from the state, but its protection; and is often in himself its most intelligent and respectable member. Even in China, we are informed, where pilfering, fraud, and corruption, are the reigning practice with all the other orders of men, the great merchant is ready to give, and to procure confidence: While his countrymen act on the plans, and under the restrictions of a police adjusted to knaves, he acts on the reasons of trade, and the maxims of mankind.

IF population be connected with national wealth, liberty and personal security is the great foundation of both: And if this foundation be laid in the state, nature has secured the increase and industry of its members; the one by desires the most ardent in the human frame; the other by a consideration the most uniform and constant of any that possesses the mind. The great object of policy, therefore, with respect to both, is, to secure to the family its means of subsistence and settlement; to protect the industrious in the pursuit of his occupation; to reconcile the restrictions of police, and the social affections of mankind, with their separate and interested pursuits.

IN matters of particular profession, industry, and trade, the experienced practitioner is the master, and every general reasoner is a novice. The object in commerce is to make the individual rich; the more he gains for himself, the more he augments the wealth of his country. If a protection be required, it must be granted; if crimes and frauds be committed, they must be repressed; and government can pretend to no more. When the refined politician would lend an active hand, he only multiplies interruptions and grounds of complaint; when the merchant forgets his own interest to lay plans for his country, the period of visions and chimera is near, and the solid basis of commerce withdrawn. He might be told, that while he pursues his advantage, and gives no cause of complaint, the interest of commerce is safe.

THE general police of France, proceeding on a supposition that the exportation of corn must drain the country where it has grown, had, till of late, laid that branch of commerce under a severe prohibition. The English landholder and the farmer had credit enough to obtain a premium for exportation, to favour the sale of their commodity; and the event has shewn, that private interest is a better patron of commerce and plenty, than the refinements of state. One nation lays the refined plan of a settlement on the continent of North America, and trusts little to the conduct of traders and short-sighted men; another leaves men to find their own position in a state of freedom, and to think for themselves. The active industry and the limited views of the one, made a thriving settlement; the great projects of the other were still in idea.

BUT I willingly quit a subject in which I am not much conversant, and still less engaged by the object for which I write. Speculations on commerce and wealth have been delivered by the ablest writers; and the public will probably soon be furnished with a theory of national æconomy, equal to what has ever appeared on any subject of science whatever*. But in the view which I have taken of human affairs, nothing seems more important than the general caution which the authors to whom I refer so well understand, not to consider these articles as making the sum of national felicity, or the principal object of any state. In science we consider our objects apart; in practice it were an error not to have them all in our view at once.

ONE nation, in search of gold and of precious metals, neglect the domestic sources of wealth, and become dependent on their neighbours for the necessaries of life: Another so intent on improving their internal resources, and on increasing their commerce, that they become dependent on foreigners for the defence of what they acquire. It is even painful in conversation to find the interest of merchants give the tone to our reasonings, and to find a subject perpetually offered as the great business of national councils, to which any interposition of government is seldom, with propriety, applied, or never beyond the protection it affords.

WE complain of a want of public spirit; but whatever may be the effect of this error in practice, in speculation it is none of our faults: We reason per-

*By Mr. Smith, author of the Theory of Moral Sentiment.

petually for the public; but the want of national views were frequently better than the possession of those we express: We would have nations, like a company of merchants, think of nothing but monopolies, and the profit of trade; and, like them, too, intrust their protection to a force which they do not possess in themselves.

BECAUSE men, like other animals, are maintained in multitudes, where the necessaries of life are amassed, and the store of wealth is enlarged, we drop our regards for the happiness, the moral and political character of a people; and, anxious for the herd we would propagate, carry our views no farther than the stall and the pasture. We forget that the few have often made a prey of the many; that to the poor there is nothing so enticing as the coffers of the rich; and that when the price of freedom comes to be paid, the heavy sword of the victor may fall into the opposite scale.

WHATEVER be the actual conduct of nations in this matter, it is certain, that many of our arguments would hurry us, for the sake of wealth and of population, into a scene where mankind being exposed to corruption, are unable to defend their possessions; and where they are, in the end, subject to oppression and ruin. We cut off the roots, while we would extend the branches, and thicken the foliage.

IT is possibly from an opinion that the virtues of men are secure, that some who turn their attention to public affairs, think of nothing but the numbers and wealth of a people: It is from a dread of corruption, that others think of nothing but how to preserve the national virtues. Human society has great obligations to both. They are opposed to one another only by mistake; and even when united, have not strength sufficient to combat the wretched party, that refers every object to personal interest, and that cares not for the safety or increase of any stock but its own.

FRÉDÉRIC BASTIAT

The good Frédéric Bastiat (1801–1850) is one of the most endearing of libertarian thinkers. His great *Harmonies of Political Economy,* nowadays hardly read at all, was one of the most influential economic treatises of the 19th century. Bastiat was greatly admired in England and America, but never managed to achieve the same recognition in his native France. He was by profession a farmer, and the simplicity of his rural background is evident in his unadorned, but eloquent, defense of liberty. His address to the youth of France has never been more relevant than it is today.

From *Harmonies of Political Economy,* trans. John Murray (London, 1860).

FRÉDÉRIC BASTIAT

To the Youth of France.

Love of study, and lack of fixed opinions,—a mind free from prejudice, a heart devoid of hate, zeal for the propagation of truth,—ardent sympathies, disinterestedness, devotion, candour,—enthusiasm for all that is good and fair, simple and great, honest and religious,—such are the precious attributes of youth. It is for this reason that I dedicate my work to you. And the seed must have in it no principle of life if it fail to take root in a soil so generous.

I had thought to offer you a picture, and all I have given you is a sketch; but you will pardon me; for who, in times like the present,* can sit down to finish a grave and important work? My hope is that some one among you, on seeing it, will be led to exclaim, with the great artist, *Anch' io son pittore!* and, seizing the pencil, impart to my rude canvass colour and flesh, light and shade, sentiment and life.

You may think the title of the work somewhat ambitious; and assuredly I make no pretension to reveal the designs of Providence in the social order, and to explain the mechanism of all the forces with which God has endowed man for the realization of progress. All that I have aimed at is to put you on the right track, and make you acquainted with the truth, that *all legitimate interests are in harmony.* That is the predominant idea of my work, and it is impossible not to recognize its importance.

For some time it has been the fashion to laugh at what has been called the *social problem;* and no doubt some of the solutions which have been pro-

*First Edition of the *Harmonies Économiques* appeared in 1850.—TRANSLATOR.

posed afford but too much ground for raillery. But in the problem itself there is nothing laughable. It is the ghost of Banquo at the feast of Macbeth—and no dumb ghost either; for in formidable accents it calls out to terror-stricken society—a solution or death!

Now this solution, you will at once see, must be different according as men's interests are held to be naturally harmonious or naturally antagonistic.

In the one case, we must seek for the solution in Liberty—in the other, in Constraint. In the one case, we have only to be passive—in the other, we must necessarily offer opposition.

But Liberty assumes only one shape. Once convinced that each of the molecules which compose a fluid possesses in itself the force by which the general level is produced, we conclude that there is no surer or simpler way of seeing that level realized than not to interfere with it. All, then, who set out with this fundamental principle, that *men's interests are harmonious,* will agree as to the practical solution of the social problem,—to abstain from displacing or thwarting these interests.

Constraint, on the other hand, may assume a thousand shapes, according to the views which we take of it, and which are infinitely varied. Those schools which set out with the principle, that *men's interests are antagonistic,* have done nothing yet towards the solution of the problem, unless it be that they have thrust aside Liberty. Among the infinite forms of Constraint, they have still to choose the one which they consider good, if indeed any of them be so. And then, as a crowning difficulty, they have to obtain universal acceptance, among men who are free agents, for the particular form of Constraint to which they have awarded the preference.

But, on this hypothesis, if human interests are, by their very nature, urged into fatal collision, and if this shock can be avoided only by the accidental invention of an artificial social order, the destiny of the human race becomes very hazardous, and we ask in terror,

1st, If any man is to be found who has discovered a satisfactory form of Constraint?

2d, Can this man bring to his way of thinking the innumerable schools who give the preference to other forms?

3d, Will mankind give in to that particular form which, by hypothesis, runs counter to all individual interests?

4th, Assuming that men will allow themselves to be rigged out in this new attire, what will happen if another inventor presents himself, with a coat of a different and improved cut? Are we to persevere in a vicious organization, knowing it to be vicious; or must we resolve to change that organization every morning according as the caprices of fashion and the fertility of inventors' brains may dictate?

5th, Would not all the inventors whose plans have been rejected unite together against the particular organization which had been selected, and would not their success in disturbing society be in exact proportion to the degree in which that particular form of organization ran counter to all existing interests?

6th, And, last of all, it may be asked, Does there exist any human force capable of overcoming an antagonism which we presuppose to be itself the very essence of human force?

I might multiply such questions *ad infinitum*, and propose, for example, this difficulty:

If individual interest is opposed to the general interest, where are we to place the active principle of Constraint? Where is the fulcrum of the lever to be placed? Beyond the limits of human society? It must be so if we are to escape the consequences of your law. If we are to intrust some men with arbitrary power, prove first of all that these men are formed of a different clay from other mortals; that they in their turn will not be acted upon by the fatal principle of self-interest; and that, placed in a situation which excludes the idea of any curb, any effective opposition, their judgments will be exempt from error, their hands from rapacity, and their hearts from covetousness.

The radical difference between the various Socialist schools (I mean here, those which seek the solution of the social problem in an artificial organization) and the Economist school, does not consist in certain views of detail or of governmental combination. We encounter that difference at the starting point, in the preliminary and pressing question—Are human interests, when left to themselves, antagonistic or harmonious?

It is evident that the Socialists have set out in quest of an artificial organization only because they judge the natural organization of society bad or insufficient; and they have judged the latter bad and insufficient only because they think they see in men's interests a radical antagonism, for otherwise they would not have had recourse to Constraint. It is not necessary to constrain into harmony what is in itself harmonious.

Thus they have discovered antagonism everywhere:

Between the proprietor and the *prolétaire;**
Between capital and labour;
Between the masses and the *bourgeoisie;*
Between agriculture and manufactures;
Between the rustic and the burgess;
Between the native and the foreigner;
Between the producer and the consumer;
Between civilisation and organization;
    In a word,
Between Liberty and Harmony.

And this explains why it happens that, although a certain kind of sentimental philanthropy finds a place in their hearts, gall and bitterness flow continually from their lips. Each reserves all his love for the new state of society he has dreamt of; but as regards the society in which we actually live and move, it cannot, in their opinion, be too soon crushed and overthrown, to make room for the New Jerusalem they are to rear upon its ruins.

I have said that the *Economist* school, setting out with the natural harmony of interests, is the advocate of Liberty.

And yet I must allow that if Economists in general stand up for Liberty, it is unfortunately not equally true that their principles establish solidly the foundation on which they build—the harmony of interests.

Before proceeding further, and to forewarn you against the conclusions which will no doubt be drawn from this avowal, I must say a word on the situations which Socialism and Political Economy respectively occupy.

---

*The author employs the term *prolétaire,* for which we have no equivalent word, to distinguish the man who lives by wages from the man who lives upon realized property—"les hommes qui n'ont que leurs bras, les salariés."—TRANSLATOR.

It would be folly in me to assert that Socialism has never lighted upon a truth, and that Political Economy has never fallen into an error.

What separates, radically and profoundly, the two schools is their difference of methods. The one school, like the astrologer and the alchemist, proceeds on hypothesis; the other, like the astronomer and the chemist, proceeds on observation.

Two astronomers, observing the same fact, may not be able to arrive at the same result.

In spite of this transient disagreement, they feel themselves united by the common process which sooner or later will cause that disagreement to disappear. They recognise each other as of the same communion. But between the astronomer, who observes, and the astrologer, who imagines, the gulf is impassable, although accidentally they may sometimes approximate.

The same thing holds of Political Economy and Socialism.

The Economists observe man, the laws of his organization, and the social relations which result from those laws. The Socialists conjure up an imaginary society, and then create a human heart to suit that society.

Now, if philosophy never errs, philosophers often do. I deny not that Economists may make false observations; I will add, that they must necessarily begin by doing so.

But then, what happens? If men's interests are harmonious, it follows that every incorrect observation will lead logically to antagonism. What, then, are the Socialist tactics? They gather from the works of Economists certain incorrect observations, follow them out to their consequences, and show those consequences to be disastrous. Thus far they are right. Then they set to work upon the observer, whom we may assume to be Malthus or Ricardo. Still they have right on their side. But they do not stop there. They turn against the science of Political Economy itself, accusing it of being heartless, and leading to evil. Here they do violence to reason and justice, inasmuch as science is not responsible for incorrect observation. At length they proceed another step. They lay the blame on society itself:— they threaten to overthrow it for the purpose of reconstructing the edifice:—and why? Because, say they, it is proved by science that society as now constituted is urged onwards to destruction. In this they outrage good sense—for either science is not mistaken, and then why attack it?—or it is mistaken, and in that case they should leave society in repose, since society is not menaced.

But these tactics, illogical as they are, have not been the less fatal to economic science, especially when the cultivators of that science have had the misfortune, from a chivalrous and not unnatural feeling, to render themselves liable, *singuli in solidum,* for their predecessors and for one another. Science is a queen whose gait should be frank and free:—the atmosphere of the *coterie* stifles her.

I have already said that in Political Economy every erroneous proposition must lead ultimately to antagonism. On the other hand, it is impossible that the voluminous works of even the most eminent economists should not include some erroneous propositions. It is ours to mark and to rectify them in the interest of science and of society. If we persist in maintaining them for the honour of the fraternity, we shall not only expose ourselves, which is of little consequence, but we shall expose truth itself, which is a serious affair, to the attcks of Socialism.

To return: the conclusion of the Economists is for Liberty. For in order that this conclusion should take hold of men's minds and hearts, it must be solidly based on this fundamental principle, that interests, left to themselves, tend to harmonious combinations, and to the progressive preponderance of the general good.

Now many Economists, some of them writers of authority, have advanced propositions, which, step by step, lead logically to *absolute evil,* necessary injustice, fatal and progressive inequality, and inevitable pauperism, &c.

Thus, there are very few of them who, so far as I know, have not attributed *value* to natural agents, to the gifts which God has vouchsafed *gratuitously* to his creatures. The word *value* implies that we do not give away the portion of it which we possess except for an equivalent consideration. Here, then, we have men, especially proprietors of land, bartering for effective labour the gifts of God, and receiving recompense for utilities in the creation of which their labour has had no share—an evident, but a necessary, injustice, say these writers.

Then comes the famous theory of Ricardo, which may be summed up in a few words: The price of the necessaries of life depends on the labour required to produce them on the least productive land in cultivation. Then the increase of population obliges us to have recourse to soils of lower and lower fertility. Consequently mankind at large (all except the landowners) are forced to give a larger and larger amount of labour for the same amount of subsistence; or, what comes to the same thing, to receive a less and less amount of subsistence for the same amount of labour,—whilst the landowners see their rental swelling by every new descent to soils of an inferior quality. Conclusion: Progressive opulence of men of leisure—progressive poverty of men of labour; in other words, fatal inequality.

Finally, we have the still more celebrated theory of Malthus, that population has a tendency to increase more rapidly than the means of subsistence, and that at every given moment of the life of man. Now, men cannot be happy, to live in peace, if they have not the means of support; and there are but two obstacles to this increase of population which is always threatening us, namely, a diminished number of births, or an increase of mortality in all its dreadful forms. Moral restraint, to be efficacious, must be universal, and no one expects that. There remains, then, only the repressive obstacles—vice, poverty, war, pestilence, famine; in other words, pauperism and death.

I forbear to mention other systems of a less general bearing, which tend in the same way to bring us to a dead-stand. Monsieur de Tocqueville, for example, and many others, tell us, if we admit the right of primogeniture, we arrive at the most concentrated aristocracy—if we do not admit it, we arrive at ruin and sterility.

And it is worthy of remark, that these four melancholy theories do not in the least degree run foul of each other. If they did, we might console ourselves with the reflection that they are alike false, since they refute each other. But no,—they are in unison, and make part of one and the same general theory, which, supported by numerous and specious facts, would seem to explain the spasmodic state of modern society, and fortified by the assent of many masters in the science, presents itself with frightful authority to the mind of the confused and discouraged inquirer.

We have still to discover how the authors of this melancholy theory have been able to lay down, as their principle, the *harmony of interests*, and, as their conclusion, Liberty.

For if mankind are indeed urged on by the laws of Value towards Injustice,—by the laws of Rent towards Inequality,—by the laws of Population towards Poverty,—by the laws of Inheritance towards Sterility,—we can no longer affirm that God has made the moral as he has made the natural world— a harmonious work; we must bow the head, and confess that it has pleased Him to base it on revolting and irremediable dissonance.

You must not suppose, young men, that the socialists have refuted and repudiated what, in order to wound no one's susceptibilities, I shall call the theory of dissonances. No; let them say as they will, they have assumed the truth of that theory, and it is just because they have assumed its truth that they propose to substitute Constraint for Liberty, artificial for natural organization, their own inventions for the work of God. They say to their opponents (and in this, perhaps, they are more consistent than the latter),—if, as you have told us, human interests when left to themselves tend to harmonious combination, we cannot do better than welcome and magnify Liberty as you do. But you have demonstrated unanswerably that those interests, if allowed to develop themselves freely, urge mankind towards injustice, inequality, pauperism, and sterility. Your theory, then, provokes reaction precisely because it is true.

We desire to break up the existing fabric of society just because it is subject to the fatal laws which you have described; we wish to make trial of our own powers, seeing that the power of God has miscarried.

Thus they are agreed as regards the premises, and differ only on the conclusion.

The Economists to whom I have alluded say that *the great providential laws urge on society to evil;* but that we must take care not to disturb the action of those laws, because such action is happily impeded by the secondary laws which retard the final catastrophe; and arbitrary intervention can only enfeeble the embankment, without stopping the fatal rising of the flood.

The Socialists say that *the great providential laws urge on society to evil;* we must therefore abolish them, and select others from our inexhaustible storehouse.

The Catholics say that *the great providential laws urge on society to evil;* we must therefore escape from them by renouncing worldly interests, and taking refuge in abnegation, sacrifice, asceticism, and resignation.

It is in the midst of this tumult, of these cries of anguish and distress, of these exhortations to subversion, or to resignation and despair, that I endeavour to obtain a hearing for this assertion, in presence of which, if it be correct, all difference of opinion must disappear—*it is not true that the great providential laws urge on society to evil.*

It is with reference to the conclusions to be deduced from their common premises that the various schools are divided and combat each other. I deny those premises, and I ask, Is not that the best way of putting an end to these disputes?

The leading idea of this work, the harmony of interests, is *simple.* Is simplicity not the touchstone of truth? The laws of light, of sound, of motion, appear to us to be all the truer for being simple—Why should it be otherwise with the law of interests?

This idea is *conciliatory.* What is more fitted to reconcile parties than to demonstrate the harmony of the various branches of industry: the harmony of classes, of nations, even of doctrines?

It is *consoling,* seeing that it points out what is false in those systems which adopt, as their conclusion, progressive evil.

It is *religious,* for it assures us that it is not only the celestial but the social mechanism which reveals the wisdom of God, and declares His glory.

It is *practical,* for one can scarcely conceive anything more easily reduced to practice than this,—to allow men to labour, to exchange, to learn, to associate, to act and react on each other,—for, according to the laws of Providence, nothing can result from their intelligent spontaneity but order, harmony, progress, good, and better still; better *ad infinitum.*

Bravo, you will say; here we have the optimism of the Economists with a vengeance! These Economists are so much the slaves of their own systems that they shut their eyes to facts for fear of seeing them. In the face of all the poverty, all the injustice, all the oppressions which desolate humanity, they coolly deny the existence of evil. The smell of revolutionary gunpowder does not reach their blunted senses— the pavement of the barricades has no voice for them; and were society to crumble to pieces before their eyes, they would still keep repeating; "All is for the best in the best of worlds."

No indeed,—we do not think that all is for the best;

but I have faith in the wisdom of the laws of Providence, and for the same reason I have faith in Liberty.

The question is, Have we Liberty?

The question is, Do these laws act in their plenitude, or is their action not profoundly troubled by the countervailing action of human institutions?

Deny evil! deny suffering! Who can? We must forget that our subject is man. We must forget that we are ourselves men. The laws of Providence may be regarded as harmonious without their necessarily excluding evil. Enough that evil has its explanation and its mission, that it checks and limits itself, that it destroys itself by its own action, and that each suffering prevents a greater suffering by repressing the cause of suffering.

Society has for its element man, who is a *free* agent; and since man is free, he may choose,—since he may choose, he may be mistaken,—since he may be mistaken, he may suffer.

I go further. I say he must be mistaken and suffer —for he begins his journey in ignorance, and for ignorance there are endless and unknown roads, all of which, except one, lead to error.

Now, every Error engenders suffering; but either suffering reacts upon the man who errs, and then it brings Responsibility into play,—or, if it affects others who are free from error, it sets in motion the marvellous reactionary machinery of Solidarity.

The action of these laws, combined with the faculty which has been vouchsafed to us of connecting effects with their causes, must bring us back, by means of this very suffering, into the way of what is good and true.

Thus, not only do we not deny the existence of evil,

but we acknowledge that it has a mission in the social, as it has in the material world.

But, in order that it should fulfil this mission, we must not stretch Solidarity artificially, so as to destroy Responsibility,—in other words, we must respect Liberty.

Should human institutions step in to oppose in this respect the divine laws, evil would not the less flow from error, only it would shift its position. It would strike those whom it ought not to strike. It would be no longer a warning and a monitor. It would no longer have the tendency to diminish and die away by its own proper action. Its action would be continued, and increase, as would happen in the physiological world if the imprudences and excesses of the men of one hemisphere were felt in their unhappy effects only by the inhabitants of the opposite hemisphere.

Now this is precisely the tendency not only of most of our governmental institutions, but likewise, and above all, of those which we seek to establish as remedies for the evils which we suffer. Under the philanthropical pretext of developing among men a factitious Solidarity, we render Responsibility more and more inert and inefficacious. By an improper application of the public force, we alter the relation of labour to its remuneration, we disturb the laws of industry and of exchange, we offer violence to the natural development of education, we give a wrong direction to capital and labour, we twist and invert men's ideas, we inflame absurd pretensions, we dazzle with chimerical hopes, we occasion a strange loss of human power, we change the centres of population, we render experience itself useless,—in a word, we give to all interests artificial foundations, we set them by the ears, and then we exclaim that—Interests are antagonistic: Liberty has done all the evil,—let us denounce and stifle Liberty.

And yet, as this sacred word has still power to stir men's hearts and make them palpitate, we despoil Liberty of its *prestige* by depriving it of its name; and it is under the title of *Competition* that the unhappy victim is led to the sacrificial altar, amid the applause of a mob stretching forth their hands to receive the shackles of servitude.

It is not enough, then, to exhibit, in their majestic harmony, the natural laws of the social order; we must also explain the disturbing causes which paralyze their action; and this is what I have endeavoured to do in the second part of this work.

I have striven to avoid controversy; and, in doing so, I have no doubt lost an opportunity of giving to the principles which I desire to disseminate the stability which results from a thorough and searching discussion. And yet, might not the attention of the reader, seduced by digressions, have been diverted from the argument taken as a whole? If I exhibit the edifice as it stands, what matters it in what light it has been regarded by others, even by those who first taught me to look at it?

And now I would appeal with confidence to men of all schools, who prefer truth, justice, and the public good to their own systems.

Economists! like you, I am the advocate of LIBERTY; and if I succeed in shaking some of those premises which sadden your generous hearts, perhaps you will see in this an additional incentive to love and to serve our sacred cause.

Socialists! you have faith in ASSOCIATION. I conjure you, after having read this book, to say whether society as it is now constituted, apart from its abuses and shackles, that is to say, under the condition of Liberty, is not the most beautiful, the most complete, the most durable, the most universal, the most equitable, of all Associations.

Egalitaires! You admit but one principle, the MUTUALITY OF SERVICES. Let human transactions be free, and I assert that they are not and cannot be anything else than a reciprocal exchange of *services,* —services always diminishing in *value,* always increasing in *utility.*

Communists! you desire that men, become brothers, should enjoy in common the goods which Providence has lavished on them. My aim is to demonstrate that society as it exists has only to acquire freedom in order to realize and surpass your wishes and your hopes. For all things are common to all, on the single condition that each man takes the trouble to gather what God has given, which is very natural; or remunerate freely those who take that trouble for him, which is very just.

Christians of all communions! unless you stand alone in casting doubt on the divine wisdom, manifested in the most magnificent of all God's works which have come within the range of our knowledge, you will find in this book no expression which can shock the severest morals, or the most mysterious dogmas of your faith.

Proprietors! whatever be the extent of your possessions, if I establish that your rights, now so much contested, are limited, like those of the most ordinary workman, to the receiving of services in exchange for real and substantial services which have been actually rendered by you, or by your forefathers, those rights will henceforth repose on a basis which cannot be shaken.

Prolétaires! men who live by wages! I undertake to demonstrate that you obtain the fruits of the land of which you are not the owners with less pain and effort than if you were obliged to raise those fruits by your own direct labour,—with less than if that land had been given to you in its primitive state, and before being prepared for cultivation by labour.

Capitalists and labourers! I believe myself in a position to establish the law that, in proportion as capital is accumulated, the *absolute* share of the total product falling to the capitalist increases, and his *proportional* share is diminished; while both the *absolute* and *relative* share of the product falling to the labourer is augmented,—the reverse effects being produced when capital is lessened or dissipated.*
If this law be established, the obvious deduction is, a harmony of interests between labourers and those who employ them.

Disciples of Malthus! sincere and calumniated philanthropists, whose only fault has been in warning mankind against the effects of a law which you believe to be fatal, I shall have to submit to you another law more reassuring:— *"Cæteris paribus,* increasing density of population is equivalent to increasing facility of production."* And if it be so, I am certain it will not be you who will grieve to see a

---

*I shall explain this law by figures: Suppose three periods during which capital increases, labour remaining the same. Let the total production at these three periods be as 80—100—120. It will be thus divided:

	Capitalist's share.	Labourer's share.	Total.
First Period,	...45	35	80
Second Period,	...50	50	100
Third Period,	...55	65	120

Of course these proportions are merely given for the sake of illustration.

a stumbling-block removed from the threshold of our favourite science.

Men of spoliation! you who, by force or fraud, by law or in spite of law, batten on the people's substance; you who live by the errors you propagate, by the ignorance you cherish, by the wars you light up, by the trammels with which you hamper trade; you who tax labour after having rendered it unproductive, making it lose a sheaf for every handful you yourselves pluck from it; you who cause yourselves to be paid for creating obstacles, in order to get afterwards paid for partially removing those obstacles; incarnations of egotism in its worst sense; parasitical excrescences of a vicious policy, prepare for the sharpest and most unsparing criticism. To you, alone, I make no appeal, for the design of this book is to sacrifice you, or rather to sacrifice your unjust pretensions. In vain we cherish conciliation. There are two principles which can never be reconciled— Liberty and Constraint.

If the laws of Providence are harmonious, it is when they act with freedom, without which there is no harmony. Whenever, then, we remark an absence of harmony, we may be sure that it proceeds from an absence of liberty, an absence of justice. Oppressors, spoliators, contemners of justice, you can have no part in the universal harmony, for it is you who disturb it.

Do I mean to say that the effect of this work may be to enfeeble power, to shake its stability, to diminish its authority? My design is just the opposite. But let me not be misunderstood.

It is the business of political science to distinguish between what ought and what ought not to fall under State control; and in making this important distinction we must not forget that the State always acts through the intervention of Force. The services which it renders us, and the services which it exacts from us in return, are alike imposed upon us under the name of contributions.

The question then comes back to this: What are the things which men have a right to impose upon each other *by force?* Now I know but one thing in this situation, and that is *Justice.* I have no right to *force* any one whatever to be religious, charitable, well educated, or industrious; but I have a right to *force* him to be *just,*—this is a case of legitimate defence.

Now, individuals in the aggregate can possess no right which did not pre-exist in individuals as such. If, then, the employment of individual force is justified only by legitimate defence, the fact that the action of government is always manifested by Force should lead us to conclude that it is essentially limited to the maintenance of order, security, and justice.

All action of governments beyond this limit is a usurpation upon conscience, upon intelligence, upon industry; in a word, upon human Liberty.

This being granted, we ought to set ourselves unceasingly and without compunction to emancipate the entire domain of private enterprise from the encroachments of power. Without this we shall not have gained Freedom, or the free play of those laws of harmony which God has provided for the development and progress of the human race.

Will Power by this means be enfeebled? Will it have lost in stability because it has lost in extent? Will it have less authority because it has fewer functions to discharge? Will it attract to itself less respect because it calls forth fewer complaints? Will it be more the sport of factions, when it has reduced those enormous budgets and that coveted influence which are the baits and allurements of faction? Will it encounter greater danger when it has less responsibility?

To me it seems evident, that to confine public force to its one, essential, undisputed, beneficent mission,—a mission desired and accepted by all,—would be the surest way of securing to it respect and universal support. In that case, I see not whence could proceed systematic opposition, parliamentary struggles, street insurrections, revolutions, sudden changes of fortune, factions, illusions, the pretensions of all to govern under all forms, those dangerous and absurd systems which teach the people to look to government for everything, that compromising diplomacy, those wars which are always in perspective, or armed truces which are nearly as fatal, those crushing taxes which it is impossible to levy on any equitable principle, that absorbing and unnatural mixing up of politics with everything, those great artificial displacements of capital and labour, which are the source of fruitless heartburnings, fluctuations, stoppages, and commercial crises. All those causes of trouble, of irritation, of disaffection, of covetousness, and of disorder, and a thousand others, would no longer have any foundation, and the depositaries of power, instead of disturbing, would contribute to the universal harmony,—a harmony which does not indeed exclude evil, but which leaves less and less room for those ills which are inseparable from the ignorance and perversity of our feeble nature, and whose mission it is to prevent or chastise that ignorance and perversity.

Young men! in these days in which a grievous

Scepticism would seem to be at once the effect and the punishment of the anarchy of ideas which prevails, I shall esteem myself happy if this work, as you proceed in its perusal, should bring to your lips the consoling words, I BELIEVE,—words of a sweet-smelling savour, which are at once a refuge and a force, which are said to remove mountains, and stand at the head of the Christian's creed—I believe. "I believe, not with a blind and submissive faith, for we are not concerned here with the mysteries of revelation, but with a rational and scientific faith, befitting things which are left to man's investigation.—I believe that He who has arranged the material universe has not withheld His regards from the arrangements of the social world.—I believe that He has combined, and caused to move in harmony, free agents as well as inert molecules.—I believe that His over-ruling Providence shines forth as strikingly, if not more so, in the laws to which He has subjected men's interests and men's wills, as in the laws which He has imposed on weight and velocity.—I believe that everything in human society, even what is apparently injurious, is the cause of improvement and of progress.—I believe that Evil tends to Good, and calls it forth, whilst Good cannot tend to Evil; whence it follows that Good must in the end predominate.—I believe that the invincible social tendency is a constant approximation of men towards a common moral, intellectual, and physical level, with, at the same time, a progressive and indefinite elevation of that level.—I believe that all that is necessary to the gradual and peaceful development of humanity is that its tendencies should not be disturbed, but have the liberty of their movements restored.—I believe these things, not because I desire them, not because they satisfy my heart, but because my judgment accords to them a deliberate assent."

Ah! whenever you come to pronounce these words, I BELIEVE, you will be anxious to propagate your creed, and the social problem will soon be resolved, for let them say what they will it is not of difficult solution. Men's interests are harmonious,—the solution then lies entirely in this one word—LIBERTY.

LORD ACTON

John Emerich Edward Dalberg-Acton (1834–1902) was considered to be the most learned man of his era. His famous *mot,* "Power tends to corrupt and absolute power tends to corrupt absolutely," has become an accepted dogma. He was a liberal in the classical sense, but he was also a conservative. The liberalism of Mill and Macaulay had little in common with *his* liberalism, as Gertrude Himmelfarb has noted. Their liberalism was lacking in religion. They never considered what was right or wrong, innocent or sinful; but only what was good and bad. To the typical 19th-century liberal, politics was a series of compromises, deals, expediences. This did not appeal to Acton the devout Catholic, and it was his Catholicism that made him a conservative. The combination of political liberalism and spiritual conservatism makes Acton a writer rather close to being a conservative in the 20th-century sense of the word. While he was to attack Burke in his later writings, readers will note a subtle Burkean influence when he deals with the French Revolution. Like Burke, he wrote, "Government by Idea tends to take in everything, to make the whole of society obedient to the idea. Spaces not so governed are unconquered, beyond the border, unconverted, unconvinced of future danger."

From *Essays on Freedom and Power,* ed. G. Himmelfarb (Glencoe, Ill., 1948).

LORD ACTON

Nationality

Whenever great intellectual cultivation has been combined with that suffering which is inseparable from extensive changes in the condition of the people, men of speculative or imaginative genius have sought in the contemplation of an ideal society a remedy, or at least a consolation, for evils which they were practically unable to remove. Poetry has always preserved the idea, that at some distant time or place, in the Western islands or the Arcadian region, an innocent and contented people, free from the corruption and restraint of civilised life, have realised the legends of the golden age. The office of the poets is always nearly the same, and there is little variation in the features of their ideal world; but when philosophers attempt to admonish or reform mankind by devising an imaginary state, their motive is more definite and immediate, and their commonwealth is a satire as well as a model. Plato and Plotinus, More and Campanella, constructed their fanciful societies with those materials which were omitted from the fabric of the actual communities, by the defects of which they were inspired. The Republic, the Utopia, and the City of the Sun were protests against a state of things which the experience of their authors taught them to condemn, and from the faults of which they took refuge in the opposite extremes. They remained without influence, and have never passed from literary into political history, because something more than discontent

NOTE: This essay first appeared in *The Home and Foreign Review*, I (July, 1862), 146–74; reprinted in *The History of Freedom and Other Essays* (London, Macmillan Co., 1907), pp. 270–300.

and speculative ingenuity is needed in order to invest a political idea with power over the masses of mankind. The scheme of a philosopher can command the practical allegiance of fanatics only, not of nations; and though oppression may give rise to violent and repeated outbreaks, like the convulsions of a man in pain, it cannot mature a settled purpose and plan of regeneration, unless a new notion of happiness is joined to the sense of present evil.

The history of religion furnishes a complete illustration. Between the later mediæval sects and Protestantism there is an essential difference, that outweighs the points of analogy found in those systems which are regarded as heralds of the Reformation, and is enough to explain the vitality of the last in comparison with the others. Whilst Wycliffe and Hus contradicted certain particulars of the Catholic teaching, Luther rejected the authority of the Church, and gave to the individual conscience an independence which was sure to lead to an incessant resistance. There is a similar difference between the Revolt of the Netherlands, the Great Rebellion, the War of Independence, or the rising of Brabant, on the one hand, and the French Revolution on the other. Before 1789, insurrections were provoked by particular wrongs, and were justified by definite complaints and by an appeal to principles which all men acknowledged. New theories were sometimes advanced in the cause of controversy, but they were accidental, and the great argument against tyranny was fidelity to the ancient laws. Since the change produced by the French Revolution, those aspirations which are awakened by the evils and defects of the social state have come to act as permanent and energetic forces throughout the civilised world.

They are spontaneous and aggressive, needing no prophet to proclaim, no champion to defend them, but popular, unreasoning, and almost irresistible. The Revolution effected this change, partly by its doctrines, partly by the indirect influence of events. It taught the people to regard their wishes and wants as the supreme criterion of right. The rapid vicissitudes of power, in which each party successively appealed to the favour of the masses as the arbiter of success, accustomed the masses to be arbitrary as well as insubordinate. The fall of many governments, and the frequent redistribution of territory, deprived all settlements of the dignity of permanence. Tradition and prescription ceased to be guardians of authority; and the arrangements which proceeded from revolutions, from the triumphs of war, and from treaties of peace, were equally regardless of established rights. Duty cannot be dissociated from right, and nations refuse to be controlled by laws which are no protection.

In this condition of the world, theory and action follow close upon each other, and practical evils easily give birth to opposite systems. In the realms of free-will, the regularity of natural progress is preserved by the conflict of extremes. The impulse of the reaction carries men from one extremity towards another. The pursuit of a remote and ideal object, which captivates the imagination by its splendour and the reason by its simplicity, evokes an energy which would not be inspired by a rational, possible end, limited by many antagonistic claims, and confined to what is reasonable, practicable, and just. One excess or exaggeration is the corrective of the other, and error promotes truth, where the masses are concerned, by counterbalancing a contrary error. The few have not strength to achieve great changes unaided; the many have not wisdom to be moved by truth unmixed. Where the disease is various, no particular definite remedy can meet the wants of all. Only the attraction of an abstract idea, or of an ideal state, can unite in a common action multitudes who seek a universal cure for many special evils, and a common restorative applicable to many different conditions. And hence false principles, which correspond with the bad as well as with the just aspirations of mankind, are a normal and necessary element in the social life of nations.

Theories of this kind are just, inasmuch as they are provoked by definite ascertained evils, and undertake their removal. They are useful in opposition, as a warning or a threat, to modify existing things, and keep awake the consciousness of wrong. They cannot serve as a basis for the reconstruction of civil society, as medicine cannot serve for food; but they may influence it with advantage, because they point out the direction, though not the measure, in which reform is needed. They oppose an order of things which is the result of a selfish and violent abuse of power by the ruling classes, and of artificial restriction on the natural progress of the world, destitute of an ideal element or a moral purpose. Practical extremes differ from the theoretical extremes they provoke, because the first are both arbitrary and violent, whilst the last, though also revolutionary, are at the same time remedial. In one case the wrong is voluntary, in the other it is inevitable. This is the general character of the contest between the existing order and the subversive theories that deny its legitimacy. There are three principal theories of this kind, impugning the present distribution of power, of property, and of territory, and attacking respectively the aristocracy, the middle class, and the sovereignty. They are the theories of equality, communism, and nationality. Though sprung from a common origin, opposing cognate evils, and connected by many links, they did not appear simultaneously. Rousseau proclaimed the first, Babæuf the second, Mazzini the third; and the third is the most recent in its appearance, the most attractive at the present time, and the richest in promise of future power.

In the old European system, the rights of nationalities were neither recognised by governments nor asserted by the people. The interest of the reigning families, not those of the nations, regulated the frontiers; and the administration was conducted generally without any reference to popular desires. Where all liberties were suppressed, the claims of national independence were necessarily ignored, and a princess, in the words of Fénelon, carried a monarchy in her wedding portion. The eighteenth century acquiesced in this oblivion of corporate rights on the Continent, for the absolutists cared only for the State, and the liberals only for the individual. The Church, the nobles, and the nation had no place in the popular theories of the age; and they devised none in their own defence, for they were not openly attacked. The aristocracy retained its privileges, and the Church her property; and the dynastic interest, which overruled the natural inclination of the nations, and destroyed their independence, nevertheless maintained their integrity. The national sentiment was not wounded in its most sensitive part. To dispossess a sovereign of his hereditary crown, and to annex his dominions, would have been held to inflict an injury upon all monarchies, and to furnish their subjects with a dangerous example, by depriving royalty of its inviolable character. In time of war, as there was no national cause at stake, there was no attempt to rouse national feeling. The courtesy of the rulers towards each other was proportionate to the contempt for the lower orders. Compliments passed between the commanders of hostile armies; there was no bitterness, and no excitement; battles were fought with the pomp and pride of a parade. The art of war became a slow and learned game. The monarchies were united not only by a natural community of interests, but by family alliances. A marriage contract sometimes became the signal for an interminable war, whilst family connections often set a barrier to ambition. After the wars of religion came to an end in 1648, the only wars were those which were waged for an inheritance or a dependency, or against countries whose system of government exempted them from the common law of dynastic States, and made them not only unprotected but obnoxious. These countries were England and Holland, until Holland ceased to be a republic, and until, in England, the defeat of the Jacobites in the forty-five terminated the struggle for the Crown. There was one country, however, which still continued to be an exception; one monarch whose place was not admitted in the comity of kings.

Poland did not possess those securities for stability which were supplied by dynastic connections and the theory of legitimacy, wherever a crown could be obtained by marriage or inheritance. A monarch without royal blood, a crown bestowed by the nation, were an anomaly and an outrage in that age of dynastic absolutism. The country was excluded from the European system by the nature of its institutions. It excited a cupidity which could not be satisfied. It gave the reigning families of Europe no hope of permanently strengthening themselves by intermarriage with its rulers, or of obtaining it by request or by inheritance. The Hapsburgs had contested the possession of Spain and the Indies with the French Bourbons, of Italy with the Spanish Bourbons, of the empire with the house of Wittelsbach, of Silesia with the house of Hohenzollern. There had been wars between rival houses for half the territories of Italy and Germany. But none could hope to redeem their losses or increase their power in a country to which marriage and descent gave no claim. Where they could not permanently inherit they endeavoured, by intrigues, to prevail at each election, and after contending in support of candidates who were their partisans, the neighbours at last appointed an instrument for the final demolition of the Polish State. Till then no nation had been deprived of its political existence by the Christian Powers, and whatever disregard had been shown for national interests and sympathies, some care had been taken to conceal the wrong by a hypocritical perversion of law. But the partition of Poland was an act of wanton violence, committed in open defiance not only of popular feeling but of public law. For the first time in modern history a great State was suppressed, and a whole nation divided among its enemies.

This famous measure, the most revolutionary act of the old absolutism, awakened the theory of nationality in Europe, converting a dormant right into an aspiration, and a sentiment into a political claim. "No wise or honest man," wrote Edmund Burke, "can approve of that partition, or can contemplate it without prognosticating great mischief from it to all countries at some future time."[1]   Thenceforward there was a nation demanding to be united in a State, —a soul, as it were, wandering in search of a body in which to begin life over again; and, for the first time, a cry was heard that the arrangement of States was unjust—that their limits were unnatural, and that a whole people was deprived of its right to constitute an independent community. Before that claim could be efficiently asserted against the overwhelming power of its opponents,—before it gained energy, after the last partition, to overcome the influence of long habits of submission, and of the contempt which previous disorders had brought upon Poland, —the ancient European system was in ruins, and a new world was rising in its place.

The old despotic policy which made the Poles its prey had two adversaries,—the spirit of English liberty, and the doctrines of that revolution which destroyed the French monarchy with its own weapons; and these two contradicted in contrary ways the theory that nations have no collective rights. At the present day, the theory of nationality is not only the most powerful auxiliary of revolution, but its actual substance in the movements of the last three years. This, however, is a recent alliance, unknown to the first French Revolution. The modern theory of nationality arose partly as a legitimate consequence, partly as a reaction against it. As the system which overlooked national division was opposed by liberalism in two forms, the French and the English, so the system which insists upon them proceeds from two distinct sources, and exhibits the character either of

[1]"Observations on the Conduct of the Minority," *Works,* V, 112.

1688 or of 1789. When the French people abolished the authorities under which it lived, and became its own master, France was in danger of dissolution: for the common will is difficult to ascertain, and does not readily agree. "The laws," said Vergniaud, in the debate on the sentence of the king, "are obligatory only as the presumptive will of the people, which retains the right of approving or condemning them. The instant it manifests its wish the work of the national representation, the law, must disappear." This doctrine resolved society into its natural elements, and threatened to break up the country into as many republics as there were communes. For true republicanism is the principle of self-government in the whole and in all the parts. In an extensive country, it can prevail only by the union of several independent communities in a single confederacy, as in Greece, in Switzerland, in the Netherlands, and in America; so that a large republic not founded on the federal principle must result in the government of a single city, like Rome and Paris, and, in a less degree, Athens, Berne, and Amsterdam; or, in other words, a great democracy must either sacrifice self-government to unity, or preserve it by federalism.

The France of history fell together with the French State, which was the growth of centuries. The old sovereignty was destroyed. The local authorities were looked upon with aversion and alarm. The new central authority needed to be established on a new principle of unity. The state of nature, which was the ideal of society, was made the basis of the nation; descent was put in the place of tradition, and the French people was regarded as a physical product: an ethnological, not historic, unit. It was assumed that a unity existed separate from the rep-

resentation and the government, wholly independent of the past, and capable at any moment of expressing or of changing its mind. In the words of
Siéyès, it was no longer France, but some unknown
country to which the nation was transported. The
central power possessed authority, inasmuch as it
obeyed the whole, and no divergence was permitted
from the universal sentiment. This power, endowed
with volition, was personified in the Republic One
and Indivisible. The title signified that a part could
not speak or act for the whole,—that there was a
power supreme over the State, distinct from, and
independent of, its members; and it expressed, for
the first time in history, the notion of an abstract
nationality. In this manner the idea of the sovereignty of the people, uncontrolled by the past, gave
birth to the idea of nationality independent of the
political influence of history. It sprang from the rejection of the two authorities,—of the State and of
the past. The kingdom of France was, geographically
as well as politically, the product of a long series of
events, and the same influences which built up the
State formed the territory. The Revolution repudiated alike the agencies to which France owed her
boundaries and those to which she owed her government. Every effaceable trace and relic of national
history was carefully wiped away,—the system of
administration, the physical divisions of the country, the classes of society, the corporations, the
weights and measures, the calendar. France was no
longer bounded by the limits she had received from
the condemned influence of her history; she could
recognise only those which were set by nature. The
definition of the nation was borrowed from the
material world, and, in order to avoid a loss of terri-

tory, it became not only an abstraction but a fiction.

There was a principle of nationality in the ethnological character of the movement, which is the source of the common observation that revolution is more frequent in Catholic than in Protestant countries. It is, in fact, more frequent in the Latin than in the Teutonic world, because it depends partly on a national impulse, which is only awakened where there is an alien element, the vestige of a foreign dominion, to expel. Western Europe has undergone two conquests—one by the Romans and one by the Germans, and twice received laws from the invaders. Each time it rose again against the victorious race; and the two great reactions, while they differ according to the different characters of the two conquests, have the phenomenon of imperialism in common. The Roman republic laboured to crush the subjugated nations into a homogeneous and obedient mass; but the increase which the proconsular authority obtained in the process subverted the republican government, and the reaction of the provinces against Rome assisted in establishing the empire. The Cæsarean system gave an unprecedented freedom to the dependencies, and raised them to a civil equality which put an end to the dominion of race over race and of class over class. The monarchy was hailed as a refuge from the pride and cupidity of the Roman people; and the love of equality, the hatred of nobility, and the tolerance of despotism implanted by Rome became, at least in Gaul, the chief feature of the national character. But among the nations whose vitality had been broken down by the stern republic, not one retained the materials necessary to enjoy independence, or to develop a new history. The political faculty which organises states and finds society in a moral order was exhausted, and the Christian doctors looked in vain over the waste of ruins for a people by whose aid the Church might survive the decay of Rome. A new element of national life was brought to that declining world by the enemies who destroyed it. The flood of barbarians settled over it for a season, and then subsided; and when the landmarks of civilisation appeared once more, it was found that the soil had been impregnated with a fertilising and regenerating influence, and that the inundation had laid the germs of future states and of a new society. The political sense and energy came with the new blood, and was exhibited in the power exercised by the younger race upon the old, and in the establishment of a graduated freedom. Instead of universal equal rights, the actual enjoyment of which is necessarily contingent on, and commensurate with, power, the rights of the people were made dependent on a variety of conditions, the first of which was the distribution of property. Civil society became a classified organism instead of a formless combination of atoms, and the feudal system gradually arose.

Roman Gaul had so thoroughly adopted the ideas of absolute authority and undistinguished equality during the five centuries between Cæsar and Clovis, that the people could never be reconciled to the new system. Feudalism remained a foreign importation, and the feudal aristocracy an alien race, and the common people of France sought protection against both in the Roman jurisprudence and the power of the crown. The development of absolute monarchy by the help of democracy is the one constant character of French history. The royal power, feudal at first, and limited by the immunities and the great

vassals, became more popular as it grew more absolute; while the suppression of aristocracy, the removal of the intermediate authorities, was so particularly the object of the nation, that it was more
energetically accomplished after the fall of the
throne. The monarchy which had been engaged from
the thirteenth century in curbing the nobles, was at
last thrust aside by the democracy, because it was too
dilatory in the work, and was unable to deny its own
origin and effectually ruin the class from which it
sprang. All those things which constitute the peculiar character of the French Revolution,—the demand for equality, the hatred of nobility and
feudalism, and of the Church which was connected
with them, the constant reference to pagan examples, the suppression of monarchy, the new code of
law, the breach with tradition, and the substitution
of an ideal system for everything that had proceeded
from the mixture and mutual action of the races,—
all these exhibit the common type of a reaction
against the effects of the Frankish invasion. The hatred of royalty was less than the hatred of aristocracy; privileges were more detested than tyranny;
and the king perished because of the origin of his
authority rather than because of its abuse. Monarchy
unconnected with aristocracy became popular in
France, even when most uncontrolled; whilst the attempt to reconstitute the throne, and to limit and
fence it with its peers, broke down, because the old
Teutonic elements on which it relied—hereditary
nobility, primogeniture, and privilege—were no
longer tolerated. The substance of the ideas of 1789
is not the limitation of the sovereign power, but the
abrogation of intermediate powers. These powers,
and the classes which enjoyed them, come in Latin

Europe from a barbarian origin; and the movement which calls itself liberal is essentially national. If liberty were its object, its means would be the establishment of great independent authorities not derived from the State, and its model would be England. But its object is equality; and it seeks, like France in 1789, to cast out the elements of inequality which were introduced by the Teutonic race. This is the object which Italy and Spain have had in common with France, and herein consists the natural league of the Latin nations.

This national element in the movement was not understood by the revolutionary leaders. At first, their doctrine appeared entirely contrary to the idea of nationality. They taught that certain general principles of government were absolutely right in all States; and they asserted in theory the unrestricted freedom of the individual, and the supremacy of the will over every external necessity or obligation. This is in apparent contradiction to the national theory, that certain natural forces ought to determine the character, the form, and the policy of the State, by which a kind of fate is put in the place of freedom. Accordingly the national sentiment was not developed directly out of the revolution in which it was involved, but was exhibited first in resistance to it, when the attempt to emancipate had been absorbed in the desire to subjugate, and the republic had been succeeded by the empire. Napoleon called a new power into existence by attacking nationality in Russia, by delivering it in Italy, by governing in defiance of it in Germany and Spain. The sovereigns of these countries were deposed or degraded; and a system of administration was introduced which was French in its origin, its spirit, and its instruments.

The people resisted the change. The movement against it was popular and spontaneous, because the rulers were absent or helpless; and it was national, because it was directed against foreign institutions. In Tyrol, in Spain, and afterwards in Prussia, the people did not receive the impulse from the government, but undertook of their own accord to cast out the armies and the ideas of revolutionised France. Men were made conscious of the national element of the revolution by its conquests, not in its rise. The three things which the Empire most openly oppressed—religion, national independence, and political liberty—united in a short-lived league to animate the great uprising by which Napoleon fell. Under the influence of that memorable alliance a political spirit was called forth on the Continent, which clung to freedom and abhorred revolution, and sought to restore, to develop, and to reform the decayed national institutions. The men who proclaimed these ideas, Stein and Görres, Humboldt, Müller, and De Maistre,[2] were as hostile to Bonapartism as to the absolutism of the old governments, and insisted on the national rights, which had been in-

[2]There are some remarkable thoughts on nationality in the State Papers of the Count de Maistre: "En premier lieu les nations sont quelque chose dans le monde, il n'est pas permis de les compter pour rien, de les affliger dans leurs convenances, dans leurs affections, dans leurs intérêts les plus chers. . . . Or le traité du 30 mai aneantit complétement la Savoie; il divise l'indivisible; il partage en trois portions une malheureuse nation de 400,000 hommes, une par la langue, une par la religion, une par le caractère, une par l'habitude invétérée, une enfin par les limites naturelles. . . . L'union des nations ne souffre pas de difficultés sur la carte géographique; mais dans la réalité, c'est autre chose; il y a des nations *immiscibles.* . . . Je lui parlai par occasion de l'esprit italien qui s'agite dans ce moment; il (Count Nesselrode) me répondit: 'Oui, Monsieur; mais cet esprit est un grand mal, car il peut gêner les arrangements de l'Italie.' "—*Correspondance Diplomatique de J. de Maistre,* II, 7, 8, 21, 25. In the same year, 1815, Görres wrote: "In Italien wie allerwarts ist das Volk gewecht; es will etwas grossartiges, es will Ideen haben, die, wenn es sie auch nicht ganz begreift, doch einen freien unendlichen Gesichtskreis seiner Einbildung eröffnen. . . . Es ist reiner Naturtrieb, dass ein Volk, also scharf und deutlich in seine natürlichen Gränzen eingeschlossen, aus der Zerstreuung in die Einheit sich zu sammeln sucht."— *Werke,* II, 20.

vaded equally by both, and which they hoped to restore by the destruction of the French supremacy. With the cause that triumphed at Waterloo the friends of the Revolution had no sympathy, for they had learned to identify their doctrine with the cause of France. The Holland House Whigs in England, the Afrancesados in Spain, the Muratists in Italy, and the partisans of the Confederation of the Rhine, merging patriotism in their revolutionary affections, regretted the fall of the French power, and looked with alarm at those new and unknown forces which the War of Deliverance had evoked, and which were as menacing to French liberalism as to French supremacy.

But the new aspirations for national and popular rights were crushed at the restoration. The liberals of those days cared for freedom, not in the shape of national independence, but of French institutions; and they combined against the nations with the ambition of the governments. They were as ready to sacrifice nationality to their ideal as the Holy Alliance was to the interests of absolutism. Talleyrand indeed declared at Vienna that the Polish question ought to have precedence over all other questions, because the partition of Poland had been one of the first and greatest causes of the evils which Europe had suffered; but dynastic interests prevailed. All the sovereigns represented at Vienna recovered their dominions, except the King of Saxony, who was punished for his fidelity to Napoleon; but the States that were unrepresented in the reigning families—Poland, Venice, and Genoa—were not revived, and even the Pope had great difficulty in recovering the Legations from the grasp of Austria. Nationality, which the old *regime* had ignored, which had been outraged by the revolution and the empire, received, after its first open demonstration, the hardest blow at the Congress of Vienna. The principle which the first partition had generated, to which the revolution had given a basis of theory, which had been lashed by the empire into a momentary convulsive effort, was matured by the long error of the restoration into a consistent doctrine, nourished and justified by the situation of Europe.

The governments of the Holy Alliance devoted themselves to suppress with equal care the revolutionary spirit by which they had been threatened, and the national spirit by which they had been restored. Austria, which owed nothing to the national movement, and had prevented its revival after 1809, naturally took the lead in repressing it. Every disturbance of the final settlements of 1815, every aspiration for changes or reforms, was condemned as sedition. This system repressed the good with the evil tendencies of the age; and the resistance which it provoked, during the generation that passed away from the restoration to the fall of Metternich, and again under the reaction which commenced with Schwarzenberg and ended with the administrations of Bach and Manteuffel, proceeded from various combinations of the opposite forms of liberalism. In the successive phases of that struggle, the idea that national claims are above all other rights gradually rose to the supremacy which it now possesses among the revolutionary agencies.

The first liberal movement, that of the Carbonari in the south of Europe, had no specific national character, but was supported by the Bonapartists both in Spain and Italy. In the following years the opposite ideas of 1813 came to the front, and a revolutionary movement, in many respects hostile to the principles of revolution, began in defence of liberty, religion, and nationality. All these causes were united in the Irish agitation, and in the Greek, Belgian, and Polish revolutionists. Those sentiments which had been insulted by Napoleon, and had risen against him, rose against the governments of the restoration. They had been oppressed by the sword, and then by the treaties. The national principle added force, but not justice, to this movement, which, in every case but Poland, was successful. A period followed in which it degenerated into a purely national idea, as the agitation for repeal succeeded emancipation, and Panslavism and Panhellenism arose under the auspices of the Eastern Church. This was the third phase of the resistance to the settlement of Vienna, which was weak, because it failed to satisfy national or constitutional aspirations, either of which would have been a safeguard against the other, by a moral if not by a popular justification. At first, in 1813, the people rose against their conquerors, in defence of their legitimate rulers. They refused to be governed by usurpers. In the period between 1825 and 1831, they resolved that they would not be misgoverned by strangers. The French administration was often better than that which it displaced, but there were prior claimants for the authority exercised by the French, and at first the national contest was a contest for legitimacy. In the second period this element was wanting. No dispossessed princes led the Greeks, the Belgians, or the Poles. The Turks, the Dutch, and the Russians were attacked, not as usurpers, but as oppressors,—because they misgoverned, not because they were of a different race. Then began a time when the text simply was, that nations would not be

governed by foreigners. Power legitimately obtained, and exercised with moderation, was declared
invalid. National rights, like religion, had borne part
in the previous combinations, and had been auxiliaries in the struggles for freedom, but now nationality
became a paramount claim, which was to assert itself alone, which might put forward as pretexts the
rights of rulers, the liberties of the people, the safety
of religion, but which, if no such union could be
formed, was to prevail at the expense of every other
cause for which nations make sacrifices.

Metternich is, next to Napoleon, the chief pro-
moter of this theory; for the anti-national character
of the restoration was most distinct in Austria, and
it is in opposition to the Austrian Government that
nationality grew into a system. Napoleon, who, trust-
ing to his armies, despised moral forces in politics,
was overthrown by their rising. Austria committed
the same fault in the government of her Italian provinces. The kingdom of Italy had united all the northern part of the Peninsula in a single State; and the
national feelings, which the French repressed elsewhere, were encouraged as a safeguard of their
power in Italy and in Poland. When the tide of victory turned, Austria invoked against the French the
aid of the new sentiment they had fostered. Nugent
announced, in his proclamation to the Italians, that
they should become an independent nation. The
same spirit served different masters, and contributed first to the destruction of the old States, then
to the expulsion of the French, and again, under
Charles Albert, to a new revolution. It was appealed
to in the name of the most contradictory principles
of government, and served all parties in succession,
because it was one in which all could unite. Begin-

ning by a protest against the dominion of race over race, its mildest and least-developed form, it grew into a condemnation of every State that included different races, and finally became the complete and consistent theory, that the State and the nation must be co-extensive. "It is," says Mr. Mill, "in general a necessary condition of free institutions, that the boundaries of governments should coincide in the main with those of nationalities."[3]

The outward historical progress of this idea from an indefinite aspiration to be the keystone of a political system, may be traced in the life of the man who gave to it the element in which its strength resides, —Giuseppe Mazzini. He found Carbonarism impotent against the measures of the governments, and resolved to give new life to the liberal movement by transferring it to the ground of nationality. Exile is the nursery of nationality, as oppression is the school of liberalism; and Mazzini conceived the idea of Young Italy when he was a refugee at Marseilles. In the same way, the Polish exiles are the champions of every national movement; for to them all political rights are absorbed in the idea of independence, which, however they may differ with each other, is the one aspiration common to them all. Towards the year 1830 literature also contributed to the national idea. "It was the time," says Mazzini, "of the great conflict between the romantic and the classical school, which might with equal truth be called a conflict between the partisans of freedom and of authority." The romantic school was infidel in Italy, and Catholic in Germany; but in both it had the common effect of encouraging national history and literature,

[3]Mill's *Considerations on Representative Government*, p. 298.

and Dante was as great an authority with the Italian democrats as with the leaders of the mediæval revival at Vienna, Munich, and Berlin. But neither the influence of the exiles, nor that of the poets and critics of the new party, extended over the masses. It was a sect without popular sympathy or encouragement, a conspiracy founded not on a grievance, but on a doctrine; and when the attempt to rise was made in Savoy, in 1834, under a banner with the motto "Unity, Independence, God and Humanity," the people were puzzled at its object, and indifferent to its failure. But Mazzini continued his propaganda, developed his *Giovine Italia* into a *Giovine Europa*, and established in 1847 the international league of nations. "The people," he said, in his opening address, "is penetrated with only one idea, that of unity and nationality. . . . There is no international question as to forms of government, but only a national question."

The revolution of 1848, unsuccessful in its national purpose, prepared the subsequent victories of nationality in two ways. The first of these was the restoration of the Austrian power in Italy, with a new and more energetic centralisation, which gave no promise of freedom. Whilst that system prevailed, the right was on the side of the national aspirations, and they were revived in a more complete and cultivated form by Manin. The policy of the Austrian Government, which failed during the ten years of the reaction to convert the tenure by force into a tenure by right, and to establish with free institutions the condition of allegiance, gave a negative encouragement to the theory. It deprived Francis Joseph of all active support and sympathy in 1859, for he was more clearly wrong in his conduct than his enemies in their doctrines. The real cause of the energy which the national theory has acquired is, however, the triumph of the democratic principle in France, and its recognition by the European Powers. The theory of nationality is involved in the democratic theory of the sovereignty of the general will. "One hardly knows what any division of the human race should be free to do, if not to determine with which of the various collective bodies of human beings they choose to associate themselves."[4] It is by this act that a nation constitutes itself. To have a collective will, unity is necessary, and independence is requisite in order to assert it. Unity and nationality are still more essential to the notion of the sovereignty of the people than the cashiering of monarchs, or the revocation of laws. Arbitrary acts of this kind may be prevented by the happiness of the people or the popularity of the king, but a nation inspired by the democratic idea cannot with consistency allow a part of itself to belong to a foreign State, or the whole to be divided into several native States. The theory of nationality therefore proceeds from both the principles which divide the political world, —from legitimacy, which ignores its claims, and from the revolution, which assumes them; and for the same reason it is the chief weapon of the last against the first.

In pursuing the outward and visible growth of the national theory we are prepared for an examination of its political character and value. The absolutism which has created it denies equally that absolute right of national unity which is a product of democracy, and that claim of national liberty which be-

[4]Mill's *Considerations,* p. 296.

longs to the theory of freedom. These two views of nationality, corresponding to the French and to the English systems, are connected in name only, and are in reality the opposite extremes of political thought. In one case, nationality is founded on the perpetual supremacy of the collective will, of which the unity of the nation is the necessary condition, to which every other influence must defer, and against which no obligation enjoys authority, and all resistance is tyrannical. The nation is here an ideal unit founded on the race, in defiance of the modifying action of external causes, of tradition, and of existing rights. It overrules the rights and wishes of the inhabitants, absorbing their divergent interests in a fictitious unity; sacrifices their several inclinations and duties to the higher claim of nationality, and crushes all natural rights and all established liberties for the purpose of vindicating itself.[5] Whenever a single definite object is made the supreme end of the State, be it the advantage of a class, the safety or the power of the country, the greatest happiness of the greatest number, or the support of any speculative idea, the State becomes for the time inevitably absolute. Liberty alone demands for its realisation the limitation of the public authority, for liberty is the only object which benefits all alike, and provokes no sincere opposition. In supporting the claims of national unity, governments must be subverted in whose title there is no flaw, and whose policy is beneficent and equitable, and subjects must be com-

[5]"Le sentiment d'indépendance nationale est encore plus général et plus profondément gravé dans le cœur des peuples que l'amour d'une liberté constitutionnelle. Les nations les plus soumises au despotisme éprouvent ce sentiment avec autant de vivacité que les nations libres; les peuples les plus barbares le sentent même encore plus vivement que les nations policées."— *L'Italie au Dixneuvième Siècle*, p. 148, Paris, 1821.

pelled to transfer their allegiance to an authority for which they have no attachment, and which may be practically a foreign domination. Connected with this theory in nothing except in the common enmity of the absolute state, is the theory which represents nationality as an essential, but not a supreme element in determining the forms of the State. It is distinguished from the other, because it tends to diversity and not to uniformity, to harmony and not to unity; because it aims not at an arbitrary change, but at careful respect for the existing conditions of political life, and because it obeys the laws and results of history, not the aspirations of an ideal future. While the theory of unity makes the nation a source of despotism and revolution, the theory of liberty regards it as the bulwark of self-government, and the foremost limit to the excessive power of the State. Private rights, which are sacrificed to the unity, are preserved by the union of nations. No power can so efficiently resist the tendencies of centralisation, of corruption, and of absolutism, as that community which is the vastest that can be included in a State, which imposes on its members a consistent similarity of character, interest, and opinion, and which arrests the action of the sovereign by the influence of a divided patriotism. The presence of different nations under the same sovereignty is similar in its effect to the independence of the Church in the State. It provides against the servility which flourishes under the shadow of a single authority, by balancing interests, multiplying associations, and giving to the subject the restraint and support of a combined opinion. In the same way it promotes independence by forming definite groups of public opinion, and by affording a great source and centre of political sentiments, and of notions of duty not derived from the sovereign will. Liberty provokes diversity, and diversity preserves liberty by supplying the means of organisation. All those portions of law which govern the relations of men with each other, and regulate social life, are the varying result of national custom and the creation of private society. In these things, therefore, the several nations will differ from each other; for they themselves have produced them, and they do not owe them to the State which rules them all. This diversity in the same State is a firm barrier against the intrusion of the government beyond the political sphere which is common to all into the social department which escapes legislation and is ruled by spontaneous laws. This sort of interference is characteristic of an absolute government, and is sure to provoke a reaction, and finally a remedy. That intolerance of social freedom which is natural to absolutism is sure to find a corrective in the national diversities, which no other force could so efficiently provide. The co-existence of several nations under the same State is a test, as well as the best security of its freedom. It is also one of the chief instruments of civilisation; and, as such, it is in the natural and providential order, and indicates a state of greater advancement than the national unity which is the ideal of modern liberalism.

The combination of different nations in one state is as necessary a condition of civilised life as the combination of men in society. Inferior races are raised by living in political union with races intellectually superior. Exhausted and decaying nations are revived by the contact of a younger vitality. Nations in which the elements of organisation and the capacity for government have been lost, either through the

demoralising influence of despotism, or the disinte-
grating action of democracy, are restored and educated anew under the discipline of a stronger and
less corrupted race. This fertilising and regenerating process can only be obtained by living under one
government. It is in the cauldron of the State that the
fusion takes place by which the vigour, the knowledge, and the capacity of one portion of mankind
may be communicated to another. Where political
and national boundaries coincide, society ceases to
advance, and nations relapse into a condition corresponding to that of men who renounce intercourse
with their fellow-men. The difference between the
two unites mankind not only by the benefits it confers on those who live together, but because it con-
nects society either by a political or a national bond,
gives to every people an interest in its neighbours,
either because they are under the same government
or because they are of the same race, and thus promotes the interests of humanity, of civilisation, and
of religion.

Christianity rejoices at the mixture of races, as
paganism identifies itself with their differences, because truth is universal, and errors various and particular. In the ancient world idolatry and nationality
went together, and the same term is applied in Scrip-
ture to both. It was the mission of the Church to
overcome national differences. The period of her undisputed supremacy was that in which all Western
Europe obeyed the same laws, all literature was contained in one language, and the political unit of
Christendom was personified in a single potentate,
while its intellectual unity was represented in one
university. As the ancient Romans concluded their
conquests by carrying away the gods of the con-

quered people, Charlemagne overcame the national resistance of the Saxons only by the forcible destruction of their pagan rites. Out of the mediæval period, and the combined action of the German race and the Church, came forth a new system of nations and a new conception of nationality. Nature was overcome in the nation as well as in the individual. In pagan and uncultivated times, nations were distinguished from each other by the widest diversity, not only in religion, but in customs, language, and character. Under the new law they had many things in common; the old barriers which separated them were removed, and the new principle of self-government, which Christianity imposed, enabled them to live together under the same authority, without necessarily losing their cherished habits, their customs, or their laws. The new idea of freedom made room for different races in one State. A nation was no longer what it had been to the ancient world,—the progeny of a common ancestor, or the aboriginal product of a particular region,—a result of merely physical and material causes,—but a moral and political being; not the creation of geographical or physiological unity, but developed in the course of history by the action of the State. It is derived from the State, not supreme over it. A State may in course of time produce a nationality; but that a nationality should constitute a State is contrary to the nature of modern civilisation. The nation derives its rights and its power from the memory of a former independence.

The Church has agreed in this respect with the tendency of political progress, and discouraged wherever she could the isolation of nations; admonishing them of their duties to each other, and regarding conquest and feudal investitude as the natural means of raising barbarous or sunken nations to a higher level. But though she has never attributed to national independence an immunity from the accidental consequences of feudal law, of hereditary claims, or of testamentary arrangements, she defends national liberty against uniformity and centralisation with an energy inspired by perfect community of interests. For the same enemy threatens both; and the State which is reluctant to tolerate differences, and to do justice to the peculiar character of various races, must from the same cause interfere in the internal government of religion. The connection of religious liberty with the emancipation of Poland or Ireland is not merely the accidental result of local causes; and the failure of the Concordat to unite the subjects of Austria is the natural consequence of a policy which did not desire to protect the provinces in their diversity and autonomy, and sought to bribe the Church by favours instead of strengthening her by independence. From this influence of religion in modern history has proceeded a new definition of patriotism.

The difference between nationality and the State is exhibited in the nature of patriotic attachment. Our connection with the race is merely natural or physical, whilst our duties to the political nation are ethical. One is a community of affections and instincts infinitely important and powerful in savage life, but pertaining more to the animal than to the civilised man; the other is an authority governing by laws, imposing obligations, and giving a moral sanction and character to the natural relations of society. Patriotism is in political life what faith is in religion, and it stands to the domestic feelings and to homesickness as faith to fanaticism and to superstition. It has one aspect derived from private life and nature, for it is an extension of the family affections, as the tribe is an extension of the family. But in its real political character, patriotism consists in the development of the instinct of self-preservation into a moral duty which may involve self-sacrifice. Self-preservation is both an instinct and a duty, natural and involuntary in one respect, and at the same time a moral obligation. By the first it produces the family; by the last the State. If the nation could exist without the State, subject only to the instinct of self-preservation, it would be incapable of denying, controlling, or sacrificing itself; it would be an end and a rule to itself. But in the political order moral purposes are realised and public ends are pursued to which private interests and even existence must be sacrificed. The great sign of true patriotism, the development of selfishness into sacrifice, is the product of political life. That sense of duty which is supplied by race is not entirely separated from its selfish and instinctive basis; and the love of country, like married love, stands at the same time on a material and a moral foundation. The patriot must distinguish between the two causes or objects of his devotion. The attachment which is given only to the country is like obedience given only to the State—a submission to physical influences. The man who prefers his country before every other duty shows the same spirit as the man who surrenders every right to the State. They both deny that right is superior to authority.

There is a moral and political country, in the language of Burke, distinct from the geographical, which may be possibly in collision with it. The Frenchmen who bore arms against the Convention were as patriotic as the Englishmen who bore arms against King Charles, for they recognised a higher duty than that of obedience to the actual sovereign.

"In an address to France," said Burke, "in an attempt to treat with it, or in considering any scheme at all relative to it, it is impossible we should mean the geographical, we must always mean the moral and political, country. . . . The truth is, that France is out of itself—the moral France is separated from the geographical. The master of the house is expelled, and the robbers are in possession. If we look for the corporate people of France, existing as corporate in the eye and intention of public law (that corporate people, I mean, who are free to deliberate and to decide, and who have a capacity to treat and conclude), they are in Flanders and Germany, in Switzerland, Spain, Italy, and England. There are all the princes of the blood, there are all the orders of the State, there are all the parliaments of the kingdom. . . . I am sure that if half that number of the same description were taken out of this country, it would leave hardly anything that I should call the people of England."[6] Rousseau draws nearly the same distinction between the country to which we happen to belong and that which fulfils towards us the political functions of the State. In the *Emile* he has a sentence of which it is not easy in a translation to convey the point: "Qui n'a pas une patrie a du moins un pays." And in his tract on Political Economy he writes: "How shall men love their country if it is nothing more for them than for strangers, and bestows on them only that which it can refuse to none?" It is in the same sense he says, further on, "La patrie ne peut subsister sans la liberté."[7]

---

[6]Burke's "Remarks on the Policy of the Allies," *Works*, V. 26, 29, 30.

[7] *œuvres*, I, 593, 595; II, 717. Bossuet, in a passage of great beauty on the love of country, does not attain to the political definition of the word: "La société humaine demande qu'on aime la terre où l'on habite ensemble, ou la regarde comme une mère et une nourrice commune. . . . Les hommes en effet se sentent

The nationality formed by the State, then, is the only one to which we owe political duties, and it is, therefore, the only one which has political rights. The Swiss are ethnologically either French, Italian, or German; but no nationality has the slightest claim upon them, except the purely political nationality of Switzerland. The Tuscan or the Neapolitan State has formed a nationality, but the citizens of Florence and of Naples have no political community with each other. There are other States which have neither succeeded in absorbing distinct races in a political nationality, nor in separating a particular district from a larger nation. Austria and Mexico are instances on the one hand, Parma and Baden on the other. The progress of civilisation deals hardly with the last description of States. In order to maintain their integrity they must attach themselves by confederations, or family alliances, to greater Powers, and thus lose something of their independence. Their tendency is to isolate and shut off their inhabitants, to narrow the horizon of their views, and to dwarf in some degree the proportions of their ideas. Public opinion cannot maintain its liberty and purity in such small dimensions, and the currents that come from larger communities sweep over a contracted territory. In a small and homogeneous population there is hardly room for a natural classification of society, or for inner groups of interests that set bounds to sovereign power. The government and the subjects contend with borrowed weapons. The resources of the one and the aspirations of the other are derived from some external source, and the

liés par quelque chose de fort, lorsqu'ils songent, que le même terre qui les a portés et nourris étant vivants, les recevra dans son sein quand ils seront morts." "Politique tirée de l'Ecriture Sainte," *œuvres,* X, 317.

consequence is that the country becomes the instrument and the scene of contests in which it is not interested. These States, like the minuter communities of the Middle Ages, serve a purpose, by constituting partitions and securities of self-government in the larger States; but they are impediments to the progress of society, which depends on the mixture of races under the same governments.

The vanity and peril of national claims founded on no political tradition, but on race alone, appear in Mexico. There the races are divided by blood, without being grouped together in different regions. It is, therefore, neither possible to unite them nor to convert them into the elements of an organised State. They are fluid, shapeless, and unconnected, and cannot be precipitated, or formed into the basis of political institutions. As they cannot be used by the State, they cannot be recognised by it; and their peculiar qualities, capabilities, passions, and attachments are of no service, and therefore obtain no regard. They are necessarily ignored, and are therefore perpetually outraged. From this difficulty of races with political pretensions, but without political position, the Eastern world escaped by the institution of castes. Where there are only two races there is the resource of slavery; but when different races inhabit the different territories of one Empire composed of several smaller States, it is of all possible combinations the most favourable to the establishment of a highly developed system of freedom. In Austria there are two circumstances which add to the difficulty of the problem, but also increase its importance. The several nationalities are at very unequal degrees of advancement, and there is no single nation which is so predominant as to overwhelm or absorb the others.

These are the conditions necessary for the very highest degree of organisation which government is capable of receiving. They supply the greatest variety of intellectual resource; the perpetual incentive to progress which is afforded not merely by competition, but by the spectacle of a more advanced people; the most abundant elements of self-government, combined with the impossibility for the State to rule all by its own will; and the fullest security for the preservation of local customs and ancient rights. In such a country as this, liberty would achieve its most glorious results, while centralisation and absolutism would be destruction.

The problem presented to the government of Austria is higher than that which is solved in England, because of the necessity of admitting the national claims. The parliamentary system fails to provide for them, as it presupposes the unity of the people. Hence in those countries in which different races dwell together, it has not satisfied their desires, and is regarded as an imperfect form of freedom. It brings out more clearly than before the differences it does not recognise, and thus continues the work of the old absolutism, and appears as a new phase of centralisation. In those countries, therefore, the power of the imperial parliament must be limited as jealously as the power of the crown, and many of its functions must be discharged by provincial diets, and a descending series of local authorities.

The great importance of nationality in the State consists in the fact that it is the basis of political capacity. The character of a nation determines in great measure the form and vitality of the State. Certain political habits and ideas belong to particular nations, and they vary with the course of the national history. A people just emerging from barbarism, a people effete from the excesses of a luxurious civilisation, cannot possess the means of governing itself; a people devoted to equality, or to absolute monarchy, is incapable of producing an aristocracy; a people averse to the institution of private property is without the first element of freedom. Each of these can be converted into efficient members of a free community only by the contact of a superior race, in whose power will lie the future prospects of the State. A system which ignores these things, and does not rely for its support on the character and aptitude of the people, does not intend that they should administer their own affairs, but that they should simply be obedient to the supreme command. The denial of nationality, therefore, implies the denial of political liberty.

The greatest adversary of the rights of nationality is the modern theory of nationality. By making the State and the nation commensurate with each other in theory, it reduces practically to a subject condition all other nationalities that may be within the boundary. It cannot admit them to an equality with the ruling nation which constitutes the State, because the State would then cease to be national, which would be a contradiction of the principle of its existence. According, therefore, to the degree of humanity and civilisation in that dominant body which claims all the rights of the community, the inferior races are exterminated, or reduced to servitude, or outlawed, or put in a condition of dependence.

If we take the establishment of liberty for the realisation of moral duties to be the end of civil society, we must conclude that those states are substantially the most perfect which, like the British and Austrian Empires, include various distinct nationalities without oppressing them. Those in which no mixture of races has occurred are imperfect; and those in which its effects have disappeared are decrepit. A State which is incompetent to satisfy different races condemns itself; a State which labours to neutralise, to absorb, or to expel them, destroys its own vitality; a State which does not include them is destitute of the chief basis of self-government. The theory of nationality, therefore, is a retrograde step in history. It is the most advanced form of the revolution, and must retain its power to the end of the revolutionary period, of which it announces the approach. Its great historical importance depends on two chief causes.

First, it is a chimera. The settlement at which it aims is impossible. As it can never be satisfied and exhausted, and always continues to assert itself, it prevents the government from ever relapsing into the condition which provoked its rise. The danger is too threatening, and the power over men's minds too great, to allow any system to endure which justifies the resistance of nationality. It must contribute, therefore, to obtain that which in theory it condemns,—the liberty of different nationalities as members of one sovereign community. This is a service which no other force could accomplish; for it is a corrective alike of absolute monarchy, of democracy, and of constitutionalism, as well as of the centralisation which is common to all three. Neither the monarchical nor the revolutionary, nor the parliamentary system can do this; and all the ideas which have excited enthusiasm in past times are impotent for the purpose except nationality alone.

And secondly, the national theory marks the end of the revolutionary doctrine and its logical exhaustion. In proclaiming the supremacy of the rights of nationality, the system of democratic equality goes beyond its own extreme boundary, and falls into contradiction with itself. Between the democratic and the national phase of the revolution, socialism had intervened, and had already carried the consequences of the principle to an absurdity. But that phase was passed. The revolution survived its offspring, and produced another further result. Nationality is more advanced than socialism, because it is a more arbitrary system. The social theory endeavours to provide for the existence of the individual beneath the terrible burdens which modern society heaps upon labour. It is not merely a development of the notion of equality, but a refuge from real misery and starvation. However false the solution, it was a reasonable demand that the poor should be saved from destruction; and if the freedom of the State was sacrificed to the safety of the individual, the more immediate object was, at least in theory, attained. But nationality does not aim either at liberty or prosperity, both of which it sacrifices to the imperative necessity of making the nation the mould and measure of the State. Its course will be marked with material as well as moral ruin, in order that a new invention may prevail over the works of God and the interests of mankind. There is no principle of change, no phase of political speculation conceivable, more comprehensive, more subversive, or more arbitrary than this. It is a confutation of democracy, because it sets limits to the exercise of the popular will, and substitutes for it a higher principle. It prevents not only the division, but the extension of the State, and forbids to terminate war by conquest, and to obtain a security for peace. Thus, after surrendering the individual to the collective will, the revolutionary system makes the collective will subject to conditions which are independent of it, and rejects all law, only to be controlled by an accident.

Although, therefore, the theory of nationality is more absurd and more criminal than the theory of socialism, it has an important mission in the world, and marks the final conflict, and therefore the end, of two forces which are the worst enemies of civil freedom,—the absolute monarchy and the revolution.

WALTER BAGEHOT

Walter Bagehot (1826–1877) remains one of the most quoted political theorists of the 19th century. As the editor of *The Economist* of London, he wrote on a limitless range of subjects, sometimes with almost prophetic insight. A liberal-conservative of the old school, his influence has been particularly strong on the British Conservative Party in the 20th century. His analysis of the British monarchy is notable for its cool, unreverential approach, quite different from that of a de Maistre or a Donoso Cortés.

From *The English Constitution* (London, 1867).

WALTER BAGEHOT

The Monarchy

The use of the Queen, in a dignified capacity, is incalculable. Without her in England, the present English Government would fail and pass away. Most
people when they read that the Queen walked on the
slopes at Windsor—that the Prince of Wales went to
the Derby—have imagined that too much thought
and prominence were given to little things. But they
have been in error; and it is nice to trace how the
actions of a retired widow and an unemployed youth
become of such importance.

The best reason why Monarchy is a strong government is, that it is an intelligible government. The
mass of mankind understand it, and they hardly anywhere in the world understand any other. It is often
said that men are ruled by their imaginations; but it
would be truer to say they are governed by the weakness of their imaginations. The nature of a constitution, the action of an assembly, the play of parties,
the unseen formation of a guiding opinion, are complex facts, difficult to know, and easy to mistake. But
the action of a single will, the fiat of a single mind,
are easy ideas: anybody can make them out, and no
one can ever forget them. When you put before the
mass of mankind the question, 'Will you be governed
by a king, or will you be governed by a constitution?'
the inquiry comes out thus—'Will you be governed in
a way you understand, or will you be governed in a
way you do not understand?' The issue was put to the
French people; they were asked, 'Will you be governed by Louis Napoleon, or will you be governed by
an assembly?' The French people said, 'We will be

governed by the one man we can imagine, and not by the many people we cannot imagine.'

The best mode of comprehending the nature of the two governments, is to look at a country in which the two have within a comparatively short space of years succeeded each other.

'The political condition,' says Mr. Grote, 'which Grecian legend everywhere presents to us, is in its principal features strikingly different from that which had become universally prevalent among the Greeks in the time of the Peloponnesian war. Historical oligarchy, as well as democracy, agreed in requiring a certain established system of government, comprising the three elements of specialized functions, temporary functionaries, and ultimate responsibility (under some forms or other) to the mass of qualified citizens—either a Senate or an Ecclesia, or both. There were, of course, many and capital distinctions between one government and another, in respect to the qualification of the citizen, the attributes and efficiency of the general assembly, the admissibility to power, &c.; and men might often be dissatisfied with the way in which these questions were determined in their own city. But in the mind of every man, some determining rule or system— something like what in modern times is called a *constitution*—was indispensable to any government entitled to be called legitimate, or capable of creating in the mind of a Greek a feeling of moral obligation to obey it. The functionaries who exercise authority under it might be more or less competent or popular; but his personal feelings toward them were commonly lost in his attachment or aversion to the general system. If any energetic man could by audacity or craft break down the constitution, and render himself permanent ruler according to his own will and pleasure, even though he might govern well, he could never inspire the people with any sentiment of duty towards him: his sceptre was illegitimate from the beginning, and even the taking of his life, far from being interdicted by that moral feeling which condemned the shedding of blood in other cases, was considered meritorious: he could not even be mentioned in the language except by a name (τύραννος *despot*) which branded him as an object of mingled fear and dislike.

'If we carry our eyes back from historical to legendary Greece, we find a picture the reverse of what has been here sketched. We discern a government in which there is little or no scheme or system, still less any idea of responsibility to the governed, but in which the mainspring of obedience on the part of the people consists in their personal feeling and reverence towards the chief. We remark, first and foremost, the King; next, a limited number of subordinate kings or chiefs; afterwards, the mass of armed freemen, husbandmen, artisans, freebooters, &c.; lowest of all, the free labourers for hire and the bought slaves. The King is not distinguished by any broad, or impassable boundary from the other chiefs, to each of whom the title *Basileus* is applicable as well as to himself: his supremacy has been inherited from his ancestors, and passes by inheritance, as a general rule, to his eldest son, having been conferred upon the family as a privilege by the favour of Zeus. In war, he is the leader, foremost in personal prowess, and directing all military movements; in peace, he is the general protector of the injured and oppressed; he offers up moreover those public prayers and sacrifices which are intended to obtain for the whole people the favour of the gods. An ample domain is assigned to him as an appurtenance of his lofty position, and the produce of his fields and his cattle is consecrated in part to an abundant, though rude hospitality. Moreover he receives frequent presents, to avert his enmity, to conciliate his favour, or to buy off his exactions; and when plunder is taken from the enemy, a large previous share, comprising probably the most alluring female captive, is reserved for him apart from the general distribution.

'Such is the position of the King in the heroic times of Greece—the only person (if we except the heralds and priests, each both special and subordinate) who is then presented to us as clothed with any individual authority—the person by whom all the executive functions, then few in number, which the society requires, are either performed or directed. His personal ascendancy—derived from divine countenance bestowed both upon himself individually and upon his race, and probably from accredited divine descent—is the salient feature in the picture: the people hearken to his voice, embrace his propositions, and obey his orders: not merely resistance, but even criticism upon his acts, is generally exhibited in an odious point of view, and is indeed never heard of except from some one or more of the subordinate princes.'

The characteristic of the English Monarchy is that it retains the feelings by which the heroic kings governed their rude age, and has added the feelings by which the constitutions of later Greece ruled in more refined ages. We are a more mixed people than the Athenians, or probably than any political Greeks. We have progressed more unequally. The slaves in ancient times were a separate order; not ruled by the same laws, or thoughts, as other men. It was not necessary to think of them in making a constitution: it was not necessary to improve them in order to make a constitution possible. The Greek legislator had not to combine in his polity men like the labourers of Somersetshire, and men like Mr. Grote. He had not to deal with a community in which primitive barbarism lay as a recognized basis to acquired civilization. *We have.* We have no slaves to keep down by special terrors and independent legislation. But we have whole classes unable to comprehend the idea of a constitution—unable to feel the least attachment to impersonal laws. Most do indeed vaguely know that there are some other institutions besides the Queen, and some rules by which she governs. But a vast number like their minds to dwell more upon her than upon anything else, and therefore she is inestimable. A Republic has only difficult ideas in government; a Constitutional Monarchy has an easy idea too; it has a comprehensible element for the vacant many, as well as complex laws and notions for the inquiring few.

A *family* on the throne is an interesting idea also. It brings down the pride of sovereignty to the level of petty life. No feeling could seem more childish than the enthusiasm of the English at the marriage of the Prince of Wales. They treated as a great political event, what, looked at as a matter of pure business, was very small indeed. But no feeling could be more like common human nature as it is, and as it is likely to be. The women—one half the human race at least —care fifty times more for a marriage than a ministry. All but a few cynics like to see a pretty novel touching for a moment the dry scenes of the grave world. A princely marriage is the brilliant edition of a universal fact, and as such, it rivets mankind. We smile at the *Court Circular;* but remember how many people read the *Court Circular!* Its use is not in what it says, but in those to whom it speaks. They say that the Americans were more pleased at the Queen's letter to Mrs. Lincoln, than at any act of the English Government. It was a spontaneous act of intelligible feeling in the midst of confused and tiresome business. Just so a royal family sweetens politics by the seasonable addition of nice and pretty events. It introduces irrelevant facts into the business of government, but they are facts which speak to 'men's bosoms' and employ their thoughts.

To state the matter shortly, Royalty is a government in which the attention of the nation is concentrated on one person doing interesting actions. A Republic is a government in which that attention is divided between many, who are all doing uninteresting actions. Accordingly, so long as the human heart is strong and the human reason weak, Royalty will be strong because it appeals to diffused feeling, and Republics weak because they appeal to the understanding.

Secondly. The English Monarchy strengthens our government with the strength of religion. It is not easy to say why it should be so. Every instructed theologian would say that it was the duty of a person born under a Republic as much to obey that Republic as it is the duty of one born under a Monarchy to obey the monarch. But the mass of the English people do not think so; they agree with the oath of allegiance; they say it is their duty to obey the 'Queen'; and they have but hazy notions as to obeying laws without a queen. In former times, when our constitution was incomplete, this notion of local holiness in one part was mischievous. All parts were struggling, and it was necessary each should have its full growth. But superstition said one should grow where it would, and no other part should grow without its leave. The whole cavalier party said it was their duty to obey the king, whatever the king did. There was to be 'passive obedience' to him, and there was no religious obedience due to any one else. He was the 'Lord's anointed', and no one else had been anointed at all. The parliament, the laws, the press were human institutions; but the Monarchy was a Divine institution. An undue advantage was given to a part of the constitution, and therefore the progress of the whole was stayed.

After the Revolution this mischievous sentiment was much weaker. The change of the line of sovereigns was at first conclusive. If there was a mystic right in any one, that right was plainly in James II; if it was an English duty to obey any one whatever he did, he was the person to be so obeyed; if there was an inherent inherited claim in any king, it was in the Stuart king to whom the crown had come by descent, and not in the Revolution king to whom it had come by vote of Parliament. All through the reign of William III there was (in common speech) one king whom man had made, and another king whom God had made. The king who ruled had no consecrated loyalty to build upon; although he ruled in fact, according to sacred theory there was a king in France who ought to rule. But it was very hard for the English people, with their plain sense and slow imagination, to keep up a strong sentiment of veneration for a foreign adventurer. He lived under the protection of a French king; what he did was commonly stupid, and what he left undone was very often wise.

As soon as Queen Anne began to reign there was a change of feeling; the old sacred sentiment began to cohere about her. There were indeed difficulties which would have baffled most people; but an Englishman whose heart is in a matter is not easily baffled. Queen Anne had a brother living and a father living, and by every rule of descent, their right was better than hers. But many people evaded both claims. They said James II had 'run away', and so abdicated, though he only ran away because he was in duress and was frightened, and though he claimed the allegiance of his subjects day by day. The Pretender, it was said, was not legitimate, though the birth was proved by evidence which any Court of Justice would have accepted. The English people were 'out of' a sacred monarch, and so they tried very hard to make a new one. Events, however, were too strong for them. They were ready and eager to take Queen Anne as the stock of a new dynasty; they were ready to ignore the claims of her father and the claims of her brother, but they could not ignore the fact that at the critical period she had no children. She had once had thirteen, but they all died in her lifetime, and it was necessary either to revert to the Stuarts or to make a new king by Act of Parliament.

According to the Act of Settlement passed by the Whigs, the crown was settled on the descendants of the 'Princess Sophia' of Hanover, a younger daughter of a daughter of James I. There were before her James II, his son, the descendants of a daughter of Charles I, and elder children of her own mother. But the Whigs passed these over because they were Catholics, and selected the Princess Sophia, who, if she was anything, was a Protestant. Certainly this selection was statesmanlike, but it could not be very popular. It was quite impossible to say that it was the duty of the English people to obey the House of Hanover upon any principles which do not concede the right of the people to choose their rulers, and which do not degrade monarchy from its solitary pinnacle of majestic reverence, and make it one only among many expedient institutions. If a king is a useful public functionary who may be changed, and in whose place you may make another, you cannot regard him with mystic awe and wonder: and if you are bound to worship him, of course you cannot change him. Accordingly, during the whole reigns of George I and George II the sentiment of religious loyalty altogether ceased to support the Crown. The prerogative of the king had no strong party to support it; the Tories, who naturally would support it, disliked the actual king; and the Whigs, according to their creed, disliked the king's office. Until the accession of George III the most vigorous opponents of the Crown were the country gentlemen, its natural friends, and the representatives of quiet rural districts, where loyalty is mostly to be found, if anywhere. But after the accession of George III the common feeling came back to the same point as in Queen Anne's time. The English were ready to take the new young prince as the beginning of a sacred line of sovereigns, just as they had been willing to take an old lady who was the second cousin of his great-great-grandmother. So it is now. If you ask the immense majority of the Queen's subjects by what right she rules, they would never tell you that she rules by Parliamentary right, by virtue of 6 Anne, c. 7. They will say she rules by 'God's grace'; they believe that they have a mystic obligation to obey her. When her family came to the Crown it was a sort of treason to maintain the inalienable right of lineal sovereignty, for it was equivalent to saying that the claim of another family was better than hers; but now, in the strange course of human events, that very sentiment has become her surest and best support.

But it would be a great mistake to believe that at the accession of George III the instinctive sentiment of hereditary loyalty at once became as useful as now. It began to be powerful, but it hardly began to be useful. There was so much harm done by it as well as so much good, that it is quite capable of being argued whether on the whole it was beneficial or hurtful. Throughout the greater part of his life George III was a kind of 'consecrated obstruction'. Whatever he did had a sanctity different from what any one else did, and it perversely happened that he was commonly wrong. He had as good intentions as any one need have, and he attended to the business of his country, as a clerk with his bread to get attends to the business of his office. But his mind was small, his education limited, and he lived in a changing time. Accordingly he was always resisting what ought to be, and prolonging what ought not to be. He was the sinister but sacred assailant of half his ministries; and when the French revolution excited the horror of the world, and proved democracy to be 'impious', the piety of England concentrated upon him, and gave him tenfold strength. The monarchy by its religious sanction now confirms all our political order; in George III's time it confirmed little except itself. It gives now a vast strength to the entire constitution, by enlisting on its behalf the credulous obedience of enormous masses; then it lived aloof, absorbed all the holiness into itself, and turned over all the rest of the polity to the coarse justification of bare expediency.

A principal reason why the monarchy so well consecrates our whole state is to be sought in the peculiarity many Americans and many utilitarians smile at. They laugh at this 'extra', as the Yankee called it, at the solitary transcendent element. They quote Napoleon's saying, 'that he did not wish to be fatted in idleness,' when he refused to be grand elector in Sièyes' constitution, which was an office copied, and M. Thiers says, well copied, from constitutional monarchy. But such objections are wholly wrong. No doubt it was absurd enough in the Abbé Sièyes to propose that a new institution, inheriting no reverence, and made holy by no religion, should be created to fill the sort of post occupied by a constitutional king in nations of monarchical history. Such an institution, far from being so august as to spread reverence around it, is too novel and artificial to get reverence for itself; if, too, the absurdity could anyhow be augmented, it was so by offering an office of inactive uselessness and pretended sanctity to Napoleon, the most active man in France, with the greatest genius for business, only not sacred, and exclusively fit for action. But the blunder of Sièyes brings the excellence of real monarchy to the best light. When a monarch can bless, it is best that he should not be touched. It should be evident that he does no wrong. He should not be brought too closely to real measurement. He should be aloof and solitary. As the functions of English royalty are for the most part latent, it fulfils this condition. It seems to order, but it never seems to struggle. It is commonly hidden like a mystery, and sometimes paraded like a pageant, but in neither case is it contentious. The nation is divided into parties, but the Crown is of no party. Its apparent separation from business is that which removes it both from enmities and from desecration, which preserves its mystery, which enables it to combine the affection of conflicting parties—to be a visible symbol of unity to those still so imperfectly educated as to need a symbol.

Thirdly. The Queen is the head of our society. If she did not exist the Prime Minister would be the first person in the country. He and his wife would have to receive foreign ministers, and occasionally foreign princes, to give the first parties in the country; he and she would be at the head of the pageant of life; they would represent England in the eyes of foreign nations; they would represent the Government of England in the eyes of the English.

It is very easy to imagine a world in which this change would not be a great evil. In a country where people did not care for the outward show of life, where the genius of the people was untheatrical, and they exclusively regarded the substance of things, this matter would be trifling. Whether Lord and Lady Derby received the foreign ministers, or Lord and Lady Palmerston, would be a matter of indifference; whether they gave the nicest parties would be important only to the persons at those parties. A nation of unimpressible philosophers would not care at all how the externals of life were managed. Who is the showman is not material unless you care about the show.

But of all nations in the world the English are perhaps the least a nation of pure philosophers. It would be a very serious matter to us to change every four or five years the visible head of our world. We are now remarkable for the highest sort of ambition;

but we are remarkable for having a great deal of the lower sort of ambition and envy. The House of Commons is thronged with people who get there merely for 'social purposes', as the phrase goes; that is, that they and their families may go to parties else impossible. Members of Parliament are envied by thousands merely for this frivolous glory, as a thinker calls it. If the highest post in conspicuous life were thrown open to public competition, this low sort of ambition and envy would be fearfully increased. Politics would offer a prize too dazzling for mankind; clever base people would strive for it, and stupid base people would envy it. Even now a dangerous distinction is given by what is exclusively called public life. The newspapers describe daily and incessantly a certain conspicuous existence; they comment on its characters, recount its details, investigate its motives, anticipate its course. They give a precedent and a dignity to that world which they do not give to any other. The literary world, the scientific world, the philosophic world, not only are not comparable in dignity to the political world, but in comparison are hardly worlds at all. The newspaper makes no mention of them, and could not mention them. As are the papers, so are the readers; they, by irresistible sequence and association, believe that those people who constantly figure in the papers are cleverer, abler, or at any rate, somehow higher, than other people. 'I wrote books', we heard of a man saying, 'for twenty years, and I was nobody; I got into Parliament, and before I had taken my seat I had become somebody.' English politicians are the men who fill the thoughts of the English public; they are the actors on the scene, and it is hard for the admiring spectators not to believe that the admired actor is greater than themselves. In this present age and country it would be very dangerous to give the slightest addition to a force already perilously great. If the highest social rank was to be scrambled for in the House of Commons, the number of social adventurers there would be incalculably more numerous, and indefinitely more eager.

A very peculiar combination of causes has made this characteristic one of the most prominent in English society. The Middle Ages left all Europe with a social system headed by Courts. The government was made the head of all society, all intercourse, and all life; everything paid allegiance to the sovereign, and everything ranged itself round the sovereign— what was next to be greatest, and what was farthest least. The idea that the head of the government is the head of society is so fixed in the ideas of mankind that only a few philosophers regard it as historical and accidental, though when the matter is examined, that conclusion is certain and even obvious.

In the first place, society as society does not naturally need a head at all. Its constitution, if left to itself, is not monarchical, but aristocratical. Society, in the sense we are now talking of, is the union of people for amusement and conversation. The making of marriages goes on in it, as it were, incidentally, but its common and main concern is talking and pleasure. There is nothing in this which needs a single supreme head; it is a pursuit in which a single person does not of necessity dominate. By nature it creates an 'upper ten thousand'; a certain number of persons and families possessed of equal culture, and equal faculties, and equal spirit, get to be on a level —and that level a high level. By boldness, by cultivation, by 'social science' they raise themselves above others; they become the 'first families', and all the rest come to be below them. But they tend to be much about a level among one another; no one is recognized by all or by many others as superior to them all. This is society as it grew up in Greece or Italy, as it grows up now in any American or colonial town. So far from the notion of a 'head of society' being a necessary notion, in many ages it would scarcely have been an intelligible notion. You could not have made Socrates understand it. He would have said, 'If you tell me that one of my fellows is chief magistrate, and that I am bound to obey him, I understand you, and you speak well; or that another is a priest, and that he ought to offer sacrifices to the gods, which I or any one not a priest ought not to offer, again I understand and agree with you. But if you tell me that there is in some citizen a hidden charm by which his words become better than my words, and his house better than my house, I do not follow you, and should be pleased if you will explain yourself.'

And even if a head of society were a natural idea, it certainly would not follow that the head of the civil government should be that head. Society as such has no more to do with civil polity than with ecclesiastical. The organization of men and women for the purpose of amusement is not necessarily identical with their organization for political purposes, any more than with their organization for religious purposes; it has of itself no more to do with the State than it has with the Church. The faculties which fit a man to be a great ruler are not those of society; some great rulers have been unintelligible like Cromwell, or brusque like Napoleon, or coarse and barbarous like Sir Robert Walpole. The light nothings of the drawing-room and the grave things of office are as different from one another as two human occupations can be. There is no naturalness in uniting the two; the end of it always is, that you put a man at the head of society who very likely is remarkable for social defects, and is not eminent for social merits.

The best possible commentary on these remarks is the 'History of English Royalty'. It has not been sufficiently remarked that a change has taken place in the structure of our society exactly analogous to the change in our polity. A Republic has insinuated itself beneath the folds of a Monarchy. Charles II was really the head of society; Whitehall, in his time, was the centre of the best talk, the best fashion, and the most curious love affairs of the age. He did not contribute good morality to society, but he set an example of infinite agreeableness. He concentrated around him all the light part of the high world of London, and London concentrated around it all the light part of the high world of England. The Court was the focus where everything fascinating gathered, and where everything exciting centered. Whitehall was an unequalled club, with female society of a very clever and sharp sort superadded. All this, as we know, is now altered. Buckingham Palace is as unlike a club as any place is likely to be. The Court is a separate part, which stands aloof from the rest of the London world, and which has but slender relations with the more amusing part of it. The two first Georges were men ignorant of English, and wholly unfit to guide and lead English society. They both preferred one or two German ladies of bad character to all else in London. George III had no social vices, but he had no social pleasures. He was a family man, and a man of business, and sincerely preferred a leg of mutton and turnips after a good day's work, to the best fashion and the most exciting talk. In consequence, society in London, though still in form under the domination of a Court, assumed in fact its natural and oligarchical structure. It, too, has become an 'upper ten thousand'; it is no more monarchical in fact than the society of New York. Great ladies give the tone to it with little reference to the particular Court world. The peculiarly masculine world of the clubs and their neighbourhood has no more to do in daily life with Buckingham Palace than with the Tuileries. Formal ceremonies of presentation and attendance are retained. The names of levee and drawing-room still sustain the memory of the time when the king's bed-chamber and the queen's 'withdrawing room' were the centres of London life, but they no longer make a part of social enjoyment: they are a sort of ritual in which nowadays almost every decent person can if he likes take part. Even Court balls, where pleasure is at least supposed to be possible, are lost in a London July. Careful observers have long perceived this, but it was made palpable to every one by the death of the Prince Consort. Since then the Court has been always in a state of suspended animation, and for a time it was quite annihilated. But everything went on as usual. A few people who had no daughters and little money made it an excuse to give fewer parties, and if very poor, stayed in the country, but upon the whole the difference was not perceptible. The queen bee was taken away, but the hive went on.

Refined and original observers have of late objected to English royalty that it is not splendid enough. They have compared it with the French Court, which is better in show, which comes to the surface everywhere so that you cannot help seeing it, which is infinitely and beyond question the most splendid thing in France. They have said, 'that in old times the English Court took too much of the nation's money, and spent it ill; but now, when it could be trusted to spend well, it does not take enough of the nation's money. There are arguments for not having a Court, and there are arguments for having a splendid Court; but there are no arguments for having a mean Court. It is better to spend a million in dazzling when you wish to dazzle, than three-quarters of a million in trying to dazzle and yet not dazzling.' There may be something in this theory; it may be that the Court of England is not quite as gorgeous as we might wish to see it. But no comparison must ever be made between it and the French Court. The Emperor represents a different idea from the Queen. He is not the head of the State; he *is* the State. The theory of his government is that every one in France is equal, and that the Emperor embodies the principle of equality. The greater you make him, the less, and therefore the more equal, you make all others. He is magnified that others may be dwarfed. The very contrary is the principle of English royalty. As in politics it would lose its principal use if it came forward into the public arena, so in society if it advertised itself it would be pernicious. We have voluntary show enough already in London; we do not wish to have it encouraged and intensified, but quieted and mitigated. Our Court is but the head of an unequal, competing, aristocratic society: its splendour would not keep others down, but incite others to come on. It is of use so long as it keeps others out of the first place, and is guarded and retired in that place. But it would do evil if it added a new example

to our many examples of showy wealth—if it gave
the sanction of its dignity to the race of expenditure.

Fourthly. We have come to regard the Crown as
the head of our *morality*. The virtues of Queen Victoria and the virtues of George III have sunk deep
into the popular heart. We have come to believe that
it is natural to have a virtuous sovereign, and that
the domestic virtues are as likely to be found on
thrones as they are eminent when there. But a little
experience and less thought show that royalty cannot take credit for domestic excellence. Neither
George I, nor George II, nor William IV were patterns
of family merit; George IV was a model of family
demerit. The plain fact is, that to the disposition of
all others most likely to go wrong, to an excitable
disposition, the place of a constitutional king has
greater temptations than almost any other, and
fewer suitable occupations than almost any other.
All the world and all the glory of it, whatever is most
attractive, whatever is most seductive, has always
been offered to the Prince of Wales of the day, and
always will be. It is not rational to expect the best
virtue where temptation is applied in the most trying form at the frailest time of human life. The occupations of a constitutional monarch are grave,
formal, important, but never exciting; they have
nothing to stir eager blood, awaken high imagination, work off wild thoughts. On men like George III,
with a predominant taste for business occupations,
the routine duties of constitutional royalty have
doubtless a calm and chastening effect. The insanity
with which he struggled, and in many cases struggled very successfully, during many years, would
probably have burst out much oftener but for the
sedative effect of sedulous employment. But how

few princes have ever felt the anomalous impulse for real work; how uncommon is that impulse anywhere; how little are the circumstances of princes calculated to foster it; how little can it be relied on as an ordinary breakwater to their habitual temptations! Grave and careful men may have domestic virtues on a constitutional throne, but even these fail sometimes, and to imagine that men of more eager temperaments will commonly produce them, is to expect grapes from thorns and figs from thistles.

Lastly. Constitutional royalty has the function which I insisted on at length in my last essay, and which, though it is by far the greatest, I need not now enlarge upon again. It acts as a *disguise.* It enables our real rulers to change without heedless people knowing it. The masses of Englishmen are not fit for an elective government; if they knew how near they were to it, they would be surprised, and almost tremble.

Of a like nature is the value of constitutional royalty in times of transition. The greatest of all helps to the substitution of a cabinet government for a preceding absolute monarchy, is the accession of a king favourable to such a government, and pledged to it. Cabinet government, when new, is weak in time of trouble. The prime minister—the chief on whom everything depends, who must take responsibility if any one is to take it, who must use force if any one is to use it—is not fixed in power. He holds his place, by the essence of the government, with some uncertainty. Among a people well-accustomed to such a government such a functionary may be bold; he may rely, if not on the parliament, on the nation which understands and values him. But when that govern-

ment has only recently been introduced, it is difficult
for such a minister to be as bold as he ought to be. His
power rests too much on human reason, and too little
on human instinct. The traditional strength of the
hereditary monarch is at these times of incalculable
use. It would have been impossible for England to get
through the first years after 1688 but for the singular
ability of William III. It would have been impossible
for Italy to have attained and kept her freedom without the help of Victor Emmanuel; neither the work
of Cavour nor the work of Garibaldi were more
necessary than his. But the failure of Louis Philippe
to use his reserve power as constitutional monarch
is the most instructive proof how great that reserve
power is. In February, 1848, Guizot was weak because his tenure of office was insecure. Louis Philippe should have made that tenure certain. Parliamentary reform might afterwards have been
conceded to instructed opinion, but nothing ought to
have been conceded to the mob. The Parisian populace ought to have been put down, as Guizot wished.
If Louis Philippe had been a fit king to introduce free
government, he would have strengthened his ministers when they were the instruments of order, even
if he afterwards discarded them when order was
safe, and policy could be discussed. But he was one
of the cautious men who are 'noted' to fail in old age:
though of the largest experience, and of great ability,
he failed and lost his crown for want of petty and
momentary energy, which at such a crisis a plain
man would have at once put forth.

Such are the principal modes in which the institution of royalty by its august aspect influences mankind, and in the English state of civilization they are

invaluable. Of the actual business of the sovereign—the real work the Queen does—I shall speak in my next paper.

The House of Commons has inquired into most things, but has never had a committee on 'the Queen'. There is no authentic blue-book to say what she does. Such an investigation cannot take place; but if it could, it would probably save her much vexatious routine, and many toilsome and unnecessary hours.

The popular theory of the English Constitution involves two errors as to the sovereign. First, in its oldest form at least, it considers him as an 'Estate of the Realm', a separate co-ordinate authority with the House of Lords and the House of Commons. This and much else the sovereign once was, but this he is no longer. That authority could only be exercised by a monarch with a legislative veto. He should be able to reject bills, if not as the House of Commons rejects them, at least as the House of Peers rejects them. But the Queen has no such veto. She must sign her own death-warrant if the two Houses unanimously send it up to her. It is a fiction of the past to ascribe to her legislative power. She has long ceased to have any. Secondly, the ancient theory holds that the Queen is the executive. The American Constitution was made upon a most careful argument, and most of that argument assumes the king to be the administrator of the English Constitution, and an unhereditary substitute for him—viz., a president—to be peremptorily necessary. Living across the Atlantic, and misled by accepted doctrines, the acute framers of the Federal Constitution, even after the keenest attention, did not perceive the prime minister to be the principal executive of the British Constitution, and the sover-

eign a cog in the mechanism. There is, indeed, much
excuse for the American legislators in the history of
that time. They took their idea of our constitution
from the time when they encountered it. But in the
so-called government of Lord North, George III was
the government. Lord North was not only his appointee, but his agent. The minister carried on a war
which he disapproved and hated, because it was a
war which his sovereign approved and liked. Inevitably, therefore, the American Convention believed
the king, from whom they had suffered, to be the real
executive, and not the minister, from whom they
had not suffered.

If we leave literary theory, and look to our actual
old law, it is wonderful how much the sovereign can
do. A few years ago the Queen very wisely attempted
to make life-Peers, and the House of Lords very unwisely, and contrary to its own best interests, refused
to admit her claim. They said her power had decayed
into non-existence; she once had it, they allowed, but
it had ceased by long disuse. If any one will run over
the pages of Comyn's 'Digest', or any other such
book, title 'Prerogative', he will find the Queen has a
hundred such powers which waver between reality
and desuetude, and which would cause a protracted
and very interesting legal argument if she tried to
exercise them. Some good lawyer ought to write a
careful book to say which of these powers are really
usable, and which are obsolete. There is no authentic
explicit information as to what the Queen can do,
any more than of what she does.

In the bare superficial theory of free institutions
this is undoubtedly a defect. Every power in a popular government ought to be known. The whole notion
of such a government is that the political people—

the governing people—rules as it thinks fit. All the acts of every administration are to be canvassed by it; it is to watch if such acts seem good, and in some manner or other to interpose if they seem not good. But it cannot judge if it is to be kept in ignorance; it cannot interpose if it does not know. A secret prerogative is an anomaly—perhaps the greatest of anomalies. That secrecy is, however, essential to the utility of English royalty as it now is. Above all things our royalty is to be reverenced, and if you begin to poke about it you cannot reverence it. When there is a select committee on the Queen, the charm of royalty will be gone. Its mystery is its life. We must not let in daylight upon magic. We must not bring the Queen into the combat of politics, or she will cease to be reverenced by all combatants; she will become one combatant among many. The existence of this secret power is, according to abstract theory, a defect in our constitutional polity, but it is a defect incident to a civilization such as ours, where august and therefore unknown powers are needed, as well as known and serviceable powers.

If we attempt to estimate the working of this inner power by the evidence of those, whether dead or living, who have been brought in contact with it, we shall find a singular difference. Both the courtiers of George III and the courtiers of Queen Victoria are agreed as to the magnitude of the royal influence. It is with both an accepted secret doctrine that the Crown does more than it seems. But there is a wide discrepancy in opinion as to the quality of that action. Mr. Fox did not scruple to describe the hidden influence of George III as the undetected agency of 'an infernal spirit'. The action of the Crown at that period was the dread and terror of Liberal politicians. But now the best Liberal politicians say, 'We shall never know, but when history is written our children may know, what we owe to the Queen and Prince Albert'. The mystery of the constitution, which used to be hated by our calmest, most thoughtful, and instructed statesmen, is now loved and reverenced by them.

Before we try to account for this change, there is one part of the duties of the Queen which should be struck out of the discussion. I mean the formal part. The Queen has to assent to and sign countless formal documents, which contain no matter of policy, of which the purport is insignificant, which any clerk could sign as well. One great class of documents George III used to read before he signed them, till Lord Thurlow told him, 'It was nonsense his looking at them, for he could not understand them'. But the worst case is that of commissions in the army. Till an Act passed only three years since, the Queen used to sign *all* military commissions, and she still signs all fresh commissions. The inevitable and natural consequence is that such commissions were, and to some extent still are, in arrears by thousands. Men have often been known to receive their commissions for the first time years after they have left the service. If the Queen had been an ordinary officer she would long since have complained, and long since have been relieved of this slavish labour. A cynical statesman is said to have defended it on the ground 'that you *may* have a fool for a sovereign, and then it would be desirable he should have plenty of occupation in which he can do no harm'. But it is in truth childish to heap formal duties of business upon a person who has of necessity so many formal duties of society. It is a remnant of the old days when

George III would know everything, however trivial, and assent to everything, however insignificant. These labours of routine may be dismissed from the discussion. It is not by them that the sovereign acquires his authority either for evil or for good.

The best mode of testing what we owe to the Queen is to make a vigorous effort of the imagination, and see how we should get on without her. Let us strip cabinet government of all its accessories, let us reduce it to its two necessary constituents—a representative assembly (a House of Commons) and a cabinet appointed by that assembly—and examine how we should manage with them only. We are so little accustomed to analyse the constitution; we are so used to ascribe the whole effect of the constitution to the whole constitution, that a great many people will imagine it to be impossible that a nation should thrive or even live with only these two simple elements. But it is upon that possibility that the general imitability of the English Government depends. A monarch that can be truly reverenced, a House of Peers that can be really respected, are historical accidents nearly peculiar to this one island, and entirely peculiar to Europe. A new country, if it is to be capable of a cabinet government, if it is not to degrade itself to presidential government, must create that cabinet out of its native resources—must not rely on these old world debris.

Many modes might be suggested by which a parliament might do in appearance what our parliament does in reality, viz., appoint a premier. But I prefer to select the simplest of all modes. We shall then see the bare skeleton of this polity, perceive in what it differs from the royal form, and be quite free from the imputation of having selected an unduly charming and attractive substitute.

Let us suppose the House of Commons—existing alone and by itself—to appoint the premier quite simply, just as the shareholders of a railway choose a director. At each vacancy, whether caused by death or resignation, let any member or members have the right of nominating a successor; after a proper interval, such as the time now commonly occupied by a ministerial crisis, ten days or a fortnight, let the members present vote for the candidate they prefer; then let the Speaker count the votes, and the candidate with the greatest number be premier. This mode of election would throw the whole choice into the hands of party organization, just as our present mode does, except in so far as the Crown interferes with it; no outsider would ever be appointed, because the immense number of votes which every great party brings into the field would far outnumber every casual and petty minority. The premier should not be appointed for a fixed time, but during good behaviour or the pleasure of parliament. *Mutatis mutandis,* subject to the differences now to be investigated, what goes on now would go on then. The premier then, as now, must resign upon a vote of want of confidence, but the volition of parliament would then be the overt and single force in the selection of a successor, whereas it is now the predominant though latent force.

It will help the discussion very much if we divide it into three parts. The whole course of a representative government has three stages—first, when a ministry is appointed; next, during its continuance; last, when it ends. Let us consider what is the exact use of the Queen at each of these stages, and how our present form of government differs in each, whether for good or for evil, from that simpler form of cabinet government which might exist without her.

At the beginning of an administration there would not be much difference between the royal and un-royal species of cabinet governments when there were only two great parties in the State, and when the greater of those parties was thoroughly agreed within itself who should be its parliamentary leader, and who therefore should be its premier. The sovereign must now accept that recognized leader; and if the choice were directly made by the House of Commons, the House must also choose him; its supreme section, acting compactly and harmoniously, would sway its decisions without substantial resistance, and perhaps without even apparent competition. A predominant party, rent by no intestine demarcation, would be despotic. In such a case cabinet government would go on without friction whether there was a queen or whether there was no queen. The best sovereign could then achieve no good, and the worst effect no harm.

But the difficulties are far greater when the predominant party is not agreed who should be its leader. In the royal form of cabinet government the sovereign then has sometimes a substantial selection; in the unroyal, who would choose? There must be a meeting at 'Willis's Rooms'; there must be that sort of interior despotism of the majority over the minority within the party, by which Lord John Russell in 1859 was made to resign his pretensions to the supreme government, and to be content to serve as a subordinate to Lord Palmerston. The tacit compression which a party anxious for office would exercise over leaders who divided its strength, would be used and must be used. Whether such a party would always choose precisely the best man may well be doubted. In a party once divided it is very difficult to secure unanimity in favour of the very person whom a disinterested bystander would recommend. All manner of jealousies and enmities are immediately awakened, and it is always difficult, often impossible, to get them to sleep again. But though such a party might not select the very best leader, they have the strongest motives to select a very good leader. The maintenance of their rule depends on it. Under a presidential constitution the preliminary caucuses which choose the president need not care as to the ultimate fitness of the man they choose. They are solely concerned with his attractiveness as a candidate; they need not regard his efficiency as a ruler. If they elect a man of weak judgement, he will reign his stated term; even though he show the best judgement, at the end of that term there will be by constitutional destiny another election. But under a ministerial government there is no such fixed destiny. The government is a removable government; its tenure depends upon its conduct. If a party in power were so foolish as to choose a weak man for its head, it would cease to be in power. Its judgement is its life. Suppose in 1859 that the Whig Party had determined to set aside both Earl Russell and Lord Palmerston, and to choose for its head an incapable nonentity, the Whig Party would probably have been exiled from office at the Schleswig-Holstein difficulty. The nation would have deserted them, and Parliament would have deserted them, too; neither would have endured to see a secret negotiation, on which depended the portentous alternative of war or peace, in the hands of a person who was thought to be weak—who had been promoted because of his mediocrity—whom his own friends did not respect. A ministerial government, too, is carried on in the face of day. Its life is in debate. A president may be a weak man; yet if he keep good ministers to the end of his administration, he may not be found out—it may still be a dubious controversy whether he is wise or foolish. But a prime minister must show what he is. He must meet the House of Commons in debate; he must be able to guide that assembly in the management of its business, to gain its ear in every emergency, to rule it in its hours of excitement. He is conspicuously submitted to a searching test, and if he fails he must resign.

Nor would any party like to trust to a weak man the great power which a cabinet government commits to its premier. The premier, though elected by parliament, can dissolve parliament. Members would be naturally anxious that the power which might destroy their coveted dignity should be lodged in fit hands. They dare not place in unfit hands a power which, besides hurting the nation, might altogether ruin them. We may be sure, therefore, that whenever the predominant party is divided, the *un*-royal form of cabinet government would secure for us a fair and able parliamentary leader—that it would give us a good premier, if not the very best. Can it be said that the royal form does more?

In one case I think it may. If the constitutional monarch be a man of singular discernment, of unprejudiced disposition, and great political knowledge, he may pick out from the ranks of the divided party its very best leader, even at a time when the party, if left to itself, would not nominate him. If the sovereign be able to play the part of that thoroughly intelligent but perfectly disinterested spectator who is so prominent in the works of certain moralists, he may be able to choose better for his subjects than they would choose for themselves. But if the monarch be not so exempt from prejudice, and have not this nearly miraculous discernment, it is not likely that he will be able to make a wiser choice than the choice of the party itself. He certainly is not under the same motive to choose wisely. His place is fixed whatever happens, but the failure of an appointing party depends on the capacity of their appointee.

There is great danger, too, that the judgement of the sovereign may be prejudiced. For more than forty years the personal antipathies of George III materially impaired successive administrations. Almost at the beginning of his career he discarded Lord Chatham: almost at the end he would not permit Mr. Pitt to coalesce with Mr. Fox. He always preferred mediocrity; he generally disliked high ability; he always disliked great ideas. If constitutional monarchs be ordinary men of restricted experience and common capacity (and we have no right to suppose that *by miracle* they will be more), the judgement of the sovereign will often be worse than the judgement of the party, and he will be very subject to the chronic danger of preferring a respectful commonplace man, such as Addington, to an independent first-rate man, such as Pitt.

We shall arrive at the same sort of mixed conclusion if we examine the choice of a premier under both systems in the critical case of cabinet government—the case of three parties. This is the case in which that species of government is most sure to exhibit its defects, and least likely to exhibit its merits. The defining characteristic of that government is the choice of the executive ruler by the legislative assembly; but when there are three parties a satisfactory choice is impossible. A really good selection is a selection by a large majority which trusts those it chooses, but when there are three parties there is no such trust. The numerically weakest has the casting vote—it can determine which candidate shall be chosen. But it does so under a penalty. It forfeits the right of voting for its own candidate. It settles which of other people's favourites shall be chosen, on condition of abandoning its own favourite. A choice based on such self-denial can never be a firm choice —it is a choice at any moment liable to be revoked. The events of 1858, though not a perfect illustration of what I mean, are a sufficient illustration. The Radical Party, acting apart from the moderate Liberal Party, kept Lord Derby in power. The ultra-movement party thought it expedient to combine with the non-movement party. As one of them coarsely but clearly put it, 'We get more of our way under these men than under the other men'; he meant that, in his judgement, the Tories would be more obedient to the Radicals than the Whigs. But it is obvious that a union of opposites so marked could not be durable. The Radicals bought it by choosing the men whose principles were most adverse to them; the Conservatives bought it by agreeing to measures whose scope was most adverse to them. After a short interval the Radicals returned to their natural alliance and their natural discontent with the moderate Whigs. They used their determining vote first for a government of the contrary opinion.

I am not blaming this policy. I am using it merely as an illustration. I say that if we imagine this sort of action greatly exaggerated and greatly prolonged parliamentary government becomes impossible. If there are three parties, no two of which will steadily combine for mutual action, but of which the weakest

gives a rapidly oscillating preference to the two others, the primary condition of a cabinet polity is not
satisfied. We have not a parliament fit to choose; we
cannot rely on the selection of a sufficiently permanent executive, because there is no fixity in the
thoughts and feelings of the choosers.

Under every species of cabinet government,
whether the royal or the unroyal, this defect can be
cured in one way only. The moderate people of every
party must combine to support the government
which, on the whole, suits every party best. This is
the mode in which Lord Palmerston's administration has been lately maintained: a ministry in many
ways defective, but more beneficially vigorous
abroad, and more beneficially active at home, than
the vast majority of English ministries. The moderate Conservatives and the moderate Radicals have
maintained a steady government by a sufficiently
coherent union with the moderate Whigs. Whether
there is a king or no king, this preservative self-
denial is the main force on which we must rely for
the satisfactory continuance of a parliamentary government at this its period of greatest trial. Will that
moderation be aided or impaired by the addition of
a sovereign? Will it be more effectual under the royal
sort of ministerial government, or will it be less
effectual?

If the sovereign has a genius for discernment, the
aid which he can give at such a crisis will be great.
He will select for his minister, and if possible maintain as his minister, the statesman upon whom the
moderate party will ultimately fix their choice, but
for whom at the outset it is blindly searching; being
a man of sense, experience, and tact, he will discern
which is the combination of equilibrium, which is

the section with whom the milder members of the other sections will at last ally themselves. Amid the shifting transitions of confused parties, it is probable that he will have many opportunities of exercising a selection. It will rest with him to call either on A B to form an administration or upon X Y, and either may have a chance of trial. A disturbed state of parties is inconsistent with fixity, but it abounds in momentary tolerance. Wanting something, but not knowing with precision what, parties will accept for a brief period anything, to see whether it may be that unknown something—to see what it will do. During the long succession of weak governments which begins with the resignation of the Duke of Newcastle in 1762 and ends with the accession of Mr. Pitt in 1784, the vigorous will of George III was an agency of the first magnitude. If at a period of complex and protracted division of parties, such as are sure to occur often and last long in every enduring parliamentary government, the extrinsic force of royal selection were always exercised discreetly, it would be a political benefit of incalculable value.

But will it be so exercised? A constitutional sovereign must in the common course of government be a man of but common ability. I am afraid, looking to the early acquired feebleness of hereditary dynasties, that we must expect him to be a man of inferior ability. Theory and experience both teach that the education of a prince can be but a poor education, and that a royal family will generally have less ability than other families. What right have we then to expect the perpetual entail on any family of an exquisite discretion, which if it be not a sort of genius, is at least as rare as genius?

Probably in most cases the greatest wisdom of a

constitutional king would show itself in well considered inaction. In the confused interval between 1857 and 1859 the Queen and Prince Albert were far too wise to obtrude any selection of their own. If they had chosen, perhaps they would not have chosen Lord Palmerston. But they saw, or may be believed to have seen, that the world was settling down without them, and that by interposing an extrinsic agency, they would but delay the beneficial crystallization of intrinsic forces. There is, indeed, a permanent reason which would make the wisest king, and the king who feels most sure of his wisdom, very slow to use that wisdom. The responsibility of parliament should be felt by parliament. So long as parliament thinks it is the sovereign's business to find a government it will be sure not to find a government itself. The royal form of ministerial government is the worst of all forms if it erect the subsidiary apparatus into the principal force, if it induce the assembly which ought to perform paramount duties to expect some one else to perform them.

It should be observed, too, in fairness to the unroyal species of cabinet government, that it is exempt from one of the greatest and most characteristic defects of the royal species. Where there is no court there can be no evil influence from a court. What these influences are every one knows; though no one, hardly the best and closest observer, can say with confidence and precision how great their effect is. Sir Robert Walpole, in language too coarse for our modern manners, declared after the death of Queen Caroline, that he would pay no attention to the king's daughters ('those girls', as he called them), but would rely exclusively on Madame de Walmoden, the king's mistress. 'The king', says a writer in George IV's time, 'is in our favour, and what is more to the purpose, the Marchioness of Conyngham is so too.' Everybody knows to what sort of influences several Italian changes of government since the unity of Italy have been attributed. These sinister agencies are likely to be most effective just when everything else is troubled, and when, therefore, they are particularly dangerous. The wildest and wickedest king's mistress would not plot against an invulnerable administration. But very many will intrigue when parliament is perplexed, when parties are divided, when alternatives are many, when many evil things are possible, when cabinet government must be difficult.

It is very important to see that a good administration can be stated without a sovereign, because some colonial statesmen have doubted it. 'I can conceive', it has been said, 'that a ministry would go on well enough without a governor when it was launched, but I do not see how to launch it.' It has even been suggested that a colony which broke away from England, and had to form its own government, might not unwisely choose a governor for life, and solely trusted with selecting ministers, something like the Abbé Sieyes's grand elector. But the introduction of such an officer into such a colony would in fact be the voluntary erection of an artificial encumbrance to it. He would inevitably be a party man. The most dignified post in the State must be an object of contest to the great sections into which every active political community is divided. These parties mix in everything and meddle in everything; and they neither would nor could permit the most honoured and conspicuous of all stations to be filled, except at their pleasure. They know, too, that the grand elector, the great chooser of ministries, might be, at a sharp crisis, either a good friend or a bad enemy. The strongest party would select some one who would be on their side when he had to take a side, who would incline to them when he did incline, who should be a constant auxiliary to them and a constant impediment to their adversaries. It is absurd to choose by contested party election an unpartial chooser of ministers.

But it is during the continuance of a ministry, rather than at its creation, that the functions of the sovereign will mainly interest most persons, and that most people will think them to be of the gravest importance. I own I am myself of that opinion. I think it may be shown that the post of sovereign over an intelligent and political people under a constitutional monarchy is the post which a wise man would choose above any other—where he would find the intellectual impulses best stimulated and the worst intellectual impulses best controlled.

On the duties of the Queen during an administration we have an invaluable fragment from her own hand. In 1851 Louis Napoleon had his *coup d'état;* in 1852 Lord John Russell had his—he expelled Lord Palmerston. By a most instructive breach of etiquette he read in the House a royal memorandum on the duties of his rival. It is as follows: 'The Queen requires, first that Lord Palmerston will distinctly state what he proposes in a given case, in order that the Queen may know as distinctly to what she is giving her royal sanction. Secondly, having once given her sanction to such a measure that it be not arbitrarily altered or modified by the minister. Such an act she must consider as failing in sincerity towards the Crown, and justly to be visited by the exercise of her constitutional right of dismissing that minister. She expects to be kept informed of what passes between him and foreign ministers before important decisions are taken based upon that intercourse; to receive the foreign dispatches in good time; and to have the drafts for her approval sent to her in sufficient time to make herself acquainted with their contents before they must be sent off.'

In addition to the control over particular ministers, and especially over the foreign minister, the Queen has a certain control over the Cabinet. The first minister, it is understood, transmits to her authentic information of all the most important decisions, together with what the newspapers would do equally well, the more important votes in Parliament. He is bound to take care that she knows everything which there is to know as to the passing politics of the nation. She has by rigid usage a right to complain if she does not know of every great act of her ministry, not only before it is done, but while there is yet time to consider it—while it is still possible that it may not be done.

To state the matter shortly, the sovereign has, under a constitutional monarchy such as ours, three rights—the right to be consulted, the right to encourage, the right to warn. And a king of great sense and sagacity would want no others. He would find that his having no others would enable him to use these with singular effect. He would say to his minister: 'The responsibility of these measures is upon you. Whatever you think best must be done. Whatever you think best shall have my full and effectual support. *But* you will observe that for this reason and that reason what you propose to do is bad; for this reason and that reason what you do not propose is better. I do not oppose, it is my duty not to oppose; but observe that I *warn.*' Supposing the king to be right, and to have what kings often have, the gift of effectual expression, he could not help moving his minister. He might not always turn his course, but he would always trouble his mind.

In the course of a long reign a sagacious king would acquire an experience with which few ministers could contend. The king could say: 'Have you referred to the transactions which happened during such and such an administration, I think about fourteen years ago? They afford an instructive example of the bad results which are sure to attend the policy which you propose. You did not at that time take so prominent a part in public life as you now do, and it is possible you do not fully remember all the events. I should recommend you to recur to them, and to discuss them with your older colleagues who took part in them. It is unwise to recommence a policy which so lately worked so ill.' The king would indeed have the advantage which a permanent under-secretary has over his superior the parliamentary secretary—that of having shared in the proceedings of the previous parliamentary secretaries. These proceedings were part of his own life; occupied the best of his thoughts, gave him perhaps anxiety, perhaps pleasure, were commenced in spite of his dissuasion, or were sanctioned by his approval. The parliamentary secretary vaguely remembers that something was done in the time of some of his predecessors, when he very likely did not know the least or care the least about that sort of public business. He has to begin by learning painfully and imperfectly what the permanent secretary knows by clear and instant memory. No doubt a parliamentary secretary always can, and sometimes does, silence his subordinate by the tacit might of his superior dignity. He says: 'I do not think there is much in all that. Many errors were committed at the time you refer to which we need not now discuss.' A pompous man easily sweeps away the suggestions of those beneath him. But though a minister may so deal with his subordinate, he cannot so deal with his king. The social force of admitted superiority by which he overturned his under-secretary is now not with him but against him. He has no longer to regard the deferential hints of an acknowledged inferior, but to answer the arguments of a superior to whom he has himself to be respectful. George III in fact knew the forms of public business as well or better than any statesman of his time. If, in addition to his capacity as a man of business and to his industry, he had possessed the higher faculties of a discerning statesman, his influence would have been despotic. The old Constitution of England undoubtedly gave a sort of power to the Crown which our present Constitution does not give. While a majority in parliament was principally purchased by royal patronage, the king was a party to the bargain either with his minister or without his minister. But even under our present Constitution a monarch like George III, with high abilities, would possess the greatest influence. It is known to all Europe that in Belgium King Leopold has exercised immense power by the use of such means as I have described.

It is known, too, to every one conversant with the real course of the recent history of England, that Prince Albert really did gain great power in precisely the same way. He had the rare gifts of a constitutional monarch. If his life had been prolonged

twenty years, his name would have been known to
Europe as that of King Leopold is known. While he
lived he was at a disadvantage. The statesmen who
had most power in England were men of far greater
experience than himself. He might, and no doubt did,
exercise a great, if not a commanding influence over
Lord Malmesbury, but he could not rule Lord Palmerston. The old statesman who governed England, at
an age when most men are unfit to govern their own
families, remembered a whole generation of statesmen who were dead before Prince Albert was born.
The two were of different ages and different natures.
The elaborateness of the German prince—an elaborateness which has been justly and happily compared with that of Goethe—was wholly alien to the
half-Irish, half-English, statesman. The somewhat
boisterous courage in minor dangers, and the obtru-
sive use of an always effectual, but not always
refined, commonplace, which are Lord Palmerston's
defects, doubtless grated on Prince Albert, who had
a scholar's caution and a scholar's courage. The facts
will be known to our children's children, though not
to us. Prince Albert did much, but he died ere he
could have made his influence felt on a generation of
statesmen less experienced than he was, and anxious to learn from him.

It would be childish to suppose that a conference
between a minister and his sovereign can ever be a
conference of pure argument. 'The divinity which
doth hedge a king' may have less sanctity than it had,
but it still has much sanctity. No one, or scarcely any
one, can argue with a cabinet minister in his own
room as well as he would argue with another man in
another room. He cannot make his own points as
well; he cannot unmake as well the points presented

to him. A monarch's room is worse. The best instance is Lord Chatham, the most dictatorial and imperious of English statesmen, and almost the first English statesman who was borne into power against the wishes of the king and against the wishes of the nobility—the first popular minister. We might have expected a proud tribune of the people to be dictatorial to his sovereign—to be to the king what he was to all others. On the contrary, he was the slave of his own imagination; there was a kind of mystic enchantment in vicinity to the monarch which divested him of his ordinary nature. 'The least peep into the king's closet', said Mr. Burke, 'intoxicates him, and will to the end of his life.' A wit said that, even at the levee, he bowed so low that you could see the tip of his hooked nose between his legs. He was in the habit of kneeling at the bedside of George III while transacting business. Now no man can *argue* on his knees. The same superstitious feeling which keeps him in that physical attitude will keep him in a corresponding mental attitude. He will not refute the bad arguments of the king as he will refute another man's bad arguments. He will not state his own best arguments effectively and incisively when he knows that the king would not like to hear them. In a nearly balanced argument the king must always have the better, and in politics many most important arguments are nearly balanced. Whenever there was much to be said for the king's opinion it would have its full weight; whatever was said for the minister's opinions would only have a lessened and enfeebled weight.

The king, too, possesses a power, according to theory, for extreme use on a critical occasion, but which he can in law use on any occasion. He can dissolve;

he can say to his minister in fact, if not in words, 'This parliament sent you here, but I will see if I cannot get another parliament to send some one else here'. George III well understood that it was best to take his stand at times and on points when it was perhaps likely, or at any rate not unlikely, the nation would support him. He always made a minister that he did not like tremble at the shadow of a possible successor. He had a cunning in such matters like the cunning of insanity. He had conflicts with the ablest men of his time, and he was hardly ever baffled. He understood how to help a feeble argument by a tacit threat, and how best to address it to an habitual deference.

Perhaps such powers as these are what a wise man would most seek to exercise and least fear to possess. To wish to be a despot, 'to hunger after tyranny', as the Greek phrase had it, marks in our day an uncultivated mind. A person who so wishes cannot have weighed what Butler calls the 'doubtfulness things are involved in'. To be sure you are right to impose your will, or to wish to impose it, with violence upon others; to see your own ideas vividly and fixedly, and to be tormented till you can apply them in life and practice, not to like to hear the opinions of others, to be unable to sit down and weigh the truth they have, are but crude states of intellect in our present civilization. We know, at least, that facts are many; that progress is complicated; that burning ideas (such as young men have) are mostly false and always incomplete. The notion of a far-seeing and despotic statesman, who can lay down plans for ages yet unborn, is a fancy generated by the pride of the human intellect to which facts give no support. The plans of Charlemagne died with him; those of Richelieu were

mistaken; those of Napoleon gigantesque and fran-
tic. But a wise and great constitutional monarch attempts no such vanities. His career is not in the air;
he labours in the world of sober fact; he deals with
schemes which can be effected—schemes which are
desirable—schemes which are worth the cost. He
says to the ministry his people send to him, to ministry after ministry, 'I think so and so; do you see if
there is anything in it. I have put down my reasons
in a certain memorandum, which I will give you.
Probably it does not exhaust the subject, but it will
suggest materials for your consideration.' By years
of discussion with ministry after ministry, the best
plans of the wisest king would certainly be adopted,
and the inferior plans, the impracticable plans,
rooted out and rejected. He could not be uselessly
beyond his time, for he would have been obliged to
convince the representatives, the characteristic men
of his time. He would have the best means of proving
that he was right on all new and strange matters, for
he would have won to his side probably, after years
of discussion, the chosen agents of the commonplace
world—men who were where they were, because
they had pleased the men of the existing age, who
will never be much disposed to new conceptions or
profound thoughts. A sagacious and original constitutional monarch might go to his grave in peace if
any man could. He would know that his best laws
were in harmony with his age; that they suited the
people who were to work them, the people who were
to be benefited by them. And he would have passed
a happy life. He would have passed a life in which he
could always get his arguments heard, in which he
could always make those who had the responsibility
of action think of them before they acted—in which

he could know that the schemes which he had set at work in the world were not the casual accidents of an individual idiosyncrasy, which are mostly much wrong, but the likeliest of all things to be right—the ideas of one very intelligent man at last accepted and acted on by the ordinary intelligent many.

But can we expect such a king, or, for that is the material point, can we expect a lineal series of such kings? Every one has heard the reply of the Emperor Alexander to Madame de Stael, who favoured him with a declamation in praise of beneficent despotism. 'Yes, Madame, but it is only a happy accident.' He well knew that the great abilities and the good intentions necessary to make an efficient and good despot never were continuously combined in any line of rulers. He knew that they were far out of reach of hereditary human nature. Can it be said that the characteristic qualities of a constitutional monarch are more within its reach? I am afraid it cannot. We found just now that the characteristic use of an hereditary constitutional monarch, at the outset of an administration, greatly surpassed the ordinary competence of hereditary faculties. I fear that an impartial investigation will establish the same conclusion as to his uses during the continuance of an administration.

If we look at history, we shall find that it is only during the period of the present reign that in England the duties of a constitutional sovereign have ever been well performed. The first two Georges were ignorant of English affairs, and wholly unable to guide them, whether well or ill; for many years in their time the Prime Minister had, over and above the labour of managing parliament, to manage the woman—sometimes the queen, sometimes the mistress—who managed the sovereign; George III interfered unceasingly, but he did harm unceasingly; George IV and William IV gave no steady continuing guidance, and were unfit to give it. On the Continent, in first-class countries, constitutional royalty has never lasted out of one generation. Louis Philippe, Victor Emmanuel, and Leopold are the founders of their dynasties; we must not reckon in constitutional monarchy any more than in despotic monarchy on the permanence in the descendants of the peculiar genius which founded the race. As far as experience goes, there is no reason to expect an hereditary series of useful limited monarchs.

If we look to theory, there is even less reason to expect it. A monarch is useful when he gives an effectual and beneficial guidance to his ministers. But these ministers are sure to be among the ablest men of their time. They will have had to conduct the business of parliament so as to satisfy it: they will have to speak so as to satisfy it. The two together cannot be done save by a man of very great and varied ability. The exercise of the two gifts is sure to teach a man much of the world; and if it did not, a parliamentary leader has to pass through a magnificent training before he becomes a leader. He has to gain a seat in parliament; to gain the ear of parliament; to gain the confidence of parliament; to gain the confidence of his colleagues. No one can achieve these—no one, still more, can both achieve them and retain them—without a singular ability, nicely trained in the varied detail of life. What chance has an hereditary monarch such as nature forces him to be, such as history shows he is, against men so educated and so born? He can but be an average man to begin with; sometimes he will be clever, but sometimes he will be stupid; in the long run he will be neither clever nor stupid: he will be the simple, common man who plods the plain routine of life from the cradle to the grave. His education will be that of one who has never had to struggle; who has always felt that he has nothing to gain; who has had the first dignity given him; who has never seen common life as in truth it is. It is idle to expect an ordinary man born in the purple to have greater genius than an extraordinary man born out of the purple; to expect a man whose place has always been fixed to have a better judgement than one who has lived by his judgement; to expect a man whose career will be the same whether he is discreet or whether he is indiscreet to have the nice discretion of one who has risen by his wisdom, who will fall if he ceases to be wise.

The characteristic advantage of a constitutional king is the permanence of his place. This gives him the opportunity of acquiring a consecutive knowledge of complex transactions, but it gives only an opportunity. The king must use it. There is no royal road to political affairs: their detail is vast, disagreeable, complicated, and miscellaneous. A king, to be the equal of his ministers in discussion, must work as they work; he must be a man of business as they are men of business. Yet a constitutional prince is the man who is most tempted to pleasure, and the least forced to business. A despot must feel that he is the pivot of the State. The stress of his kingdom is upon him. As he is, so are his affairs. He may be seduced into pleasure; he may neglect all else; but the risk is evident. He will hurt himself; he may cause a revolution. If he becomes unfit to govern, some one else who is fit may conspire against him. But a constitutional king need fear nothing. He may neglect his duties, but he will not be injured. His place will be as fixed, his income as permanent, his opportunities of selfish enjoyment as full as ever. Why should he work? It is true he will lose the quiet and secret influence which in the course of years industry would gain for him; but an eager young man, on whom the world is squandering its luxuries and its temptations, will not be much attracted by the distant prospect of a moderate influence over dull matters. He may form good intentions; he may say, 'Next year I *will* read these papers; I will try and ask more questions; I will not let these women talk to me so'. But they will talk to him. The most hopeless idleness is that most smoothed with excellent plans. 'The Lord Treasurer', says Swift, 'promised he will settle it to-night, and so he will say a hundred nights.' We may depend upon it, the ministry whose power will be lessened by the prince's attention will not be too eager to get him to attend.

So it is if the prince come young to the throne; but the case is worse when he comes to it old or middle-aged. He is then unfit to work. He will then have spent the whole of youth and the first part of manhood in idleness, and it is unnatural to expect him to labour. A pleasure-loving lounger in middle life will not begin to work as George III worked, or as Prince Albert worked. The only fit material for a constitutional king is a prince who begins early to reign—who in his youth is superior to pleasure—who in his youth is willing to labour—who has by nature a genius for discretion. Such kings are among God's greatest gifts, but they are also among His rarest.

An ordinary idle king on a constitutional throne will leave no mark on his time; he will do little good and as little harm; the royal form of cabinet govern-

ment will work in his time pretty much as the unroyal. The addition of a cipher will not matter
though it take precedence of the significant figures.
But *corruptio optima pessima.* The most evil case of
the royal form is far worse than the most evil case
of the unroyal. It is easy to imagine, upon a constitutional throne, an active and meddling fool who always acts when he should not, who never acts when
he should, who warns his ministers against their
judicious measures, who encourages them in their
injudicious measures. It is easy to imagine that such
a king should be the tool of others; that favourites
should guide him; that mistresses should corrupt
him; that the atmosphere of a bad court should be
used to degrade free government.

We have had an awful instance of the dangers of
constitutional royalty. We have had the case of a
meddling maniac. During great part of his life
George III's reason was half upset by every crisis.
Throughout his life he had an obstinacy akin to that
of insanity. He was an obstinate and an evil influence; he could not be turned from what was inex-
pedient; by the aid of his station he turned truer but
weaker men from what was expedient. He gave an
excellent moral example to his contemporaries, but
he is an instance of those whose good dies with them,
while their evil lives after them. He prolonged the
American war, perhaps he caused the American
war, so we inherit the vestiges of an American hatred; he forbad Mr. Pitt's wise plans, so we inherit an
Irish difficulty. He would not let us do right in time,
so now our attempts at right are out of time and
fruitless. Constitutional royalty under an active and
half-insane king is one of the worst of governments.
There is in it a secret power which is always eager,

which is generally obstinate, which is often wrong, which rules ministers more than they know themselves, which overpowers them much more than the public believe, which is irresponsible because it is inscrutable, which cannot be prevented because it cannot be seen. The benefits of a good monarch are almost invaluable, but the evils of a bad monarch are almost irreparable.

We shall find these conclusions confirmed if we examine the powers and duties of an English monarch at the break-up of an administration. But the power of dissolution and the prerogative of creating peers, the cardinal powers of that moment, are too important and involve too many complex matters to be sufficiently treated at the very end of a paper as long as this.

WILLIAM GRAHAM SUMNER

William Graham Sumner (1840–1910) was one of the founders of modern sociology. He was also one of the leading American Social Darwinists and advocates of the new capitalistic class. In good Darwinian language he argued, "The millionaires are a product of natural selection. . . . They get high wages and live in luxury, but the bargain is a good one for society." He called for total *laissez faire,* and criticized the capitalists who wanted high tariffs. "The law of the survival of the fittest," he explained—again couching his analysis in Darwinian theory— "is not man-made and cannot be abrogated by man." Borrowing heavily from Adam Smith and Herbert Spencer, he became the intellectual spokesman for private property in America. "Property," he said, "ought to be defended on account of its reality and importance, and on account of its rank among the interests of man." His case was always cogently argued with great genius and passion.

From "Equality," *Earth Hunger* (New Haven, 1913); "State Interference," *War* (New Haven, 1911).

WILLIAM GRAHAM SUMNER

Equality

The thirst for equality is a characteristic of modern mores. In the Middle Ages inequality was postulated in all social doctrines and institutions. There were some "prophets" who arose to talk of equality in the way of poetry, and some popular leaders who used the notion in popular revolts, but they were rebels and heretics, and they preached to deaf ears. The church also, which never failed to have a prescription for every human taste or appetite, had its construction of equality. Ecclesiastics and inquisitors treated all men as equal before the church, sometimes with great effect, when an unpopular king or prince was also a heretic. The doctrine of equality flattered ecclesiastical vanity.

Modern notions of equality are no doubt to be explained historically as revolts against mediæval inequality and status. Natural rights, human rights, equal rights, equality of all men, are phases of a notion which began far back in the Middle Ages, in obscure and neglected writings, or in the polemical utterances of sects and parties. They were counter-assertions against the existing system which assumed that rights were obtained from sovereigns, from which it resulted that each man had such rights as his ancestors and he had been able to get— with the further result that perhaps no two men had the same or equal rights. The case became different when, in the eighteenth century, the mediæval system was gone, the fighting value of the doctrine of equality was exhausted, and it was turned into a dogma of absolute validity and universal application.

The assertion that all men are equal is perhaps the purest falsehood in dogma that was ever put into human language; five minutes' observation of facts will show that men are unequal through a very wide range of variation. Men are not simple units; they are very complex; there is no such thing as a unit man. Therefore we cannot measure men. If we take any element of man and measure men for it, they always fall under a curve of probable error. When we say "man" for human being, we overlook distinctions of age and sex. Males of different ages are not equal; men and women are not equal in the struggle for existence. Women are handicapped by a function which causes disabilities in the struggle for existence, and this difference produces immense disparity in the sexes as to all interests through all human life.

The ground is then shifted to say that all men should be equal before the law, as an ideal of political institutions. They never have been so yet in any state; practically it seems impossible to realize such a state of things. It is an ideal. If this doctrine is a fighting doctrine, if it means that the law should create no privileges for one, or some, which others do not obtain under the same legal conditions, we should all take sides with it for the purposes of the fight. Even this, however, would remain an ideal, an object of hope and effort, not a truth.

When we come nearer to the real thing which men have in mind we find that they actually complain of inequality of fortune, of realization, of earthly lot, of luxury and comfort, of power and satisfaction. This is what they want and this craving is what is in the mores. Nearly all, when they say that they want equality, only use another form of expression to say that they want more welfare than they have, because they take as a standard all which any one has and they find many who have more than themselves. In the nineteenth century, the eighteenth-century rhetoric about natural rights, equal rights, etc., gradually took on the form of a demand for the materialistic equality of enjoyment. Every change by which rhetorical phrases are set aside and real meaning is revealed is a gain. The fact of the mores of present-day society is that there is in them an intense craving for something which is a political phantasm. There is no reason whatever why it should be expected that men should enjoy equally, for that means that all should have means of enjoyment equal to the greatest which any one has; there is nothing in history, science, religion, or politics which could give warrant for such an expectation under any circumstances. We know of no force which could act for the satisfaction of human desires so as to make the satisfaction equal for a number of men, and we know of no interference by "the State," that is, by a committee of men, which could so modify the operation of natural forces as to produce that result. There is an old distinction between commutative and distributive justice which goes back to the Greeks, and which some writers of the nineteenth century have brought out again. Distributive justice is justice in which all personal circumstances are duly allowed for so that all are made "equal" on an absolute standard. Of course equality must necessarily be carried to some such conception at last. It is evident that God alone could give distributive justice; and we find, in this world in which we are, that God has not seen fit to provide for it at all.

WILLIAM GRAHAM SUMNER

State Interference

The United States, starting on a new continent, with full chance to select the old-world traditions which they would adopt, have become the representatives and champions in modern times of all the principles of individualism and personal liberty. We have had no neighbors to fear. We have had no necessity for stringent State discipline. Each one of us has been able to pursue happiness in his own way, unhindered by the demands of a State which would have worn out our energies by expenditure simply in order to maintain the State. The State has existed of itself. The one great exception, the Civil War, only illustrates the point more completely *per contra*. The old Jeffersonian party rose to power and held it, because it conformed to the genius of the country and bore along the true destinies of a nation situated as this one was. It is the glory of the United States, and its calling in history, that it shows what the power of personal liberty is—what self-reliance, energy, enterprise, hard sense men can develop when they have room and liberty and when they are emancipated from the burden of traditions and faiths which are nothing but the accumulated follies and blunders of a hundred generations of "statesmen."

It is, therefore, the highest product of political institutions so far that they have come to a point where, under favourable circumstances, individualism is, under their protection to some extent possible. If political institutions can give security for the pursuit of happiness by each individual, according to his own notion of it, in his own way, and by his own means, they have reached their perfection. This fact, however, has two aspects. If no man can be held to serve another man's happiness, it follows that no man can call on another to serve his happiness. The different views of individualism depend on which of these aspects is under observation. What seems to be desired now is a combination of liberty for all with an obligation of each to all. That is one of the forms in which we are seeking a social philosopher's stone.

. . .

We are told that the State is an ethical person. This is the latest form of political mysticism. Now, it is true that the State is an ethical person in just the same sense as a business firm, a joint stock corporation, or a debating society. It is not a physical person, but it may be a metaphysical or legal person, and as such it has an entity and is an independent subject of rights and duties. Like the other ethical persons, however, the State is just good for what it can do to serve the interests of man, and no more. Such is far from being the meaning and utility of the dogma that the State is an ethical person. The dogma is needed as a source from which can be spun out again contents of phrases and deductions previously stowed away in it. It is only the most modern form of dogmatism devised to sacrifice the man to the institution which is not good for anything except so far as it can serve the man.

One of the newest names for the coming power is the "omnicracy." Mankind has been trying for some thousands of years to find the right-ocracy. None of those which have yet been tried have proved satisfactory. We want a new name on which to pin new hopes, for mankind "never is, but always to be blessed." Omnicracy has this much sense in it, that no one of the great dogmas of the modern political creed is true if it is affirmed of anything less than the whole population, man, woman, child, and baby. When the propositions are enunciated in this sense they are philosophically grand and true. For instance, all the propositions about the "people" are grand and true if we mean by the people every soul in the community, with all the interests and powers which give them an aggregate will and power, with capacity to suffer or to work; but then, also, the propositions remain grand abstractions beyond the realm of practical utility. On the other hand, those propositions cannot be made practically available unless they are affirmed of some limited section of the population, for instance, a majority of the males over twenty-one; but then they are no longer true in philosophy or in fact.

Consequently, when the old-fashioned theories of State interference are applied to the new democratic State, they turn out to be simply a device for setting separate interests in a struggle against each other inside the society. It is plain on the face of all the great questions which are offered to us as political questions to-day, that they are simply struggles of interests for larger shares of the product of industry. One mode of dealing with this distribution would be to leave it to free contract under the play of natural laws. If we do not do this, and if the State interferes with the distribution, how can we stop short of the mediæval plan of reiterated and endless interference, with constant diminution of the total product to be divided?

We have seen above what the tyranny was in the decay of the Roman Empire, when each was in servitude to all; but there is one form of that tyranny which may be still worse. That tyranny will be realized when the same system of servitudes is established in a democratic state; when a man's neighbors are his masters; when the "ethical power of public opinion" bears down upon him at all hours and as to all matters; when his place is assigned to him and he is held in it, not by an emperor or his satellites, who cannot be everywhere all the time, but by the other members of the "village community" who can.

So long as the struggle for individual liberty took the form of a demand that the king or the privileged classes should take their hands off, it was popular and was believed to carry with it the cause of justice and civilization. Now that the governmental machine is brought within everyone's reach, the seduction of power is just as masterful over a democratic faction as ever it was over king or barons. No governing organ has yet abstained from any function because it acknowledged itself ignorant or incompetent. The new powers in the State show no disposition to do it. Nevertheless, the activity of the State, under the new democratic system, shows itself every year more at the mercy of clamorous factions, and legislators find themselves constantly under greater pressure to act, not by their deliberate judgment of what is expedient, but in such a way as to quell clamor, although against their judgment of public interests. It is rapidly becoming the chief art of the legislator to devise measures which shall sound as if they satisfied clamor while they only cheat it.

There are two things which are often treated as if they were identical, which are as far apart as any two things in the field of political philosophy can be: (1) That everyone should be left to do as he likes, so far as possible, without any other social restraints than such as are unavoidable for the peace and order of society. (2) That "the people" should be allowed to carry out their will without any restraint from constitutional institutions. The former means that each should have his own way with his own interests; the latter, that any faction which for the time is uppermost should have its own way with all the rest.

One result of all the new State interference is that the State is being superseded in vast domains of its proper work. While it is reaching out on one side to fields of socialistic enterprise, interfering in the interests of parties in the industrial organism, assuming knowledge of economic laws which nobody possesses, taking ground as to dogmatic notions of justice which are absurd, and acting because it does not know what to do, it is losing its power to give peace, order, and security. The extra-legal power and authority of leaders over voluntary organizations of men throughout a community who are banded together in order to press their interests at the expense of other interests, and who go to the utmost verge of the criminal law, if they do not claim immunity from it, while obeying an authority which acts in secret and without responsibility, is a phenomenon which shows the inadequacy of the existing State to guarantee rights and give security. The boycott and the plan of campaign are certainly not industrial instrumentalities, and it is not yet quite certain whether they are violent and criminal instrumentalities, by which some men coerce other men in matters of material interests. If we turn our minds to the victims of these devices, we see that they do not find in the modern State that security for their interests under the competition of life which it is the first and unquestioned duty of the State to provide. The boycotted man is deprived of the peaceful enjoyment of rights which the laws and institutions of his country allow him, and he has no redress. The State has forbidden all private war on the ground that it will give a remedy for wrongs, and that private redress would distrub the peaceful prosecution of their own interests by other members of the community who are not parties to the quarrel; but we have seen an industrial war paralyze a whole section for weeks, and it was treated almost as a right of the parties that they might fight it out, no matter at what cost to bystanders. We have seen representative bodies of various voluntary associations meet and organize by the side of the regular constitutional organs of the State, in order to deliberate on proposed measures and to transmit to the authorized representatives of the people their approval or disapproval of the propositions, and it scarcely caused a comment. The plutocracy invented the lobby, but the democracy here also seems determined to better the instruction. There are various opinions as to what the revolution is which is upon us, and as to what it is which is about to perish. I do not see anything else which is in as great peril as representative institutions or the constitutional State.

I therefore maintain that it is at the present time a matter of patriotism and civic duty to resist the extension of State interference. It is one of the proudest results of political growth that we have reached the point where individualism is possible. Nothing could better show the merit and value of the institutions which we have inherited than the fact that we can afford to play with all these socialistic and semi-socialistic absurdities. They have no great importance until the question arises: Will a generation which can be led away into this sort of frivolity be able to transmit intact institutions which were made only by men of sterling thought and power, and which can be maintained only by men of the same type? I am familiar with the irritation and impatience with which remonstrances on this matter are received. Those who know just how the world ought to be reconstructed are, of course, angry when they are pushed aside as busybodies. A group of people who assail the legislature with a plan for regulating their neighbor's mode of living are enraged at the "dogma" of non-interference. The publicist who has been struck by some of the superficial roughnesses in the collision of interests which must occur in any time of great industrial activity, and who has therefore determined to waive the objections to State interference, if he can see it brought to bear on his pet reform, will object to absolute principles. For my part, I have never seen that public or private principles were good for anything except when there seemed to be a motive for breaking them. Anyone who has studied a question as to which the solution is yet wanting may despair of the power of free contract to solve it. I have examined a great many cases of proposed interference with free contract, and the only alternative to free contract which I can find is "heads I win, tails you lose" in favor of one party or the other. I am familiar with the criticisms which some writers claim to make upon individualism, but the worst individualism I can find in history is that of the Jacobins, and I believe that it is logically sound that the anti-social vices should be most developed whenever the attempt is made to put socialistic theories in practice. The only question at this point is: Which may we better trust, the play of free social forces or legislative and administrative interference? This question is as pertinent for those who expect to win by interference as for others, for whenever we try to get paternalized we only succeed in getting policed.

ANDREW CARNEGIE

To some the quintessence of the Robber Baron, to others a great industrial statesman, Andrew Carnegie (1835–1919) was clearly one of the founders of the modern industrial state. Unlike many of his industrialist colleagues, Carnegie was a well-read and eloquent man, and his book, *The Gospel of Wealth,* is the classic apologia of 19th- and early 20th-century American capitalism. The following selections from this work, imbued with Social Darwinist ideology, properly sum up his views on the new industrial capitalism, its consequences and advantages for society.

From *The Gospel of Wealth* (New York, 1900).

ANDREW CARNEGIE

The Gospel of Wealth

THE PROBLEM OF THE ADMINISTRATION OF WEALTH

The problem of our age is the proper administration of wealth, that the ties of brotherhood may still bind together the rich and poor in harmonious relationship. The conditions of human life have not only been changed, but revolutionized, within the past few hundred years. In former days there was little difference between the dwelling, dress, food, and environment of the chief and those of his retainers. The Indians are to-day where civilized man then was. When visiting the Sioux, I was led to the wigwam of the chief. It was like the others in external appearance, and even within the difference was trifling between it and those of the poorest of his braves. The contrast between the palace of the millionaire and the cottage of the laborer with us to-day measures the change which has come with civilization. This change, however, is not to be deplored, but welcomed as highly beneficial. It is well, nay, essential, for the progress of the race that the houses of some should be homes for all that is highest and best in literature and the arts, and for all the refinements of civilization, rather than that none should be so. Much better this great irregularity than universal squalor. Without wealth there can be no Mæcenas. The "good old times" were not good old times. Neither master nor servant was as well situated then as to-day. A relapse to old conditions would be disastrous to both—not the least so to him who serves—and would sweep away civilization with it. But whether the change be for good or ill, it is upon us, beyond our power to alter, and, therefore, to be accepted and made the best of. It is a waste of time to criticize the inevitable.

It is easy to see how the change has come. One illustration will serve for almost every phase of the cause. In the manufacture of products we have the whole story. It applies to all combinations of human industry, as stimulated and enlarged by the inventions of this scientific age. Formerly, articles were manufactured at the domestic hearth, or in small shops which formed part of the household. The master and his apprentices worked side by side, the latter living with the master, and therefore subject to the same conditions. When these apprentices rose to be masters, there was little or no change in their modes of life, and they, in turn, educated succeeding apprentices in the same routine. There was, substantially, social equality, and even political equality, for those engaged in industrial pursuits had then little or no voice in the State.

The inevitable result of such a mode of manufacture was crude articles at high prices. To-day the world obtains commodities of excellent quality at prices which even the preceding generation would have deemed incredible. In the commercial world similar causes have produced similar results, and the race is benefited thereby. The poor enjoy what the rich could not before afford. What were the luxuries have become the necessaries of life. The laborer has now more comforts than the farmer had a few generations ago. The farmer has more luxuries than the landlord had, and is more richly clad and better housed. The landlord has books and pictures rarer and appointments more artistic than the king could then obtain.

The price we pay for this salutary change is, no

doubt, great. We assemble thousands of operatives in the factory, and in the mine, of whom the employer can know little or nothing, and to whom he is little better than a myth. All intercourse between them is at an end. Rigid castes are formed, and, as usual, mutual ignorance breeds mutual distrust. Each caste is without sympathy with the other, and ready to credit anything disparaging in regard to it. Under the law of competition, the employer of thousands is forced into the strictest economies, among which the rates paid to labor figure prominently, and often there is friction between the employer and employed, between capital and labor, between rich and poor. Human society loses homogeneity.

The price which society pays for the law of competition, like the price it pays for cheap comforts and luxuries, is also great; but the advantages of this law are also greater still than its cost—for it is to this law that we owe our wonderful material development, which brings improved conditions in its train. But, whether the law be benign or not, we must say of it, as we say of the change in the conditions of men to which we have referred: It is here; we cannot evade it; no substitutes for it have been found; and while the law may be sometimes hard for the individual, it is best for the race, because it insures the survival of the fittest in every department. We accept and welcome, therefore, as conditions to which we must accommodate ourselves, great inequality of environment; the concentration of business, industrial and commercial, in the hands of a few; and the law of competition between these, as being not only beneficial, but essential to the future progress of the race.

*   *   *   *   *

Under the first and second modes most of the wealth of the world that has reached the few has hitherto been applied. Let us in turn consider each of these modes. The first is the most injudicious. In monarchical countries, the estates and the greatest portion of the wealth are left to the first son, that the vanity of the parent may be gratified by the thought that his name and title are to descend unimpaired to succeeding generations. The condition of this class in Europe to-day teaches the failure of such hopes or ambitions. The successors have become impoverished through their follies, or from the fall in the value of land. Even in Great Britain the strict law of entail has been found inadequate to maintain an hereditary class. Its soil is rapidly passing into the hands of the stranger. Under republican institutions the division of property among the children is much fairer; but the question which forces itself upon thoughtful men in all lands is, Why should men leave great fortunes to their children? If this is done from affection, is it not misguided affection? Observation teaches that, generally speaking, it is not well for the children that they should be so burdened. Neither is it well for the State. Beyond providing for the wife and daughters moderate sources of income, and very moderate allowances indeed, if any, for the sons, men may well hesitate; for it is no longer questionable that great sums bequeathed often work more for the injury than for the good of the recipients. Wise men will soon conclude that, for the best interests of the members of their families, and of the State, such bequests are an improper use of their means.

It is not suggested that men who have failed to educate their sons to earn a livelihood shall cast them adrift in poverty. If any man has seen fit to rear his sons with a view to their living idle lives, or, what is highly commendable, has instilled in them the sentiment that they are in a position to labor for public ends without reference to pecuniary considerations, then, of course, the duty of the parent is to see that such are provided for in moderation. There are instances of millionaires' sons unspoiled by wealth, who, being rich, still perform great services to the community. Such are the very salt of the earth, as valuable as, unfortunately, they are rare. It is not the exception, however, but the rule, that men must regard; and, looking at the usual result of enormous sums conferred upon legatees, the thoughtful man must shortly say, "I would as soon leave to my son a curse as the almighty dollar," and admit to himself that it is not the welfare of the children, but family pride, which inspires these legacies.

As to the second mode, that of leaving wealth at death for public uses . . . the cases are not few in which the real object sought by the testator is not attained, nor are they few in which his real wishes are thwarted. In many cases the bequests are so used as to become only monuments of his folly. It is well to remember that it requires the exercise of not less ability than that which acquires it, to use wealth so as to be really beneficial to the community. Besides this, it may fairly be said that no man is to be extolled for doing what he cannot help doing, nor is he to be thanked by the community to which he only leaves wealth at death. Men who leave a vast sum in this way may fairly be thought men who would not have left it at all had they been able to take it with them. The memories of such cannot be held in grateful remembrance, for there is no grace in their gifts. It is not to be wondered at that such bequests seem so generally to lack the blessing. . . .

There remains, then, only one mode of using great fortunes; but in this we have the true antidote for the temporary unequal distribution of wealth, the reconciliation of the rich and the poor—a reign of harmony, another ideal, differing, indeed, from that of the Communist in requiring only the further evolution of existing conditions, not the total overthrow of our civilization. It is founded upon the present most intense Individualism, and the race is prepared to put it in practice by degrees whenever it pleases. Under its sway we shall have an ideal State, in which the surplus wealth of the few will become, in the best sense, the property of the many, because administered for the common good: and this wealth, passing through the hands of the few, can be made a much more potent force for the elevation of our race than if distributed in small sums to the people themselves. Even the poorest can be made to see this, and to agree that great sums gathered by some of their fellow-citizens and spent for public purposes, from which the masses reap the principal benefit, are more valuable to them than if scattered among themselves in trifling amounts through the course of many years. . . .

The best uses to which surplus wealth can be put have already been indicated. Those who would administer wisely must, indeed, be wise; for one of the serious obstacles to the improvement of our race is indiscriminate charity. It were better for mankind that the millions of the rich were thrown into the sea than so spent as to encourage the slothful, the drunken, the unworthy. Of every thousand dollars spent in so-called charity to-day, it is probable that nine hundred and fifty dollars is unwisely spent—so spent, indeed, as to produce the very evils which it hopes to mitigate or cure. A well-known writer of philosophic books admitted the other day that he had given a quarter of a dollar to a man who approached him as he was coming to visit the house of his friend. He knew nothing of the habits of this beggar, knew not the use that would be made of this money, although he had every reason to suspect that it would be spent improperly. This man professed to be a disciple of Herbert Spencer; yet the quarter-dollar given that night will probably work more injury than all the money will do good which its thoughtless donor will ever be able to give in true charity. He only gratified his own feelings, saved himself from annoyance—and this was probably one of the most selfish and very worst actions of his life, for in all respects he is most worthy.

In bestowing charity, the main consideration should be to help those who will help themselves; to provide part of the means by which those who desire to improve may do so; to give those who desire to rise the aids by which they may rise; to assist, but rarely or never to do all. Neither the individual nor the race is improved by almsgiving. Those worthy of assistance, except in rare cases, seldom require assistance. The really valuable men of the race never do, except in case of accident or sudden change. Every one has, of course, cases of individuals brought to his own knowledge where temporary assistance can do genuine good, and these he will not overlook. But the amount which can be wisely given by the individual for individuals is necessarily limited by his lack of knowledge of the circumstances connected with each. He is the only true reformer who is as careful and as anxious not to aid the unworthy as he is to aid the worthy, and, perhaps, even more so, for in alms-giving more injury is probably done by rewarding vice than by relieving virtue.

The rich man is thus almost restricted to following the examples of Peter Cooper, Enoch Pratt of Baltimore, Mr. Pratt of Brooklyn, Senator Stanford, and others, who know that the best means of benefiting the community is to place within its reach the ladders upon which the aspiring can rise—free libraries, parks, and means of recreation, by which men are helped in body and mind; works of art, certain to give pleasure and improve the public taste; and public institutions of various kinds, which will improve the general condition of the people; in this manner returning their surplus wealth to the mass of their fellows in the forms best calculated to do them lasting good.

Thus is the problem of rich and poor to be solved. The laws of accumulation will be left free, the laws of distribution free. Individualism will continue, but the millionaire will be but a trustee for the poor, intrusted for a season with a great part of the increased wealth of the community, but administering it for the community far better than it could or would have done for itself. The best minds will thus have reached a stage in the development of the race in which it is clearly seen that there is no mode of disposing of surplus wealth creditable to thoughtful and earnest men into whose hands it flows, save by using it year by year for the general good. This day already dawns. Men may die without incurring the pity of their fellows, still sharers in great business enterprises from which their capital cannot be or has not been withdrawn, and which is left chiefly at death for public uses; yet the day is not far distant when the man who dies leaving behind him millions of available wealth, which was free for him to administer during life, will pass away "unwept, unhonored, and unsung," no matter to what uses he leaves the dross which he cannot take with him. Of such as these the public verdict will then be: "The man who dies thus rich dies disgraced."

Such, in my opinion, is the true gospel concerning wealth, obedience to which is destined some day to solve the problem of the rich and the poor, and to bring "Peace on earth, among men good will."

POPULAR ILLUSIONS ABOUT TRUSTS

. . . The day of small concerns within the means of many able men seems to be over, never to return. The rise to partnership in vast concerns must come chiefly through such means as these permitted by the laws of limited partnership.

To-day we hear little of the joint-stock corporation, which has settled into its proper sphere and escapes notice. It was succeeded by the "syndicate," a combination of corporations which pulled together for a time, and expected to destroy destructive competition. The word has already almost passed out of use, and now the syndicate has given place to the trust.

We see in all these efforts of men the desire to furnish opportunities to mass capital, to concentrate the small savings of the many and to direct them to one end. The conditions of human society create for this an imperious demand; the concentration of capital is a necessity for meeting the demands of our day, and as such should not be looked at askance, but be encouraged. There is nothing detrimental to human society in it, but much that is, or is bound soon to become, beneficial. It is an evolution from the heterogeneous to the homogeneous [*sic*], and is clearly another step in the upward path of development.

Abreast of this necessity for massing the wealth of the many in even larger and larger sums for huge enterprises, another law is seen in operation in the invariable tendency from the beginning till now to lower the cost of all articles produced by man. Through the operation of this law the home of the laboring man of our day boasts luxuries which even in the palaces of monarchs as recent as Queen Elizabeth were unknown. It is a trite saying that the comforts of to-day were the luxuries of yesterday, and conveys only a faint impression of the contrast, until one walks through the castles and palaces of older countries, and learns that two or three centuries ago these had for carpets only rushes, small open spaces for windows, glass being little known, and were without gas or water-supply, or any of what we consider to-day the conveniences of life. As for those chief treasures of life, books, there is scarcely a workingman's family which has not at its command, without money and without price, access to libraries to which the palace was recently a stranger.

If there be in human history one truth clearer and more indisputable than another, it is that the cheapening of articles, whether of luxury or of necessity or of those classed as artistic, insures their more general distribution, and is one of the most potent factors in refining and lifting a people, and in adding to its happiness. In no period of human activity has this great agency been so potent or so wide-spread as in our own. Now, the cheapening of all these good things, whether it be in the metals, in textiles, or in food, or especially in books and prints, is rendered possible only through the operation of the law, which may be stated thus: cheapness is in proportion to the scale of production. To make ten tons of steel a day would cost many times as much per ton as to make one hundred tons; to make one hundred tons would cost double as much per ton as a thousand; and to make one thousand tons per day would cost greatly more than to make ten thousand tons. Thus, the larger the scale of operation the cheaper the product. The huge steamship of twenty thousand tons burden carries its tons of freight at less cost, it is stated, than the first steamships carried a pound. It is, fortunately, impossible for man to impede, much less to change, this great and beneficent law, from which flow most of his comforts and luxuries, and also most of the best and most improving forces in his life.

In an age noted for its inventions, we see the same law running through these. Inventions facilitate big operations, and in most instances require to be worked upon a great scale. Indeed, as a rule, the great invention which is beneficent in its operation would be useless unless operated to supply a thousand people where ten were supplied before. Every agency in our day labors to scatter the good things of life, both for mind and body, among the toiling millions. Everywhere we look we see the inexorable law ever producing bigger and bigger things. One of the most notable illustrations of this is seen in the railway freight-car. When the writer entered the service of the Pennsylvania Railroad from seven to eight tons were carried upon eight wheels; to-day they carry fifty tons. The locomotive has quadrupled in power. The steamship to-day is ten times bigger, the blast-furnace has seven times more capacity, and the tendency everywhere is still to increase. The contrast between the hand printing-press of old and the elaborate newspaper printing-machine of to-day is even more marked.

We conclude that this overpowering, irresistible tendency toward aggregation of capital and increase of size in every branch of product cannot be arrested or even greatly impeded, and that, instead of attempting to restrict either, we should hail every increase as something gained, not for the few rich, but for the millions of poor, seeing that the law is salutary, working for good and not for evil. Every enlargement is an improvement, step by step, upon what has preceded. It makes for higher civilization, for the enrichment of human life, not for one, but for all classes of men. It tends to bring to the laborer's cottage the luxuries hitherto enjoyed only by the rich, to remove from the most squalid homes much of their squalor, and to foster the growth of human happiness relatively more in the workman's home than in the millionaire's palace. It does not tend to make the rich poorer, but it does tend to make the poor richer in the possession of better things, and greatly lessens the wide and deplorable gulf between the rich and the poor. Superficial politicians, may, for a time, deceive the uninformed, but more and more will all this be clearly seen by those who are now led to regard aggregations as injurious.

In all great movements, even of the highest value, there is cause for criticism, and new dangers arising from new conditions, which must be guarded against. There is no nugget free from more or less impurity, and no good cause without its fringe of scoria. The sun itself has spots, but, as has been wisely said, these are rendered visible only by the light it itself sends forth. . . .

AN EMPLOYER'S VIEW OF THE LABOR QUESTION

. . . A strike or lockout is, in itself, a ridiculous affair. Whether a failure or a success, it gives no direct proof of its justice or injustice. In this it resembles war between two nations. It is simply a question of strength and endurance between the contestants. The gage of battle, or the duel, is not more senseless, as a means of establishing what is just and fair, than an industrial strike or lockout. It would be folly to conclude that we have reached any permanent adjustment between capital and labor until strikes and lockouts are as much things of the past as the gage of battle or the duel have become in the most advanced communities.

Taking for granted, then, that some further modifications must be made between capital and labor, I propose to consider the various plans that have been suggested by which labor can advance another stage in its development in relation to capital. And, as a preliminary, let it be noted that it is only labour and capital in their greatest masses which it is necessary to consider. It is only in large establishments that the industrial unrest of which I have spoken ominously manifests itself. The farmer who hires a man to assist him, or the gentleman who engages a groom or a butler, is not affected by strikes. The innumerable cases in which a few men only are directly concerned, which comprise in the aggregate the most of labor, present upon the whole a tolerably satisfactory condition of affairs. This clears the ground of much, and leaves us to deal only

with the immense mining and manufacturing concerns of recent growth, in which capital and labor
often array themselves in alarming antagonism.

Among the expedients suggested for their better
reconciliation, the first place must be assigned to the
idea of coöperation, or the plan by which the workers
are to become part-owners in enterprises, and share
their fortunes. There is no doubt that if this could be
effected it would have the same beneficial effect
upon the workman which the ownership of land has
upon the man who has hitherto tilled the land for
another. The sense of ownership would make of him
more of a man as regards himself, and hence more
of a citizen as regards the commonwealth. But we
are here met by a difficulty which I confess I have not
yet been able to overcome, and which renders me
less sanguine than I should like to be in regard to
coöperation. The difficulty is this, and it seems to me
to be inherent in all gigantic manufacturing, mining, and commercial operations. Two men or two
combinations of men will erect blast-furnaces, iron-
mills, cotton-mills, or piano manufactories adjoin-
ing each other, or engage in shipping or commercial
business. They will start with equal capital and
credit; and to those only superficially acquainted
with the personnel of these concerns, success will
seem as likely to attend the one as the other. Nevertheless, one will fail after dragging along a lifeless
existence, and pass into the hands of its creditors;
while the neighboring mill or business will make a
fortune for its owners. Now, the successful manufacturer, dividing every month or every year a proportion of his profits among his workmen, either as
a bonus or as dividends upon shares owned by them,
will not only have a happy and contented body of

operatives, but he will inevitably attract from his rival the very best workmen in every department. His rival, having no profits to divide among his workmen, and paying them only a small assured minimum to enable them to live, finds himself despoiled of foremen and of workmen necessary to carry on his business successfully. His workmen are discontented and, in their own opinion, defrauded of the proper fruits of their skill, through incapacity or inattention of their employers. Thus, unequal business capacity in the management produces unequal results.

It will be precisely the same if one of these manufactories belongs to the workmen themselves; but in this case, in the present stage of development of the workmen, the chances of failure will be enormously increased. It is, indeed, greatly to be doubted whether any body of working-men in the world could to-day organize and successfully carry on a mining or manufacturing or commercial business in competition with concerns owned by men trained to affairs. If any such coöperative organization succeeds, it may be taken for granted that it is principally owing to the exceptional business ability of one of the managers, and only in a very small degree to the efforts of the mass of workmen-owners. This business ability is excessively rare, as is proved by the incredibly large proportion of those who enter upon the stormy sea of business only to fail. I should say that twenty coöperative concerns would fail to every one that would succeed. There are, of course, a few successful establishments, notably two in France and one in England, which are organized upon the coöperative plan, in which the workmen participate directly in the profits. But these were all created by the present owners, who now generously share the profits with their workmen, and are making the success of their manufactories upon the coöperative plan the proud work of their lives. What these concerns will become when the genius for affairs is no longer with them to guide, is a matter of grave doubt and, to me, of foreboding. I can, of course, picture in my mind a state of civilization in which the most talented business men shall find their most cherished work in carrying on immense concerns, not primarily for their own personal aggrandizement, but for the good of the masses of workers engaged therein, and their families; but this is only a foreshadowing of a dim and distant future. When a class of such men has evolved, the problem of capital and labor will be permanently solved to the entire satisfaction of both. But as this manifestly belongs to a future generation, I cannot consider coöperation, or common ownership, as the next immediate step in advance which it is possible for labor to make in its upward path.

The next suggestion is that peaceful settlement of differences should be reached through arbitration. Here we are upon firmer ground. I would lay it down as a maxim that there is no excuse for a strike or a lockout until arbitration of differences has been offered by one party and refused by the other. No doubt serious trouble attends even arbitration at present, from the difficulty of procuring suitable men to judge intelligently between the disputants. There is a natural disinclination among business men to expose their business to men in whom they have not entire confidence. We lack, so far, in America a retired class of men of affairs. Our vile practice is to keep on accumulating more dollars until we die. If it were the custom here, as it is in England, for men to withdraw from active business after acquiring a fortune, this class would furnish the proper arbitrators. . . .

The influence of trades-unions upon the relations between the employer and employed has been much discussed. Some establishments in America have refused to recognize the right of the men to form themselves into these unions, although I am not aware that any concern in England would dare to take this position. This policy, however, may be regarded as only a temporary phase of the situation. The right of the working-men to combine and to form trades-unions is no less sacred than the right of the manufacturer to enter into associations and conferences with his fellows, and it must sooner or later be conceded. Indeed, it gives one but a poor opinion of the American workman if he permits himself to be deprived of a right which his fellow in England long since conquered for himself. My experience has been that trades-unions, upon the whole, are beneficial both to labor and capital. They certainly educate the working-men, and give them a truer conception of the relations of capital and labor than they could otherwise form. The ablest and best workmen eventually come to the front in these organizations; and it may be laid down as a rule that the more intelligent the workman the fewer the contests with employers. It is not the intelligent workman, who knows that labor without his brother capital is helpless, but the blatant ignorant man, who regards capital as the natural enemy of labor, who does so much to embitter the relations between employer and employed; and the power of this ignorant demagogue arises chiefly from the lack of proper organization among the men through which their real voice can be expressed. This voice will always be found in favor of the judicious and intelligent representative. Of course, as men become intelligent more deference must be paid to them personally and to their rights, and even to their opinions and prejudices; and, upon the whole, a greater share of profits must be paid in the day of prosperity to the intelligent than to the ignorant workman. He cannot be imposed upon so readily. On the other hand, he will be found much readier to accept reduced compensation when business is depressed; and it is better in the long run for capital to be served by the highest intelligence, and to be made well aware of the fact that it is dealing with men who know what is due to them, both as to treatment and compensation.

One great source of the trouble between employers and employed arises from the fact that the immense establishments of to-day, in which alone we find serious conflicts between capital and labor, are not managed by their owners, but by salaried officers, who cannot possibly have any permanent interest in the welfare of the working men. These officials are chiefly anxious to present a satisfactory balance-sheet at the end of the year, that their hundreds of shareholders may receive the usual dividends, and that they may therefore be secure in their positions, and be allowed to manage the business without unpleasant interference either by directors or shareholders. It is notable that bitter strikes seldom occur in small establishments where the owner comes into direct contact with his men, and knows their qualities, their struggles, and their aspirations. It is the chairman, situated hundreds of miles away from his men, who only pays a flying visit to the works and perhaps finds time to walk through the mill or mine once or twice a year, that is chiefly responsible for the disputes which break out at intervals. I have noticed that the manager who confers oftenest with a committee of his leading men has the least trouble with his workmen. Although it may be impracticable for the presidents of these large corporations to know the working-men personally, the manager at the mills, having a committee of his best men to present their suggestions and wishes from time to time, can do much to maintain and strengthen amicable relations, if not interfered with from headquarters. I, therefore, recognize in trades-unions, or, better still, in organizations of the men of each establishment, who select representatives to speak for them, a means, not of further embittering the relations between employer and employed, but of improving them. . . .

Whatever the future may have in store for labor, the evolutionist, who sees nothing but certain and steady progress for the race, will never attempt to set bounds to its triumphs, even to its final form of complete and universal industrial coöperation, which I hope is some day to be reached. But I am persuaded that the next step forward is to be in the direction I have here ventured to point out; and as one who is now most anxious to contribute his part toward helping forward the day of amicable relations between the two forces of capital and labor, which are not enemies, but are really auxiliaries who stand or fall together, I ask at the hands of both capital and labor a careful consideration of these views.

LUDWIG VON MISES

A leader of the great Austrian School of classical economics, Ludwig von Mises (1881–   ) has been associated with libertarianism since the early days of the 20th century. His seminal book, *Human Action,* along with his other numerous writings in economics, sociology, and philosophy, has inspired students of freedom for years. His ideas have been anathematized by both the Nazis and the Communists; and his analysis of "Etatism" and anti-Semitism is heavily tinged with his own experience in confronting the modern omnipotent state.

From the *Omnipotent Government: The Rise of the Total State and Total War* (New Rochelle, N.Y.: Arlington House, 1969). Reprinted with permission of the publisher.

LUDWIG VON MISES

Etatism

I. THE NEW MENTALITY

The most important event in the history of the last hundred years is the displacement of liberalism by etatism. Etatism appears in two forms: socialism and interventionism. Both have in common the goal of subordinating the individual unconditionally to the state, the social apparatus of compulsion and coercion.

Etatism too, like liberalism in earlier days, originated in Western Europe and only later came into Germany. It has been asserted that autochthonous German roots of etatism could be found in Fichte's socialist utopia and in the sociological teachings of Schelling and Hegel. However, the dissertations of these philosophers were so foreign to the problems and tasks of social and economic policies that they could not directly influence political matters. What use could practical politics derive from Hegel's assertion: "The state is the actuality of the ethical idea. It is ethical mind *qua* the substantial will manifest and revealed to itself, knowing and thinking itself, accomplishing what it knows and in so far as it knows it." Or from his dictum: "The state is absolutely rational inasmuch as it is the actuality of the substantial will which it possesses in the particular self-consciousness once that consciousness has been raised to consciousness of its universality."*

Etatism assigns to the state the task of guiding the citizens and of holding them in tutelage. It aims at restricting the individual's freedom to act. It seeks to mold his destiny and to vest all initiative in the gov-

---

*Hegel, *Philosophy of Right*, translated by T. M. Knox (Oxford, 1942), pp. 155–156.

ernment alone. It came into Germany from the West.* Saint Simon, Owen, Fourier, Pecqueur, Sismondi, Auguste Comte laid its foundations. Lorenz von Stein was the first author to bring the Germans comprehensive information concerning these new doctrines. The appearance in 1842 of the first edition of his book, *Socialism and Communism in Present-Day France,* was the most important event in pre-Marxian German socialism. The elements of government interference with business, labor legislation, and trade-unionism† also reached Germany from the West. In America Frederick List became familiar with the protectionist theories of Alexander Hamilton.

Liberalism had taught the German intellectuals to absorb Western political ideas with reverential awe. Now, they thought, liberalism was already outstripped; government interference with business had replaced old-fashioned liberal orthodoxy and would inexorably result in socialism. He who did not want to appear backward had to become "social," i.e., either interventionist or socialist. New ideas succeed only after some lapse of time; years have to pass before they reach the broader strata of intellectuals. List's *National System of Political Economy* was published in 1841, a few months before Stein's book. In 1847 Marx and Engels produced the Communist Manifesto. In the middle 'sixties the prestige of liberalism began to melt away. Very soon the economic, philosophical, historical, and juridical university lectures were representing liberalism in caricature.

*Hayek, "The Counter-Revolution of Science," *Economica,* VIII, 9–36, 119–150, 281–320.
†Adolf Weber (*Der Kampf zwischen Kapital und Arbeit,* 3d and 4th eds. Tubingen, 1921, p. 68) says quite correctly in dealing with German trade-unionism: "Form and spirit . . . came from abroad."

The social scientists outdid each other in emotional criticism of British free trade and laissez faire; the philosophers disparaged the "stock-jobber" ethics of utilitarianism, the superficiality of enlightenment, and the negativity of the nation of liberty; the lawyers demonstrated the paradox of democratic and parliamentary institutions; and the historians dealt with the moral and political decay of France and of Great Britain. On the other hand, the students were taught to admire the "social kingdom of the Hohenzollerns" from Frederick William I, the "noble socialist," to William I, the great Kaiser of social security and labor legislation. The Social Democrats despised Western "plutodemocracy" and "pseudoliberty" and ridiculed the teachings of "bourgeois economics."

The boring pedantry of the professors and the boastful oratory of the Social Democrats failed to impress critical people. The élite were conquered for etatism by other men. From England penetrated the ideas of Carlyle, Ruskin, and the Fabians, from France Solidarism. The churches of all creeds joined the choir. Novels and plays propagated the new doctrine of the state. Shaw and Wells, Spielhagen and Gerhart Hauptmann, and hosts of other writers, less gifted, contributed to the popularity of etatism.

II. THE STATE

The state is essentially an apparatus of compulsion and coercion. The characteristic feature of its activities is to compel people through the application or the threat of force to behave otherwise than they would like to behave.

But not every apparatus of compulsion and coercion is called a state. Only one which is powerful enough to maintain its existence, for some time at least, by its own force is commonly called a state. A gang of robbers, which because of the comparative weakness of its forces has no prospect of successfully resisting for any length of time the forces of another organization, is not entitled to be called a state. The state will either smash or tolerate a gang. In the first case the gang is not a state because its independence lasts for a short time only; in the second case it is not a state because it does not stand on its own might. The pogrom gangs in imperial Russia were not a state because they could kill and plunder only thanks to the connivance of the government.

This restriction of the notion of the state leads directly to the concepts of state territory and sovereignty. Standing on its own power implies that there is a space on the earth's surface where the operation of the apparatus is not restricted by the intervention of another organization; this space is the state's territory. Sovereignty (*suprema potestas,* supreme power) signifies that the organization stands on its own legs. A state without territory is an empty concept. A state without sovereignty is a contradiction in terms.

The total complex of the rules according to which those at the helm employ compulsion and coercion is called law. Yet the characteristic feature of the state is not these rules, as such, but the application or threat of violence. A state whose chiefs recognize but one rule, to do whatever seems at the moment to be expedient in their eyes, is a state without law. It does not make any difference whether or not these tyrants are "benevolent."

The term law is used in a second meaning too. We call international law the complex of agreements which sovereign states have concluded expressly or tacitly in regard to their mutual relations. It is not, however, essential to the statehood of an organization that other states should recognize its existence through the conclusion of such agreements. It is the fact of sovereignty within a territory that is essential, not the formalities.

The people handling the state machinery may take over other functions, duties, and activities. The government may own and operate schools, railroads, hospitals, and orphan asylums. Such activities are only incidental to the conception of a state. Whatever other functions it may assume, the state is always characterized by the compulsion and coercion exercised.

With human nature as it is, the state is a necessary and indispensable institution. The state is, if properly administered, the foundation of society, of human coöperation and civilization. It is the most beneficial and most useful instrument in the endeavors of man to promote human happiness and welfare. But it is a tool and a means only, not the ultimate goal. It is not God. It is simply compulsion and coercion; it is the police power.

It has been necessary to dwell upon these truisms because the mythologies and metaphysics of etatism have succeeded in wrapping them in mystery. The state is a human institution, not a superhuman being. He who says "state" means coercion and compulsion. He who says: There should be a law concerning this matter, means: The armed men of the government should force people to do what they do not want to do, or not to do what they like. He who says: This law should be better enforced, means: The police should force people to obey this law. He who says: The state is God, deifies arms and prisons. The worship of the state is the worship of force. There is no more dangerous menace to civilization than a government of incompetent, corrupt, or vile men. The worst evils which mankind ever had to endure were inflicted by bad governments. The state can be and has often been in the course of history the main source of mischief and disaster.

The apparatus of compulsion and coercion is always operated by mortal men. It has happened time and again that rulers have excelled their contemporaries and fellow citizens both in competence and in fairness. But there is ample historical evidence to the contrary too. The thesis of etatism that the members of the government and its assistants are more intelligent than the people, and that they know better what is good for the individual than he himself knows, is pure nonsense. The Führers and the Duces are neither God nor God's vicars.

The essential characteristic features of state and government do not depend on their particular structure and constitution. They are present both in despotic and in democratic governments. Democracy too is not divine. We shall later deal with the benefits that society derives from democratic government. But great as these advantages are, it should never be forgotten that majorities are no less exposed to error and frustration than kings and dictators. That a fact is deemed true by the majority does not prove its truth. That a policy is deemed expedient by the majority does not prove its expediency. The individuals who form the majority are not gods and their joint conclusions are not necessarily godlike.

III. THE POLITICAL AND SOCIAL DOCTRINES OF
LIBERALISM

There is a school of thought which teaches that social coöperation of men could be achieved without compulsion or coercion. Anarchism believes that a social order could be established in which all men would recognize the advantages to be derived from coöperation and be prepared to do voluntarily everything which the maintenance of society requires and to renounce voluntarily all actions detrimental to society. But the anarchists overlook two facts. There are people whose mental abilities are so limited that they cannot grasp the full benefits that society brings to them. And there are people whose flesh is so weak that they cannot resist the temptation of striving for selfish advantage through actions detrimental to society. An anarchistic society would be exposed to the mercy of every individual. We may grant that every sane adult is endowed with the faculty of realizing the good of social coöperation and of acting accordingly. However, it is beyond doubt that there are infants, the aged, and the insane. We may agree that he who acts antisocially should be considered mentally sick and in need of cure. But as long as not all are cured, and as long as there are infants and the senile, some provision must be taken lest they destroy society.

Liberalism differs radically from anarchism. It has nothing in common with the absurd illusions of the anarchists. We must emphasize this point because etatists sometimes try to discover a similarity. Liberalism is not so foolish as to aim at the abolition of the state. Liberals fully recognize that no social coöperation and no civilization could exist without some amount of compulsion and coercion. It is the task of government to protect the social system against the attacks of those who plan actions detrimental to its maintenance and operation.

The essential teaching of liberalism is that social coöperation and the division of labor can be achieved only in a system of private ownership of the means of production, i.e., within a market society, or capitalism. All the other principles of liberalism—democracy, personal freedom of the individual, freedom of speech and of the press, religious tolerance, peace among the nations—are consequences of this basic postulate. They can be realized only within a society based on private property.

From this point of view liberalism assigns to the state the task of protecting the lives, health, freedom, and property of its subjects against violent or fraudulent aggression.

That liberalism aims at private ownership of the means of production implies that it rejects public ownership of the means of production, i.e., socialism. Liberalism therefore objects to the socialization of the means of production. It is illogical to say, as many etatists do, that liberalism is hostile to or hates the state, because it is opposed to the transfer of the ownership of railroads or cotton mills to the state. If a man says that sulphuric acid does not make a good hand lotion, he is not expressing hostility to sulphuric acid as such; he is simply giving his opinion concerning the limitations of its use.

It is not the task of this study to determine whether the program of liberalism or that of socialism is more adequate for the realization of those aims which are common to all political and social endeavors, i.e., the achievement of human happiness and welfare. We are only tracing the role played by liberalism and by antiliberalism—whether socialist or interventionist—in the evolution which resulted in the establishment of totalitarianism. We can therefore content ourselves with briefly sketching the outlines of the social and political program of liberalism and its working.

In an economic order based on private ownership of the means of production the market is the focal point of the system. The working of the market mechanism forces capitalists and entrepreneurs to produce so as to satisfy the consumers' needs as well and cheaply as the quantity and quality of material resources and of man power available and the state of technological knowledge allow. If they are not equal to this task, if they produce poor goods, or at too great cost, or not the commodities that the consumers demand most urgently, they suffer losses. Unless they change their methods to satisfy the consumers' needs better, they will finally be thrown out of their positions as capitalists and entrepreneurs. Other people who know better how to serve the consumer will replace them. Within the market society the working of the price mechanism makes the consumers supreme. They determine through the prices they pay and through the amount of their purchases both the quantity and quality of production. They determine directly the prices of consumers' goods, and thereby indirectly the prices of all material factors of production and the wages of all hands employed.

Within the market society each serves all his fellow citizens and each is served by them. It is a system of mutual exchange of services and commodities, a mutual giving and receiving. In that endless rotating mechanism the entrepreneurs and capitalists are the servants of the consumers. The consumers are the masters, to whose vestments and methods of production. The market chooses the whims the entrepreneurs and the capitalists must adjust their inentrepreneurs and the capitalists, and removes them as soon as they prove failures. The market is a democracy in which every penny gives a right to vote and where voting is repeated every day.

Outside of the market stands the social apparatus of compulsion and coercion, and its steersmen, the government. To state and government the duty is assigned of maintaining peace both at home and abroad. For only in peace can the economic system achieve its ends, the fullest satisfaction of human needs and wants.

But who should command the apparatus of compulsion and coercion? In other words, who should rule? It is one of the fundamental insights of liberal thought that government is based on opinion, and that therefore in the long run it cannot subsist if the men who form it and the methods they apply are not accepted by the majority of those ruled. If the conduct of political affairs does not suit them, the citizens will finally succeed in overthrowing the government by violent action and in replacing the rulers by men deemed more competent. The rulers are always a minority. They cannot stay in office if the majority is determined to turn them out. Revolution and civil war are the ultimate remedy for unpopular rule. For the sake of domestic peace, liberalism aims at democratic government. Democracy is therefore not a revolutionary institution. On the contrary, it is the very means of preventing revolutions. Democracy is a system providing for the peaceful adjustment of government to the will of the majority.

When the men in office and their methods no longer please the majority of the nation, they will—in the next election—be eliminated, and replaced by other men and another system. Democracy aims at safeguarding peace within the country and among the citizens.

The goal of liberalism is the peaceful coöperation of all men. It aims at peace among nations too. When there is private ownership of the means of production everywhere and when the laws, the tribunals, and the administration treat foreigners and citizens on equal terms, it is of little importance where a country's frontiers are drawn. Nobody can derive any profit from conquest, but many can suffer losses from fighting. War no longer pays; there is no motive for aggression. The population of every territory is free to determine to which state it wishes to belong, or whether it prefers to establish a state of its own. All nations can coexist peacefully, because no nation is concerned about the size of its state.

This is, of course, a very cool and dispassionate plea for peace and democracy. It is the outcome of a utilitarian philosophy. It is as far from the mystical mythology of the divine right of kings as it is from the metaphysics of natural law or the natural and imprescriptible rights of man. It is founded upon considerations of common utility. Freedom, democracy, peace, and private property are deemed good because they are the best means for promoting human happiness and welfare. Liberalism wants to secure to man a life free from fear and want. That is all.

About the middle of the nineteenth century liberals were convinced that they were on the eve of the realization of their plans. It was an illusion.

IV. SOCIALISM

Socialism aims at a social system based on public ownership of the means of production. In a socialist community all material resources are owned and operated by the government. This implies that the government is the only employer, and that no one can consume more than the government allots to him. The term "state socialism" is pleonastic; socialism is necessarily always state socialism. Planning is nowadays a popular synonym for socialism. Until 1917 communism and socialism were usually used as synonyms. The fundamental document of Marxian socialism, which all socialist parties united in the different International Working Men's Associations considered and still consider the eternal and unalterable gospel of socialism, is entitled the *Communist Manifesto.* Since the ascendancy of Russian Bolshevism most people differentiate between communism and socialism. But this differentiation refers only to political tactics. Present-day communists and socialists disagree only in respect to the methods to be applied for the achievement of ends which are common to both.

The German Marxian socialists called their party the Social Democrats. It was believed that socialism was compatible with democratic government—indeed that the program of democracy could be fully realized only within a socialist community. In Western Europe and in America this opinion is still current. In spite of all the experience which events since 1917 have provided, many cling stubbornly to the belief that true democracy and true socialism are identical. Russia, the classical country of dictatorial oppression, is considered democratic because it is socialist.

However, the Marxians' love of democratic institutions was a strategem only, a pious fraud for the deception of the masses.* Within a socialist community there is no room left for freedom. There can be no freedom of the press where the government owns every printing office. There can be no free choice of profession or trade where the government is the only employer and assigns everyone the task he must fulfill. There can be no freedom to settle where one chooses when the government has the power to fix one's place of work. There can be no real freedom of scientific research where the government owns all the libraries, archives, and laboratories and has the right to send anyone to a place where he cannot continue his investigations. There can be no freedom in art and literature where the government determines who shall create them. There can be neither freedom of conscience nor of speech where the government has the power to remove any opponent to a climate which is detrimental to his health, or to assign him duties which surpass his strength and ruin him both physically and intellectually. In a socialist community the individual citizen can have no more freedom than a soldier in the army or an inmate in an orphanage.

But, object the socialists, the socialist commonwealth differs in this essential respect from such organizations: the inhabitants have the right to choose the government. They forget, however, that the right to vote becomes a sham in a socialist state. The citizens have no sources of information but those provided by the government. The press, the radio, and the meeting halls are in the hands of the

*Bukharin, *Program of the Communists (Bolshevists),* p. 29.

administration. No party of opposition can be organized or can propagate its ideas. We have only to look
to Russia or Germany to discover the true meaning
of elections and plebiscites under socialism.

The conduct of economic affairs by a socialist government cannot be checked by the vote of parliamentary bodies or by the control of the citizens.
Economic enterprises and investments are designed
for long periods. They require many years for prepa-
ration and realization; their fruits ripen late. If a
penal law has been promulgated in May, it can be
repealed without harm or loss in October. If a minister of foreign affairs has been appointed, he can be
discharged a few months later. But if industrial investments have been once started, it is necessary to
cling to the undertaking until it is achieved and to
exploit the plant erected as long as it seems profitable. To change the original plan would be wasteful.
This necessarily implies that the personnel of the
government cannot be easily disposed of. Those who
made the plan must execute it. They must later operate the plants erected, because others cannot take
over the responsibility for their proper management. People who once agree to the famous four- and
five-year plans virtually abandon their right to
change the system and the personnel of government
not only for the duration of four or five years but for
the following years too, in which the planned investments have to be utilized. Consequently a socialist
government must stay in office for an indefinite period. It is no longer the executor of the nation's will;
it cannot be discharged without sensible detriment if
its actions no longer suit the people. It has irrevocable powers. It becomes an authority above the people; it thinks and acts for the community in its own

right and does not tolerate interference with "its own business" by outsiders.*

The entrepreneur in a capitalist society depends upon the market and upon the consumers. He has to obey the orders which the consumers transmit to him by their buying or failure to buy, and the mandate with which they have charged him can be revoked at any hour. Every entrepreneur and every owner of means of production must daily justify his social function through subservience to the wants of the consumers.

The management of a socialist economy is not under the necessity of adjusting itself to the operation of a market. It has an absolute monopoly. It does not depend on the wants of the consumers. It itself decides what must be done. It does not serve the consumers as the businessman does. It provides for them as the father provides for his children or the headmaster of a school for the students. It is the authority bestowing favors, not a businessman eager to attract customers. The salesman thanks the customer for patronizing his shop and asks him to come again. But the socialists say: Be grateful to Hitler, render thanks to Stalin; be nice and submissive, then the great man will be kind to you later too.

The prime means of democratic control of the administration is the budget. Not a clerk may be appointed, not a pencil bought, if Parliament has not made an allotment. The government must account for every penny spent. It is unlawful to exceed the allotment or to spend it for other purposes than those fixed by Parliament. Such restrictions are impracticable for the management of plants, mines, farms,

*Hayek, *Freedom and the Economic System* (Chicago, 1939), pp. 10 ff.

and transportation systems. Their expenditure must be adjusted to the changing conditions of the moment. You cannot fix in advance how much is to be spent to clear fields of weeds or to remove snow from railroad tracks. This must be decided on the spot according to circumstances. Budget control by the people's representatives, the most effective weapon of democratic government, disappears in a socialist state.

Thus socialism must lead to the dissolution of democracy. The sovereignty of the consumers and the democracy of the market are the characteristic features of the capitalist system. Their corollary in the realm of politics is the people's sovereignty and democratic control of government. Pareto, Georges Sorel, Lenin, Hitler, and Mussolini were right in denouncing democracy as a capitalist method. Every step which leads from capitalism toward planning is necessarily a step nearer to absolutism and dictatorship.

The advocates of socialism who are keen enough to realize this tell us that liberty and democracy are worthless for the masses. People, they say, want food and shelter; they are ready to renounce freedom and self-determination to obtain more and better bread by submitting to a competent paternal authority. To this the old liberals used to reply that socialism will not improve but on the contrary will impair the standard of living of the masses. For socialism is a less efficient system of production than capitalism. But this rejoinder also failed to silence the champions of socialism. Granted, many of them replied, that socialism may not result in riches for all but rather in a smaller production of wealth; nevertheless the masses will be happier under socialism, because they will share their worries with all their fellow citizens, and here will not be wealthier classes to be envied by poorer ones. The starving and ragged workers of Soviet Russia, they tell us, are a thousand times more joyful than the workers of the West who live under conditions which are luxurious compared to Russian standards; equality in poverty is a more satisfactory state than well-being where there are people who can flaunt more luxuries than the average man.

Such debates are vain because they miss the central point. It is useless to discuss the alleged advantages of socialist management. Complete socialism is simply impracticable; it is not at all a system of production; it results in chaos and frustration.

The fundamental problem of socialism is the problem of economic calculation. Production within a system of division of labor, and thereby social coöperation, requires methods for the computation of expenditures asked for by different thinkable and possible ways of achieving ends. In capitalist society market prices are the units of this calculation. But within a system where all factors of production are owned by the state there is no market, and consequently there are no prices for these factors. Thus it becomes impossible for the managers of a socialist community to calculate. They cannot know whether what they are planning and achieving is reasonable or not. They have no means of finding out which of the various methods of production under consideration is the most advantageous. They cannot find a genuine basis of comparison between quantities of different material factors of production and of different services; so they cannot compare the outlays necessary with the anticipated outputs. Such comparisons need a common unit; and there is no such unit available but that provided by the price system of the market. The socialist managers cannot know whether the construction of a new railroad line is more advantageous than the construction of a new motor road. And if they have once decided on the construction of a railroad, they cannot know which of many possible routes it should cover. Under a system of private ownership money calculations are used to solve such problems. But no such calculation is possible by comparing various classes of expenditures and incomes in kind. It is out of the question to reduce to a common unit the quantities of various kinds of skilled and unskilled labor, iron, coal, building materials of different types, machinery, and everything else that the building, the upkeep, and the operation of railroads necessitates. But without such a common unit it is impossible to make these plans the subject of economic calculations. Planning requires that all the commodities and services which we have to take into account can be reduced to money. The management of a socialist community would be in a position like that of a ship captain who had to cross the ocean with the stars shrouded by a fog and without the aid of a compass or other equipment of nautical orientation.

Socialism as a universal mode of production is impracticable because it is impossible to make economic calculations within a socialist system. The choice for mankind is not between two economic systems. It is between capitalism and chaos.

V. SOCIALISM IN RUSSIA AND IN GERMANY

The attempts of the Russian Bolsheviks and of the German Nazis to transform socialism from a program into reality have not had to meet the problem of economic calculation under socialism. These two socialist systems have been working within a world the greater part of which still clings to a market economy. The rulers of these socialist states base the calculations on which they make their decisions on the prices established abroad. Without the help of these prices their actions would be aimless and planless. Only in so far as they refer to this price system are they able to calculate, keep books, and prepare their plans. With this fact in mind we may agree with the statement of various socialist authors and politicians that socialism in only one or a few countries is not yet true socialism. Of course these men attach a quite different meaning to their assertions. They are trying to say that the full blessings of socialism can be reaped only in a world-embracing socialist community. The rest of us, on the contrary, must recognize that socialism will result in complete chaos precisely if it is applied in the greater part of the world.

The German and the Russian systems of socialism have in common the fact that the government has full control of the means of production. It decides what shall be produced and how. It allots to each individual a share of consumer's goods for his consumption. These systems would not have to be called socialist if it were otherwise.

But there is a difference between the two systems —though it does not concern the essential features of socialism.

The Russian pattern of socialism is purely bureaucratic. All economic enterprises are departments of the government, like the administration of the army or the postal system. Every plant, shop, or farm stands in the same relation to the superior central organization as does a post office to the office of the postmaster general.

The German pattern differs from the Russian one in that it (seemingly and nominally) maintains private ownership of the means of production and keeps the appearance of ordinary prices, wages, and markets. There are, however, no longer entrepreneurs but only shop managers *(Betriebsführer)*. These shop managers do the buying and selling, pay the workers, contract debts, and pay interest and amortization. There is no labor market; wages and salaries are fixed by the government. The government tells the shop managers what and how to produce, at what prices and from whom to buy, at what prices and to whom to sell. The government decrees to whom and under what terms the capitalists must entrust their funds and where and at what wages laborers must work. Market exchange is only a sham. All the prices, wages, and interest rates are fixed by the central authority. They are prices, wages, and interest rates in appearance only; in reality they are merely determinations of quantity relations in the government's orders. The government, not the consumers, directs production. This is socialism in the outward guise of capitalism. Some labels of capitalistic market economy are retained but they mean something entirely different from what they mean in a genuine market economy.

The execution of the pattern in each country is not so rigid as not to allow for some concessions to the other pattern. There are, in Germany too, plants and shops directly managed by government clerks; there is especially the national railroad system; there are the government's coal mines and the national telegraph and telephone lines. Most of these institutions are remnants of the nationalization carried out by the previous governments under the regime of German militarism. In Russia, on the other hand, there are some seemingly independent shops and farms left. But these exceptions do not alter the general characteristics of the two systems.

It is not an accident that Russia adopted the bureaucratic pattern and Germany the *Zwangswirtschaft* pattern. Russia is the largest country in the world and is thinly inhabited. Within its borders it has the richest resources. It is much better endowed by nature than any other country. It can without too great harm to the well-being of its population renounce foreign trade and live in economic self-sufficiency. But for the obstacles which Czarism first put in the way of capitalist production, and for the later shortcomings of the Bolshevik system, the Russians even without foreign trade could have long enjoyed the highest standard of living in the world. In such a country the application of the bureaucratic system of production is not impossible, provided the management is in a position to use for economic calculation the prices fixed on the markets of foreign capitalist countries, and to apply the techniques developed by the enterprise of foreign capitalism. Under these circumstances socialism results not in complete chaos but only in extreme poverty. A few years ago in the Ukraine, the most fertile land of Europe, many millions literally died of starvation.

In a predominantly industrial country conditions are different. The characteristic feature of a predominantly industrial country is that its population must live to a great extent on imported food and imported raw materials.* It must pay for these im-

---

*The United States, although the country with the most efficient and greatest industry, is not a *predominantly* industrial country, as it enjoys an equilibrium between its processing industries and its production of food and raw materials.

ports by the export of manufactured goods, which it produces mainly from imported raw materials. Its vital strength lies in its factories and in its foreign trade. Jeopardizing the efficiency of industrial production is equivalent to imperiling the basis of sustenance. If the plants produce worse or at higher cost they cannot compete in the world market, where they must outdo commodities of foreign origin. If exports drop, imports of food and other necessities drop correspondingly; the nation loses its main source of living.

Now Germany is a predominantly industrial country. It did very well when, in the years preceding the first World War, its entrepreneurs steadily expanded their exports. There was no other country in Europe in which the standard of living of the masses improved faster than in imperial Germany. For German socialism there could be no question of imitating the Russian model. To have attempted this would have immediately destroyed the apparatus of German export trade. It would have suddenly plunged into misery a nation pampered by the achievements of capitalism. Bureaucrats cannot meet the competition of foreign markets; they flourish only where they are sheltered by the state, with its compulsion and coercion. Thus the German socialists were forced to take recourse to the methods which they called German socialism. These methods, it is true, are much less efficient than that of private initiative. But they are much more efficient than the bureaucratic system of the Soviets.

This German system has an additional advantage.

On the other hand Austria, whose industry is small compared with that of America, is predominantly industrial because it depends to a great extent on the import of food and raw materials and must export almost half of its industrial output.

The German capitalists and the Betriebsführer, the former entrepreneurs, do not believe in the eternity of the Nazi regime. They are, on the contrary, convinced that the rule of Hitler will collapse one day and that then they will be restored to the ownership of the plants which in pre-Nazi days were their property. They remember that in the first World War too the Hindenburg program had virtually dispossessed them, and that with the breakdown of the imperial government they were *de facto* reinstated. They believe that it will happen again. They are therefore very careful in the operation of the plants whose nominal owners and shop managers they are. They do their best to prevent waste and to maintain the capital invested. It is only thanks to these selfish interests of the Betriebsführer that German socialism secured an adequate production of armaments, planes, and ships.

Socialism would be impracticable altogether if established as a world-wide system of production, and thus deprived of the possibility of making economic calculations. When confined to one or a few countries in the midst of a world capitalist economy it is only an inefficient system. And of the two patterns for its realization the German is less inefficient than the Russian one.

VI. INTERVENTIONISM

All civilizations have up to now been based on private ownership of the means of production. In the past civilization and private ownership have been linked together. If history could teach us anything, it would be that private property is inextricably linked with civilization.

Governments have always looked askance at private property. Governments are never liberal from inclination. It is in the nature of the men handling the apparatus of compulsion and coercion to overrate its power to work, and to strive at subduing all spheres of human life to its immediate influence. Etatism is the occupational disease of rulers, warriors, and civil servants. Governments become liberal only when forced to by the citizens.

From time immemorial governments have been eager to interfere with the working of the market mechanism. Their endeavors have never attained the ends sought. People used to attribute these failures to the inefficacy of the measures applied and to the leniency of their enforcement. What was wanted, they thought, was more energy and more brutality; then success would be assured. Not until the eighteenth century did men begin to understand that interventionism is necessarily doomed to fail. The classical economists demonstrated that each constellation of the market has a corresponding price structure. Prices, wages, and interest rates are the result of the interplay of demand and supply. There are forces operating in the market which tend to restore this—natural—state if it is disturbed. Government decrees, instead of achieving the particular ends they seek, tend only to derange the working of the market and imperil the satisfaction of the needs of the consumers.

In defiance of economic science the very popular doctrine of modern interventionism asserts that there is a system of economic coöperation, feasible as a permanent form of economic organization, which is neither capitalism nor socialism. This third system is conceived as an order based on private ownership of the means of production in which, however, the government intervenes, by orders and prohibitions, in the exercise of ownership rights. It is claimed that this system of interventionism is as far from socialism as it is from capitalism; that it offers a third solution of the problem of social organization; that it stands midway between socialism and capitalism; and that while retaining the advantages of both it escapes the disadvantages inherent in each of them. Such are the pretensions of interventionism as advocated by the older German school of etatism, by the American Institutionalists, and by many groups in other countries. Interventionism is practiced—except for socialist countries like Russia and Nazi Germany—by every contemporary government. The outstanding examples of interventionist policies are the *Sozialpolitik* of imperial Germany and the New Deal policy of present-day America.

Marxians do not support interventionism. They recognize the correctness of the teachings of economics concerning the frustration of interventionist measures. In so far as some Marxian doctrinaires have recommended interventionism they have done so because they consider it an instrument for paralyzing and destroying the capitalist economy, and hope thereby to accelerate the coming of socialism. But the consistent orthodox Marxians scorn interventionism as idle reformism detrimental to the interests of the proletarians. They do not expect to bring about the socialist utopia by hampering the evolution of capitalism; on the contrary, they believe that only a full development of the productive forces of capitalism can result in socialism. Consistent Marxians abstain from doing anything to interfere with what they deem to be the *natural* evolution of capitalism. But consistency is a very rare quality among Marxians. So most Marxian parties and the trade-unions operated by Marxians are enthusiastic in their support of interventionism.

A mixture of capitalist and socialist principles is not feasible. If, within a society based on private ownership of the means of production, some of these means are publicly owned and operated, this does not make for a mixed system which combines socialism and capitalism. The enterprises owned and operated by the state or by municipalities do not alter the characteristic features of a market economy. They must fit themselves, as buyers of raw materials, of equipment and of labor, and as sellers of goods and services, into the scheme of the market economy. They are subject to the laws determining production for the needs of consumers. They must strive for profits or, at least, to avoid losses. When the government tries to eliminate or to mitigate this dependence by covering the losses of its plants and shops by drawing on the public funds, the only result is that this dependence is shifted to another field. The means for covering the losses must be raised by the imposition of taxes. But this taxation has its effect on the market. It is the working of the market mechanism, and not the government collecting the taxes, that decides upon whom the incidence of the taxes falls and how it affects production and consumption. The market, not the government, determines the working of those publicly operated enterprises.

Nor should interventionism be confused with the German pattern of socialism. It is the essential feature of interventionism that it does not aim at a total abolition of the market; it does not want to reduce private ownership to a sham and the entrepreneurs to the status of shop managers. The interventionist government does not want to do away with private enterprise; it wants only to regulate its working through isolated measures of interference. Such measures are not designed as cogs in an all-round system of orders and prohibitions destined to control the whole apparatus of production and distribution; they do not aim at replacing private ownership and a market economy by socialist planning.

In order to grasp the meaning and the effects of interventionism it is sufficient to study the working of the two most important types of intervention: interference by restriction and interference by price control.

Interference by restriction aims directly at a diversion of production from the channels prescribed by the market and the consumers. The government either forbids the manufacture of certain goods or the application of certain methods of production, or makes such methods more difficult by the imposition of taxes or penalties. It thus eliminates some of the means available for the satisfaction of human needs. The best-known examples are import duties and other trade barriers. It is obvious that all such measures make the people as a whole poorer, not richer. They prevent men from using their knowledge and ability, their labor and material resources as efficiently as they can. In the unhampered market forces are at work tending to utilize every means of production in a way that provides for the highest satisfaction of human wants. The interference of the government brings about a different employment of resources and thereby impairs the supply.

We do not need to ask here whether some restrictive measures could not be justified, in spite of the diminution of supply they cause, by advantages in other fields. We do not need to discuss the problem of whether the disadvantage of raising the price of bread by an import duty on wheat is outweighed by the increase in income of domestic farmers. It is enough for our purpose to realize that restrictive measures cannot be considered as measures of increasing wealth and welfare, but are instead expenditures. They are, like subsidies which the government pays out of the revenue collected by taxing the citizens, not measures of production policy but measures of spending. They are not parts of a system of creating wealth but a method of consuming it.

The aim of price control is to decree prices, wages, and interest rates different from those fixed by the market. Let us first consider the case of maximum prices, where the government tries to enforce prices lower than the market prices.

The prices set on the unhampered market correspond to an equilibrium of demand and supply. Everybody who is ready to pay the market price can buy as much as he wants to buy. Everybody who is ready to sell at the market price can sell as much as he wants to sell. If the government, without a corresponding increase in the quantity of goods available for sale, decrees that buying and selling must be done at a lower price, and thus makes it illegal either to ask or to pay the potential market price, then this equilibrium can no longer prevail. With unchanged supply there are now more potential buyers on the market, namely, those who could not afford the higher market price but are prepared to buy at the lower official rate. There are now potential buyers who cannot buy, although they are ready to pay the price fixed by the government or even a higher price.

The price is no longer the means of segregating those potential buyers who may buy from those who may not. A different principle of selection has come into operation. Those who come first can buy; others are too late in the field. The visible outcome of this state of things is the sight of housewives and children standing in long lines before the groceries, a spectacle familiar to everybody who has visited Europe in this age of price control. If the government does not want only those to buy who come first (or who are personal friends of the salesman), while others go home empty handed, it must regulate the distribution of the stocks available. It has to introduce some kind of rationing.

But price ceilings not only fail to increase the supply, they reduce it. Thus they do not attain the ends which the authorities wish. On the contrary, they result in a state of things which from the point of view of the government and of public opinion is even less desirable than the previous state which they had intended to alter. If the government wants to make it possible for the poor to give their children more milk, it has to buy the milk at the market price and sell it to these poor parents with a loss, at a cheaper rate. The loss may be covered by taxation. But if the government simply fixes the price of milk at a lower rate than the market, the result will be the contrary of what it wants. The marginal producers, those with the highest costs, will, in order to avoid losses, go out of the business of producing and selling milk. They will use their cows and their skill for other, more profitable purposes. They will, for example, produce cheese, butter, or meat. There will be less milk available for the consumers, not more. Then the government has to choose between two alternatives: either to refrain from any endeavors to control the price of milk and to abrogate its decree, or to add to its first measure a second one. In the latter case it must fix the prices of the factors of production necessary for the production of milk at such a rate that the marginal producers will no longer suffer losses and will abstain from restricting the output. But then the same problem repeats itself on a remoter plane. The supply of the factors of production necessary for the production of milk drops, and again the government is back where it started, facing failure in its interference. If it keeps stubbornly on pushing forward its schemes, it has to go still further. It has to fix the prices of the factors of production necessary for the production of those factors of production which are needed for the production of milk. Thus the government is forced to go further and further, fixing the prices of all consumer goods and of all factors of production—both human (i.e., labor) and material— and to force every entrepreneur and every worker to continue work at these prices and wages. No branch of industry can be omitted from this all-round fixing of prices and wages and from this general order to produce those quantities which the government wants to see produced. If some branches were to be left free, the result would be a shifting of capital and labor to them and a corresponding fall of the supply of goods whose prices the government has fixed. However, it is precisely these goods which the government considers especially important for the satisfaction of the needs of the masses.*

But when this state of all-round control of business

---

*For the two situations in which price-control measures can be used effectively within a narrowly confined sphere, the reader is referred to Mises' *Nationalökonomie,* pp. 674–675.

is achieved, the market economy has been replaced by the German pattern of socialist planning. The government's board of production management now exclusively controls all business activities and decides how the means of production—men and material resources—must be used.

The isolated measures of price fixing fail to attain the ends sought. In fact, they produce effects contrary to those aimed at by the government. If the government, in order to eliminate these inexorable and unwelcome consequences, pursues its course further and further, it finally transforms the system of capitalism and free enterprise into socialism.

Many American and British supporters of price control are fascinated by the alleged success of Nazi price control. They believe that the German experience has proved the practicability of price control within the framework of a system of market economy. You have only to be as energetic, impetuous, and brutal as the Nazis are, they think, and you will succeed. These men who want to fight Nazism by adopting its methods do not see that what the Nazis have achieved has been the building up of a system of socialism, not a reform of conditions within a system of market economy.

There is no third system between a market economy and socialism. Mankind has to choose between those two systems—unless chaos is considered an alternative.†

It is the same when the government takes recourse to minimum prices. Practically the most important case of fixing prices at a higher level than the established on the unhampered market is the case of

---

†We pass over the fact that, because of the impossibility of economic calculation under it, socialism too must result in chaos.

minimum wages. In some countries minimum wage rates are decreed directly by the government. The governments of other countries interfere only indirectly with wages. They give a free hand to the labor unions by acquiescing in the use of compulsion and coercion by unions against reluctant employers and employees. If it were otherwise strikes would not attain the ends which the trade-unions want to attain. The strike would fail to force the employer to grant higher wages than those fixed by the unhampered market, if he were free to employ men to take the place of the strikers. The essence of labor-union policy today is the application or threat of violence under the benevolent protection of the government. The unions represent, therefore, a vital part of the state apparatus of compulsion and coercion. Their fixing of minimum wage rates is equivalent to a government intervention establishing minimum wages.

The labor unions succeed in forcing the entrepreneurs to grant higher wages. But the result of their endeavors is not what people usually ascribe to them. The artificially elevated wage rates cause permanent unemployment of a considerable part of the potential labor force. At these higher rates the marginal employments for labor are no longer profitable. The entrepreneurs are forced to restrict output, and the demand on the labor market drops. The unions seldom bother about this inevitable result of their activities; they are not concerned with the fate of those who are not members of their brotherhood. But it is different for the government, which aims at the increase of the welfare of the whole people and wants to benefit not only union members but all those who have lost their jobs. The government wants to raise the income of all workers; that a great many of them cannot find employment is contrary to its intentions.

These dismal effects of minimum wages have become more and more apparent the more trade-unionism has prevailed. As long as only one part of labor, mostly skilled workers, was unionized, the wage rise achieved by the unions did not lead to unemployment but to an increased supply of labor in those branches of business where there were no efficient unions or no unions at all. The workers who lost their jobs as a consequence of union policy entered the market of the free branches and caused wages to drop in those branches. The corollary of the rise in wages for organized workers was a drop in wages for unorganized workers. But with the spread of unionism conditions have changed. Workers now losing their jobs in one branch of industry find it harder to get employment in other lines. They are victimized.

There is unemployment even in the absence of any government or union interference. But in an unhampered labor market there prevails a tendency to make unemployment disappear. The fact that the unemployed are looking for jobs must result in fixing wage rates at a height which makes it possible for the entrepreneurs to employ all those eager to work and to earn wages. But if minimum wage rates prevent an adjustment of wage rates to the conditions of demand and supply, unemployment tends to become a permanent mass phenomenon.

There is but one means to make market wage rates rise for all those eager to work: an increase in the amount of capital goods available which makes it possible to improve technological methods of production and thereby to raise the marginal productivity of labor. It is a sad fact that a great war, in destroying a part of the stock of capital goods, must result in a temporary fall in real wage rates, when the shortage of man power brought about by the enlistment of millions of men is once overcome. It is precisely because they are fully aware of this undesirable consequence that liberals consider war not only a political but also an economic disaster.

Government spending is not an appropriate means to brush away unemployment. If the government finances its spending by collecting taxes or by borrowing from the public, it curtails the private citizens' power to invest and to spend to the same extent that it increases its own spending capacity. If the government finances its spending by inflationary methods (issue of additional paper money or borrowing from the commercial banks) it brings about a general rise of commodity prices. If then *money wage rates* do not rise at all or not to the same extent as commodity prices, mass unemployment may disappear. But it disappears precisely because *real wage rates* have dropped.

Technological progress increases the productivity of human effort. The same amount of capital and labor can now produce more than before. A surplus of capital and labor becomes available for the expansion of already existing industries and for the development of new ones. "Technological unemployment" may occur as a transitory phenomenon. But very soon the unemployed will find new jobs either in the new industries or in the expanding old ones. Many millions of workers are today employed in industries which were created in the last decades. And the wage earners themselves are the main buyers of the products of these new industries.

There is but one remedy for lasting unemployment of great masses: the abandonment of the policy of raising wage rates by government decree or by the application of the threat of violence.

Those who advocate interventionism because they want to sabotage capitalism and thereby finally to achieve socialism are at least consistent. They know what they are aiming at. But those who do not wish to replace private property by German Zwangswirtschaft or Russian Bolshevism are sadly mistaken in recommending price control and labor-union compulsion.

The more cautious and sophisticated supporters of interventionism are keen enough to recognize that government interference with business fails in the long run to attain the ends sought. But, they assert, what is needed is immediate action, a short-run policy. Interventionism is good because its immediate effects are beneficial, even if its remoter consequences may be disastrous. Do not bother about tomorrow; only today counts. With regard to this attitude two points must be emphasized: (1) today, after years and decades of interventionist policies, we are already confronted with the long-run consequences of interventionism; (2) wage interventionism is bound to fail even in the short run, if not accompanied by corresponding measures of protectionism.

VII. ETATISM AND PROTECTIONISM

Etatism—whether interventionism or socialism—is a national policy. The national governments of various countries adopt it. Their concern is whatever they consider favors the interests of their own nations. They are not troubled about the fate or the happiness of foreigners. They are free from any inhibitions which would prevent them from inflicting harm on aliens.

We have dealt already with how the policies of etatism hurt the well-being of the whole nation and even of the groups or classes which they are intended to benefit. For the purpose of this book it is still more important to emphasize that no national system of etatism can work within a world of free trade. Etatism and free trade in international relations are incompatible, not only in the long run but even in the short run. Etatism must be accompanied by measures severing the connections of the domestic market with foreign markets. Modern protectionism, with its tendency to make every country economically self-sufficient as far as possible, is inextricably linked with interventionism and its inherent tendency to turn into socialism. Economic nationalism is the unavoidable outcome of etatism.

In the past various doctrines and considerations induced governments to embark upon a policy of protectionism. Economics has exposed all these arguments as fallacious. Nobody tolerably familiar with economic theory dares today to defend these long since unmasked errors. They still play an important role in popular discussion; they are the preferred theme of demagogic fulminations; but they have nothing to do with present-day protectionism. Present-day protectionism is a necessary corollary of the domestic policy of government interference with business. Interventionism begets economic nationalism. It thus kindles the antagonisms resulting in war. An abandonment of economic nationalism is not feasible if nations cling to interference with business. Free trade in international relations requires domestic free trade. This is fundamental to any understanding of contemporary international relations.

It is obvious that all interventionist measures aiming at a rise in domestic prices for the benefit of domestic producers, and all measures whose immediate effect consists in a rise in domestic costs of production, would be frustrated if foreign products were not either barred altogether from competition on the domestic market or penalized when imported. When, other things being unchanged, labor legislation succeeds in shortening the hours of work or in imposing on the employer in another way additional burdens to the advantage of the employees, the immediate effect is a rise in production costs. Foreign producers can compete under more favorable conditions, both on the home market and abroad, than they could before.

The acknowledgment of this fact has long since given impetus to the idea of equalizing labor legislation in different countries. These plans have taken on more definite form since the international conference called by the German Government in 1890. They led finally in 1919 to the establishment of the International Labor Office in Geneva. The results obtained were rather meager. The only efficient way to equalize labor conditions all over the world would be freedom of migration. But it is precisely this which unionized labor of the better-endowed and comparatively underpopulated countries fights with every means available.

The workers of those countries where natural conditions of production are more favorable and the population is comparatively thin enjoy the advantages of a higher marginal productivity of labor.

They get higher wages and have a higher standard of living. They are eager to protect their advantageous position by barring or restricting immigration.* On the other hand, they denounce as "dumping" the competition of goods produced abroad by foreign labor remunerated at a lower scale; and they ask for protection against the importation of such goods.

The countries which are comparatively over-populated—i.e., in which the marginal productivity of labor is lower than in other countries—have but one means to compete with the more favored countries: lower wages and a lower standard of living. Wage rates are lower in Hungary and in Poland than in Sweden or in Canada because the natural resources are poorer and the population is greater in respect to them. This fact cannot be disposed of by an international agreement, or by the interference of an international labor office. The average standard of living is lower in Japan than in the United States because the same amount of labor produces less in Japan than in the United States.

Such being the conditions, the goal of international agreements concerning labor legislation and trade-union policies cannot be the equalization of wage rates, hours of work, or other such "pro-labor" measures. Their only aim could be to coördinate these things so that no changes in the previously prevailing conditions of competition resulted. If, for example, American laws or trade-union policies re-

---

*Many Americans are not familiar with the fact that, in the years between the two world wars, almost all European nations had recourse to very strict anti-immigration laws. These laws were more rigid than the American laws, since most of them did not provide for any immigration quotas. Every nation was eager to protect its wage level—a low one when compared with American conditions—against the immigration of men from other countries in which wage rates were still lower. The result was mutual hatred and—in face of a threatening common danger—disunion.

sulted in a 5 per cent rise in construction costs, it would be necessary to find out how much this increased the cost of production in the various branches of industry in which America and Japan are competing or could compete if the relation of production costs changed. Then it would be necessary to investigate what kind of measures could burden Japanese production to such an extent that no change in the competitive power of both nations would take place. It is obvious that such calculations would be extremely difficult. Experts would disagree with regard both to the methods to be used and the probable results. But even if this were not the case an agreement could not be reached. For it is contrary to the interests of Japanese workers to adopt such measures of compensation. It would be more advantageous for them to expand their export sales to the disadvantage of American exports; thus the demand for their labor would rise and the condition of Japanese workers improve effectively. Guided by this idea, Japan would be ready to minimize the rise in production costs effected by the American measures and would be reluctant to adopt compensatory measures. It is chimerical to expect that international agreements concerning socio-economic policies could be substituted for protectionism.

We must realize that practically every new pro-labor measure forced on employers results in higher costs of production and thereby in a change in the conditions of competition. If it were not for protectionism such measures would immediately fail to attain the ends sought. They would result only in a restriction of domestic production and consequently in an increase of unemployment. The unemployed could find jobs only at lower wage rates; if they were not prepared to acquiesce in this solution they would remain unemployed. Even narrow-minded people would realize that economic laws are inexorable, and that government interference with business cannot attain its ends but must result in a state of affairs which—from the point of view of the government and the supporters of its policy—is even less desirable than the conditions which it was designed to alter.

Protectionism, of course, cannot brush away the unavoidable consequences of interventionism. It can only improve conditions in appearance; it can only conceal the true state of affairs. Its aim is to raise domestic prices. The higher prices provide a compensation for the rise in costs of production. The worker does not suffer a cut in money wages but he has to pay more for the goods he wants to buy. As far as the home market is concerned the problem is seemingly settled.

But this brings us to a new problem: monopoly.

VIII. ECONOMIC NATIONALISM AND DOMESTIC MONOPOLY PRICES

The aim of the protective tariff is to undo the undesired consequences of the rise in domestic costs of production caused by government interference. The purpose is to preserve the competitive power of domestic industries in spite of the rise in costs of production.

However, the mere imposition of an import duty can attain this end only in the case of those commodities whose domestic production falls short of domestic demand. With industries producing more than is needed for domestic consumption a tariff alone would be futile unless supplemented by monopoly.

In an industrial European country, for example Germany, an import duty on wheat raises the domestic price to the level of the world market price plus the import duty. Although the rise in the domestic wheat price results in an expansion of domestic production on the one hand and a restriction of domestic consumption on the other hand, imports are still necessary for the satisfaction of domestic demand. As the costs of the marginal wheat dealer include both the world market price and the import duty, the domestic price goes up to this height.

It is different with those commodities that Germany produces in such quantities that a part can be exported. A German import duty on manufactures which Germany produces not only for the domestic market but for export too would be, as far as export trade is concerned, a futile measure to compensate for a rise in domestic costs of production. It is true that it would prevent foreign manufacturers from selling on the German market. But export trade must continue to be hampered by the rise in domestic production costs. On the other hand the competition between the domestic producers on the home market would eliminate those German plants in which production no longer paid with the rise in costs due to government interference. At the new equilibrium the domestic price would reach the level of the world market price plus a part of the import duty. Domestic consumption would now be lower than it was before the rise in domestic production costs and the imposition of the import duty. The restriction of domestic consumption and the falling off of exports mean a shrinking of production with consequent unemployment and an increased pressure on the labor market resulting in a drop in wage rates. The failure of the Sozialpolitik becomes manifest.*

But there is still another way out. The fact that the import duty has insulated the domestic market provides domestic producers with the opportunity to build up a monopolistic scheme. They can form a cartel and charge the domestic consumers monopoly prices which can go up to a level only slightly lower than the world market price plus the import duty. With their domestic monopoly profits they can afford to sell at lower prices abroad. Production goes on. The failure of the Sozialpolitik is skillfully concealed from the eyes of an ignorant public. But the domestic consumers must pay higher prices. What the worker gains by the rise in wage rates and by pro-labor legislation burdens him in his capacity as consumer.

But the government and the trade-union leaders have attained their goal. They can then boast that the entrepreneurs were wrong in predicting that higher wages and more labor legislation would make their plants unprofitable and hamper production.

Marxian myths have succeeded in surrounding the problem of monopoly with empty babble. According to the Marxian doctrines of imperialism, there prevails within an unhampered market society a tendency toward the establishment of monopolies. Monopoly, according to these doctrines, is an evil originating from the operation of the forces working

---

*We need not consider the case of import duties so low that only a few or none of the domestic plants can continue production for the home market. In this case foreign competitors could penetrate the domestic market, and prices would reach the level of the world market price plus the whole import duty. The failure of the tariff would be even more manifest.

in an unhampered capitalism. It is, in the eyes of the reformers, the worst of all drawbacks of the laissez faire system; its existence is the best justification of interventionism; it must be the foremost aim of government interference with business to fight it. One of the most serious consequences of monopoly is that it begets imperialism and war.

There are, it is true, instances in which a monopoly —a world monopoly—of some products could possibly be established without the support of governmental compulsion and coercion. The fact that the natural resources for the production of mercury are very few, for example, might engender a monopoly even in the absence of governmental encouragement. There are instances, again, in which the high cost of transportation makes it possible to establish local monopolies for bulky goods, e.g., for some building materials in places unfavorably located. But this is not the problem with which most people are concerned when discussing monopoly. Almost all the monopolies that are assailed by public opinion and against which governments pretend to fight are government made. They are national monopolies created under the shelter of import duties. They would collapse with a regime of free trade.

The common treatment of the monopoly question is thoroughly mendacious and dishonest. No milder expression can be used to characterize it. It is the aim of the government to raise the domestic price of the commodities concerned above the world market level, in order to safeguard in the short run the operation of its pro-labor policies. The highly developed manufactures of Great Britain, the United States, and Germany would not need any protection against foreign competition were it not for the policies of their own governments in raising costs of domestic production. But these tariff policies, as shown in the case described above, can work only when there is a cartel charging monopoly prices on the domestic market. In the absence of such a cartel domestic production would drop, as foreign producers would have the advantage of producing at lower costs than those due to the new pro-labor measure. A highly developed trade-unionism, supported by what is commonly called "progressive labor legislation," would be frustrated even in the short run if domestic prices were not maintained at a higher level than that of the world market, and if the exporters (if exports are to be continued) were not in a position to compensate the lower export prices out of the monopolistic profits drawn on the home market. Where the domestic cost of production is raised by government interference, or by the coercion and compulsion exercised by trade-unions, export trade will need to be subsidized. The subsidies may be openly granted as such by the government, or they may be disguised by monopoly. In this second case the domestic consumers pay the subsidies in the form of higher prices for the commodities which the monopoly sells at a lower price abroad. If the government were sincere in its antimonopolistic gestures, it could find a very simple remedy. The repeal of the import duty would brush away at one stroke the danger of monopoly. But governments and their friends are eager to raise domestic prices. Their struggle against monopoly is only a sham.

The correctness of the statement that it is the aim of the governments to raise prices can easily be demonstrated by referring to conditions in which the imposition of an import duty does not result in the establishment of a cartel monopoly. The American farmers producing wheat, cotton, and other agricultural products cannot, for technical reasons, form a cartel. Therefore the administration developed a scheme to raise prices through restriction of output and through withholding huge stocks from the market by means of government buying and government loans. The ends arrived at by this policy are a substitute for an infeasible farming cartel and farming monopoly.

No less conspicuous are the endeavors of various governments to create international cartels. If the protective tariff results in the formation of a national cartel, international cartelization could in many cases be attained by agreements between the national cartels. Such agreements are often very well served by another pro-monopoly activity of governments, the patents and other privileges granted to new inventions. However, where technical obstacles prevent the construction of national cartels—as is almost always the case with agricultural production—no such international agreements can be built up. Then the governments interfere again. History between the two world wars is an open record of state intervention to foster monopoly and restriction by international agreements. There were schemes for wheat pools, rubber and tin restrictions, and so on.* Of course, most of them collapsed very quickly.

Such is the true story of modern monopoly. It is not an outcome of unhampered capitalism and of an inherent trend of capitalist evolution, as the Marxians would have us believe. It is, on the contrary, the result of government policies aiming at a reform of market economy.

---

*G. L. Schwartz, "Back to Free Enterprise," *Nineteenth Century and After*, CXXXI (1942), 130.

IX. AUTARKY

Interventionism aims at state control of market conditions. As the sovereignty of the national state is limited to the territory subject to its supremacy and has no jurisdiction outside its boundaries, it considers all kinds of international economic relations as serious obstacles to its policy. The ultimate goal of its foreign trade policy is economic self-sufficiency. The avowed tendency of this policy is, of course, only to reduce imports as far as possible; but as exports have no purpose but to pay for imports, they drop concomitantly.

The striving after economic self-sufficiency is even more violent in the case of socialist governments. In a socialist community production for domestic consumption is no longer directed by the tastes and wishes of the consumers. The central board of production management provides for the domestic consumer according to its own ideas of what serves him best; it *takes care of the people* but it no longer *serves* the consumer. But it is different with production for export. Foreign buyers are not subject to the authorities of the socialist state; they have to be served; their whims and fancies have to be taken into account. The socialist government is sovereign in purveying to the domestic consumers, but in its foreign-trade relations it encounters the sovereignty of the foreign consumer. On foreign markets it has to compete with other producers producing better commodities at lower cost. We have mentioned earlier how the dependence on foreign imports and consequently on exports influences the whole structure of German socialism.

The essential goal of socialist production, according to Marx, is the elimination of the market. As long as a socialist community is still forced to sell a part of its production abroad—whether to foreign socialist governments or to foreign business—it still produces for a market and is subject to the laws of the market economy. A socialist system is defective as such as long as it is not economically self-sufficient.

The international division of labor is a more efficient system of production than is the economic autarky of every nation. The same amount of labor and of material factors of production yields a higher output. This surplus production benefits everyone concerned. Protectionism and autarky always result in shifting production from the centers where conditions are more favorable—i.e., from where the output for the same amount of physical input is higher —to centers where they are less favorable. The more productive resources remain unused while the less productive are utilized. The effect is a general drop in the productivity of human effort, and thereby a lowering of the standard of living all over the world.

The economic consequences of protectionist policies and of the trend toward autarky are the same for all countries. But there are qualitative and quantitative differences. The social and political results are different for comparatively overpopulated industrial countries and for comparatively underpopulated agricultural countries. In the predominantly industrial countries the prices of the most urgently needed foodstuffs are going up. This interferes more and sooner with the well-being of the masses than the corresponding rise in the prices of manufactured goods in the predominantly agricultural countries. Besides, the workers in the industrial countries are in a better position to make their complaints heard than the farmers and farm hands in the agricultural countries. The statesmen and economists of the predominantly industrial countries become frightened. They realize that natural conditions are putting a check on their country's endeavors to replace imports of food and raw materials by domestic production. They clearly understand that the industrial countries of Europe can neither feed nor clothe their population out of domestic products alone. They foresee that the trend toward more protection, more insulation of every country, and finally self-sufficiency will bring about a tremendous fall in the standard of living, if not actual starvation. Thus they look around for remedies.

German aggressive nationalism is animated by these considerations. For more than sixty years German nationalists have been depicting the consequences which the protectionist policies of other nations must eventually have for Germany. Germany, they pointed out, cannot live without importing food and raw materials. How will it pay for these imports when one day the nations producing these materials have succeeded in the development of their domestic manufactures and bar access to German exports? There is, they told themselves, only one redress: We must conquer more dwelling space, more Lebensraum.

The German nationalists are fully aware that many other nations—for example, Belgium—are in the same unfavorable position. But, they say, there is a very important difference. These are small nations. They are therefore helpless. Germany is strong enough to conquer more space. And, happily for Germany, they say today, there are two other powerful nations, which are in the same position as Germany, namely, Italy and Japan. They are the natural allies of Germany in these wars of the have-nots against the haves.

Germany does not aim at autarky because it is eager to wage war. It aims at war because it wants autarky—because it wants to live in economic self-sufficiency.

X. GERMAN PROTECTIONISM

The second German Empire, founded at Versailles in 1871, was not only a powerful nation; it was—in spite of the depression which started in 1873—economically very prosperous. Its industrial plants were extremely successful in competing—abroad and at home—with foreign products. Some grumblers found fault with German manufactures; German goods, they said, were cheap but inferior. But the great foreign demand was precisely for such cheap goods. The masses put more stress upon cheapness than upon fine quality. Whoever wanted to increase sales had to cut prices.

In those optimistic 1870's everybody was fully convinced that Europe was on the eve of a period of peace and prosperity. There were to be no more wars; trade barriers were doomed to disappear; men would be more eager to build up and to produce than to destroy and to kill each other. Of course, far-sighted men could not overlook the fact that Europe's cultural preëminence would slowly vanish. Natural conditions for production were more favorable in overseas countries. Capitalism was on the point of developing the resources of backward nations. Some branches of production would not be able to stand the competition of the newly opened areas. Agricultural production and mining would drop in Europe; Europeans would buy such goods by exporting manufactures. But people did not worry. Intensification of the international division of labor was in their eyes not a disaster but on the contrary a source of richer supply. Free trade was bound to make all nations more flourishing.

The German liberals advocated free trade, the gold standard, and freedom of domestic business. German manufacturing did not need any protection. It triumphantly swept the world market. It would have been nonsensical to bring forward the infant-industry argument. German industry had reached its maturity.

Of course, there were still many countries eager to penalize imports. However, the inference from Ricardo's free-trade argument was irrefutable. Even if all other countries cling to protection, every nation serves its own interest best by free trade. Not for the sake of foreigners but for the sake of their own nation, the liberals advocated free trade. There was the great example set by Great Britain, and by some smaller nations, like Switzerland. These countries did very well with free trade. Should Germany adopt their policies? Or should it imitate half-barbarian nations like Russia?

But Germany chose the second path. This decision was a turning point in modern history.

There are many errors current concerning modern German protectionism.

It is important to recognize first of all that the teachings of Frederick List have nothing to do with modern German protectionism. List did not advocate tariffs for agricultural products. He asked for protection of infant industries. In doing this he underrated the competitive power of contemporary German manufacturing. Even in those days, in the early

1840's, German industrial production was already much stronger than List believed. Thirty to forty years later it was paramount on the European continent and could very successfully compete on the world market. List's doctrines played an important role in the evolution of protectionism in Eastern Europe and in Latin America. But the German supporters of protectionism were not justified in referring to List. He did not unconditionally reject free trade; he advocated protection of manufacturing only for a period of transition, and he nowhere suggested protection for agriculture. List would have violently opposed the trend of German foreign-trade policy of the last sixty-five years.

The representative literary champion of modern German protectionism was Adolf Wagner. The essence of his teachings is this: All countries with an excess production of foodstuffs and raw materials are eager to develop domestic manufacturing and to bar access to foreign manufactures; the world is on the way to economic self-sufficiency for each nation. In such a world what will be the fate of those nations which can neither feed nor clothe their citizens out of domestic foodstuffs and raw materials? They are doomed to starvation.

Adolf Wagner was not a keen mind. He was a poor economist. The same is true of his partisans. But they were not so dull as to fail to recognize that protection is not a panacea against the dangers which they depicted. The remedy they recommended was conquest of more space—war. They asked for protection of German agriculture in order to encourage production on the poor soil of the country, because they wanted to make Germany independent of foreign supplies of food for the impending war. Import duties for food were in their eyes a short-run remedy only, a measure for a period of transition. The ultimate remedy was war and conquest.

It would be wrong, however, to assume that the incentive to Germany's embarking upon protectionism was a propensity to wage war. Wagner, Schmoller, and the other socialists of the chair, in their lectures and seminars, long preached the gospel of conquest. But before the end of the 'nineties they did not dare to propagate such views in print. Considerations of war economy, moreover, could justify protection only for agriculture; they were not applicable in the case of protection for the processing industries. The military argument of war preparedness did not play an important role in the protection of Germany's industrial production.

The main motive for the tariff on manufactures was the Sozialpolitik. The pro-labor policy raised the domestic costs of production and made it necessary to safeguard the policy's short-run effects. Domestic prices had to be raised above the world market level in order to escape the dilemma of either lower money wages or a restriction of exports and increase of unemployment. Every new progress of the Sozialpolitik, and every successful strike, disarranged conditions to the disadvantage of the German enterprises and made it harder for them to outdo foreign competitors both on the domestic and on the foreign markets. The much glorified Sozialpolitik was only possible within an economic body sheltered by tariffs.

Thus Germany developed its characteristic system of cartels. The cartels charged the domestic consumers high prices and sold cheaper abroad. What the worker gained from labor legislation and union wages was absorbed by higher prices. The government and the trade-union leaders boasted of the apparent success of their policies: the workers received higher *money* wages. But *real* wages did not rise more than the marginal productivity of labor.

Only a few observers saw through all this, however. Some economists tried to justify industrial protectionism as a measure for safe-guarding the fruits of Sozialpolitik and of unionism; they advocated *social protectionism (den sozialen Schutzzoll)*. They failed to recognize that the whole process demonstrated the futility of coercive government and union interference with the conditions of labor. The greater part of public opinion did not suspect at all that Sozialpolitik and protection were closely linked together. The trend toward cartels and monopoly was in their opinion one of the many disastrous consequences of capitalism. They bitterly indicted the greediness of capitalists. The Marxians interpreted it as that concentration of capital which Marx had predicted. They purposely ignored the fact that it was not an outcome of the free evolution of capitalism but the result of government interference, of tariffs and—in the case of some branches, like potash and coal—of direct government compulsion. Some of the less shrewd socialists of the chair (Lujo Brentano, for example) went so far in their inconsistency as to advocate at the same time free trade and a more radical pro-labor policy.

In the thirty years preceding the first World War Germany could eclipse all other European countries in pro-labor policies because it above all indulged in protectionism and subsequently in cartelization.

When, later, in the course of the depression of 1929 and the following years, unemployment figures went up conspicuously because trade-unions would not accept a reduction of boom wage rates, the comparatively mild tariff protectionism turned into the hyper-protectionist policies of the quota system, monetary devaluation, and foreign exchange control. At that time Germany was no longer ahead in pro-labor policies; other countries had surpassed it. Great Britain, once the champion of free trade, adopted the German idea of social protection. So did all other countries. Up-to-date hyper-protectionism is the corollary of present-day Sozialpolitik.

There cannot be any doubt that for nearly sixty years Germany set the example in Europe both of Sozialpolitik and of protectionism. But the problems involved are not Germany's problems alone.

The most advanced countries of Europe have poor domestic resources. They are comparatively overpopulated. They are in a very unlucky position indeed in the present trend toward autarky, migration barriers, and expropriation of foreign investments. Insulation means for them a severe fall in standards of living. After the present war Great Britain—with its foreign assets gone—will be in the same position as Germany. The same will be true for Italy, Belgium, Switzerland. Perhaps France is better off because it has long had a low birth rate. But even the smaller, predominantly agricultural countries of the European East are in a critical position. How should they pay for imports of cotton, coffee, various minerals, and so on? Their soil is much poorer than that of Canada or the American wheat belt; its products cannot compete on the world market.

Thus the problem is not a German one; it is a European problem. It is a German problem only to the extent that the Germans tried—in vain—to solve it by war and conquest.

LUDWIG VON MISES

Anti-Semitism and Racism

I. THE ROLE OF RACISM

Nazism is frequently regarded as primarily a theory of racism.

German chauvinism claims for the Germans a lofty ancestry. They are the scions of the Nordic-Aryan master race, which includes all those who have contributed to the development of human civilization. The Nordic is tall, slim, with fair hair and blue eyes; he is wise, a gallant fighter, heroic, ready to sacrifice, and animated by "Faustic" ardor. The rest of mankind are trash, little better than apes. For, says Hitler, "the gulf which separates the lowest so-called human beings from our most noble races is broader than the gulf between the lowest men and the highest apes."* It is obvious that this noble race has a fair claim to world hegemony.

In this shape the Nordic myth serves the national vanity. But political nationalism has nothing in common with chauvinistic self-praise and conceit. The German nationalists do not strive for world domination because they are of noble descent. The German racists do not deny that what they are saying of the Germans could be said, with better justification, of the Swedes or Norwegians. Nevertheless, they would call these Scandinavians lunatics if they ventured to adopt the policies which they recommend for their own German nation. For the Scandinavians lack both of the conditions which underlie German aggressivism: high population figures and a strategically advantageous geographical position.

The idiomatic congeniality of the Indo-European

*Speech at the party meeting at Nuremberg, September 3, 1933. *Frankfurter Zeitung,* September 4, 1933.

languages was once explained on the hypothesis of a common descent of all these peoples. This Aryan hypothesis was scientifically disproved long ago. The Aryan race is an illusion. Scientific anthropology does not recognize this fable.*

The first Mosaic book tells us that Noah is the ancestor of all men living today. Noah had three sons. From one of them, Shem, stem the old Hebrews, the people whom Moses delivered from Egyptian slavery. Judiasm teaches that all persons embracing the Jewish religion are the scions of this people. It is impossible to prove this statement; no attempt has ever been made to prove it. There are no historical documents reporting the immigration of Jews from Palestine to Central or Eastern Europe; on the other hand, there are documents available concerning the conversion of European non-Jews to Judaism. Nevertheless, this ancestry hypothesis is widely accepted as an unshakable dogma. The Jews maintain it because it forms an essential teaching of their religion; others because it can justify a policy of discrimination against Jews. The Jews are called Asiatic strangers because, according to this hypothesis, they immigrated into Europe only some 1800 years ago. This explains also the use of the term Semites to signify people professing the Jewish religion and their offspring. The term Semitic languages is used in philosophy to signify the family of languages to which Hebrew, the idiom of the Old Testament, belongs. It is a fact, of course, that Hebrew is the religious language of Judaism, as Latin is of Catholicism and Arabic of Islam.

For more than a hundred years anthropologists

---

*Houzé, *L'Aryen et l'Anthroposociologie* (Brussels, 1906), pp. 3 ff.; Hertz, *Rasse und Kultur* (3d ed. Leipzig, 1925), pp. 102 ff.

have studied the bodily features of various races. The undisputed outcome of these scientific investigations is that the peoples of white skin, Europeans and non-European descendants of emigrated European ancestors, represent a mixture of various bodily characteristics. Men have tried to explain this fact as the result of intermarriage between the members of pure primitive stocks. Whatever the truth of this, it is certain that there are today no pure stocks within the class or race of white-skinned people.

Further efforts have been made to coördinate certain bodily features—racial characteristics—with certain mental and moral characteristics. All these endeavors have also failed.

Finally people have tried, especially in Germany, to discover the physical characteristics of an alleged Jewish or Semitic race as distinguished from the characteristics of European non-Jews. These quests, too, have failed completely. It has proved impossible to differentiate the Jewish Germans anthropologically from the non-Jewish ones. In the field of anthropology there is neither a Jewish race nor Jewish racial characteristics. The racial doctrine of the anti-Semites pretends to be natural science. But the material from which it is derived is not the result of the observation of natural phenomena. It is the genealogy of Genesis and the dogma of the rabbis' teaching that all members of their religious community are descended from the subjects of King David.

Men living under certain conditions often acquire in the second, sometimes even in the first generation, a special physical or mental conformation. This is, of course, a rule to which there are many exceptions. But very often poverty or wealth, urban or rural environment, indoor or outdoor life, mountain peaks or lowlands, sedentary habits or hard physical labor stamp their peculiar mark on a man's body. Butchers and watchmakers, tailors and lumbermen, actors and accountants can often be recognized as such by their expression or physical constitution. Racists intentionally ignore these facts. However, they alone can account for the origin of those types which are in everyday speech called aristocratic or plebeian, an officers' type, a scholarly type, or a Jewish type.

The laws promulgated by the Nazis for discrimination against Jews and the offspring of Jews have nothing at all to do with racial considerations proper. A law discriminating against people of a certain race would first have to enumerate with biological and physiological exactitude the characteristic features of the race concerned. It would then have to decree the legal procedure and proper formalities by which the presence or absence of these characteristics could be duly established for every individual. The validly executed final decisions of such procedures would then have to form the basis of the discrimination in each case. The Nazis have chosen a different way. They say, it is true, that they want to discriminate not against people professing the Jewish religion but against people belonging to the Jewish race. Yet they define the members of the Jewish race as people professing the Jewish religion or descended from people professing the Jewish religion. The characteristic legal feature of the Jewish race is, in the so-called racial legislation of Nuremberg, the membership of the individual concerned or of his ancestors in the religious community of Judaism. If a law pretends that it tends toward a discrimina-

tion against the shortsighted but defines shortsight-
edness as the quality of being bald, people using the
generally accepted terminology would not call it a
law to the disadvantage of the shortsighted but of the
bald. If Americans want to discriminate against
Negroes, they do not go to the archives in order to
study the racial affiliation of the people concerned;
they search the individual's body for traces of Negro
descent. Negroes and whites differ in racial—i.e.,
bodily—features; but it is impossible to tell a Jewish
German from a non-Jewish one by any racial characteristic.

The Nazis continually speak of race and racial
purity. They call their policies an outcome of modern anthropology. But it is useless to search their
policies for racial considerations. They consider—
with the exception of Jews and the offspring of Jews
—all white men speaking German as Aryans. They
do not discriminate among them according to bodily
features. German-speaking people are in their opinion Germans, even if it is beyond doubt that they are
the scions of Slavonic, Romanic, or Mongol (Magyar
or Finno-Ugric) ancestors. The Nazis have claimed
that they were fighting the decisive war between the
Nordic master race and the human underdogs. Yet
for this struggle they were allied with the Italians,
whom their racial doctrines depicted as a mongrel
race, and with the slit-eyed, yellow-skinned, dark-
haired Japanese Mongols. On the other hand, they
despise the Scandinavian Nordics who do not sympathize with their own plans for world supremacy. The
Nazis call themselves anti-Semites but they aid the
Arab tribes in their fight against the British, whom
they themselves consider as Nordic. The Arabs
speak a Semitic idiom, and the Nazis scholars call

them Semites. Who, in the Palestinian struggles, has the fairer claim to the appellation "anti-Semites"?

Even the racial myth itself is not a product of Germany. It is of French origin. Its founders, especially Gobineau, wanted to justify the privileges of the French aristocracy by demonstrating the gentle Frankish birth of the nobility. Hence originated in Western Europe the mistaken belief that the Nazis too recognize the claims of princes and noblemen to political leadership and caste privileges. The German nationalists, however, consider the whole German people—with the exception of the Jews and the offspring of Jews—a homogeneous race of noblemen. Within this noble race they make no discriminations. No higher degree of nobility than Germanhood is conceivable. Under the laws of the Nazis all German-speaking people are comrades *(Volksgenossen)* and as such equal. The only discrimination which the Nazis make among Germans is according to the intensity of their zeal in the display of those qualities which are regarded as genuinely German. Every non-Jewish German—prince, nobleman, or commoner—has the same right to serve his nation and to distinguish himself in this service.

It is true that in the years preceding the first World War the nationalists too clung to the prejudice, once very popular in Germany, that the Prussian Junkers were extraordinarily gifted for military leadership. In this respect only did the old Prussian legend survive until 1918. The lessons taught by the failure of the Prussian officers in the campaign of 1806 were long since forgotten. Nobody cared about Bismarck's skepticism. Bismarck, himself the son of a nonaristocratic mother, observed that Prussia was breeding officers of lower ranks up to the position of regimental commanders of a quality unsurpassed by any other country; but that as far as the higher ranks were concerned, the native Prussian stock was no longer so fertile in producing able leaders as it had been in the days of Frederick II.* But the Prussian historians had extolled the deeds of the Prussian Army until all critics were silenced. Pan-Germans, Catholics, and Social Democrats were united in their dislike of the arrogant Junkers but fully convinced that these Junkers were especially fitted for military leadership and for commissions. People complained about the exclusion of nonaristocratic officers from the Royal Guards and from many regiments of the cavalry, and about the disdainful treatment they received in the rest of the army; but they never ventured to dispute the Junkers' paramount military qualifications. Even the Social Democrats had full confidence in the active officers of the Prussian Army. The firm conviction that the war would result in a smashing German victory, which all strata of the German nation held in 1914, was primarily founded on this overestimation of the military genius of the Junkers.

People did not notice that the German nobility, who had long since ceased to play a leading role in political life, were now on the point of losing the army's reins. They had never excelled in science, art, and literature. Their contributions in these fields cannot be compared with the achievements of British, French, and Italian aristocrats. Yet in no other modern country was the position of the aristocrats more favorable or that of the commoners less auspicious than in Germany. At the peak of his life and

*Bismarck, *op. cit.,* I, 6.

success Goethe wrote, full of bitterness: "I do not
know how conditions are in foreign countries, but in
Germany only the nobleman can attain a certain
universal and personal perfection. A commoner may
acquire merit, he may, at best, cultivate his mind;
but his personality goes astray, whatever he tries."*
But it was commoners and not noblemen who
created the works which led Germany to be called
the "nation of poets and thinkers."

In the ranks of the authors who formed the nation's political thought there were no noblemen.
Even the Prussian conservatives got their ideologies
from plebeians, from Stahl, Rodbertus, Wagener,
Adolf Wagner. Among the men who developed German nationalism there was hardly a member of the
aristocracy. Pan-Germanism and Nazism are in this
sense "bourgeois" movements like socialism, Marxism, and interventionism. Within the ranks of the
higher bureaucracy there was a steady penetration
of nonaristocratic elements.

It was the same with the armed forces. The hard
work in the offices of the General Staff, in the technical services, and in the navy did not suit the tastes
and desires of the Junkers. Many important posts in
the General Staff were occupied by commoners. The
outstanding personality in German prewar militarism was Admiral Tirpitz, who attained nobility only
in 1900. Ludendorff, Groener, and Hoffmann were
also commoners.

But it was the defeat in the first World War which
finally destroyed the military prestige of the Junkers. In the present German Army there are still
many aristocrats in higher ranks, because the offi-

*Goethe, *Wilhelm Meister's Lehrjahre,* Book V, chap. iii.

cers who got their commissions in the last years preceding the first World War have now reached the top of the ladder. But there is no longer any preference given to aristocrats. Among the political leaders of Nazism there are few nobles—and the titles even of these are often questionable.

The German princes and nobles, who unswervingly disparaged liberalism and democracy and until 1933 stubbornly fought for the preservation of their privileges, have completely surrendered to Nazism and connive at its egalitarian principles. They are to be found in the ranks of the most fanatical admirers of the Führer. Princes of the blood take pride in serving as satellites of notorious racketeers who hold party offices. One may wonder whether they act out of sincere conviction or out of cowardice and fear. But there can be no doubt that the belief, common to many members of the British aristocracy, that a restoration of the German dynasties would change the German mentality and the temper of politics is entirely mistaken.*

II. THE STRUGGLE AGAINST THE JEWISH MIND

Nazism wants to combat the Jewish mind. But it has not succeeded so far in defining its characteristic features. The Jewish mind is no less mythical than the Jewish race.

The earlier German nationalists tried to oppose to the Jewish mind the "Christian-Teutonic" worldview. The combination of Christian and Teutonic is, however, untenable. No exegetical tricks can justify a German claim to a preferred position within the realm of Christianity. The Gospels do not mention

*The last sovereign duke of Saxe-Coburg-Gotha, born and brought up in Great Britain as a grandson of Queen Victoria, was the first German prince who—long before 1933—took office in the Nazi party.

the Germans. They consider all men equal under God. He who is anxious to discriminate not only against Jews but against the Christian descendants of Jews has no use for the Gospels. Consistent anti-Semites must reject Christianity.

We do not need to decide here whether or not Christianity itself can be called Jewish.† At any rate Christianity developed out of the Jewish creed. It recognizes the Ten Commandments as eternal law and the Old Testament as Holy Writ. The Apostles and the members of the primitive community were Jews. It could be objected that Christ did not agree in his teachings with the rabbis. But the facts remain that God sent the Saviour to the Jews and not to the Vandals, and that the Holy Spirit inspired books in Hebrew and in Greek but not in German. If the Nazis were prepared to take their racial myths seriously and to see in them more than oratory for their party meetings, they would have to eradicate Christianity with the same brutality they use against liberalism and pacifism. They failed to embark upon such an enterprise, not because they regarded it as hopeless, but because their *politics* had nothing at all to do with racism.

It is strange indeed in a country in which the authorities officially outrage Jews and Judaism in filthy terms, which has outlawed the Jews on account of their Judaism, and in which mathematical theorems, physical hypotheses, and therapeutical procedures are boycotted, if their authors are suspected of being "non-Aryans," that priests continue in many thousands of churches of various creeds to praise the Ten Commandments, revealed to the Jew

†Pope Pius XI is credited with the dictum: "Spirtually we are Semites." G. Seldes, *The Catholic Crisis* (New York, 1939), p. 45.

Moses, as the foundation of moral law. It is strange that in a country in which no word of a Jewish author must be printed or read, the Psalms and their German translations, adaptations, and imitations are sung. It is strange that the German armies, which exult in Eastern Europe in cowardly slaughtering thousands of defenseless Jewish women and children, are accompanied by army chaplains with Bibles in their hands. But the Third Reich is full of such contradictions.

Of course, the Nazis do not comply with the moral teachings of the Gospels. Neither do any other conquerors and warriors. Christianity is no more allowed to become an obstacle in the way of Nazi politics than it was in the way of other aggressors.

Nazism not only fails explicitly to reject Christianity; it solemnly declares itself a Christian party. The twenty-fourth point of the "*unalterable* Party Program" proclaims that the party stands for *positive Christianity,* without linking itself with one of the various Christian churches and denominations. The term "positive" in this connection means neutrality in respect to the antagonisms between the various churches and sects.*

Many Nazi writers, it is true, take pleasure in denouncing and deriding Christianity and in drafting plans for the establishment of a new German religion. The Nazi party as such, however, does not combat Christianity but the Christian churches as autonomous establishments and independent agencies. Its totalitarianism cannot tolerate the existence of any institution not completely subject to the Führer's

---

*For another interpretation of the term "positiv" see *Die Grundlagen des Nationalsozialismus* (Leipzig, 1937, p. 59) by Bishop Alois Hudal, the outstanding Catholic champion of Nazism.

sovereignty. No German is granted the privilege of defying an order issued by the state by referring to an independent authority. The separation of church and state is contrary to the principles of totalitarianism. Nazism must consequently aim at a return to the conditions prevailing in the German Lutheran churches and likewise in the Prussian Union Church before the Constitution of Weimar. Then the civil authority was supreme in the church too. The ruler of the country was the supreme bishop of the Lutheran Church of his territory. His was the *jus circa sacra.*

The conflict with the Catholic Church is of a similar character. The Nazis will not tolerate any link between German citizens and foreigners or foreign institutions. They dissolved even the German Rotary Clubs because they were tied up with the Rotary International, whose headquarters are located in Chicago. A German citizen owes allegiance to his Führer and nation only; any kind of internationalism is an evil. Hitler could tolerate Catholicism only if the Pope were a resident of Germany and a subordinate of the party machine.

Except for Christianity, the Nazis reject as Jewish everything which stems from Jewish authors. This condemnation includes the writings of those Jews who, like Stahl, Lassalle, Gumplowicz, and Rathenau, have contributed many essential ideas to the system of Nazism. But the Jewish mind is, as the Nazis say, not limited to the Jews and their offspring only. Many "Aryans" have been imbued with Jewish mentality—for instance the poet, writer, and critic Gotthold Ephraim Lessing, the socialist Frederick Engels, the composer Johannes Brahms, the writer Thomas Mann, and the theologian Karl Barth. They too are damned. Then there are whole schools of thought, art, and literature rejected as Jewish. Internationalism and pacifism are Jewish, but so is warmongering. So are liberalism and capitalism, as well as the "spurious" socialism of the Marxians and of the Bolsheviks. The epithets Jewish and Western are applied to the philosophies of Descartes and Hume, to positivism, materialism and empiro-criticism, to the economic theories both of the classics and of modern subjectivism. Atonal music, the Italian opera style, the operetta and the paintings of impressionism are also Jewish. In short, Jewish is what any Nazi dislikes. If one put together everything that various Nazis have stigmatized as Jewish, one would get the impression that our whole civilization has been the achievement only of Jews.

On the other hand, many champions of German racism have tried to demonstrate that all the eminent men of non-German nations were Aryan Nordics of German extraction. The ex-Marxian Woltmann, for example, has discovered features of Germanism in Petrarch, Dante, Ariosto, Raphael, and Michelangelo, who have their genius as an inheritance from their Teutonic ancestors. Woltmann is fully convinced that he has proved that "the entire European civilization, even in the Slavonic and Latin countries, is an achievement of the German race."[*]

It would be a waste of time to dwell upon such statements. It is enough to remark that the various representatives of German racism contradict one another both in establishing the racial characteris-

*See Woltmann's books: *Politische Anthropologie* (Eisenach, 1903); *Die Germanen und die Renaissance in Italien* (Leipzig, 1905); *Die Germanen in Frankreich* (Jena, 1907).

tics of the noble race and in the racial classification of the same individuals. Very often they contradict even what they themselves have said elsewhere. The myth of the master race has been elaborated carelessly indeed.

All Nazi champions insist again and again that Marxism and Bolshevism are the quintessence of the Jewish mind, and that it is the great historic mission of Nazism to root out this pest. It is true that this attitude did not prevent the German nationalists either from coöperating with the German communists in undermining the Weimar Republic, or from training their black guards in Russian artillery and aviation camps in the years 1923–1933, or—in the period from August, 1939, until June, 1941—from entering into a close political and military complicity with Soviet Russia. Nevertheless, public opinion supports the view that Nazism and Bolshevism are philosophies—Weltanschauungen—implacably opposed to each other. Actually there have been in these last years all over the world two main political parties: the anti-Fascists, i.e., the friends of Russia (communists, fellow travelers, self-styled liberals and progressives), and the anticommunists, i.e., the friends of Germany (parties of shirts of different colors, not very accurately called "Fascists" by their adversaries). There have been few genuine liberals and democrats in these years. Most of those who have called themselves such have been ready to support what are really totalitarian measures, and many have enthusiastically praised the Russian methods of dictatorship.

The mere fact that these two groups are fighting each other does not necessarily prove that they differ in their philosophies and first principles. There have always been wars between people who adhered to the same creeds and philosophies. The parties of the Left and of the Right are in conflict because they both aim at supreme power. Charles V used to say: "I and my cousin, the King of France, are in perfect agreement; we are fighting each other because we both aim at the same end: Milan." Hitler and Stalin aim at the same end; they both want to rule in the Baltic States, in Poland, and in the Ukraine.

The Marxians are not prepared to admit that the Nazis are socialists too. In their eyes Nazism is the worst of all evils of capitalism. On the other hand, the Nazis describe the Russian system as the meanest of all types of capitalist exploitation and as a devilish machination of World Jewry for the domination of the gentiles. Yet it is clear that both systems, the German and the Russian, must be considered from an economic point of view as socialist. And it is only the economic point of view that matters in debating whether or not a party or system is socialist. Socialism is and has always been considered a system of economic organization of society. It is the system under which the government has full control of production and distribution. As far as socialism existing merely within individual countries can be called genuine, both Russia and Germany are right in calling their systems socialist.

Whether the Nazis and the Bolsheviks are right in styling themselves workers' parties is another question. The Communist Manifesto says, "The proletarian movement is the self-conscious independent movement of the immense majority," and it is in this sense that old Marxians used to define a workers' party. The proletarians, they explained, are the immense majority of the nation; they themselves, not a benevolent government or a well-intentioned minority, seize power and establish socialism. But the Bolsheviks have abandoned this scheme. A small minority proclaims itself the vanguard of the proletariat, seizes the dictatorship, forcibly dissolves the Parliament elected by universal franchise, and rules by its own right and might. Of course, this ruling minority claims that what it does serves best the interests of the many and indeed of the whole of society, but this has always been the pretension of oligarchic rulers.

The Bolshevists set the precedent. The success of the Lenin clique encouraged the Mussolini gang and the Hitler troops. Both Italian Fascism and German Nazism adopted the political methods of Soviet Russia.* The only difference between Nazism and Bolshevism is that the Nazis got a much bigger minority in the elections preceding their coup d'état than the Bolsheviks got in the Russian elections in the fall of 1917.

The Nazis have not only imitated the Bolshevist tactics of seizing power. They have copied much more. They have imported from Russia the one-party system and the privileged role of this party and its members in public life; the paramount position of the secret police; the organization of affiliated par-

---

*Few people realize that the economic program of Italian Fascism, the *stato corporativo,* did not differ from the program of British Guild Socialism as propagated during the first World War and in the following years by the most eminent British and by some continental socialists. The most brilliant exposition of this doctrine is the book of Sidney and Beatrice Webb (Lord and Lady Passfield), *A Constitution for the Socialist Commonwealth of Great Britain,* published in 1920. Compared with this volume the speeches of Mussolini and the writings of the Italian professors of the *economia corporativa* appear clumsy. Of course, neither the British Left-wing socialists nor the Italian Fascists ever made any serious attempts to put this widely advertised program into effect. Its realization would lead to complete chaos. The economic regime of Fascist Italy was actually an abortive imitation of German Zwangswirtschaft. See Mises' *Nationalökonomie* (Geneva, 1940), pp. 705–715.

ties abroad which are employed in fighting their domestic governments and in sabotage and espionage, assisted by public funds and the protection of the diplomatic and consular service; the administrative execution and imprisonment of political adversaries; concentration camps; the punishment inflicted on the families of exiles; the methods of propaganda. They have borrowed from the Marxians even such absurdities as the mode of address, party comrade *(Parteigenosse),* derived from the Marxian comrade *(Genosse),* and the use of a military terminology for all items of civil and economic life.* The question is not in which respects both systems are alike but in which they differ.

It has already been shown wherein the socialist patterns of Russia and Germany differ. These differences are not due to any disparity in basic philosophical views; they are the necessary consequence of the differences in the economic conditions of the two countries. The Russian pattern was inapplicable in Germany, whose population cannot live in a state of self-sufficiency. The German pattern seems very inefficient when compared with the incomparably more efficient capitalist system, but it is far more efficient than the Russian method. The Russians live at a very low economic level notwithstanding the inexhaustible richness of their natural resources.

There is inequality of incomes and of standards of living in both countries. It would be futile to try to determine whether the difference in the living standards of party comrade Goering and the average party comrade is greater or smaller than that in the standards of comrade Stalin and *his* comrades. The

*For a comparison of the two systems see Max Eastman, *Stalin's Russia* (New York, 1940), pp. 83–94.

characteristic feature of socialism is not equality of income but the all-round control of business activities by the government, the government's exclusive power to use all means of production.

The Nazis do not reject Marxism because it aims at socialism but because, as they say, it advocates internationalism.* Marx's internationalism was nothing but the acceptance of eighteenth-century ideas on the root causes of war: princes are eager to fight each other because they want aggrandizement through conquest, while free nations do not covet their neighbors' land. But it never occurred to Marx that this propensity to peace depends upon the existence of an unhampered market society. Neither Marx nor his school was ever able to grasp the meaning of international conflicts within a world of etatism and socialism. They contented themselves with the assertion that in the Promised Land of socialism there would no longer be any conflicts at all.

We have already seen what a questionable role the problem of the maintenance of peace played in the Second International. For Soviet Russia the Third International has been merely a tool in its unflagging warfare against all foreign governments. The Soviets are as eager for conquest as any conqueror of the past. They did not yield an inch of the previous conquests of the Czars except where they were forced to do so. They have used every opportunity to expand their empire. Of course they no longer use the old Czarist pretexts for conquest; they have developed a new terminology for this purpose. But this

---

*In a similar way many Christian authors reject Bolshevism only because it is anti-Christian. See Berdyaew, *The Origin of Russian Communism* (London, 1937), pp. 217–225.

does not render the lot of the subdued any easier.

What the Nazis really have in mind when indicting the Jewish mind for internationalism is the liberal theory of free trade and the mutual advantages of international division of labor. The Jews, they say, want to corrupt the innate Aryan spirit of heroism by the fallacious doctrines of the advantages of peace. One could hardly overrate in a more inaccurate way the contribution of Jews to modern civilization. Peaceful coöperation between nations is certainly more than an outcome of Jewish machinations. Liberalism and democracy, capitalism and international trade are not Jewish inventions.

Finally, the Nazis call the business mentality Jewish. Tacitus informs us that the German tribes of his day considered it clumsy and shameful to acquire with sweat what could be won by bloodshed. This is also the first moral principle of the Nazis. They despise individuals and nations eager to profit by serving other people; in their eyes robbery is the noblest way to make a living. Werner Sombart has contrasted two specimens of human being: the peddlers (Händler) and heroes (Helden). The Britons are peddlers, the Germans heroes. But more often the appellation peddlers is assigned to the Jews.

The Nazis simply call everything that is contrary to their own doctrines and tenets Jewish and communist. When executing hostages in the occupied countries they always declare that they have punished Jews and communists. They call the President of the United States a Jew and a communist. He who is not prepared to surrender to them is by that token unmistakably a Jew. In the Nazi dictionary the terms Jew and communist are synonymous with non-Nazi.

III. INTERVENTIONISM AND LEGAL DISCRIMINATION AGAINST JEWS

In the days before the ascendancy of liberalism the individuals professing a certain religious creed formed an order, a caste, of their own. The creed determined the membership in a group which assigned to each member privileges and disqualifications (*privilegia odiosa.*) In only a few countries has liberalism abolished this state of affairs. In many European countries, in which in any other respect freedom of conscience and of the practice of religion and equality of all citizens under the law are granted, matrimonial law and the register of births, marriages, and deaths remain separate for each religious group. Membership within a church or religious community preserves a peculiar legal character. Every citizen is bound to belong to one of the religious groups, and he bestows this quality upon his children. The membership and procedure to be observed in cases of change of religious allegiance are regulated by public law. Special provisions are made for people who do not want to belong to any religious community. This state of things makes it possible to establish the religious allegiance of a man and of his ancestors with legal precision in the same unquestionable way in which kinship can be ascertained in inheritance cases.

The bearing of this fact can be elucidated by contrasting it with conditions concerning attachment to a linguistic group. Membership within a linguistic group never had a caste quality. It was and is a matter of fact but not a legal status.* It is as a rule impossible to establish the linguistic group to which a

---

*We may disregard some occasional attempts, made in old Austria, to give legal status to a man's linguistic character.

man's dead ancestors belonged. The only exceptions are those ancestors who were eminent personalities, writers, or political leaders of linguistic groups. It is further for the most part impossible to establish whether or not a man changed his linguistic allegiance at some time in his past. He who speaks German and declares himself to be a German need seldom fear that his statement could be disproved by documentary evidence that his parents or he himself in the past were not German. Even a foreign accent need not betray him. In countries with a linguistically mixed population the accent and inflection of each group influence the other. Among the leaders of German nationalism in the eastern parts of Germany, and in Austria, Czechoslovakia, and the other eastern countries there were numerous men who spoke German with a sharp Slavonic, Hungarian, or Italian accent, whose names sounded foreign, or who had only a short time before substituted German-sounding names for their native ones. There were even Nazi Storm Troopers whose still living parents understood no German. It happened often that brothers and sisters belonged to different linguistic groups. One could not attempt to discriminate legally against such neophytes, because it was impossible to determine the facts in a legally unquestionable way.

In an unhampered market society there is no legal discrimination against anybody. Everyone has the right to obtain the place within the social system in which he can successfully work and make a living. The consumer is free to discriminate, provided that he is ready to pay the cost. A Czech or a Pole may prefer to buy at higher cost in a shop owned by a Slav instead of buying cheaper and better in a shop owned by a German. An anti-Semite may forego being cured of an ugly disease by the employment of the "Jewish" drug Salvarsan and have recourse to a less efficacious remedy. In this arbitrary power consists what economists call consumer's sovereignty.

Interventionism means compulsory discrimination, which furthers the interests of a minority of citizens at the expense of the majority. Nevertheless discrimination can be applied in a democratic community too. Various minority groups form an alliance and thereby a majority group in order to obtain privileges for each. For instance, a country's wheat producers, cattle breeders, and wine growers form a farmers' party; they succeed in obtaining discrimination against foreign competitors and thus privileges for each of the three groups. The costs of the privilege granted to the wine growers burden the rest of the community—including the cattle breeders and wheat producers—and so on for each of the others.

Whoever sees the facts from this angle—and logically they cannot be viewed from any other—realizes that the arguments brought forward in favor of this so-called producer's policy are untenable. One minority group alone could not obtain any such privilege because the majority would not tolerate it. But if all minority groups or enough of them obtain a privilege, every group that did not get a more valuable privilege than the rest suffers. The political ascendancy of interventionism is due to the failure to recognize this obvious truth. People favor discrimination and privileges because they do not realize that they themselves are consumers and as such must foot the bill. In the case of protectionism, for example, they believe that only the foreigners against whom the import duties discriminate are hurt. It is true the foreigners are hurt, but not they alone: the consumers who must pay higher prices suffer with them.

Now wherever there are Jewish minorities—and in every country the Jews are only a minority—it is as easy to discriminate against them legally as against foreigners, because the quality of being a Jew can be established in a legally valid way. Discrimination against this helpless minority can be made to seem very plausible; it seems to further the interests of all non-Jews. People do not realize that it is certain to hurt the interests of the non-Jews as well. If Jews are barred from access to a medical career, the interests of non-Jewish doctors are favored, but the interests of the sick are hurt. Their freedom to choose the doctor whom they trust is restricted. Those who did not want to consult a Jewish doctor do not gain anything but those who wanted to do so are injured.

In most European countries it is technically feasible to discriminate legally against Jews and the offspring of Jews. It is furthermore politically feasible, because Jews are usually insignificant minorities whose votes do not count much in elections. And finally, it is considered economically sound in an age in which government interference for the protection of the less efficient producer against more efficient and cheaper competitors is regarded as a beneficial policy. The non-Jewish grocer asks, Why not protect me too? You protect the manufacturer and the farmer against the foreigners producing better and at lower cost; you protect the worker against the competition of immigrant labor; you should protect me against the competition of my neighbor, the Jewish grocer.

Discrimination need have nothing to do with hatred or repugnance toward those against whom it is applied. The Swiss and Italians do not hate the Americans or Swedes; nevertheless, they discriminate against American and Swedish products. People always dislike competitors. But for the consumer the foreigners who supply him with commodities are not competitors but purveyors. The non-Jewish doctor may hate his Jewish competitor. But he asks for the exclusion of Jews from the medical profession precisely because many non-Jewish patients not only do not hate Jewish doctors but prefer them to many non-Jewish doctors and patronize them. The fact that the Nazi racial laws impose heavy penalties for sexual intercourse between Jews and "Aryans" does not indicate the existence of hatred between these two groups. It would be needless to keep people who hate each other from sexual relations. However, in an investigation devoted to the political problems of nationalism and Nazism we need not deal with the issues of sex pathology involved. To study the inferiority complexes and sexual perversity responsible for the Nuremberg racial laws and for the sadistic bestialities exhibited in killing and torturing Jews is the task of psychiatry.

In a world in which people have grasped the meaning of a market society, and therefore advocate a consumer's policy, there is no legal discrimination against Jews. Whoever dislikes the Jews may in such a world avoid patronizing Jewish shopkeepers, doctors, and lawyers. On the other hand, in a world of interventionism only a miracle can in the long run hinder legal discrimination against Jews. The policy of protecting the less efficient domestic producer against the more efficient foreign producer, the artisan against the manufacturer, and the small shop against the department store and the chain stores would be incomplete if it did not protect the "Aryan" against the Jew.

Many decades of intensive anti-Semitic propaganda did not succeed in preventing German "Aryans" from buying in shops owned by Jews, from consulting Jewish doctors and lawyers, and from reading books by Jewish authors. They did not patronize the Jews unawares—"Aryan" competitors were careful to tell them again and again that these people were Jews. Whoever wanted to get rid of his Jewish competitors could not rely on an alleged hatred of Jews; he was under the necessity of asking for legal discrimination against them.

Such discrimination is not the result of nationalism or of racism. It is basically—like nationalism—a result of interventionism and the policy of favoring the less efficient producer to the disadvantage of the consumer.

Nearly all writers dealing with the problem of anti-Semitism have tried to demonstrate that the Jews have in some way or other, through their behavior or attitudes, excited anti-Semitism. Even Jewish authors and non-Jewish opponents of anti-Semitism share this opinion; they too search for Jewish faults driving non-Jews toward anti-Semitism. But if the cause of anti-Semitism were really to be found in distinctive features of the Jews, these properties would have to be extraordinary virtues and merits which would qualify the Jews as the elite of mankind. If the Jews themselves are to blame for the fact that those whose ideal is perpetual war and bloodshed, who worship violence and are eager to destroy freedom, consider them the most dangerous opponents of their endeavors, it must be because the Jews are foremost among the champions of freedom, justice, and peaceful coöperation among nations. If the Jews have incurred the Nazis' hatred through their own conduct, it is no doubt because what was great and noble in the German nation, all the immortal achievements of Germany's past, were either accomplished by the Jews or congenial to the Jewish mind. As the parties seeking to destroy modern civilization and return to barbarism have put anti-Semitism at the top of their programs, this civilization is apparently a creation of the Jews. Nothing more flattering could be said of an individual or of a group than that the deadly foes of civilization have well-founded reasons to persecute them.

The truth is that while the Jews are the objects of anti-Semitism, their conduct and qualities did not play a decisive role in inciting and spreading its modern version. That they form everywhere a minority which can be legally defined in a precise way makes it tempting, in an age of interventionism, to discriminate against them. Jews have, of course, contributed to the rise of modern civilization; but this civilization is neither completely nor predominantly their achievement. Peace and freedom, democracy and justice, reason and thought are not specifically Jewish. Many things, good and bad, happen on the earth without the participation of Jews. The anti-Semites grossly exaggerate when they see in the Jews the foremost representatives of modern culture and make them alone responsible for the fact that the world has changed since the centuries of the barbarian invasions.*

In the dark ages heathens, Christians, and Mos-

---

*We are dealing here with conditions in Central and Western Europe and in America. In many parts of Eastern Europe things were different. There modern civilization was really predominantly an achievement of Jews.

lems persecuted the Jews on account of their religion. This motive has lost much of its strength and is still valid only for a comparatively few Catholics and Fundamentalists who make the Jews responsible for the spread of free thinking. And this too is a mistaken idea. Neither Hume nor Kant, neither Laplace nor Darwin were Jews. Higher criticism of the Bible was developed by Protestant theologians.† The Jewish rabbis opposed it bitterly for many years.

Neither were liberalism, capitalism, or a market economy Jewish achievements. There are those who try to justify anti-Semitism by denouncing the Jews as capitalists and champions of laissez faire. Other anti-Semites—and often the same ones—blame the Jews for being communists. These contradictory charges cancel each other. But it is a fact that anticapitalist propaganda has contributed a good deal to the popularity of anti-Semitism. Simple minds do not grasp the meaning of the abstract terms capital and exploitation, capitalists and exploiters; they substitute for them the terms Jewry and Jews. However, even if the Jews were more unpopular with some people than is really the case, there would be no discrimination against them if they were not a minority clearly distinguishable legally from other people.

IV. THE "STAB IN THE BACK"

The end of the first World War glaringly exposed the nucleus of German nationalism's dogma. Ludendorff, idol of the nationalists, himself had to confess that the war was lost, that the Reich had suffered a

---

†Bishop Hudal calls David Friedrich Strauss, the outstanding figure in German higher criticism, a "non-Aryan." (*op.cit.,* p. 23). This is incorrect; Strauss had no Jewish ancestors (see his biography by Th. Ziegler, I, 4–6). On the other hand, Nazi anti-Catholics say that Ignatius of Loyola, the founder of the Jesuit order, was of Jewish origin (Seldes, *op. cit.,* p. 261). There is no proof of this statement.

crushing defeat. The news of this failure was not anticipated by the nation. For more than four years the government had told the credulous people that Germany was victorious. It was beyond doubt that the German armies had occupied almost the whole territory of Belgium and several departments of France, while the Allied armies held only a few square miles of the Reich's territory. German armies had conquered Brussels, Warsaw, Belgrade, and Bucharest. Russia and Rumania had been forced to sign peace treaties dictated by Germany. Look at the map, said the German statesmen, if you want to see who is victorious. The British Navy, they boasted, had been swept from the North Sea and was creeping into port; the British Merchant Marine was an easy prey for German U-boats. The English were starving. The citizens of London could not sleep for fear of Zeppelins. America was not in a position to save the Allies; the Americans had no army, and if they had had, they would have lacked the ships to send it to Europe. The German generals had given proof of ingenuity: Hindenburg, Ludendorff, and Mackensen were equal to the most famous leaders of the past: and in the German armed forces everybody was a hero, above all the intrepid pilots and the unflinching crews of the submarines.

And now, the collapse! Something horrible and ghastly had happened, for which the only explanation could be treason. Once again a traitor had ambushed the victor from a safely hidden corner. Once again Hagen had murdered Siegfried. The victorious army had been stabbed in the back. While the German men were fighting the enemy, domestic foes had stirred up the people at home to rise in the November rebellion, that most infamous crime of

the ages. Not the front but the hinterland had failed.
The culprits were neither the soldiers nor the generals but the weaklings of the civil government and of
the Reichstag who failed to curb the rebellion.

Shame and contrition for the events of November,
1918, were the greater with aristocrats, officers, and
nationalist notables because they had behaved in
those days in a way that they themselves very soon
were bound to regard as scandalous. Several officers
on battleships had tried to stop the mutineers, but
almost all over officers had bowed to the revolution.
Twenty-two German thrones were smashed without
any attempt at resistance. Court dignitaries, adju-
tants, orderly officers, and bodyguards quietly acquiesced when the princes to whom they had sworn
oaths of personal allegiance unto death were dethroned. The example once set by the Swiss Guards
who died for Louis XVI and his consort was not imitated. There was not a trace of the Fatherland party
and of the nationalists when the masses assaulted
the castles of the various kings and dukes.

It was salvation for the self-esteem of all these
disheartened souls when some generals and nationalist leaders found a justification and an excuse: it
had been the work of the Jews. Germany was victorious by land and sea and air, but the Jews had stabbed
the victorious forces in the back. Whoever ventured
to refute this legend was himself denounced as a Jew
or a bribed servant of the Jews. No rational argument could shake the legend. It has been picked to
pieces; each of its points has been disproved by documentary evidence; an overwhelming mass of
material has been brought to its refutation—in vain.

It must be realized that German nationalism managed to survive the defeat of the first World War only

by means of the legend of the stab in the back. Without it the nationalists would have been forced to drop
their program, which was founded wholly on the thesis of Germany's military superiority. In order to
maintain this program it was indispensable to be
able to tell the nation: "We have given new proof of
our invincibility. But our victories did not bring us
success because the Jews have sabotaged the country. If we eliminate the Jews, our victories will bring
their due reward."

Up to that time anti-Semitism had played but a
small role in the structure of the doctrines of German nationalism. It was mere byplay, not a political
issue. The endeavors to discriminate against the
Jews stemmed from interventionism, as did nationalism. But they had no vital part in the system of
German political nationalism. Now anti-Semitism
became the focal point of the nationalist creed, its
main issue. That was its meaning in domestic politics. And very soon it acquired an equal importance
in foreign affairs.

V. ANTI-SEMITISM AS A FACTOR IN INTERNATIONAL POLITICS

It was a very strange constellation of political forces
that turned anti-Semitism into an important factor
in world affairs.

In the years after the first World War Marxism
swept triumphantly over the Anglo-Saxon countries.
Public opinion in Great Britain came under the spell
of the neo-Marxian doctrines on imperialism, according to which wars are fought only for the sake of
the selfish class interests of capital. The intellectuals and the parties of the Left felt rather ashamed of

England's participation in the World War. They were convinced that it was both morally unfair and politically unwise to oblige Germany to pay reparations and to restrict its armaments. They were firmly resolved never again to let Great Britain fight a war. They purposely shut their eyes to every unpleasant fact that could weaken their naïve confidence in the omnipotence of the League of Nations. They overrated the efficacy of sanctions and of such measures as outlawing war by the Briand-Kellogg Pact. They favored for their country a policy of disarmament which rendered the British Empire almost defenseless within a world indefatigably preparing for new wars.

But at the same time the same people were asking the British government and the League to check the aspirations of the "dynamic" powers and to safeguard with every means—short of war—the independence of the weaker nations. They indulged in strong language against Japan and against Italy; but they practically encouraged, by their opposition to armaments and their unconditional pacifism, the imperialistic policies of these countries. They were instrumental in Great Britain's rejecting Secretary Stimson's proposals to stop Japan's expansion in China. They frustrated the Hoare-Laval plan, which would have left at least a part of Abyssinia independent; but they did not lift a finger when Italy occupied the whole country. They did not change their policy when Hitler seized power and immediately began to prepare for the wars which were meant to make Germany paramount first on the European continent and later in the whole world. Theirs was an ostrich policy in the face of the most serious situation that Britain ever had to encounter.*

The parties of the Right did not differ in principle from those of the Left. They were only more moderate in their utterances and eager to find a rational pretext for the policy of inactivity and indolence in which the Left acquiesced lightheartedly and without a thought of the future. They consoled themselves with the hope that Germany did not plan to attack France but only to fight Soviet Russia. It was all wishful thinking, refusing to take account of Hitler's schemes as exposed in *Mein Kampf.* The Left became furious. Our reactionaries, they shouted, are aiding Hitler because they are putting their class interests over the welfare of the nation. Yet the encouragement which Hitler got from England came not so much from the anti-Soviet feelings of some members of the upper classes as from the state of British armament, for which the Left was even more responsible than the Right. The only way to stop Hitler would have been to spend large sums for rearmament and to return to conscription. The whole British nation, not only the aristocracy, was strongly opposed to such measures. Under these conditions it was not unreasonable that a small group of lords and rich commoners should try to improve relations between the two countries. It was, of course, a plan without prospect of success. The Nazis could not be dissuaded from their aims by comforting speeches from socially prominent Englishmen. British popular repugnance to armaments and conscription was an important factor in the Nazi plans, but the sym-

*An amazing manifestation of this mentality is Bertrand Russell's book, *Which Way to Peace?*, published in 1936. Devastating criticism of the British Labor party's foreign policy is provided in the editorial, "The Obscurantists," in *Nineteenth Century and After,* No. 769 (March, 1941), pp. 209–229.

pathies of a dozen lords were not. It was no secret that Great Britain would be unable, right at the outbreak of a new war, to send an expeditionary force of seven divisions to France as it did in 1914; that the Royal Air Force was numerically much inferior to the German Air Force; or that even the British Navy was less formidable than in the years 1914–18. The Nazis knew very well that many politicians in South Africa opposed the dominion's participating in a new war, and they were in close touch with the anti-British parties in the East Indies, in Egypt, and the Arabian countries.

The problem which Great Britain had to face was simply this: Is it in the interest of the nation to permit Germany to conquer the whole European continent? It was Hitler's great plan to keep England neutral at all costs, until the conquest of France, Poland, Czechoslovakia, and the Ukraine should be completed. Should Great Britain render him this service? Whoever answered this question in the negative must not talk but act. But the British politicians buried their heads in the sand.

Given the state of British public opinion, France should have understood that it was isolated and must meet the Nazi danger by itself. The French know little about the German mentality and German political conditions. Yet when Hitler seized power every French politician should have realized that the main point in his plans was the annihilation of France. Of course the French parties of the Left shared the prejudices, illusions, and errors of the British Left. But there was in France an influential nationalist group which had always mistrusted Germany and favored an energetic anti-German policy. If the

French nationalists in 1933 and the years following had seriously advocated measures to prevent German rearmament, they would have had the support of the whole nation with the exception of the intransigent communists. Germany had already started to rearm under the Weimar Republic. Nevertheless in 1933 it was not ready for a war with France, nor for some years thereafter. It would have been forced either to yield to a French threat or to wage a war without prospect of success. At that time it was still possible to stop the Nazis with threats. And even had war resulted, France would have been strong enough to win.

But then something amazing and unexpected happened. Those nationalists who for more than sixty years had been fanatically anti-German, who had scorned everything German, and who had always demanded an energetic policy against the Weimar Republic changed their minds overnight. Those who had disparaged as Jewish all endeavors to improve Franco-German relations, who had attacked as Jewish machinations the Dawes and Young plans and the Locarno agreement, and who had held the League suspect as a Jewish institution suddenly began to sympathize with the Nazis. They refused to recognize the fact that Hitler was eager to destroy France once and for all. Hitler, they hinted, is less a foe of France than of the Jews; as an old warrior he sympathizes with his French fellow warriors. They belittled German rearmament. Besides, they said, Hitler rearms only in order to fight Jewish Bolshevism. Nazism is Europe's shield against the assault of World Jewry and its foremost representative, Bolshevism. The Jews are eager to push France into a war against the Nazis. But France is wise enough not to pull any chestnuts out of the fire for the Jews. France will not bleed for the Jews.

It was not the first time in French history that the nationalists put their anti-Semitism above their French patriotism. In the Dreyfus Affair they fought vigorously in order to let a treacherous officer quietly evade punishment while an innocent Jew languished in prison.

It has been said that the Nazis corrupted the French nationalists. Perhaps some French politicians really took bribes. But politically this was of little importance. The Reich would have wasted its funds. The anti-Semitic newspapers and periodicals had a wide circulation; they did not need German subsidies. Hitler left the League; he annulled the disarmament clauses of the Treaty of Versailles; he occupied the demilitarized zone on the Rhine; he stirred anti-French tendencies in North Africa. The French nationalists for the most part criticized these acts only in order to put all the blame on their political adversaries in France: it was they who were guilty, because they had adopted a hostile attitude toward Nazism.

Then Hitler invaded Austria. Seven years earlier France had vigorously opposed the plan of an Austro-German customs union. But now the French Government hurried to recognize the violent annexation of Austria. At Munich—in coöperation with Great Britain and Italy—it forced Czechoslovakia to yield to the German claims. All this met with the approval of the majority of the French nationalists. When Mussolini, instigated by Hitler, proclaimed the Italian aspirations for Savoy, Nice, Corsica, and Tunis, the nationalists' objections were ventured timidly. No Demosthenes rose to warn the nation against

Philip. But if a new Demosthenes had presented himself the nationalists would have denounced him as the son of a rabbi or a nephew of Rothschild.

It is true that the French Left did not oppose the Nazis either, and in this respect they did not differ from their British friends. But that is no excuse for the nationalists. They were influential enough to induce an energetic anti-Nazi policy in France. But for them every proposal seriously to resist Hitler was a form of Jewish treachery.

It does credit to the French nation that it loved peace and was ready to avoid war even at the price of sacrifice. But that was not the question. Germany openly prepared a war for the total annhilation of France. There was no doubt about the intentions of the Nazis. Under such conditions the only policy appropriate would have been to frustrate Hitler's plans at all costs. Whoever dragged in the Jews in discussing Franco-German relations forsook the cause of his nation. Whether Hitler was a friend or foe of the Jews was irrelevant. The existence of France was at stake. This alone had to be considered, not the desire of French shopkeepers or doctors to get rid of their Jewish competitors.

That France did not block Hitler's endeavors in time, that it long neglected its military preparations, and that finally, when war could no longer be avoided, it was not ready to fight was the fault of anti-Semitism. The French anti-Semites served Hitler well. Without them the new war might have been avoided, or at least fought under much more favorable conditions.

When war came, it was stigmatized by the French Right as a war for the sake of the Jews and by the French communists as a war for the sake of capitalism. The unpopularity of the war paralyzed the hands of the military chiefs. It slowed down work in the armament factories. From a military point of view matters in June, 1940, were not worse than in early September, 1914, and less unfavorable than in September, 1870. Gambetta, Clemenceau, or Briand would not have capitulated. Neither would Georges Mandel. But Mandel was a Jew and therefore not eligible for political leadership. Thus the unbelievable happened: France disavowed its past, branded the proudest memories of its history Jewish, and hailed the loss of its political independence as a national revolution and a regeneration of its true spirit.

Not alone in France but the world over anti-Semitism made propaganda for Nazism. Such was the detrimental effect of interventionism and its tendencies toward discrimination that a good many people became unable to appreciate problems of foreign policy from any viewpoint but that of their appetite for discrimination against successful competitors. The hope of being delivered from a Jewish competitor fascinated them while they forgot everything else, their nation's independence, freedom, religion, civilization. There were and are pro-Nazi parties all over the world. Every European country has its Quislings. Quislings commanded armies whose duty it was to defend their country. They capitulated ignominiously; they coöperated with invaders; they had the impudence to style their treachery true patriotism. The Nazis have an ally in every town or village where there is a man eager to get rid of a Jewish competitor. The secret weapon of Hitler is the anti-Jewish inclinations of many millions of shopkeepers and grocers, of doctors and lawyers, professors and writers.

The present war would never have originated but for anti-Semitism. Only anti-Semitism made it possible for the Nazis to restore the German people's faith in the invincibility of its armed forces and thus to drive Germany again into the policy of aggression and the struggle for hegemony. Only the anti-Semitic entanglement of a good deal of French public opinion prevented France from stopping Hitler when he could still be stopped without war. And it was anti-Semitism that helped the German armies find in every European country men ready to open the doors to them.

Mankind has paid a high price indeed for anti-Semitism.

BARRY MORRIS GOLDWATER

More than any other contemporary politician, Senator Barry M. Goldwater (1909–   ) deserves the credit for helping to revive conservatism as a mainstream American political movement. His book, *The Conscience of a Conservative,* was a major best-seller. As a presidential candidate he carried the conservative message to every state in the Union. In his quiet, subdued manner, Goldwater delivered speeches of great controversy and wisdom. His acceptance speech at the Republican Convention in San Francisco in 1964, reprinted below, was widely misinterpreted for political reasons, but nevertheless remains an important document in the history of American conservatism. The late Professor Willmoore Kendall described it as the most important contribution by a politician to political philosophy in our century.

BARRY MORRIS GOLDWATER

From this moment, united and determined, we will go forward together—dedicated to the ultimate and undeniable greatness of the whole man.

I accept your nomination with a deep sense of humility. I accept the responsibility that goes with it. I seek your continued help and guidance.

Our cause is too great for any man to feel worthy of it.

Our task would be too great for any man, did he not have with him the hearts and hands of this great Republican Party.

I promise you that every fibre of my being is consecrated to our cause, that nothing shall be lacking from the struggle that can be brought to it by enthusiasm and devotion—and hard work!

In this world, no person—no party—can guarantee anything. What we *can* do, and what we *shall* do, is to *deserve* victory.

The good Lord raised up this mighty Republic to be a home for the brave and to flourish as the land of the free—*not* to stagnate in the swampland of collectivism—*not* to cringe before the bullying of Communism.

The tide has been running against freedom. Our people have followed false prophets. We must and we *shall* return to proven ways—*not* because they are old, but because they are *true*. We must and we shall set the tides running again in the cause of freedom.

This Party, with its every action, every word, every breath, and every heartbeat, has but a single resolve:

Freedom!

Freedom—made orderly for this nation by our Constitutional government.

Freedom—under a government limited by the laws of nature and of nature's God.

Freedom—balanced so that order, lacking liberty, will not become the slavery of the prison cell; balanced so that liberty, lacking order, will not become the license of the mob and the jungle.

We Americans understand freedom. We have earned it, lived for it, and died for it.

This nation and its people are freedom's model in a searching world. We *can be* freedom's missionaries in a doubting world. But first we *must renew* freedom's vision in our own hearts and in our own homes.

During four futile years, the Administration which we shall replace has distorted and lost that vision.

It has talked and talked and talked the *words* of freedom. But it has failed and failed and failed in the *works* of freedom.

Failures cement the wall of shame in Berlin. Failures blot the sands of shame at the Bay of Pigs. Failures mark the slow death of freedom in Laos. Failures infest the jungles of Vietnam. Failures haunt the houses of our once great alliances, and undermine the greatest bulwark ever erected by free nations—the NATO community.

Failures proclaim lost leadership, obscure purpose, weakening will, and the risk of inciting our sworn enemies to new aggressions and new excesses.

Because of this Administration, we are a world divided—we are a nation becalmed.

We have lost the brisk pace of diversity and the genius of individual creativity. We are plodding at a pace set by centralized planning, red tape, rules without responsibility, and regimentation without recourse.

Rather than useful jobs, our people have been offered bureaucratic make-work. Rather than moral leadership, they have been given bread and circuses, spectacle and even scandal.

There is violence in our streets, corruption in our highest offices, aimlessness among our youth, anxiety among our elders. There is virtual despair among the many who look beyond material success for the inner meaning of their lives.

Where examples of morality should be set, the opposite is seen. Small men, seeking great wealth or power, have too often and too long turned even the highest levels of public service into mere personal opportunity.

Certainly, simple honesty is not too much to demand of men in government. We find it in most. Republicans demand it from everyone—no matter how exalted or protected his position.

The growing menace to personal safety, to life, limb, and property, in homes, churches, playgrounds, and places of business, particularly in our great cities, is the mounting concern of every thoughtful citizen. Security from domestic violence, no less than from foreign aggression, is the most elementary and fundamental purpose of any government. A government that cannot fulfill this purpose is one that cannot long command the loyalty of its citizens. History demonstrates that nothing prepares the way for tyranny more than the failure of public officials to keep the streets safe from bullies and marauders.

We Republicans see all this as more, *much* more than the result of mere political differences, or mere political mistakes. We see this as the result of a fundamentally and absolutely wrong view of man, his nature, and his destiny.

Those who seek to live your lives for you, to take

your liberties in return for relieving you of your responsibilities—those who elevate the state and downgrade the citizen—must see ultimately a world in which earthly power can be substituted for divine will. This nation was founded upon the rejection of that notion and upon the acceptance of God as the author of freedom.

Those who seek absolute power, even though they seek it to do what they regard as good, are simply demanding the right to enforce *their* version of heaven on earth. They are the very ones who always create the most hellish tyrannies.

Absolute power *does* corrupt. And those who seek it must be suspect and must be opposed.

Their mistaken course stems from false notions of equality.

Equality, rightly understood, as our Founding Fathers understood it, leads to liberty and to the emancipation of creative differences.

Wrongly understood, as it has been so tragically in our time, it leads first to conformity and then to despotism.

It is the cause of Republicanism to resist concentrations of power, *private* or *public,* which enforce such conformity and inflict such despotism.

It is the cause of Republicanism to ensure that power remains in the hands of the people. And, so help us God, that is exactly what a Republican President will do—with the help of a Republican Congress.

It is the cause of Republicanism to restore a clear understanding of the tyranny of man over man in the world at large. It is our cause to dispel the foggy thinking which avoids hard decisions in the delusion that a world of conflict will mysteriously resolve itself into a world of harmony—if we just don't rock the boat or irritate the forces of aggression.

It is the cause of Republicanism to remind ourselves and the world that only the strong *can* remain free—that only the strong *can* keep the peace!

Republicans have shouldered this hard responsibility and marched in this cause before. It was Republican leadership under Dwight David Eisenhower that kept the peace and passed along to this Administration the mightiest arsenal for defense the world has ever known.

It was the strength and believable will of the Eisenhower years that kept the peace by using our strength—by using it in the Formosa Straits and in Lebanon, and by showing it *courageously* at all times.

It was during those Republican years that the thrust of Communist imperialism was blunted. It was during those years of Republican leadership that this world moved closer to *peace* than at any other time in the last three decades.

It has been during *Democratic* years that our strength to deter war has stood still and even gone into a planned decline.

It has been during *Democratic* years that we have weakly stumbled into conflict—*timidly* refusing to draw our own lines against aggression—*deceitfully* refusing to tell even our own people of our full participation—and *tragically* letting our finest men die on battlefields unmarked by purpose, pride, or the prospect of victory.

Yesterday it was Korea. Today it is Vietnam.

We are at war in Vietnam—yet the President who is the Commander in Chief of our forces refuses to say whether or not the objective is victory. His Secretary of Defense continues to mislead and misinform the American people.

It has been during *Democratic* years that a billion persons were cast into Communist captivity and their fate cynically sealed. Today, we have an Administration which seems eager to deal with Communism in every coin known—from gold to wheat, from consulates to confidences, and even human freedom itself.

The Republican cause demands that we brand Communism as the principal disturber of peace in the world today—indeed, the only significant disturber of the peace. We must make clear that until its goals of conquest are absolutely renounced, and its relations with all nations tempered, Communism and the governments it now controls are enemies of every man on earth who is or wants to be free.

We can keep the peace only if we remain vigilant and strong. Only if we keep our eyes open and keep our guard up can we prevent war.

I do not intend to let peace *or* freedom be torn from our grasp because of lack of strength or lack of will. *That* I promise you.

I believe that we must must look beyond the defense of freedom today to its extension tomorrow. I believe that the Communism which boasts it will "bury us," will instead give way to the forces of freedom.

And I can see, in the distant and yet recognizable future, the outlines of a world worthy of our dedication, our every risk, our every effort, our every sacrifice along the way. Yes, a world that will redeem the suffering of those who *will* be liberated from tyranny.

I can see, and I suggest that all thoughtful men

must contemplate, the flowering of an Atlantic civilization: the *whole* of Europe reunified and freed, trading openly across its borders, communicating openly across the world.

This is a goal more meaningful than a moon shot —a truly inspiring goal for all free men to set for themselves during the latter half of the twentieth century.

I can see, and all free men must thrill to, the advance of this Atlantic civilization joined by its great ocean highway to the United States. What a destiny can be ours—to stand as a great central pillar linking Europe, the Americas, and the venerable and vital peoples and cultures of the Pacific.

I can see a day when all the Americas, North and South, will be linked in a mighty system, a system in which the errors and misunderstandings of the past will be submerged, one by one, in a rising tide of prosperity and interdependence. We know that the misunderstandings of centuries are not to be wiped away in a day or an hour. But we pledge that human sympathy—what our neighbors to the South call an attitude that is *simpatico*—no less than enlightened self-interest, will be our guide.

I can see this Atlantic civilization galvanizing and *guiding* emergent nations everywhere.

I know that freedom is not the fruit of every soil. I know that our own freedom was achieved through centuries by the unremitting efforts of brave and wise men. I know that the road to freedom is a long and a challenging road. I know that some men may walk away from it, that some men resist challenge —accepting the false security of governmental paternalism.

I pledge that the America I envision in the years

ahead will extend its hand in help, in teaching, and in cultivation, so that all new nations will at least be *encouraged* to go *our* way—so that they will not wander down the dark alleys of tyranny, or the dead-end streets of collectivism.

We do *no* man a service by hiding freedom's light under a bushel of mistaken humility.

I seek an America proud of its past, proud of its ways, proud of its dreams, and determined actively to proclaim them.

But our example to the world must, like charity, begin at home.

In our vision of a good and decent future, free and peaceful, there must be room for the liberation of the energy and the talent of the individual—otherwise our vision is blind at the outset.

We must assure a society here which, while never abandoning the needy or forsaking the helpless, nurtures incentives and opportunities for the creative and the productive.

We must know the *whole* good as the product of many single contributions.

I cherish a day when our children, once again, will restore as heroes the sort of men and women who—unafraid and undaunted—pursue the truth, strive to cure disease, subdue and make fruitful our natural environment, and produce the inventive engines of production, science, and technology.

This nation, whose creative people have enhanced this entire span of history, should again thrive upon the greatness of all those things which we—as individual citizens—can and should do.

During Republican years this again will be a nation of men and women, of families proud of their roles, jealous of their responsibilities, unlimited in their aspirations—a nation where all who *can, will* be self-reliant.

We Republicans see in our Constitutional form of government the great framework which assures the orderly but dynamic fulfillment of the whole man— and we see the whole man as the *great* reason for instituting orderly government in the first place.

We see, in private property and an economy based upon and fostering private property, the one way to make government a durable ally of the whole man, rather than his determined enemy. We see, in the sanctity of private property, the only durable foundation for Constitutional government in a free society.

And beyond that, we see and cherish diversity of ways, diversity of thoughts, of motives and accomplishments. We do not seek to live anyone's life for him—we seek only to secure his rights, guarantee him opportunity to strive, with government performing only those needed and Constitutionally-sanctioned tasks which cannot otherwise be performed.

We seek a government that attends to its inherent responsibilities of maintaining a stable monetary and fiscal climate—encouraging a free and competitive economy, and enforcing law and order.

Thus do we seek inventiveness, diversity, and creative difference within a stable order. For we Republicans define government's role, where needed, at *many* levels, preferably the one *closest* to the people involved.

Our towns and our cities, then our counties and states, then our regional compacts—and *only then* the national government! *That* is the ladder of liberty built by decentralized power. On it, also, we must have balance *between* branches of government at *every* level.

Balance, diversity, creative difference—*these* are the elements of the Republican equation. Republicans agree on these elements and they heartily agree to disagree on many, many of their applications.

This is a party for free men—*not* for blind followers and *not* for conformists.

In 1858, Lincoln said of the Republican Party that it was composed of "strange, discordant, and even hostile elements." Yet all of the elements agreed on one paramount objective—to arrest the progress of slavery and place it in the course of ultimate extinction.

Today as then, but more urgently and more broadly than then, the task of preserving and enlarging freedom at home, and of safeguarding it from the forces of tyranny abroad, is great enough to challenge *all* our resources and to require *all* our strength.

Any who join us in all sincerity, we welcome. Those who do not care for our cause we do not expect to enter our ranks in any case.

And let our Republicanism, so focused and so dedicated, not be made fuzzy and futile by unthinking labels.

Extremism in the defense of liberty is no vice. Moderation in the pursuit of justice is no virtue.

The beauty of the very system we Republicans are pledged to restore and revitalize, the beauty of this Federal system of ours, is in its reconciliation of diversity with unity. We must not see malice in honest differences of opinion, no matter how great, so long as they are not inconsistent with the pledges we have given to each other in and through the Constitution.

Our Republican cause is not to level out the world or make its people conform in computer-regimented sameness.

Our Republican cause is to free our people and light the way for liberty throughout the world.

Ours is a very human cause for very *humane* goals.

This party, its good people, and its unquenchable devotion to freedom will not fulfill the high purpose of the campaign—which we launch *here and now*—until our cause has won the day, inspired the world, and shown the way to a tomorrow worthy of all our yesterdays.

JOHN ENOCH POWELL

Enoch Powell (1912–   ) is one of the most brilliant and controversial Conservative politicians of our time. After winning every possible academic prize at Cambridge University, he went on to become the youngest Professor of Greek in the history of the University of Sydney. A Brigadier in the British Army during World War II (he rose through the ranks from private soldier), he was first elected to Parliament in 1950. He served under Prime Minister Macmillan as Parliamentary Secretary to the Ministry of Housing, and later as Financial Secretary and Minister of Health. He was the opposition spokesman on defense until his ouster from the "shadow cabinet" in 1968. He has published books of poetry, translation, history, and economics, and has become the leading advocate of market economics in Britain.

From *Freedom and Reality* (New Rochelle, N. Y.: Arlington House, 1970). Reprinted by permission of the publisher.

JOHN ENOCH POWELL

How Intervention Spreads

As a frontal assault on the free economy the National Plan failed. But the attack became more insidious and more subtle. So far from Socialist ideas having retreated, they seemed to have become all the more deeply entrenched, not least within organisations that would not describe themselves as Socialist.

All revolutionaries become conservative in the very act of effecting their revolution. From the moment a change has been brought about, their concern is to prevent it from being reversed. They seek means to guard the power they have taken into their hands against all possibility of a counter-revolution. The Socialist Party and Government will be determined that the people at large shall not by any manner of means regain those liberties of choice and decision of which Socialism is engaged in depriving them.

The methods which revolutionaries, thus turned conservative, adopt are much the same everywhere and in every age. The student of history might find a wry interest in watching those methods being applied once again here and now. As usual, the least dangerous of those methods are the most obvious. Obviously almost every single act of this administration not only transfers to the state from individuals some piece of ownership, some right of decision, but creates new instruments of control and power. But these instruments—these statutory powers, these commissions, boards, authorities, these arbitrary influences exercised so often without legal authority at all—are in themselves inert and unprotected until

they can be surrounded with entrenchments and fortifications, manned by resolute defenders.

These fortifications we see rising before our eyes;
these forces we see being enlisted.

Power and patronage are at work. The very representatives of capitalism and free enterprise, the
most distinguished exponents of material or financial markets, those who have attained eminence by
using successfully the very mechanisms of individual decision and free choice which Socialism aims to
destroy, are persuaded to collaborate in the work. It
is called 'co-operating with the government of the
day'. They man committees, sit in the chairs of
boards, they advise on this piece of nationalisation,
undertake to operate that set of controls. Then they
discover that it is impracticable to denounce, attack
and oppose the very Ministers and policies with
which they are co-operating. Reluctantly at first, but
habit is a wonderful healer, they come to recognise
on which side their bread is buttered. It is now buttered on the state side. So they turn advocates of the
state.

THE PATRON'S LIVERY

Already substantial numbers of defenders, then,
have been thus recruited by the force of patronage
and wear the patron's livery—a rather medieval
term, I am afraid, but it will serve.

But these are the officers, rather than the troops.
At the very least they would be suitable for sending
to an OCTU. It is a different kind of patronage which
recruits the rank and file. This is the patronage of
the state as employer. Every act, every advance, of
Socialism brings into existence a new vested interest, for it creates new dependents of the state. The

new administrators, the new managers, the new employees—all look to the state in future for their job, their livelihood, their advancement. The same people, in the same industry, in the same place, are now different in an essential respect: they have a vested interest in the new order, the state order, continuing.

Those revolutions in history have been most permanent which have known how to create the largest vested interests. When Henry VIII had sold the lands of the dissolved monasteries to a multitude of private owners, there had come into existence an exactly equal number of people with a vested interest in the Protestant religion. They wanted the change to be permanent; they did not want to see anything disturbed any more. As Socialism proceeds, the number of people grow apace who do not want what has been done to be upset.

But there is a still more pervasive sort of vested interest in the permanence of revolutionary changes which springs up rapidly and is soon the most powerful force preserving them. This is opinion: the settled belief that things could not be otherwise, that there is no practicable alternative, that what is is bound to be. In the last analysis all power rests upon opinion. The great object of the Socialist is therefore to get people to believe that management, ownership and control by the state are inevitable. Once that belief has taken hold in a sufficient part of the nation, the task is done. The safest prisoners are those who are convinced they could not live outside the gaol: they cannot escape, because they do not want to.

SOCIALIST PROPOSITIONS

The creation of this ultimate vested interest in the Socialist state has already proceeded dangerously far. If anyone thinks that assertion imaginative or alarmist, let him consider the following propositions. 'Only the state could raise enough capital for the electricity and atomic power industries.' 'Without state direction we should put our industries down in the wrong parts of the country.' 'We cannot balance our payments unless the state helps us to export.' 'The state is responsible for providing people with homes.' 'The state ought to plan for economic growth.' 'Prices and wages will get out of hand unless the state controls them.' 'You cannot have a free market in land.' Every one of those propositions, and dozens more like them with which I could weary you, are accepted by vast numbers of people already—not as a matter of opinion but as self-evidently true. There is not one of them which you could venture to dispute without making a large number of people, including a large number who vote Conservative, extremely angry. Yet every one of these propositions leads directly and automatically to an extension of state Socialism.

INTERVENING IN INVESTMENT

Take, for example, the first of the propositions I mentioned—that 'only the state can find the capital' for huge investment like that required in the power-producing industries. The statement is absurd on the face of it. The capital is found by the state from the same source as that from which private investment is found: it comes out of the current national income. What the statement must therefore mean is that investment would not flow into the right directions unless the state directed resources compulsorily to where it thought best. The cloven hoof of Socialism is already revealed: the statement is none other than

the old, familiar Socialist claim that the state knows
what we ought to want. However, we next proceed to
ask what is the reason for supposing that the requisite investment would not flow into the production of
power in various forms as it flows into the other
directions where it is still at liberty to go. There are
two possible answers.

One, that the state knows better than anyone else
how much power of various kinds will be required at
a particular period in the future, would be greeted
with a hearty gust of belly-laughter by the very
same people who listen respectfully and credulously
to the original statement about 'only the state being
able to find the capital'. The alternative answer is
that the state has decided to sell power at lower
prices than would yield a comparable return on the
investment to what it could earn elsewhere, and
must therefore subsidise the prices by making the
capital available compulsorily. This reply opens up
an important line of discussion, but admits at the
outset that the alleged inability of anyone but the
state to find the necessary capital is an untrue statement, designed to cover up a very different one,
namely that the state ought to fix the price of power
and knows the right price at which to fix it.

This is no unpractical, theoretical point. The Government are at this time about to make a decision,
through their monopoly powers and through their
control over the nationalised gas industry, about
the price which that industry will be allowed to pay
for North Sea natural gas, potentially a tremendous
asset to this country, into which vast quantities of
private capital have flowed voluntarily. The Government have it in their power, by deliberately fixing a
price lower than what the market will bear, to do two

things. One is to keep the price of energy a little lower for the time being and reduce imports of fuel oil, an alternative source of energy. But if they do this, the other thing will follow automatically: they will discourage the exploitation of natural gas and thus eventually raise the cost of energy all round. I would like to quote to you a comment from this week's press which shows the writing on the wall.

> 'Both Shell and Esso have dropped broad hints about protest action: that if the return on their investment in the North Sea is too low they may slow down the operation. Some oil executives have even talked privately of withdrawing completely. Both measures would provoke official wrath, which is something about which the oil companies must be wary: there is already talk in the Labour Party about drawing up plans for nationalising natural gas, and any recalcitrance on the part of the explorers could be used as a reason for doing so.'

This is an understatement. In fact a Bill enabling a nationalised industry, the National Coal Board, to go into the natural gas business is already passing through the House of Commons.

Thus does the naïve acceptance of the inevitability of that Socialism which we have already, lead on to its extension, an extension which will in due course be defended and protected by the same naïve belief that it also was inevitable.

> *Eager to co-operate with the government of the day, 'to wear the patron's livery', were—of all people—the 'leaders of British industry'. They were very angry—and not only they—when told right at the outset of the Labour administration that they ought not to co-operate, but would assuredly fall victims to the temptation.*

One does feel terribly sorry for the spokesmen of industries, and of industry in general, confronted by a Socialist government. Their situation has all the pathos of the baby in the presence of the ruthless candy-stealer.

They start more than half-beaten, by the very fact that they are, or claim to be, the spokesmen and representatives. It has been their pride and occupation to 'represent' industry to the Government. Yet the safest posture for an industry confronted by Socialism would be not to have an organisation or spokesmen at all. Instead of being able to coax, browbeat or cajole a few 'representative' gentlemen into co-operation, the Government would then, unaided and at arm's length, be obliged to frame and enforce laws to control, manage or expropriate a multitude of separate undertakings—the true picture of private enterprise—with no means of getting at them except the policeman.

As soon as 'our President, Lord So-and-So' is in a position to talk about what such-and-such an industry 'wants' or 'thinks', that industry is on the road to the scaffold. Remember Caligula, who wished the Roman people had one neck, so that he could cut it? The Association of these, and the Federation of those, present just that one neck to the Socialist garotter. (And now, not content, the employers seem to be bent on *all* amalgamating into one great, soft, vulnerable neck!)

Still, this is now past remedy. It falls to contemplate these individual 'necks', as they are ushered in by the Minister's private secretary and seated, all hushed, round the mahogany conference table with the Voice of the People himself. ('Not a bad chap, is he? I rather liked him, personally. He'll soon learn that these Socialist ideas don't work and be a darned sight more competent than the fellow we had before the Election—even if he didn't go to Eton, what?') The Government, explains the Voice of the People, having regard to the financial crisis, or to the pledges on which they were elected, or to this and that, have decided that it is necessary, etc., and all this will be found set out, for greater accuracy, in the memorandum now being handed round. The Government feel sure that they can rely upon the co-operation, and indeed the advice and help, of the industry in carrying this policy through. The gentlemen, through their spokesman, explain that, while they cannot commit, etc., they will get their Executive or Council or what-not together without delay, give the matter their most urgent and careful consideration, and come back and let the Voice know the result. He thanks them and they withdraw.

Will they co-operate? You bet they will. A hundred to one they will co-operate, for two principal reasons —both dead wrong.

First, they think that if they co-operate they will get better terms, that the Government will not be so rough with them, that in fact they may be able, with luck, to talk the Government out of the more distasteful of its ideas. This is why they write letters to Opposition Members of Parliament, begging them not to raise this question, or press that subject, in the House just at present, because 'the industry' are in negotiation with the Government and 'are hopeful that it will be possible to reach a sensible conclusion behind the scenes' and therefore 'would not like there to be a row on the floor of the House at the present time.'

As any politician would have told them, this is the

exact opposite of the truth. It is a misconception to suppose that the Socialist Government will be influenced by 'what the industry thinks'. By the mechanics of politics, they are more concerned with what the Whips tell them their backbenchers think, and with what they believe their electors and potential electors think. That decided, the Government want to have no ammunition in the hands of the Opposition, no supporting 'quotes' from the industry itself to use in debate, no protests in the constituencies, no tedious quibbling about legislation, regulations or directions—in short, co-operation. Therefore the less co-operation, the more chance—a slim one at the best—there may be of modifying or delaying the action on which the Government are bent. That chance is at its maximum right at the outset—if possible, before there has been any public commitment or pronouncement.

But even if the representatives realised this, they would still co-operate—for the other big, wrong reason. They are afraid not to. They are afraid of being pilloried by the Government and its political supporters as 'unpatriotic' or simply (damning word) 'unco-operative'. They feel that the eye of the public will be upon them, and they do not like the adjectives which they foresee would be liberally used inside and outside Parliament—and will be, anyhow, before the end of the day. Of course the line of true patriotism would be the opposite to the one they are going to take. It would be to protest, by all means in their power, short of breaking the law, against every kind of error and nonsense as it comes along, and to oppose in their own industry any measure which does not commend itself to their knowledge and experience. But they shrink from this because, although they have no seats to lose and no voters to offend, it takes courage of a specialised kind—political courage—to outface authority and the popular cry of the hour. These men have commercial courage, and no doubt physical courage too; but facing the political music is something they have neither been trained nor volunteered for. So they play along with the search for an incomes policy, or export incentives, or whatever else it may be.

The effect is doubly damaging; for it also hamstrings any politicians who *are* prepared to raise their voices in protest. The public are bound to think it odd, supposing the politician's protest is sound, that no hostile noises are heard from other quarters and that instead they hear the accredited representatives of industry and commerce using the same phrases, and apparently approving the same ideas, as the Government. Thus the co-operators effectively expose the flank of the anti-Socialist opposition and compel it to fall back on positions which are better protected.

It is no comfort to the politician that when he meets the representatives of industry and commerce at dinners or on trains they are more than anxious to confide in him privately that 'of course, you were absolutely right in that speech of yours last Friday, and I'm so glad you made it'. The acknowledgment, 'Well, then, why don't *you* make one?' tends to bring the conversation to an abrupt close.

In fairness, however, be it admitted that a certain school of thought regards it as not timidity but political wisdom to play along with the follies of the passing hour. This is a special case of the general law that the expert in any subject considers himself *ipso facto* a politician and better able than the professional to judge what is politically expedient or politically practicable—like the civil servant who advises his chief that a policy otherwise sound is 'not practical politics at the present time'. Accordingly the representatives of capitalism are apt to judge the time not politically ripe for them to be candid in public.

It would be disingenuous not to add that cold terror and pseudo-political prudence are sometimes reinforced by self-interest. Governments are powerful creatures, with rewards and punishments at their disposal, which an anti-capitalist administration can operate in some ways more effectively than its opponents. What a pity it would be if years devoted at the expense of one's own business to the 'representation' of industry were not to reap their due recognition just for the lack of a little co-operation or through the utterance of a few critical sentences, which might just as well be left to others!

Perhaps, however, beneath all these causes which work, in different mixtures, to constrain acquiescence and co-operation, there lies one still deeper. Could it be that the representatives of capitalism are often at heart half-way to being anti-capitalist themselves?

One is often startled to hear a stalwart champion of private enterprise in his own industry advocating in the next breath policies elsewhere which could only be defended on Socialist assumptions. Men who would not dream of being influenced in their business decisions by Neddy targets will tell you that 'there's no question in this day and age we need economic planning'. Men who live by the market, when treated to an analysis of the principles on which they habitually act will denounce them as 'a misjudged attempt to return to nineteenth-century *laissez-*

faire'. Those who object most to government interference in the sphere which they know will often be
found among the first, when they are mere spectators, to demand government co-ordination of this
and regulation of that.

The reason is a simple one. In their own affairs
men of business learn by experience and observation. But they do not abstract from what they learn:
general principles are not their concern. Consequently, outside the limits of their own knowledge,
they adopt, like anyone else, the fashionable phrases
and prejudices of the day, regardless of whether
these are consistent with their other beliefs. Now, in
the last few years the fashion has been strongly anti-
capitalist. Everybody who was anybody has been
talking about things like economic growth, regional
development, planned economy. The whole atmosphere has been charged with the assumptions of
state control and direction.

So when a government sends for the representatives of industry and commerce and requires their
co-operation in the name of these familiar and hal-
lowed notions, they are hard put to it to know how to
refuse or argue. The enemy is within already, and
has only to open the gates to let in the main body.

*Often the free enterprise fly was to discover too late that
it had walked into the parlour of the Socialist spider.*

In politics as in war one of the greatest dangers is
that of underestimating one's opponent. I find all too
many Conservatives today who are ready to believe
that most of the objectionable parts of the Labour
Party's programme have already been put into effect
or at any rate introduced and that, to coin a phrase,

'Socialism is all over bar the shouting'. This sort of innocent has heard of steel nationalisation and thinks it is a bad thing; but if you asked him whether the Government propose to nationalise anything else, he would almost certainly reply: 'No, steel is the end of nationalisation so far as they are concerned. I understand they regard it as a bit out-of-date now.' If he was exceptionally well-informed he might burble something about Fairfields, or Beagle aircraft, or might conceivably have heard of the back staircase of nationalisation which has 'Industrial Reorganisation Corporation' written up over the door. But that would be all.

Our innocent friend is wrong, disastrously wrong. He is in for an unpleasant disillusionment. We have seen so far only the first wave, or wavelet, of Socialism; the next is coming up, with several more behind it, and they will get larger, not smaller. The more people realise this, the better; for the more chance there will be of resisting, and slowing down the process, even before the opportunity comes at a General Election to stop it altogether.

JOHN ENOCH POWELL

Intervention and the Individual

*The inevitable concomitant of interventionism is a big-
ger bureaucracy. Both expand by virtue of the assumption that the individual is capable of managing fewer
and fewer of his own affairs. Not surprisingly,*

the mania of the questionnaire bids fair to be one of
the curses of our age. The amount of time which
people who have something better to do spend in
completing perfectly futile forms and answering utterly fatuous questions would, if put to better use,
represent a considerable addition to our national income.

There are signs of this mania spreading to the
General Register Office, which conducts the national
census. I don't know whether any of you was fortunate enough to be selected as a recipient of a recent
communication from the Registrar General, enclos-
ing a questionnaire which I hold in my hand. If you
were, and have not yet completed it, you will have
received a further request, dated January this year,
telling you that 'the response has been excellent',
and that 'most of the people approached have sent in
their completed forms.' Assuming that this information makes you thoroughly ashamed of your failure
so far to co-operate, you will I hope address yourself
to filling in the questionnaire.

It starts off swimmingly: 'Have you ever had an
operation for gallstones?' to which most people
should have little difficulty in returning a straight
affirmative or negative. Things soon begin to thicken
however. You have to write down 'how many cups of
tea, coffee and other hot beverages (cocoa, chocolate,

"Ovaltine"—is that advertising?—etc.) you consume before breakfast, at breakfast, morning break, midday meal, tea-time, evening meal, bedtime and other'. I like 'other': presumably that is for the people who brew up at 2 in the morning. But that's just for a start. On the next page we get down to business. 'How many teaspoons of sugar do you take' in each beverage, and 'are the spoons level or heaped?' (One can't be too careful what one does in a modern state!) Then comes a bit of personal history: 'have you always taken the same amount of sugar in these beverages?'

We then turn to solids. On an 'average day' how many slices of bread do you eat? And don't just imagine you can slap down any old figure. You have to pick your way through 'average slice', 'extra thick' and 'extra thin' cut off 'large loaves' and 'small loaves'; so it's lucky for you if you only eat 'rolls'.

The candidate is now in a position to approach the more advanced part of the paper. For instance: 'how many fizzy drinks, non-alcoholic' by the glass do you drink per week, or, if you take sugar on your breakfast cereals, are the spoons you use tea spoons or dessert spoons and are the spoonsfuls level or heaped? Don't fill that in if you are like me, and prefer porridge; for there is a separate entry on its own for those who take porridge.

Now I am sure you will be glad to know the cost of this lark is being met out of the research funds of Queen Elizabeth College, and that you have been participating in a diet and health survey for the benefit of Professor John Yudkin, of that College.

But you may not be so pleased if you get another form, dated March of this year, also from the census office, which asks (hold it!) for details of your earnings in the financial year April 1966–March 1967. All quite confidential, of course; guaranteed no leaks even to 'other government departments' (guess which!); and you really ought to feel flattered, because this is a survey for the Department of Education and Science 'on the earnings of people with particular academic, professional, or vocational qualifications'. The questions include, for instance, whether one had 'subsidised or free housing or car for own use provided by the employer', and 'what was the total net profit before tax but after deducting expenses, from self-employment in the financial year 1966/67'.

VOLUNTEER BUREAUCRACY

Now, I have it on the authority of the Registrar General that 'surveys of this type are a relatively new development of our census work'. 'Each one', he says, 'has so far been judged on its merits.' This is just as well; for if these are a good example of the 'merit', then this promising new growth of volunteer bureaucracy had better be stamped on here and now. A glimpse of what will otherwise be in store for us is afforded by the complaisant self-satisfaction of the authors. 'We feel', says the Registrar General, 'that to use the census as a sample frame for this kind of enquiry is a valuable development and a step forward in making the fullest use of the material we have. The approach to the public has to be made by us because we cannot give anyone outside the census organisation a list of names and addresses.'

Sometimes it is a minor detail which casts a flood of light upon the malaise of a whole society. This incipient perversion of the census machinery derives from the very same general assumption which is pervading and strangling our life and our economy, namely, the conviction that the citizen is perfectly incapable of conducting his own affairs unless he is managed and controlled, planned and organised, with material distilled by experts from elaborate surveys which bureaucrats have conducted into his benighted behaviour. The National Economic Plan of the DEA—we are threatened with another, you know—and the Diet and Health Survey of the General Register Office, they are all branches, some tiny, some large, of this same pervasive, poisonous upas tree of contempt for the independence, dignity and competence of the individual.

About the same time that the Registrar General was asking questions about meals and drinks, the Ministry of Labour weighed in with some urgent inquiries into the staffing of hotels and restaurants (Anglice 'catering establishments').

The Ministry of Labour has a Manpower Research Unit. Put like that, the thing sounds harmless, sensible, even meritorious. What, one might ask, is wrong with research into manpower? Very proper, surely, very necessary. According to the official account, the Unit was 'set up to study future manpower requirements and the future distribution of manpower between industries'. Already one begins to feel a certain unease. On what assumptions are the 'future requirements of manpower' to be based? What is to be done if there turns out to be too much or too little on the assumptions made about a future year? Moreover, how can one know the future distribution of manpower between industries, when new developments and unforeseen demands are coming into existence all the time? Or is it intended to fit future developments and demands to the distribution of manpower forecast by the Ministry of Labour? Some of these questions may be answered if we look at how the Research Unit goes about its work; for it has just decided to survey, for the purpose of future manpower planning, the whole of the hotel and catering industry, and I happen to have come into possession of a copy of one of the questionnaires which it is proposed to use.

The object of the questionnaire, stated at the outset, is, I should mention, 'to compare the numbers employed in the various occupations in 1967/68 with a realistic estimate of the numbers likely to be required in 1972/73'. I turn at once to question No. 13, which starts with the words 'Do any of your staff . . . ?' and lists 42 occupations or activities. I will not trouble you with all 42, but here is a selection: 'Prepare powdered soups? Prepare tinned vegetables? Prepare frozen or dehydrated vegetables? Fillet fish?' Here I should perhaps notice that there is also a separate question lower down: 'Do any of your staff fillet Dover sole in front of customer?' However, I continue: 'Prepare basic stocks? Make Bechamel? Prepare mayonnaise? Prepare Sole Bonne Femme? Prepare Pommes Anna? Eye potatoes by hand? Put table cloths on tables? Make puff pastry? Prepare dishes with the lamp?' I must skip the rest, but cannot miss a final gem of civil servantese: 'Engage in control to eliminate dishonesty?'

THE BECHAMEL COEFFICIENT

Personally, I like the one about the Bechamel sauce the best. There seem to be two possibilities. One is that a coefficient exists known to the Ministry of

Labour, which enables one to deduce the manpower required in 1973 to make all kinds of sauces, once one has the key figure, which is the Bechamel manpower in 1968. Alternatively it may be that in the brave new world of 1973 the only sauce we shall be allowed is Bechamel sauce, which, though nice, will become monotonous.

However, I move on to the heavier parts of the questionnaire. After having 'indicated the present duties of occupational groups employed in his hotel', such as 'doorman,' 'baggage porter' and 'pageboy', the examinee finds himself asked if he is 'likely to introduce by 1973' convection ovens, micro-wave ovens, dishwashers, pan-handlers and what are called 'portion-controlled foods', and 'prefillings'. This little exercise in clairvoyance is intended to limber him up and get his prophetic powers working properly for the climax which comes, I feel, at question No. 29: 'Do you expect your future low season (February 1973) employment figures to bear the same relationship to the high season (August 1972) figures as February 1968 did to August 1967?' The question continues 'If the answer is yes'—actually they have made a mistake here, they mean no—'please indicate the occupations likely to be affected and the direction of the change.'

I want you to try to imagine the number of people engaged in this hair-raising piece of paperwork alone: the graduate staff at the Ministry devising these ludicrous questions, the junior staff typing, duplicating and posting them, then the staff co-ordinating the replies, sending reminders, making visits to clarify some point of doubt about the Bechamel or the filleted Dover sole, and finally putting it all through computers, on the good old principle 'garbage in, garbage out'. Then I want you to realise that this, though the first excursion of the Manpower Research Unit into a service industry, has been going on in a whole range of industries already and will spread to others in due course; how can one forecast future manpower requirements without covering all the employments? Each is being or will be bombarded with silly questions, to which only silly answers can be given.

I want you further to bear in mind that the Manpower Research Unit of the Ministry of Labour is itself only a tiny, obscure corner, in the great planning, enquiring, researching, questionnaire-pushing activities which are going on from one end of the government machine to the other. You must multiply the activities of the Manpower Research Unit very many fold to get any idea of the total quantity of futile effort being expended by public servants. But that is only half the picture.

TRADE ASSOCIATIONS COLLABORATE

You also have to remember all the labour and effort by management and their staffs which is being devoted to coping with this sort of nonsense, instead of doing their proper work. You might suppose that industrialists would long ere now have risen in their wrath and told the Ministry where to put its questionnaires. No doubt individually they would like to do so; but nowadays they are nearly all in one or more of their appropriate trade associations, whose alleged function is to look after their interests; and the bureaucracy of the trade associations, loyally cooperating and interacting with the bureaucracy of the state, will have committed them to fill up the forms before they know anything about it.

And so the merry games goes on, of choking and drowning Britain in a mass of paper planning. One is hard put to it to know whether to laugh or cry. It is not accident; it is the automatic and inevitable result of a policy which supposes that it is the function of government to plan the size and distribution between industries of the labour force in 1973. All the myriad, diverse, unforeseeable activities of the whole economy have to be surveyed and predicted, until the simple act of putting a tablecloth on a table or making a portion of Bechamel sauce becomes a government statistic, and no one can move or act or breathe without the agency of government. It is lunacy, yes: but it is a lunacy towards which we are heading by general connivance and with the speed of an express train.

In such a 'merry game' no one would expect the Prices and Incomes Board to be left out.

I want to tell you a story, a true story, and a sad story. It is also a cautionary story. Once upon a time there was a greengrocer with one assistant living in Wolverhampton. Not many weeks ago a large official envelope fell through his letterbox with a resounding thud. It was from the Prices and Incomes Board, far away in London. It told him to fill up the enclosed questionnaire, which it said was being sent to a sample of retailers all over the country. The reason why was explained in language so beautiful that I must quote it without alteration. It was 'to provide the Board with information relating to retailers' costs and profit margins and to give the Board some indication of the characteristic features of the retailing of fresh fruit and vegetables'.

What a lucky man I am, thought the greengrocer, to be one of those called upon to do such exalted work, though I must say I think it would have been better still if Mr. Jones and his friends would come and join me at the market tomorrow morning at 5 a.m. Then the greengrocer looked at the questionnaire, and his brow clouded. His eye fell upon such items as 'over the last five years has the percentage of fresh fruit and vegetables sold given in answer to question 6 (a) risen (b) remained the same (c) fallen slightly (d) fallen substantially? Tick where appropriate'.

Or this one: 'List below the items over and above the purchase price of produce which you pay to the suppliers of fresh fruit and vegetables'. Or this poser: 'What proportion of fresh fruit and vegetables sold by you are pre-packed?'—the space has a percentage mark after it but no indication whether the potatoes are to be valued or counted. Finally the greengrocer has to send in his trading account for the last three financial years and give reasons if any why the figures for these years are not comparable.

As he ruminated on the time, expense and general distraction which the completion of this questionnaire would involve, the greengrocer become aware that he would be liable on summary conviction to a fine of £50 if he failed to complete it or did so 'recklessly'. He also noticed another piece of paper included with the rest which gave him something of the background to his misfortune.

It appeared that there had been discussions between the Minister of Agriculture and a body called the National Federation of Fruit and Potato Trades Limited who had recommended their members to make an increase in prices to 'cover rising costs and

increased taxation'. There had also been representations by another body called the Retail Fruit Trade
Federation Limited. He rubbed his eyes when he
read, and read again, that the enquiry by the Prices
and Incomes Board had been requested—yes, requested—by the first of the above-mentioned Federations and supported—yes, supported—by the second
Federation. No wonder the First Secretary of State
and Minister of Agriculture had 'considered that this
would be desirable'. Hence the envelope through the
letterbox. So, reflected the greengrocer, it is apparently people like myself and those from whom I buy
in the market, or rather Federations who purport to
represent us, who have brought this evil upon me.
They have actually asked that I shall be plagued with
this enquiry so that the Board may have 'some indication of the characteristic features of the retailing
of fresh fruit and vegetables'. At the end presumably
somebody is going to tell me what my customers will
be willing to pay for the various goods I have to sell
them.

Now the cautionary aspect of this story is that this
envelope which came to the greengrocer is one of
many thousands which are going out all the time to
firms and persons, large and small, throughout the
country, imposing huge irritation, waste of time and
dislocation in order that the Prices and Incomes
Board may accumulate a mountain of figures of
varying value and accuracy—I forgot to tell you that
the greengrocer is allowed to insert his 'best estimate' whenever 'it is impossible to give exact per-
centages'—from which they can proceed to the
perfectly futile and absurd operation of stating what
the market price of various goods and services is, or
ought to be. They are doing so aided and abetted by

two bureaucracies: the old bureaucracy of the state, now growing apace, whose habits we know perfectly well; and the new bureaucracy of the Federation of This and the Association of That, all busily at work making jobs for themselves and hanging an additional weight round the neck of my greengrocer and the rest of British commerce and industry.

All this might be just bearable if the information given or the co-operation so willingly extended led either to a sensible result or to people's wishes being better met. But does it?

So far as the information is not wholly wasted, like that which was lavished on the National Plan, it is placed at the service of preconceptions and prejudices of a party or a bureaucracy—as for instance, the prejudice against offices and office workers.

For years past now the gentleman in Whitehall who knows best has been trying, preferably to prevent offices being provided at all—an Act to stop office building was among the most urgent legislation introduced by the present administration—but, if unfortunately that could not be completely prevented, then at least to get them built where he knew best. So he sat down to persuade or compel people to do their office work where they would not have chosen to do it. He established a bureau, deservedly called by its initials LOB, not to give people advice which would be worth their while paying for—that would be as meritorious as giving other paid advice—but advice they would not be willing to pay for.

The gentleman in Whitehall drew popular support from another prejudice of our time, the prejudice against 'congestion', against people working and living together in close proximity in increasing aggre-

gations, against that which has been the source and
condition of human progress since the beginning of
our race, whence we call it 'civilisation' or city-
dwelling.

The blitz on offices was seen as part of a larger
operation, described as 'checking the drift to the
south-east'. You may recall how until a short time
ago a neurosis, amounting almost to panic, prevailed
about the imminent prospect of the south-east choking itself to a standstill and the rest of Britain
becoming depopulated. I was much frowned upon, I
remember, for ridiculing the whole notion. Well,
would you believe it? The Registrar General, having
now got the figures, informed the world in April this
year [1967] that no such thing had been going on at
all. In the sixties there had not been any drift from
the rest of England and Wales to the south-east region. The net increase in that region had been solely
the natural increase of the population already there.
As a commentator remarked at the time: 'the myth
that everyone is moving into south-east England is
deflated'.

So the gentleman in Whitehall did not even know
what was happening or had happened. He was operating on false premises. What chance was there that
he would know what ought to happen in the future,
and who and what ought to go where?

From offices to houses. Housing has now been 'in politics'
for at least two generations, but no one yet has answered
—or even asked—the question:

Why is it that of all our personal needs and comforts
the one which has shown least progress in the last
two generations has been the rented house? While

the feeding and clothing of all classes have improved out of recognition, while cars and scooters stand outside the houses which contain new television sets, refrigerators and washing machines, one thing remains for millions of people almost as it was at the beginning of the century. That is the houses themselves. What is different about housing—above all, rented housing—that it alone has so lagged behind?

It is the state itself which has been the enemy of better and more abundant housing. The difference between the ample supplies of food, clothing and domestic appliances and the inadequate supply of rented housing is that 'governments have tried to peg rents, subsidise building and ration output.'

An American writing in our press lately [1964] said this about the British construction industry: 'For the past few years this industry has produced about 300,-000 houses and flats each year. As soon as one learns how many millions of persons in Britain live in inadequate or substandard houses or in tenement dwellings, this statistic can produce only one conclusion—it is a particularly sordid disgrace.'

I agree with him, except in one respect—the implied criticism of the industry. The industry, the very people whose business it would be to build more houses faster, are the last people who ought to be blamed.

This sordid disgrace is something which the nation as a whole has willed. It is chiefly the result of those two giant evils, rent control and housing subsidy, which the nation has not merely tolerated but insisted upon for the last 40 to 50 years.

The sum total of misery and squalor for which these evils have been responsible during their reign of half a century baffles calculation. During that period all the other elements of our material standard of living have improved out of recognition: food, clothing, transport, amusement, leisure. Housing alone has remained obstinately lagging behind. The cruel irony of this is symbolised by the television aerials on the rows of obsolete houses and the motorcars standing outside them. For decade after decade people have been prevented from demanding the one thing they wanted most after food and clothing, in the numbers which they wanted and the quality which they wanted. If the people had been allowed to demand, the industry would have supplied, as every other industry has responded with modern techniques to modern demands. Imagine what would have been the fate of our motor industry if the majority of its output since 1920 had been purchased for provision at subsidised prices to persons on 1,500 waiting lists, while all existing cars were compulsorily priced far below replacement cost. You then have some faint and distant conception of the havoc which the nation has inflicted on its house-building industry.

DESIRES THWARTED

When people's desires are thwarted, they find outlets as best they can in other directions. Much of the purchasing power which families would have preferred to put into homes has gone in other directions; but the great and continuing growth of houses for owner-occupation is some measure of the total potential demand for the products of our house-building industry. People have invested in what they were allowed to invest in, the individual owner-occupied house; but this has not produced the competitive mass market which alone would have given full scope to modern production methods and techniques, and investors have been 'warned off' the provision of what is most wanted, houses to rent.

Not content even with loading these disabilities on to itself, the nation has insisted on limiting the raw material of house-building: the ground itself. I hear people complaining about the high prices of building land for houses. But prices are only telling us the truth about the consequences of our own actions. The price an article will fetch in a given set of circumstances is its value in those circumstances. To rail at prices and threaten to control them is to behave like a petulant child who smashes the clock because he wishes it were a different time of day. Town planning is essential. The preservation of urban open space and of rural beauty are things worth paying for, as paid for they must be, in terms of somewhat higher land values. But nobody can justify the amount of land at present sterilised inside and outside our towns: in Wolverhampton, for instance, we have seen whole areas withheld from building for years at a time, almost decades, by the unholy alliance of town planning and the two evil giants.

When I consider these things, I could wish that politicians of all persuasions would spend a little less time on telling the building industry how to manage its own business. On the other hand I wish they would spend more time explaining to the electorate—this is the politician's business—that some of the evils people complain of are the result of the very laws which they mistakenly suppose to be for their protection and benefit.

One politician did his best:

The state has been interfering in housing these 50 years past. Political parties at election time have gone out to get votes by promising bigger and brighter interference. If one party has a housing target—though whoever heard of a clothing target, or a food target, or a car target, or a television set or foreign holiday target?—then the other party is expected to have a housing target too, and a bigger one if possible. So we are all of us habituated to government interference, to the point when we can hardly imagine life without it.

Yet what a hash of things the state has made! Government interference has succeeded in one thing: in organising a never-ending, self-perpetuating shortage of housing. Yet it wasn't really as difficult to do this as it may sound. Give me a year or two and I guarantee to organise you an equally squalid shortage of anything else you care to name by applying the same methods as have been so successful with houses: control the price, subsidise the product, and wait for the scarcity to come along. Players can then exercise their ingenuity by inventing systems of rationing and allocation.

You might think by now even the most purblind would have begun to suspect that something was wrong somewhere. But bad habits of long standing die hard. We never seem to ask ourselves—or at least we never seem to stay for the answer—why there is this extraordinary coincidence that the one element in the physical standard of living for which the state has taken responsibility has been the one element which has lagged behind when the rest have streaked ahead. We prefer to be taken in over and over again by the old political swindle of promising more cheaper by the simple expedient of fudging the price.

HOUSING SHORTAGE FOR EVER?

You cannot, however, have the benefits of a market when half the annual production and more than half the existing stock is kept outside the market altogether. There is one essential condition for enjoying the blessings of a market in any product. It is for that product to be sold or leased for what it will fetch in the open market. There is no burking this condition. So long as any appreciable number of houses in this country are let for less than the rent they would command in the open market, there will continue to be a housing shortage, with all the miserable and squalid consequences which I witness every week of the year as a constituency member.

People talk about charging 'economic' rents. If that means market rents—which is what the word ought to mean—then well and good. On the other hand, if it means rents calculated to cover some historical costs, then it is off the mark, for the good and sufficient reason that there is no connection whatever between the cost of making an article and what that article is worth in the market either now, or five years from now, or 50 years from now. The choice is plain and straightforward: market rents or housing shortage. Which do you prefer? Myself, I vote for houses.

The state's concern for our diet, hotels and greengroceries does not extend to holidays abroad. Political interference here is particularly high-handed.

A fortnight ago I was in West Berlin looking out over the Berlin Wall, which the Russians and the East German Government have built to keep their own citizens imprisoned.

We are used to regarding the Berlin Wall as a horrific symbol of oppression and of the denial of elementary human freedom. That such a thing could happen to us, the citizens of a free country, never enters our heads. Still less do we realise that it already *has* happened to us. There is a Berlin Wall round this country, built for the same purpose and for the same reasons by the government here, even though we are only fined or imprisoned, instead of shot, for attempting to get across it.

The freedom of a citizen to leave the country does not mean freedom to go out with what he stands up in. I remember before the War how the inhabitants of Nazi Germany had little difficulty in crossing the frontiers, provided they took with then no more than 10 Reichsmarks. You may go, but you may not take with you your possessions or such of them as you please. This is not liberty of movement. A man's freedom to dispose of his money and his goods is an indispensable part of the freedom of movement. Today we in this country do not have that liberty.

Do you wish to go on holiday? You may take £50. Do you wish to go on business? You may produce evidence that such is your purpose, or you will not be allowed to. Do you wish to travel for your health? You will need to get a pretty drastic doctor's note. Do you want to work abroad for a year or two? You will have to say that you are emigrating—it is called 'applying for emigrant status'—if you want to take with you any substantial sum.

The cause of these restrictions on our freedom is essentially the same as the cause of the Berlin Wall. It is that the Government are determined to manage affairs at home—in this case, the economy—in a manner which is inconsistent with the individual citizen's freedom of movement for himself and his goods. They wish to pursue a series of policies which weaken the value of the pound and yet to go on insisting that its value is unchanged. The contradiction is resolved by imprisoning the citizen and impounding his property. What is more, if he comes into possession of foreign currency, he must empty his pockets and hand it over—at a loss. As for gold, it is a crime to have it about, even in the form of antique coins, as though the stuff were high explosive or seditious literature.

Thus the citizen is fitted to the requirements of the régime, instead of the régime to the requirements of the citizen. This is no more than a mild version of the Communist system which will only work if those within it are not allowed to make comparisons with the outside world.

The securest prison is that from which the prisoner no longer wishes to escape. The Communist régimes have inculcated into the mass of their citizens the notion that even the wish to make comparisons with the rest of the world is unpatriotic, and that only a traitor would be guilty of a desire to travel. The régime here too have had no small success in this highest department of the gaoler's art. We are already reduced to a state of mind in which it appears not only not part of the natural order of things, but a most extraordinary and outlandish suggestion, that individuals should be free to take or send their property where they will. Millions in this country have been taught to think that no true patriot could look beyond £50 or a discretionary allowance from the Bank of England. Such is the force of habit and suggestion.

MILTON FRIEDMAN

America's premier economist, Milton Friedman (1918–) has carried his message to both professional economists—who have honored him with the Presidency of the American Economics Association —and laymen. A leader of the monetarist-oriented Chicago School, he has authored numerous books and essays of a technical nature, along with his more popular general book, *Capitalism and Freedom.* Professor Friedman is a columnist for *Newsweek,* and an advisor on economics to Presidents and Prime Ministers. In 1964 he was an economic advisor to Barry Goldwater, and in 1968, he advised Richard Nixon in his candidacy.

From *Capitalism and Freedom* (Chicago: University of Chicago Press, 1964). With the permission of the publisher.

MILTON FRIEDMAN

Introduction

In a much quoted passage in his inaugural address, President Kennedy said, "Ask not what your country can do for you—ask what you can do for your country." It is a striking sign of the temper of our times that the controversy about this passage centered on its origin and not on its content. Neither half of the statement expresses a relation between the citizen and his government that is worthy of the ideals of free men in a free society. The paternalistic "what your country can do for you" implies that government is the patron, the citizen the ward, a view that is at odds with the free man's belief in his own responsibility for his own destiny. The organismic "what you can do for your country" implies that government is the master or the deity, the citizen, the servant or the votary. To the free man, the country is the collection of individuals who compose it, not something over and above them. He is proud of a common heritage and loyal to common traditions. But he regards government as a means, an instrumentality, neither a grantor of favors and gifts, nor a master or god to be blindly worshipped and served. He recognizes no national goal except as it is the consensus of the goals that the citizens severally serve. He recognizes no national purpose except as it is the consensus of the purposes for which the citizens severally strive.

The free man will ask neither what his country can do for him nor what he can do for his country. He will ask rather "What can I and my compatriots do through government" to help us discharge our individual responsibilities, to achieve our several goals and purposes, and above all, to protect our freedom? And he will accompany this question with another: How can we keep the government we create from becoming a Frankenstein that will destroy the very freedom we establish it to protect? Freedom is a rare and delicate plant. Our minds tell us, and history confirms, that the great threat to freedom is the concentration of power. Government is necessary to preserve our freedom, it is an instrument through which we can exercise our freedom; yet by concentrating power in political hands, it is also a threat to freedom. Even though the men who wield this power initially be of good will and even though they be not corrupted by the power they exercise, the power will both attract and form men of a different stamp.

How can we benefit from the promise of government while avoiding the threat to freedom? Two broad principles embodied in our Constitution give an answer that has preserved our freedom so far, though they have been violated repeatedly in practice while proclaimed as precept.

First, the scope of government must be limited. Its major function must be to protect our freedom both from the enemies outside our gates and from our fellow-citizens: to preserve law and order, to enforce private contracts, to foster competitive markets. Beyond this major function, government may enable us at times to accomplish jointly what we would find it more difficult or expensive to accomplish severally. However, any such use of government is fraught with danger. We should not and cannot avoid using government in this way. But there should be a clear and large balance of advantages before we do. By relying primarily on voluntary co-operation and private enterprise, in both economic and other activities, we can insure that the private sector is a check on the powers of the governmental sector and an effective protection of freedom of speech, of religion, and of thought.

The second broad principle is that government power must be dispersed. If government is to exercise power, better in the county than in the state, better in the state than in Washington. If I do not like what my local community does, be it in sewage disposal, or zoning, or schools, I can move to another local community, and though few may take this step, the mere possibility acts as a check. If I do not like what my state does, I can move to another. If I do not like what Washington imposes, I have few alternatives in this world of jealous nations.

The very difficulty of avoiding the enactments of the federal government is of course the great attraction of centralization to many of its proponents. It will enable them more effectively, they believe, to legislate programs that—as they see it—are in the interest of the public, whether it be the transfer of income from the rich to the poor or from private to governmental purposes. They are in a sense right. But this coin has two sides. The power to do good is also the power to do harm; those who control the power today may not tomorrow; and, more important, what one man regards as good, another may regard as harm. The great tragedy of the drive to centralization, as of the drive to extend the scope of government in general, is that it is mostly led by men of good will who will be the first to rue its consequences.

The preservation of freedom is the protective reason for limiting and decentralizing governmental power. But there is also a constructive reason. The great advances of civilization, whether in architecture or painting, in science or literature, in industry or agriculture, have never come from centralized government. Columbus did not set out to seek a new route to China in response to a majority directive of a parliament, though he was partly financed by an absolute monarch. Newton and Leibnitz; Einstein and Bohr; Shakespeare, Milton, and Pasternak; Whitney, McCormick, Edison, and Ford; Jane Addams, Florence Nightingale, and Albert Schweitzer; no one of these opened new frontiers in human knowledge and understanding, in literature, in technical possibilities, or in the relief of human misery in response to governmental directives. Their achievements were the product of individual genius, of strongly held minority views, of a social climate permitting variety and diversity.

Government can never duplicate the variety and diversity of individual action. At any moment in time, by imposing uniform standards in housing, or nutrition, or clothing, government could undoubtedly improve the level of living of many individuals; by imposing uniform standards in schooling, road construction, or sanitation, central government could undoubtedly improve the level of performance in many local areas and perhaps even on the average of all communities. But in the process, government would replace progress by stagnation, it would substitute uniform mediocrity for the variety essential for that experimentation which can bring tomorrow's laggards above today's means.

This book discusses some of these great issues. Its major theme is the role of competitive capitalism—the organization of the bulk of economic activity through private enterprise operating in a free market—as a system of economic freedom and a necessary condition for political freedom. Its minor theme is the role that government should play in a society dedicated to freedom and relying primarily on the market to organize economic activity.

The first two chapters deal with these issues on an abstract level, in terms of principles rather than concrete application. The later chapters apply these principles to a variety of particular problems.

An abstract statement can conceivably be complete and exhaustive, though this ideal is certainly far from realized in the two chapters that follow. The application of the principles cannot even conceivably be exhaustive. Each day brings new problems and new circumstances. That is why the role of the state can never be spelled out once and for all in terms of specific functions. It is also why we need from time to time to re-examine the bearing of what we hope are unchanged principles on the problems of the day. A by-product is inevitably a retesting of the principles and a sharpening of our understanding of them.

It is extremely convenient to have a label for the political and economic viewpoint elaborated in this book. The rightful and proper label is liberalism. Unfortunately, "As a supreme, if unintended compliment, the enemies of the system of private enterprise have thought it wise to appropriate its label",[1] so that liberalism has, in the United States, come to have a very different meaning than it did in the nineteenth century or does today over much of the Continent of Europe.

[1]Joseph Schumpeter, *History of Economic Analysis* (New York: Oxford University Press, 1954) p. 394.

As it developed in the late eighteenth and early nineteenth centuries, the intellectual movement that went under the name of liberalism emphasized freedom as the ultimate goal and the individual as the ultimate entity in the society. It supported laissez faire at home as a means of reducing the role of the state in economic affairs and thereby enlarging the role of the individual; it supported free trade abroad as a means of linking the nations of the world together peacefully and democratically. In political matters, it supported the development of representative government and of parliamentary institutions, reduction in the arbitrary power of the state, and protection of the civil freedoms of individuals.

Beginning in the late nineteenth century, and especially after 1930 in the United States, the term liberalism came to be associated with a very different emphasis, particularly in economic policy. It came to be associated with a readiness to rely primarily on the state rather than on private voluntary arrangements to achieve objectives regarded as desirable. The catchwords became welfare and equality rather than freedom. The nineteenth-century liberal regarded an extension of freedom as the most effective way to promote welfare and equality; the twentieth-century liberal regards welfare and equality as either prerequisites of or alternatives to freedom. In the name of welfare and equality, the twentieth-century liberal has come to favor a revival of the very policies of state intervention and paternalism against which classical liberalism fought. In the very act of turning the clock back to seventeenth-century mercantilism, he is fond of castigating true liberals as reactionary!

The change in the meaning attached to the term

liberalism is more striking in economic matters than in political. The twentieth-century liberal, like the nineteenth-century liberal, favors parliamentary institutions, representative government, civil rights, and so on. Yet even in political matters, there is a notable difference. Jealous of liberty, and hence fearful of centralized power, whether in governmental or private hands, the nineteenth-century liberal favored political decentralization. Committed to action and confident of the beneficence of power so long as it is in the hands of a government ostensibly controlled by the electorate, the twentieth-century liberal favors centralized government. He will resolve any doubt about where power should be located in favor of the state instead of the city, of the federal government instead of the state, and of a world organization instead of a national government.

Because of the corruption of the term liberalism, the views that formerly went under that name are now often labeled conservatism. But this is not a satisfactory alternative. The nineteenth-century liberal was a radical, both in the etymological sense of going to the root of the matter, and in the political sense of favoring major changes in social institutions. So too must be his modern heir. We do not wish to conserve the state interventions that have interfered so greatly with our freedom, though, of course, we do wish to conserve those that have promoted it. Moreover, in practice, the term conservatism has come to cover so wide a range of views, and views so incompatible with one another, that we shall no doubt see the growth of hyphenated designations, such as libertarian-conservative and aristocratic-conservative.

Partly because of my reluctance to surrender the term to proponents of measures that would destroy liberty, partly because I cannot find a better alternative, I shall resolve these difficulties by using the word liberalism in its original sense—as the doctrines pertaining to a free man.

Part VII

American Conservatism:

THE OLD DISPENSATION

What we have chosen to call the "Old Dispensation" of American conservatism has been greatly ignored by students of the subject. George Washington has become a figure of mythology, no longer read or studied in any depth; James F. Cooper is known only for his literary achievement and not for his political philosophy; and Calhoun, Justice Story, Henry Cabot Lodge, and William Borah are studied only by specialists in American history. Yet all were conservative, and all have profoundly influenced not only conservative thought but also the history of this country. The writers in this section are all marked by a thoroughgoing American originality, in many ways different from the more worldly, international conservatism articulated by such contemporary thinkers as William Buckley and James Burnham.

GEORGE WASHINGTON

Historical mythology to the contrary, George Washington (1732–1799) was one of the greatest of Americans. Among our Founding Fathers, he was, in the words of Edmund Morgan, "the most limited and the strongest. His strength came not only from the fact that he had earned the unbounded confidence of the people, but from the simplicity of his mind. . . . As President of the United States he devoted himself with equal singleness of purpose, equal detachment, and equal success to making the new government respected at home and abroad." His political philosophy, as seen in the following documents, has profoundly influenced the development of our country. The Farewell Address; the letter to Jay on the tendency toward monarchy; and the letter to General Thomas, dealing with his conception of the American cause—all tend to demonstrate how important Washington has been for the development of conservative thought in the United States.

From *George Washington: Letters and Addresses,* ed. Jonas Viles (New York, 1909).

GEORGE WASHINGTON

On a Tendency Toward Monarchy

MOUNT VERNON, 1 August, 1786.

Dear Sir: Your sentiments, that our affairs are drawing rapidly to a crisis, accord with my own. What the event will be, is also beyond the reach of my foresight. We have errors to correct. We have probably had too good an opinion of human nature in forming our confederation. Experience has taught us, that men will not adopt and carry into execution measures the best calculated for their own good, without the intervention of a coercive power. I do not conceive we can exist long as a nation without having lodged some where a power, which will pervade the whole Union in as energetic a manner as the authority of the State governments extends over the several States.

To be fearful of investing Congress, constituted as that body is, with ample authorities for national purposes, appears to me the very climax of popular absurdity and madness. Could Congress exert them for the detriment of the public, without injuring themselves in an equal or greater proportion? Are not their interests inseparably connected with those of their constituents? By the rotation of appointment, must they not mingle frequently with the mass of citizens? Is it not rather to be apprehended, if they were possessed of the power before described, that their individual members would be induced to use them, on many occasions, very timidly and inefficaciously for fear of losing their popularity and future election? We must take human nature as we find it. Perfection falls not to the share of mortals. Many are of opinion, that Congress have too frequently made use of the suppliant, humble tone of requisition in applications to the States, when they had a right to assert their imperial dignity and command obedience. Be that as it may, requisitions are a perfect nullity where thirteen sovereign, independent, disunited States are in the habit of discussing and refusing compliance with them at their option. Requisitions are actually little better than a jest and a by-word throughout the land. If you tell the legislatures they have violated the treaty of peace, and invaded the prerogatives of the confederacy, they will laugh in your face. What then is to be done? Things cannot go in the same train forever. It is much to be feared, as you observe, that the better kind of people, being disgusted with the circumstances, will have their minds prepared for any revolution whatever. We are apt to run from one extreme into another. To anticipate and prevent disastrous contingencies would be the part of wisdom and patriotism.

What astonishing changes a few years are capable of producing. I am told that even respectable characters speak of a monarchical form of government without horror. From thinking proceeds speaking; thence to acting is often but a single step. But how irrevocable and tremendous! What a triumph for our enemies to verify their predictions! What a triumph for the advocates of despotism to find, that we are incapable of governing ourselves, and that systems founded on the basis of equal liberty are merely ideal and fallacious! Would to God, that wise measures may be taken in time to avert the consequences we have but too much reason to apprehend.

Retired as I am from the world, I frankly acknowledge I cannot feel myself an unconcerned spectator.

Yet, having happily assisted in bringing the ship into port, and having been fairly discharged, it is not my business to embark again on a sea of troubles. Nor could it be expected, that my sentiments and opinions would have much weight on the mind of my countrymen. They have been neglected, though given as a last legacy in the most solemn manner. I had then perhaps some claim to public attention. I consider myself as having none at present.

GEORGE WASHINGTON

Influence no Government

TO HENRY LEE, IN CONGRESS
MOUNT VERNON, 31 October, 1786.

My dear Sir: The picture which you have exhibited, and the accounts which are published of the commotions and temper of numerous bodies in the eastern States, are equally to be lamented and deprecated. They exhibit a melancholy proof of what our transatlantic foe has predicted; and of another thing perhaps, which is still more to be regretted, and is yet more unaccountable, that mankind, when left to themselves, are unfit for their own government. I am mortified beyond expression when I view the clouds, that have spread over the brightest morn that ever dawned upon any country. In a word, I am lost in amazement when I behold what intrigue, the interested views of desperate characters, ignorance, and jealousy of the minor part, are capable of effecting, as a scourge on the major part of our fellow citizens of the Union; for it is hardly to be supposed, that the great body of the people, though they will not act, can be so shortsighted or enveloped in darkness, as not to see rays of a distant sun through all this mist of intoxication and folly.

You talk, my good Sir, of employing influence to appease the present tumults in Massachusetts. I know not where that influence is to be found, or, if attainable, that it would be a proper remedy for the disorders. *Influence* is no *government*. Let us have one by which our lives, liberties, and properties will be secured, or let us know the worst at once. Under these impressions, my humble opinion is, that there is a call for decision. Know precisely what the insurgents aim at. If they have *real* grievances, redress them if possible; or acknowledge the justice of them, and your inability to do it in the present moment. If they have not, employ the force of government against them at once. If this is inadequate, *all* will be convinced, that the superstructure is bad, or wants support. To be more exposed in the eyes of the world, and more contemptible than we already are, is hardly possible. To delay one or the other of these, is to exasperate on the one hand, or to give confidence on the other, and will add their numbers; for, like snow-balls, such bodies increase by every movement, unless there is something in the way to obstruct and crumble them before the weight is too great and irresistible.

These are my sentiments. Precedents are dangerous things. Let the reins of government then be braced and held with a steady hand, and every violation of the constitution be reprehended. If defective, let it be amended, but not suffered to be trampled upon whilst it has an existence.

GEORGE WASHINGTON

On Defects of the Confederation

TO JOHN JAY
MOUNT VERNON, 10 March, 1787.

Dear Sir: How far the revision of the federal system, and giving more adequate powers of Congress may be productive of an efficient government, I will not under my present view of the matter, presume to decide.—That many inconveniences result from the present form, none can deny. Those enumerated in your letter are so obvious and sensibly felt that no logic can controvert, nor is it likely that any change of conduct will remove them, and that attempts to alter or amend it will be like the proppings of a house which is ready to fall, and which no shoars can support (as many seem to think) may also be true. But, is the public mind matured for such an important change as the one you have suggested? What would be the consequences of a premature attempt? My opinion is, that this Country must yet feel and see more, before it can be accomplished.

A thirst for power, and the bantling, I had liked to have said monster for sovereignty, which have taken such fast hold of the States individually, will when joined by the many whose personal consequence in the control of State politics will in a manner be annihilated, form a strong phalanx against it; and when to these the few who can hold posts of honor or profit in the national government, are compared with the many who will see but little prospect of being noticed, and the discontent of others who may look for appointments, the opposition will be altogether irresistable till the mass, as well as the more discerning part of the Community shall see the necessity. Among men of reflection, few will be found I believe who are not beginning to think that our system is more perfect in theory than in practice; and that notwithstanding the boasted virtue of America it is more than probable we shall exhibit the last melancholy proof, that mankind are not competent to their own government without the means of coercion in the sovereign.

Yet I would fain try what the wisdom of the proposed convention will suggest: and what can be effected by their councils. It may be the last peaceable mode of essaying the practicability of the present form, without a greater lapse of time than the exigency of our affairs will allow. In strict propriety a convention so holden may not be legal. Congress, however, may give it a coloring by recommendation, which would fit it more to the taste without proceeding to a definition of the powers. This, however constitutionally it might be done, would not, in my opinion, be expedient: for delicacy on the one hand, and jealousy on the other, would produce a mere nihil.

My name is in the delegation to this Convention; but it was put there contrary to my desire, and remains contrary to my request. Several reasons at the time of this appointment and which yet exist, conspired to make an attendance inconvenient, perhaps improper, tho' a good deal urged to it. With sentiments of great regard and friendship, &c.

GEORGE WASHINGTON

Power of Coercion Essential

TO JAMES MADISON, IN CONGRESS
MOUNT VERNON, 31 March, 1787.

My dear Sir: I am fully of opinion that those, who lean to a monarchical government, have either not consulted the public mind, or that they live in a region, which (the levelling principles in which they were bred being entirely eradicated) is much more productive of monarchical ideas, than are to be found in the southern States, where, from the habitual distinctions which have always existed among the people, one would have expected the first generation and the most rapid growth of them. I am also clear, that, even admitting the utility, nay, necessity of the form, yet that the period is not arrived for adopting the change without shaking the peace of this country to its foundation. That a thorough reform of the present system is indispensable, none, who have capacities to judge, will deny; and with hand [and heart] I hope the business will be essayed in a full convention. After which, if more powers and more decision is not found in the existing form, if it still wants energy and that secrecy and despatch (either from the non-attendance or the local views of its members), which is characteristic of good government, and if it shall be found (the contrary of which, however, I have always been more afraid of than of the abuse of them), that Congress will, upon all proper occasions, exert the powers which are given, with a firm and steady hand, instead of frittering them back to the States, where the members, in place of viewing themselves in their national character, are too apt to be looking,—I say,

after this essay is made, if the system proves inefficient, conviction of the necessity of a change will be
disseminated among all classes of the people. Then,
and not till then, in my opinion, can it be attempted
without involving all the evils of civil discord.

I confess, however, that my opinion of public virtue is so far changed, that I have my doubts whether
any system, without the means of coercion in the
sovereign, will enforce due obedience to the ordinances of a general government; without which every thing else fails. Laws or ordinances unobserved,
or partially attended to, had better never have been
made; because the first is a mere nihil, and the second is productive of much jealousy and discontent.
But what kind of coercion, you may ask. This indeed
will require thought, though the non-compliance of
the States with the late requisition is an evidence of
the necessity. It is somewhat singular that a State
(New York), which used to be foremost in all federal
measures, should now turn her face against them in
almost every instance.

GEORGE WASHINGTON

On the Constitution

TO COLONEL DAVID HUMPHREYS
MOUNT VERNON, 10 October, 1787.

My dear Humphreys: The Constitution that is submitted, is not free from imperfections, but there are as few radical defects in it as could will be expected, considering the heterogenious mass of which the Convention was composed and the diversity of interests that are to be attended to. As a Constitutional door is opened for future amendments and alterations, I think it would be wise in the People to accept what is offered to them and I wish it may be by as great a majority of them as it was by that of the Convention; but this is hardly to be expected because the importance and sinister views of too many characters, will be affected by the change.—Much will depend however upon literary abilities, and the recommendation of it by good pens should be *openly,* I mean, publickly afforded in the Gazettes.—Go matters however as they may, I shall have the consolation to reflect that no objects but the public good— and that peace and harmony which I wished to see prevail in the Convention, obtruded even for a moment in my bosom during the whole Session long as it was.

GEORGE WASHINGTON

A Defence of the Constitution

TO BUSHROD WASHINGTON
MOUNT VERNON, 10 November, 1787.

Dear Bushrod: A candid solution of a single question, to which the plainest understanding is competent, does, in my opinion, decide the dispute; namely, Is it best for the States to unite or not to unite? If there are men, who prefer the latter, then unquestionably the constitution which is offered must, in their estimation, be wrong from the words, *"We the People,"* to the signature, inclusively; but those who think differently, and yet object to parts of it, would do well to consider, that it does not lie with any *one* State, or the *minority* of the States, to superstruct a constitution for the whole. The separate interests, as far as it is practicable, must be consolidated; and local views must be attended to, as far as the nature of the case will admit. Hence it is, that every State has some objection to the present form, and these objections are directed to different points. That which is most pleasing to one is obnoxious to another, and so *vice versa.* If then the union of the whole is a desirable object, the component parts must yield a little in order to accomplish it. Without the latter, the former is unattainable; for again I repeat it, that not a single State, nor the minority of the States, can force a constitution on the majority. But, admitting the power, it will surely be granted, that it cannot be done without involving scenes of civil commotion, of a very serious nature.

Let the opponents of the proposed constitution in this State be asked, and it is a question they certainly ought to have asked themselves, what line of conduct they would advise to adopt, if nine other States, of which I think there is little doubt, should accede to the constitution. Would they recommend, that it should stand single? Will they connect it with Rhode Island? Or even with two others checkerwise, and remain with them, as outcasts from the society, to shift for themselves? Or will they return to their dependence on Great Britain? Or, lastly, have the mortification to come in when they will be allowed no credit for doing so?

The warmest friends and the best supports the constitution has, do not contend that it is free from imperfections; but they found them unavoidable, and are sensible, if evil is likely to arise therefrom, the remedy must come hereafter; for in the present moment it is not to be obtained; and, as there is a constitutional door open for it, I think the people (for it is with them to judge), can, as they will have the advantage of experience on their side, decide with as much propriety on the alterations and amendments which are necessary, as ourselves. I do not think we are more inspired, have more wisdom, or possess more virtue, than those who will come after us.

The power under the constitution will always be in the people. It is intrusted for certain defined purposes, and for a certain limited period, to representatives of their own choosing; and, whenever it is executed contrary to their interest, or not agreeable to their wishes, their servants can and undoubtedly will be recalled. It is agreed on all hands, that no government can be well administered without powers; yet, the instant these are delegated, although those, who are intrusted with the administration, are no more than the creatures of the people, act as it were but for a day, and are amenable for every false

step they take, they are, from the moment they receive it, set down as tyrants; their natures, they
would conceive from this, immediately changed, and
that they can have no other disposition but to oppress. Of these things, in a government constituted
and guarded as *ours* is, I have no idea; and do firmly
believe, that, whilst many *ostensible* reasons are assigned to prevent the adoption of it, the real ones are
concealed behind the curtains, because they are not
of a nature to appear in open day. I believe further,
supposing them pure, that as great evils result from
too great jealousy as from the want of it. We need
look, I think, no further for proof of this, than to the
constitution of some, if not all, of these States. No
man is a warmer advocate for proper restraints and
wholesome checks in every department of government, than I am; but I have never yet been able to
discover the propriety of placing it absolutely out of
the power of men to render essential services, because a possibility remains of their doing ill.

GEORGE WASHINGTON

Washington's Political Theories

TO THE MARQUIS DE LAFAYETTE

MOUNT VERNON, 7 February, 1788.

My dear Marquis: You appear to be, as might be expected from a real friend to this country, anxiously concerned about its present political situation. So far as I am able, I shall be happy in gratifying that friendly solicitude. As to my sentiments with respect to the merits of the new constitution, I will disclose them without reserve, (although by passing through the post-office they should become known to all the world,) for in truth I have nothing to conceal on that subject. It appears to me, then, little short of a miracle, that the delegates from so many different States (which States you know are also different from each other), in their manners, circumstances, and prejudices, should unite in forming a system of national government, so little liable to well-founded objections. Nor am I yet such an enthusiastic, partial, or undiscriminating admirer of it, as not to perceive it is tinctured with some real (though not radical) defects. The limits of a letter would not suffer me to go fully into an examination of them; nor would the discussion be entertaining or profitable. I therefore forbear to touch upon it. With regard to the two great points, (the pivots upon which the whole machine must move,) my creed is simply,

1st. That the general government is not invested with more powers, than are indispensably necessary to perform the functions of a good government; and consequently, that no objection ought to be made against the quantity of power delegated to it.

2ly. That these powers, (as the appointment of all

rulers will for ever arise from, and at short, stated intervals recur to, the free suffrage of the people,) are so distributed among the legislative, executive, and judical branches, into which the general government is arranged, that it can never be in danger of degenerating into a monarchy, an oligarchy, an aristocracy, or any other despotic or oppressive form, so long as there shall remain any virtue in the body of the people.

I shall not be understood, my dear Marquis, to speak of consequences, which may be produced in the revolution of ages, by corruption of morals, profligacy of manners, and listlessness for the preservation of the natural and unalienable rights of mankind, nor of the successful usurpations, that may be established at such an unpropitious juncture upon the ruins of liberty, however providently guarded and secured; as these are contingencies against which no human prudence can effectually provide. It will at least be a recommendation to the proposed constitution, that it is provided with more checks and barriers against the introduction of tyranny, and those of a nature less liable to be surmounted, than any government hitherto instituted among mortals hath possessed. We are not to expect perfection in this world; but mankind, in modern times, have apparently made some progress in the science of government. Shall that, which is now offered to the people of America, be found on experiment less perfect than it can be made, a constitutional door is left open for its amelioration.

Some respectable characters have wished, that the States, after having pointed out whatever alterations and amendments may be judged necessary, would appoint another federal convention to modify it upon those documents. For myself, I have wondered, that sensible men should not see the impracticability of this scheme. The members would go fortified with such instructions, that nothing but discordant ideas could prevail. Had I but slightly suspected, at the time when the late convention was in session, that another convention would not be likely to agree upon a better form of government, I should now be confirmed in the fixed belief that they would not be able to agree upon any system whatever; so many, I may add, such contradictory and in my opinion unfounded objections have been urged against the system in contemplation, many of which would operate equally against every efficient government that might be proposed. I will only add, as a further opinion founded on the maturest deliberation, that there is no alternative, no hope of alteration, no intermediate resting-place, between the adoption of this, and a recurrence to an unqualified state of anarchy, with all its deplorable consequences.

GEORGE WASHINGTON

On Magnanimous Devotion to the Cause

TO GENERAL THOMAS

23 July, 1775.

Sir: The retirement of a General Officer possessing the confidence of his country and the army at so critical a period, appears to me to be big with fatal consequences both to the public cause and his own reputation. While it is unexecuted I think it my duty to use this last effort to prevent it, and your own virtue and good sense must decide upon it. In the usual contests of empire and ambition, the conscience of a soldier has so little share, that he may very properly insist upon his claims of rank, and extend his pretensions even to punctilio;—but in such a cause as this, when the object is neither glory nor extent of territory, but a defence of all that is dear and valuable in private and public life, surely every post ought to be deemed honorable in which a man can serve his country. What matter of triumph will it afford our enemies, that in less than one month, a spirit of discord should show itself in the highest ranks of the army, not to be extinguished by any thing less than a total desertion of duty. How little reason shall we have to boast of American union and patriotism, if at such a time and in such a cause smaller and partial considerations cannot give way to the great and general interest. These remarks not only affect you as a member of the great American body, but as an inhabitant of Massachusetts Bay. Your own Province and the other Colonies have a peculiar and unquestionable claim to your services, and in my opinion you cannot refuse without relinquishing in some degree that character of public vir-

tue and honor which you have hitherto supported. If
our cause is just, it ought to be supported; but when
shall it find support if gentlemen of merit and experience, unable to conquer the prejudices of a competition, withdraw themselves in the hour of danger?
I admit, Sir, that your just claims and services have
not had due respect,—it is by no means a singular
case,—worthy men of all nations and countries have
had reasons to make the same complaint, but they
did not for this abandon the public cause,—they nobly stifled the dictates of resentment, and made their
enemies ashamed of their injustice. And can America afford no such instances of magnanimity? For
the sake of your bleeding country,—your devoted
Province,—your charter rights,—and by the memories of those brave men who have already fallen in
this great cause, I conjure you to banish from your
mind every suggestion of anger and disappointment;
your country will do ample justice to your merits,—
they already do it by the regret and sorrow expressed
on this occasion; and the sacrifice you are called to
make, will in the judgment of every good man and
lover of his country, do you more real honor than the
most distinguished victory. You possess the confidence and affection of the troops of this Province
particularly;—many of them are not capable of judging the propriety and reasons of your conduct,—
should they esteem themselves authorized by your
example to leave the service, the consequences may
be fatal and irretrievable. There is a reason to fear
it from the personal attachment of the officers and
men, and the obligations that are supposed to arise
from these attachments.

But, sir, the other Colonies have also their claims
upon you, not only as a native of America, but an

inhabitant of this Province. They have made common cause with it, they have sacrificed their trade, loaded themselves with taxes, and are ready to spill their blood, in vindication of the rights of Massachusetts Bay, while all the security and profit of a neutrality have been offered them. But no acts or temptations could seduce them from your side, and leave you a prey to a cruel and perfidious ministry. Sure these reflections must have some weight with a mind as generous and considerate as yours. How will you be able to answer it to your country and to your own conscience, if such a step should lead to a division of the army or the loss and ruin of America be ascribed to measures which your counsels and conduct would have prevented! Before it is too late, I entreat, sir, you would weigh well the greatness of the stake, and upon how much smaller circumstances the fate of empires has depended. Of your own honor and reputation you are the best and only judge; but allow me to say, that a people contending for life and liberty, are seldom disposed to look with a favorable eye upon either men or measures, whose passions, interests or consequences will clash with those inestimable objects. As to myself, Sir, be assured, that I shall with pleasure do all in my power to make your situation both easy and honorable, and that the sentiments I have here expressed flow from a clear opinion that your duty to your country, your posterity, and yourself, most explicitly require your continuance in the service. The order and rank of the commissions is under the consideration of the Continental Congress, whose determination will be received in a few days. It may argue a want of respect to that august body not to wait that decision. But at all events, I shall flatter myself, that these reasons,

with others which your own good judgment will suggest, will strengthen your mind against those impressions which are incident to humanity, and
laudable to a certain degree, and that the result will
be your resolution to assist your country and friends
in this day of distress. That you may reap the full
reward of honor and public esteem which such a
conduct deserves, is the sincere wish of, Sir, Yours,
&c.——

GEORGE WASHINGTON

Farewell Address, 17 September 1796

In looking forward to the moment, which is intended to terminate the career of my public life, my feelings do not permit me to suspend the deep acknowledgment of that debt of gratitude, which I owe to my beloved country,—for the many honors it has conferred upon me; still more for the stedfast confidence with which it has supported me; and for the opportunities I have thence enjoyed of manifesting my inviolable attachment, by services faithful and persevering, though in usefulness unequal to my zeal.—If benefits have resulted to our country from these services, let it always be remembered to your praise, and as an instructive example in our annals, that under circumstances in which the Passions agitated in every direction were liable to mislead, amidst appearances sometimes dubious, vicissitudes of fortune often discouraging, in situations in which not unfrequently want of success has countenanced the spirit of criticism, the constancy of your support was the essential prop of the efforts, and a guarantee of the plans by which they were effected.—Profoundly penetrated with this idea, I shall carry it with me to the grave, as a strong incitement to unceasing vows that Heaven may continue to you the choicest tokens of its beneficence—that your union and brotherly affection may be perpetual—that the free constitution which is the work of your hands, may be sacredly maintained—that its administration in every department may be stamped with wisdom and virtue—that, in fine, the happiness of the people of these States, under the auspices of liberty, may be made complete, by so careful a preservation and so prudent a use of this blessing as will acquire to them glory of recommending it to the applause, the affection, and adoption of every nation, which is yet a stranger to it.

Here, perhaps, I ought to stop.—But a solicitude for your welfare, which cannot end but with my life, and the apprehension of danger, natural to that solicitude, urge me on an occasion like the present, to offer to your solemn contemplation, and to recommend to your frequent review, some sentiments; which are the result of much reflection, of no inconsiderable observation and which appear to me all important to the permanency of your felicity as a People.—These will be offered to you with the more freedom, as you can only see in them the disinterested warnings of a parting friend, who can possibly have no personal motive to bias his counsels.—Nor can I forget, as an encouragement to it your indulgent reception of my sentiments on a former and not dissimilar occasion.

Interwoven as is the love of liberty with every ligament of your hearts, no recommendation of mine is necessary to fortify or confirm the attachment.—

The Unity of Government which constitutes you one people, is also now dear to you.—It is justly so; for it is a main Pillar in the Edifice of your real independence; the support of your tranquility at home; your peace abroad; of your safety: of your prosperity in every shape; of that very Liberty, which you so highly prize.—But as it is easy to foresee, that, from different causes, and from different quarters, much pains will be taken, many artifices employed, to weaken in your minds the conviction of this truth;— as this is the point in your political fortress against which the batteries of internal and external enemies will be most constantly and actively (though often covertly and insidiously) directed, it is of infinite moment, that you should properly estimate the immense value of your national Union to your collective and individual happiness;—that you should cherish a cordial, habitual, and immoveable attachment, to it: accustoming yourselves to think and speak of it as of the Palladium of your political safety and prosperity; watching for its preservation with jealous anxiety; discountenancing whatever may suggest even a suspicion that it can in any event be abandoned, and indignantly frowning upon the first dawning of every attempt to alienate any portion of our Country from the rest, or to enfeeble the sacred ties which now link together the various parts.

For this you have every inducement of sympathy and interest.—Citizens by birth or choice of a common country, that country has a right to concentrate your affections.—The name of AMERICAN, which belongs to you, in your national capacity, must always exalt the just pride of Patriotism, more than any appellation derived from local discriminations. —With slight shades of difference, you have the same Religion, Manners, Habits, and political Principles.—You have in a common cause fought and triumphed together. The independence and Liberty you possess are the work of joint councils, and joint efforts—of common dangers, sufferings and successes.—

But these considerations, however powerfully they address themselves to your sensibility, are greatly outweighed by those, which apply more immediately to your Interest.—Here every portion of our country finds the most commanding motives for carefully guarding and preserving the Union of the whole.

The *North* in an unrestrained intercourse with the *South*, protected by the equal Laws of a common government, finds in the productions of the latter great additional resources of maritime and commercial enterprise—and precious materials of manufacturing industry.—The *South* in the same intercourse, benefiting by the agency of the *North*, sees its agriculture grow and its commerce expand. Turning partly into its own channels the seamen of the *North*, it finds its particular navigation envigorated;—and, while it contributes, in different ways, to nourish and increase the general mass of the national navigation, it looks forward to the protection of a maritime strength to which itself is unequally adapted.—The *East*, in a like intercourse with the *West*, already finds, and in the progressive improvement of interior communications, by land and water, will more and more find, a valuable vent for the commodities which it brings from abroad, or manufactures at home.—The *West* derives from the *East* supplies requisite to its growth and comfort,— and what is perhaps of still greater consequence, it must of necessity owe the *secure* enjoyment of indispensable *outlets* for its own productions to the weight, influence, and the future maritime strength of the Atlantic side of the Union, directed by an indissoluble community of interest, as *one Nation.* Any other tenure by which the *West* can hold this essential advantage, whether derived from its own separate strength, or from an apostate and unnatural connexion with any foreign Power, must be intrinsically precarious.

While then every part of our Country thus feels an immediate and particular interest in Union, all the parts combined in the united mass of means and efforts cannot fail to find greater strength, greater resource, proportionably greater security from external danger, a less frequent interruption of their Peace by foreign Nations; and, what is of inestimable value! they must derive from Union an exemption from those broils and wars between themselves, which so frequently afflict neighboring countries, not tied together by the same government; which their own rivalships alone would be sufficient to produce; but which opposite foreign alliances, attachments, and intrigues would stimulate and embitter. —Hence likewise they will avoid the necessity of those overgrown Military establishments, which under any form of government, are inauspicious to liberty, and which are to be regarded as particularly hostile to Republican Liberty: In this sense it is, that your Union ought to be considered as a main prop of your liberty, and that the love of the one ought to endear to you the preservation of the other.

These considerations speak a persuasive language to every reflecting and virtuous mind,—and exhibit the continuance of the UNION as a primary object of Patriotic desire.—Is there a doubt, whether a common government can embrace so large a sphere?— Let experience solve it.—To listen to mere speculation in such a case were criminal.—We are authorized to hope that a proper organization of the whole, with the auxiliary agency of governments for the respective subdivisions, will afford a happy issue to the experiment. 'Tis well worth a fair and full experiment. With such powerful and obvious motives to Union, affecting all parts of our country, while experience shall not have demonstrated its impracticability, there will always be reason to distrust the patriotism of those, who in any quarter may endeavor to weaken its bands.—

In contemplating the causes which may disturb

our Union, it occurs as matter of serious concern, that any ground should have been furnished for characterizing parties by *Geographical* discriminations—*Northern* and *Southern*—*Atlantic* and *Western;* whence designing men may endeavor to excite a belief, that there is a real difference of local interests and views. One of the expedients of Party to acquire influence, within particular districts, is to misrepresent the opinions and aims of other districts.—You cannot shield yourselves too much against the jealousies and heart burnings which spring from these misrepresentations;—They tend to render alien to each other those who ought to be bound together by fraternal affection.—The inhabitants of our Western country have lately had a useful lesson on this head.—They have seen, in the negotiation by the Executive, and in the unanimous ratification by the Senate, of the treaty with Spain, and in the universal satisfaction at that event, throughout the United States, a decisive proof how unfounded were the suspicions propagated among them of a policy in the General Government and in the Atlantic States unfriendly to their interests in regard to the MISSISSIPPI.—They have been witnesses to the formation of two Treaties, that with G. Britain, and that with Spain, which secure to them every thing they could desire, in respect to our Foreign Relations, towards confirming their prosperity.—Will it not be their wisdom to rely for the preservation of these advantages on the UNION by which they were procured?—Will they not henceforth be deaf to those advisers, if such there are, who would sever them from their Brethren, and connect them with Aliens?—

To the efficacy and permanency of your Union, a

Government for the whole is indispensable.—No alliances however strict between the parts can be an adequate substitute.—They must inevitably experience the infractions and interruptions which all alliances in all time have experienced.—Sensible of this momentous truth, you have improved upon your first essay, by the adoption of a Constitution of Government, better calculated than your former for an intimate Union, and for the efficacious management of your common concerns.—This government, the offspring of our own choice uninfluenced and unawed, adopted upon full investigation and mature deliberation, completely free in its principles, in the distribution of its powers, uniting security with energy, and containing within itself a provision for its own amendment, has a just claim to your confidence and your support.—Respect for its authority, compliance with its Laws, acquiescence in its measures, are duties enjoined by the fundamental maxims of true Liberty.—The basis of our political systems is the right of the people to make and to alter their Constitutions of Government.—But the Constitution which at any time exists, 'till changed by an explicit and authentic act of the whole People, is sacredly obligatory upon all.—The very idea of the power and the right of the People to establish Government, presupposes the duty of every individual to obey the established Government.

All obstructions to the execution of the Laws, all combinations and associations, under whatever plausible character, with the real design to direct, controul, counteract, or awe the regular deliberation and action of the constituted authorities, are destructive of this fundamental principle, and of fatal tendency.—They serve to organize faction, to give it an artificial and extraordinary force—to put in the place of the delegated will of the Nation, the will of a party;—often a small but artful and enterprizing minority of the community;—and, according to the alternate triumphs of different parties, to make the public administration the mirror of the ill-concerted and incongruous projects of faction, rather than the organ of consistent and wholesome plans digested by common councils, and modified by mutual interests. —However combinations or associations of the above description may now and then answer popular ends, they are likely, in the course of time and things, to become potent engines, by which cunning, ambitious, and unprincipled men will be enabled to subvert the Power of the People and to usurp for themselves the reins of Government; destroying afterwards the very engines, which have lifted them to unjust dominion.—

Towards the preservation of your Government and the permanency of your present happy state, it is requisite, not only that you steadily discountenance irregular oppositions to its acknowledged authority, but also that you resist with care the spirit of innovation upon its principles, however specious the pretexts.—One method of assault may be to effect, in the forms of the Constitution, alterations which will impair the energy of the system, and thus to undermine what cannot be directly overthrown.—In all the changes to which you may be invited, remember that time and habit are at least as necessary to fix the true character of Governments, as of other human institutions—that experience is the surest standard, by which to test the real tendency of the existing Constitution of a Country—that facility in changes upon the credit of mere hypothesis and opinion exposes to perpetual change, from the endless variety of hypothesis and opinion:—and remember, especially, that, for the efficient management of your common interests, in a country so extensive as ours, a Government of as much vigor as is consistent with the perfect security of Liberty is indispensable.— Liberty itself will find in such a Government, with powers properly distributed and adjusted, its surest Guardian.—It is, indeed, little else than a name, where the Government is too feeble to withstand the enterprises of faction, to confine each member of the society within the limits prescribed by the laws, and to maintain all in the secure and tranquil enjoyment of the rights of person and property.

I have already intimated to you the danger of Parties in the State, with particular reference to the founding of them on Geographical discriminations. —Let me now take a more comprehensive view, and warn you in the most solemn manner against the baneful effects of the Spirit of Party, generally.

This Spirit, unfortunately, is inseparable from our nature, having its root in the strongest passions of the human mind.—It exists under different shapes in all Governments, more or less stifled, controuled, or repressed; but, in those of the popular form, it is seen in its greatest rankness, and is truly their worst enemy.—

The alternate domination of one fraction over another, sharpened by the spirit of revenge natural to party dissension, which in different ages and countries has perpetrated the most horrid enormities, is itself a frightful despotism.—But this leads at length to a more formal and permanent despotism.—The disorders and miseries, which result, gradually incline the minds of men to seek security and repose in the absolute power of an Individual: and sooner or later the chief of some prevailing faction more able or more fortunate that his competitors, turns this disposition to the purpose of his own elevation, on the ruins of Public Liberty.

Without looking forward to an extremity of this kind, (which nevertheless ought to be entirely out of sight), the common and continual mischiefs of the spirit of Party are sufficient to make it the interest and duty of a wise People to discourage and restrain it.—

It serves always to distract the Public Councils, and enfeeble the Public administration.—It agitates the community with ill founded jealousies and false alarms, kindles the animosity of one part against another, foments occasionally riot and insurrection. —It opens the doors to foreign influence and corruption, which find a facilitated access to the Government itself through the channels of party passions. Thus policy and the will of one country, are subjected to the policy and will of another.

There is an opinion that parties in free countries are useful checks upon the Administration of the Government, and serve to keep alive the Spirit of Liberty.—This within certain limits is probably true —and in Governments of a Monarchical cast, Patriotism may look with indulgence, if not with favour, upon the spirit of party.—But in those of the popular character, in Governments purely elective, it is a spirit not to be encouraged.—From their natural tendency, it is certain there will always be enough of that spirit for every salutary purpose,—and there being constant danger of excess, the effort ought to be,

by force of public opinion, to mitigate and assuage it.
—A fire not to be quenched; it demands a uniform
vigilance to prevent its bursting into a flame, lest
instead of warming, it should consume.

It is important, likewise, that the habits of thinking in a free country should inspire caution in those
entrusted with its administration, to confine themselves within their respective constitutional
spheres; avoiding in the exercise of the powers of
one department to encroach upon another.—The
spirit of encroachment tends to consolidate the powers of all the departments in one, and thus to create,
whatever the form of government, a real despotism.
—A just estimate of that love of power, and prone-
ness to abuse it, which predominates in the human
heart, is sufficient to satisfy us to the truth of this
position.—The necessity of reciprocal checks in the
exercise of political power, by dividing and distribut-
ing it into different depositories, and constituting
each the Guardian of the Public Weal against invasion by the others, had been evinced by experiments
ancient and modern; some of them in our country
and under our own eyes.—To preserve them must be
as necessary as to institute them. If in the opinion of
the People, the distribution or modification of the
Constitutional powers be in any particular wrong, let
it be corrected by an amendment in the way which
the Constitution designates.—But let there be no
change by usurpation; for though this, in one instance, may be the instrument of good, it is the cus-
tomary weapon by which free governments are
destroyed.—The precedent must always greatly
overbalance in permanent evil any partial or transient benefit which the use can at any time yield.—

Of all the dispositions and habits, which lead to

political prosperity, Religion and morality are indispensable supports.—In vain would that man claim the tribute of Patriotism, who should labour to subvert these great Pillars of human happiness, these firmest props of the duties of Men and Citizens.— The mere Politician, equally with the pious man, ought to respect and to cherish them.—A volume could not trace all their connexions with private and public felicity.—Let it simply be asked where is the security for property, for reputation, for life, if the sense of religious obligation *desert* the oaths, which are the instruments of investigation in Courts of Justice? And let us with caution indulge the supposition, that morality can be maintained without religion.— Whatever may be conceded to the influence of refined education on minds of peculiar structure— reason and experience both forbid us to expect, that national morality can prevail in exclusion of religious principle.—

'T is substantially true, that virtue or morality is a necessary spring of popular government.—The rule indeed extends with more or less force to every species of Free Government.—Who that is a sincere friend to it can look with indifference upon attempts to shake the foundation of the fabric?—

Promote, then, as an object of primary importance, institutions for the general diffusion of knowledge. In proportion as the structure of a government gives force to public opinion, it is essential that public opinion should be enlightened.—

As a very important source of strength and security, cherish public credit.—One method of preserving it is, to use it as sparingly as possible:—avoiding occasions of expense by cultivating peace, but remembering also that timely disbursements to prepare for danger frequently prevent much greater disbursements to repel it—avoiding likewise the accumulation of debt, not only by shunning occasions of expense, but by vigorous exertions in time of Peace to discharge the debts which unavoidable wars may have occasioned, not ungenerously throwing upon posterity the burthen which we ourselves ought to bear. The execution of these maxims belongs to your Representatives, but it is necessary that public opinions should coöperate.—To facilitate to them the performance of their duty, it is essential that you should practically bear in mind, that towards the payment of debts there must be Revenue —that to have Revenue there must be taxes—that no taxes can be devised which are not more or less inconvenient and unpleasant—that the intrinsic embarrassment inseparable from the selection of the proper objects (which is always a choice of difficulties) ought to be a decisive motive for a candid construction of the conduct of the Government in making it, and for a spirit of acquiescence in the measures for obtaining Revenue which the public exigencies may at any time dictate.—

Observe good faith and justice towards all Nations. Cultivate peace and harmony with all.—Religion and Morality enjoin this conduct; and can it be that good policy does not equally enjoin it?—It will be worthy of a free, enlightened, and at no distant period, a great nation, to give to mankind the magnanimous and too novel example of a People always guided by an exalted justice and benevolence.—Who can doubt that in the course of time and things, the fruits of such a plan would richly repay any temporary advantages which might be lost by a steady adherence to it? Can it be that Providence has not connected the permanent felicity of a Nation with its virtue? The experiment, at least, is recommended by every sentiment which ennobles human nature.— Alas! is it rendered impossible by its vices?

In the execution of such a plan nothing is more essential than that permanent, inveterate antipathies against particular nations and passionate attachments for others should be excluded; and that in place of them just and amicable feelings towards all should be cultivated.—The Nation, which indulges towards another an habitual hatred or an habitual fondness, is in some degree a slave. It is a slave to its animosity or to its affection, either of which is sufficient to lead it astray from its duty and its interest. —Antipathy in one nation against another disposes each more readily to offer insult and injury, to lay hold of slight causes of umbrage, and to be haughty and intractable, when accidental or trifling occasions of dispute occur.—Hence frequent collisions, obstinate, envenomed and bloody contests.—The Nation prompted by ill-will and resentment sometimes impels to War the Government, contrary to the best calculations of policy.—The Government sometimes participates in the national propensity, and adopts through passion what reason would reject;—at other times, it makes the animosity of the Nation subservient to projects of hostility instigated by pride, ambition, and other sinister and pernicious motives.— The peace often, sometimes perhaps the Liberty, of Nations has been the victim.—

So likewise a passionate attachment of one Nation for another produces a variety of evils.—Sympathy for the favourite nation, facilitating the illusion of an imaginary common interest in cases where no real common interest exists, and infusing into one the enmities of the other, betrays the former into a participation in the quarrels and wars of the latter, without adequate inducement or justification: It leads also to concessions to the favourite Nation of privileges denied to others, which is apt doubly to injure the Nation making the concessions; by unnecessarily parting with what ought to have been retained, and by exciting jealousy, ill-will, and a disposition to retaliate, in the parties from whom equal privileges are withheld; and it gives to ambitious, corrupted, or deluded citizens, (who devote themselves to the favourite Nation) facility to betray, or sacrifice the interests of their own country, without odium, sometimes even with popularity:—gilding with appearances of a virtuous sense of obligation, a commendable deference for public opinion, or a laudable zeal for public good, the base or foolish compliances of ambition, corruption or infatuation.—

As avenues to foreign influence in innumerable ways, such attachments are particularly alarming to the truly enlightened and independent Patroit.— How many opportunities do they afford to tamper with domestic factions, to practise the arts of seduction, to mislead public opinion, to influence or awe the public councils! Such an attachment of a small or weak, towards a great and powerful nation, dooms the former to be the satellite of the latter.

Against the insidious wiles of foreign influence, I conjure you to believe me, fellow-citizens, the jealousy of a free people ought to be *constantly* awake, since history and experience prove that foreign influence is one of the most baneful foes of republican Government.—But that jealousy, to be useful, must be impartial; else it becomes the instrument of the very influence to be avoided, instead of a defence against it.—Excessive partiality for one foreign nation and excessive dislike of another, cause those whom they actuate to see danger only on one side, and serve to veil and even second the arts of influence on the other.—Real Patriots, who may resist the intrigues of the favourite, are liable to become suspected and odious; while its tools and dupes usurp the applause and confidence of the people, to surrender their interests.—

The great rule of conduct for us, in regard to foreign Nations, is, in extending our commercial relations, to have with them as little *Political* connection as possible.—So far as we have already formed engagements, let them be fulfilled with perfect good faith.—Here let us stop.—

Europe has a set of primary interests, which to us have none, or a very remote relation.—Hence she must be engaged in frequent controversies, the causes of which are essentially foreign to our concerns.—Hence therefore it must be unwise in us to implicate ourselves, by artificial ties in the ordinary vicissitudes of her politics, or the ordinary combinations and collisions of her friendships, or enmities.

Our detached and distant situation invites and enables us to pursue a different course.—If we remain one People, under an efficient government, the period is not far off, when we may defy material injury from external annoyance; when we may take such an attitude as will cause the neutrality we may at any time resolve upon to be scrupulously respected. When belligerent nations, under the impossibility of making acquisitions upon us, will not lightly hazard the giving us provocation when we may choose peace or war, as our interest guided by our justice shall counsel.

Why forego the advantages of so peculiar a situation?—Why quit our own to stand upon foreign ground?—Why, by interweaving our destiny with that of any part of Europe, entangle our peace and prosperity in the toils of European ambition, rivalship, interest, humour, or caprice?—

'T is our true policy to steer clear of permanent alliances, with any portion of the foreign world;—so far, I mean, as we are now at liberty to do it—for let me not be understood as capable of patronizing infidelity to existing engagements, (I hold the maxim no less applicable to public than to private affairs, that honesty is always the best policy).—I repeat it therefore let those engagements be observed in their genuine sense.—But in my opinion it is unnecessary and would be unwise to extend them.—

Taking care always to keep ourselves, by suitable establishments, on a respectably defensive posture, we may safely trust to temporary alliances for extraordinary emergencies.—

Harmony, liberal intercourse with all nations, are recommended by policy, humanity, and interest. But even our commercial policy should hold an equal and impartial hand:—neither seeking nor granting exclusive favours or preferences;—consulting the natural course of things;—diffusing and diversifying by gentle means the streams of commerce, but forcing nothing;—establishing with Powers so disposed —in order to give trade a stable course, to define the rights of our Merchants, and to enable the Government to support them—conventional rules of intercourse, the best that present circumstances and natural opinion will permit; but temporary, and liable to be from time to time abandoned or varied, as experience and circumstances shall dictate; constantly keeping in view that 't is folly in one nation to look for disinterested favors from another,—that it must pay with a portion of its independence for whatever it may accept under that character—that by such acceptance, it may place itself in the condition of having given equivalents for nominal favours and yet of being reproached with ingratitude for not giving more.—There can be no greater error than to expect or calculate upon real favours from Nation to Nation.—'T is an allusion which experience must cure, which a just price ought to discard.

In offering to you, my Countrymen, these counsels of an old and affectionate friend, I dare not hope they will make the strong and lasting impression, I could wish,—that they will controul the usual current of the passions, or prevent our Nation from running the course which has hitherto marked the destiny of Nations.—But if I may even flatter myself, that they may be productive of some partial benefit; some occasional good; that they may now and then recur to moderate the fury of party spirit, to warn against the mischiefs of foreign intrigue, to guard against the impostures of pretended patriotism, this hope will be a full recompense for the solicitude for your welfare, by which they have been dictated.—

How far in the discharge of my official duties, I have been guided by the principles which have been delineated, the public Records and other evidences of my conduct must witness to You, and to the world. —To myself the assurance of my own conscience is, that I have at least believed myself to be guided by them.

JAMES FENIMORE COOPER

Like most early American conservatives, J. F. Cooper (1789–1851) had to come to grips with the imputation of Toryism often hurled at men with his political philosophy. His answer to such criticism came in *The American Democrat* (1838), an eloquent defense of the American Republic from a Federalist point of view. A member of the Upper New York State landed gentry—Cooperstown, New York, was founded by his family—he is best remembered for fictional accounts of the American frontier. He was the first internationally popular American novelist, and is widely read to this very day.

From *The American Democrat* (New York, 1838).

JAMES FENIMORE COOPER

On Government

Man is known to exist in no part of the world, without certain rules for the regulation of his intercourse with those around him. It is a first necessity of his weakness, that laws, founded on the immutable principles of natural justice, should be framed, in order to protect the feeble against the violence of the strong; the honest from the schemes of the dishonest; the temperate and industrious, from the waste and indolence of the dissolute and idle. These laws, though varying with circumstances, possess a common character, being formed on that consciousness of right, which God has bestowed in order that men may judge between good and evil.

Governments have many names, which names, in all cases, are dependent on some one of the leading features of the institutions. It is usual, however, to divide governments into despotisms, limited monarchies, and republicks; but these terms are too vague to answer the objects of definitions, since many aristocracies have existed under the designation of monarchies, and many monarchies have been styled republicks.

A despotism is a government of absolute power, in which the entire authority is the possession of the prince. The term "despot," as applied to a sovereign, however, is not properly one of reproach. It merely signifies a ruler who is irresponsible for his acts, and who governs without any legal restraint on his will. The word "tyrant" had originally the same meaning, though, in a measure, both have become so far corrupted as to convey an idea of abuses.

A limited monarchy is a government in which the

will of the sovereign is restrained by certain provisions of the state, that cannot lawfully be violated. In its true signification, the word monarch means any prince at the head of a state. Monarchs are known by different titles; such as emperors, kings, princes, grand dukes, dukes, &c. &c.; but it is not now common to apply the term to any below the rank of kings. The title of sovereign is of more general use, though properly meaning the same thing as that of monarch.

A republick is a government in which the pervading acknowledged principle is the right of the community as opposed to the right of a sovereign. In other words, the term implies the sovereignty of the people, in lieu of that of a monarch. Thus nations which have possessed kings, dukes, and princes at their heads, have been termed republicks, because they have reserved the right to elect the monarchs; as was formerly the case in Poland, Venice, Genoa, and in many other of the Italian states, in particular. Even Napoleon continued to style France a republick, after he had assumed the imperial diadem, because his elevation to the throne was sanctioned by the votes of the French nation. The term, in his case, however, was evidently misapplied, for the crown was made hereditary in his family, while the polity of a republick supposes a new election on the death of the last ruler, if not oftener. In the case of Napoleon, the people elected a dynasty, rather than a prince.

In a republick the chief of the state is always elective. Perhaps this fact is the most accurate technical distinction between a monarchy and this form of government, though the pervading principle of the first is the right of the sovereign, and of the last the right of the community. The term republick, (*respublica*) means the public things, or the common weal. Hence the term commonwealth, the word wealth, in its political sense, meaning prosperity in general, and not riches in particular.

If these theoretical distinctions were rigidly respected, it would be easy to infer the real character of a government from its name; but nothing can be less alike than governments ordinarily are, in their action, and in their professions. Thus despotism can scarcely be said to exist in truth, in any part of christendom; monarchs being compelled to govern according to established laws, which laws are formed on principles reasonably just, while they are restrained in the exercise of their will by an opinion that has been created by the advanced intelligence of the age.

Some kings are monarchs only in name, the power having essentially passed into the hands of a few of their nominal subjects; and, on the other hand, some princes, who, by the constitutional principles of the system, are deemed to be but a part of the state, effectually control it, by means of bribes, rewards, and political combinations, submitting to little more restraint than the nominal despots. Just at this time, Prussia is an instance of the first of these truths, England of the second, and France of the last.

Prussia, though a despotism in theory, is governed as mildly, and, apart from political justice, as equitably and legally, as any other country. The will of the sovereign is never made to interfere, arbitrarily, with the administration of law, and the law itself proceeds from the principles that properly influence

---

Res, a thing; *publica,* public—"public things."

all legislation, though it can only receive its authority from the will of the king. That country furnishes a proof of the progress of opinion, as well as of its power to check abuses. It was only the great grandfather of the present sovereign who caused tall men to marry tall women at his command, in order to gratify a silly desire to possess a regiment of the tallest troops in the world. The influence of opinion on governments has been greatly aided by the wars and revolutions of the last, and of the present century, in which privileges have been diminished, and the rights, as well as, what is perhaps of more importance, the knowledge of their rights among the people, have been greatly augmented.

England, which is called a monarchy, is in fact a complicated but efficient aristocracy. Scarcely one of the powers that is attributed to the king by the constitution, and which were in truth exercised by his predecessors, is possessed by the present monarch in fact. By the constitution, the king of England is supposed to form a balance between the nobles and the people, whereas, in truth, his utmost influence is limited to holding a balance between parties, and this only in cases of a nearly equal force between contending factions. The extent of the authority of the king of England, at the present day, amounts to little more than the influence which he is permitted to use in minor cases, the aristocracy having devised expedients to control him on all occasions that are deemed of moment. As the mode in which this change has been effected, illustrates the manner in which governments are made to take one character, while they profess to belong to another, a brief exposition will aid the reader in understanding the subject.

The king of England can do no wrong, but the ministers are responsible to parliament. As the country has no written constitution, and laws enacted by the king, lords and commons, have the force of constitutional provisions, a system has been established, by taking advantage of the necessities of different sovereigns, by which no executive act is legal, that is not sanctioned by at least one responsible minister. It follows, the monarch can do nothing to which his parliament is seriously opposed, since no minister will incur the risk of its displeasure. It is true that the nominal assent of the king is necessary to the enactment of a law, but the ministers being responsible for the consequences if it is withheld, and the parliament alone being the judge of these consequences, as well as of the criminals, while it has an active jealousy of its own power, no instance of the exercise of this authority has occurred for more than a century. The right to withhold supplies has been the most efficient agent of the parliament, in subduing the authority of the crown.

By the theory of the British constitution, the king can declare war. Formerly this prerogative was exercised by different warlike sovereigns for personal motives. Now, the right exists only in name, for no minister would consent to give the declaration the legal forms, with the certainty of being impeached, and punished, unless acting in accordance with the wishes of parliament.

Although parliament exercises this authority in all cases of importance, the ministers are permitted to perform most minor acts of authority unquestioned, so long as they have a party in the legislature to sustain them. This party, however, is necessary to their remaining in the ministry, and it follows that the majority of parliament controls the very appointment of ministers, the only important political function that the king can now, even in theory, exercise without the intervention of a responsible minister. Were he, however, to appoint a minister in opposition to the wishes of parliament, that body would refuse the required laws. The first requisite, therefore, on the formation of a new ministry, is to enquire who can "meet parliament," as it is termed; or, in other words, what ministers will be agreeable to a majority of the legislature.

Thus, while the king of England says who shall be his ministers, the parliament says who they shall not be; and, in this instance, supported as it is by a control of all legislation, the negative power is found to be stronger than the affirmative. In reality, the ministers of Great-Britain are appointed by the parliament of the country, and not by the king, and this is virtually neutralizing, if not directly annihilating, all the available authority of the latter.

In theory, the government of France and that of Great-Britain have the same general character. In practice, however, owing to the greater political advancement of the last of these two countries, France to-day, is not far from the point where England stood a century since. Then the king of England ruled through his parliament, whereas now the parliament rules through the king. On the other hand, with much of the machinery of a free state, the king of the French governs himself. A dread of the people's getting the ascendancy, causes the aristocracy to lend itself to the power of the crown, which not only dictates the law, but, in many cases, proves to be stronger than the law itself. Of the three countries, perhaps legality is more respected in Prussia and

Austria, both despotisms in theory, than in France, which has the profession of a limited monarchy. This difference is owing to the security of the two first governments, and to the insecurity of the last.

These facts show the necessity of distinguishing between names and things in governments, as well as in other matters. The institutions of no country are rigidly respected in practice, owing to the cupidity and passions of men; and vigilance in the protection of principles is even more necessary in a democracy than in a monarchy, as their violation is more certain to affect the interests of the people under such a form of government than under any other. A violation of the principles of a democracy is at the loss of the people, while, in a monarchy, it is usually their gain.

JAMES FENIMORE COOPER

On Republicks

Republics have been as liable to frauds, and to departures from their professions, as any other polities, though no government can properly be termed a republick at all, in which the predominant authority of a single hereditary ruler is acknowledged. In all republicks there must be more or less of direct representation, however much its influence is lessened by the duration and by the magnitude of the trusts.

Poland was formerly termed a republick, because the kingly office was elective, and on account of the power of the Diet. At that time any member of this body could defeat a law by exclaiming in Latin, *Veto* (I forbid it,) from which usage the word *veto* has been adopted as a substantive, in most of the languages of christendom, to express the same power in the different executive rulers; which it is now common to term the "veto-power." The exercise of this right was found so inconvenient in practice, that, at length, in cases of gravity, the nobles of the Diet would draw their swords, and menace the dissenting member with death, unless he withdrew his "veto." As a negative authority often has the efficiency of that which is affirmative, it is scarcely possible to conceive a system in which the will of a majority was less consulted than in this.

The republick of Venice was an hereditary aristocracy, as, in a great measure, was that of ancient Rome. The term, in its true signification, perhaps, infers a free government, for it means a representation of the general interests of the state, but, as in practice, this representation became confined purely to the interests of the state, and the state itself was under the control of a few who did not fail to turn their authority to their private advantage, the system has oftener resulted in abuses than even that of monarchies. The profession of a free government, in which the facts do not frankly concur, usually tends to gross wrongs, in order to conceal and protect the frauds. In Venice, such was the jealousy and tyranny of the state, that a secret council existed, with an authority that was almost despotick, while it was inquisitorial, and which was removed from the usual responsibility of opinion, by an expedient that was devised to protect its members from the ordinary liabilities of common censure. This council consisted of three nobles, who held their office for a limited period, and were appointed by drawing lots, each person concealing the fact of the lot's having fallen on himself, until he met his associates at an appointed place. It is an extraordinary fact, that the same expedient was devised to conceal the murderers, in the well known case of Morgan, who fell a victim to the exaggeration and weakness of some of the members of the Masonic Fraternity.

By examining the different republicks of ancient and modern times, it would be found that most of them had little more than the profession of liberty, though all substituted in them the right of the community for that of a monarch, as a primary principle. This feature, then, must be taken as the distinction between this form of government and that of kingdoms, or of the sovereignties in which one rules, or is supposed to rule.

Republicks may be aristocratical, or democratical; and they may so nearly approach both, as to render

it matter of doubt to which class they properly belong; for the political combinations of communities,
in a practical sense, are so numerous as almost to
defeat accurate general definitions.

JAMES FENIMORE COOPER

On the Republick of the United States of America

The government of the United States, differs from all others that have preceded it, though some imitations have been attempted in the southern parts of this continent. Its novelty, no less than its complicated nature, arising from its double system, has given birth to many errors in relation to its principles and its action, even among its own citizens, as well as among strangers.

The polity of the United States is that of a confederated republick, but the power of the federal government acting in most instances on the body of the community, without the intervention of the several states, it has been better styled a Union. This word, which is original as applied to a political system, was first given to this form of confederation, and is intended to express the greater intimacy of the relations of the parties, than those of all previous examples. It exists in the constitution however, only as it is used in setting forth the motives for substituting that instrument for the old articles of confederation: the constitution being silent as to the particular polity of the country, except as it recognizes the general term of a republick.

The word constitution, of itself, properly implies a more identified form of government, than that which is usually understood to exist under a confederation; the first inferring a social compact, fundamental and predominant, the last a league between independent sovereignties. These distinctions have a certain weight, though they are rather arbitrary than logical, since men may create any degree of allegiance, or of liability they may deem expedient, under any form, or modes of government. To deny this is to deny to bodies of human beings the right of self-government, a gift of nature. Though possessing a common end, governments are, in reality, subject to no laws but those of their own establishing.

The government of the United States was formed by the several states of the Union, as they existed at the period when the constitution was adopted, and one of its leading principles is, that all power which is not granted to the federal authority, remain in the states themselves, or what is virtually the same thing, in the people of the states. This principle follows as a necessary consequence from the nature of the grants to the federal government, but it has been clearly expressed in a clause of the instrument, that was introduced by way of amendment, in 1801. This feature distinguishes this federal government from all the federal governments that have gone before it, as it was the general and ancient rule that liberty existed as a concession from authority; whereas, here, we find authority existing as a concession from the ruled. Something like the same principle exists in the governments of the several states, and it once existed in the ancient democracies, though, in no other known system perhaps, as clearly and as unequivocally as in this, since it is a general maxim that governments should have all power, however much they may restrain themselves in its exercise.

In the conflict of parties, the question by whom the federal government was formed, has been agitated with more seriousness than the point at issue merited, since, the fact admitted that the power which framed it did not exceed its authority, it is much more essential to know what was done, than to ascertain who did it. The notion that the *people* of the United States, in the popular signification of the word, framed the government, is contrary to fact, and leads to a wrong interpretation of many of the distinctive features of the system. The constitution of the United States was formed by a convention composed of delegates elected by the different states, in modes prescribed by their several laws and usages. These delegates voted by states, and not as individuals, and the instrument was referred back to conventions in the respective states for approval, or ratification. It is a governing principle of political maxims, that the power to ratify, is the power that possesses the authority in the last resort. Thus, treaties between independent sovereignties, are never valid until ratified by the high treaty-making powers of the respective countries. As the several states of this Union first acted through delegates of their own appointing, and then ratified their acts, in conventions also chosen by constituencies of their own selection, it is not easy to establish any thing more plainly than the fact, that the constitution of the United States was framed by the states then in existence, as communities, and not by the body of the people of the Union, or by the body of the people of the states, as has been sometimes contended.

In favor of the latter opinion, it is maintained that the several states were an identified nation previously to the formation of the government, and the preamble of the constitution itself, has been quoted to prove that the compact was formed by the *people,* as distinct from the states. This preamble commences by saying that "We the people of the United States," for reasons that are then set forth, have framed the instrument that follows; but in respecting a form of phraseology, it, of necessity, neither establishes a fact, nor sets up a principle, and when we come to examine the collateral circumstances, we are irresistably led to regard it merely as a naked and vague profession.

That the several states were virtually parts of one entire nation previously to the formation of any separate general government, proves nothing in the premises, as the very circumstance that a polity distinct from that of Great Britain was established by our ancestors, who were members of the great community that was then united in one entire nation, sufficiently shows that these parts can separate, and act independently of each other. Such a circumstance might be, and probably it was, a strong motive for forming a more identified government, but it cannot properly be quoted as authority for, or against any of its provisions. The latter are a mere question of fact, and as such their construction must depend on their intention as explained in language.

The term "people," like most other substantives, has its general and its specific significations. In its general signification, the people of a country, means the population of a country; as the population of a country includes the women and children, nothing can be clearer than that the "people," in this signification, did not form the American constitution. The specific significations of this word are numerous, as rich, poor, wise, silly, good and bad people. In a political sense, the people means those who are vested with political rights, and, in this particular instance, the people vested with political rights, were the constituencies of the several states, under their various laws, modifications and constitutions, which is but another name for the governments of the states themselves. "We the *people*," as used in the preamble of the constitution, means merely, "We the *constituencies* of the several states."

It follows, that the constitution of the United States was formed by the states, and not by the people of the entire country, as contended; the term used in the preamble being used in contra-distinction to the old divine right of sovereigns, and as a mode of expressing the general republican character of the government. The states, by a prescribed majority, can also amend the constitution, altering any of its provisions, with the exception of that which guaranties the equal representation of the states in the senate. It might be shown, that states possessing a minority of all the people of the Union can alter the constitution, a fact, in itself, which proves that the government of the United States, though a republick, is not necessarily a popular government, in the broadest meaning of the word. The constitution leaves the real character of the institutions of the country, with the exception that it prohibits monarchies, to be settled by the several states themselves.

On the other hand, too much importance is attached to what is called the reserved sovereignties of the several states. A community can hardly be termed sovereign at all, which has parted with all the great powers of sovereignty, such as the control of foreign relations, the authority to make war and peace, to regulate commerce, to coin money, keep fleets and armies, with all the other powers that have been ceded by the states to the federal government. But, admitting that the rights reserved are sovereign in their ordinary nature, they are scarcely so in the conditions under which they are enjoyed, since, by an amendment of the constitution, a state may be deprived of most of them, without its own consent. A community so situated can scarcely be deemed sovereign, or even independent.

The habit of drawing particular inferences from general theories, in matters as purely practical as those of government, is at all times dangerous, and the safest mode of construing the constitution of the United States, is by looking only at the instrument itself, without adverting to other systems, except as they may serve to give the proper signification of the terms of that instrument, as these terms were understood at the time it was framed.

Many popular errors exist on the subject of the influence of the federal constitution on the rights and liberties of the citizen. The rights and liberties of the citizen, in a great degree, depend on the political institutions of the several states, and not on those of the Union. Many of these errors have arisen from mistaking the meaning of the language of the constitution. Thus, when the constitution says that no laws shall be passed abridging the rights of the citizen in any particular thing, it refers to the power which, under that particular constitution, has the authority to pass a law at all. This power, under the government of the United States, is Congress, and no other.

An example will better show the distinction. In art. 6th of the amendments to the constitution, we find the following clause: "In all criminal prosecutions, the accused shall enjoy the right of a speedy and *public* trial, by an impartial *jury,*" &c. &c. &c. It is not the meaning of this provision of the constitution, that, under the laws of the several states, the citizen shall be entitled to a *public* trial by a *jury,* but that these privileges shall be assured to those who are accused of crimes against the laws of the United

States. It is true, that similar privileges, as they are deemed essential to the liberties of their citizens, are assured to them by the constitutions of the several states, but this has been done by voluntary acts of their own, every state having full power, so far as the constitution of the United States has any control over it, to cause its accused to be tried in secret, or without the intervention of juries, as the people of that particular state may see fit.

There is nothing in the constitution of the United States, to prevent all the states, or any particular state, from possessing an established religion, from putting the press under the control of censors, from laying restrictions and penalties on the rights of speech, or from imposing most of the political and civil restraints on the citizen, that are imposed under any other form of government.

The guarantees for the liberties of the citizen, given by the constitution of the United States, are very limited, except as against the action of the government of the Union alone. Congress may not pass any law establishing a religion, or abridging the freedom of speech, or of the press, but the provisions of the constitution relating to these subjects, have no reference to the rights of the states. This distinction is very essential to a correct understanding of the institutions of the country, as many are misled on the subject. Some of the states, for example, are rigid in enforcing respect for the sabbath, and a popular notion has prevailed that their laws are unconstitutional, since the federal compact guaranties liberty of conscience. This guarantee, like most of the others of the same nature, is only against the acts of Congress, and not against the acts of the states themselves. A state may pass any law it please to restrain the abuses of the sabbath, provided it do not infringe on the provisions of its own constitution, or invade a right conceded to the United States. It cannot stop the mail for instance, or the passage of troops in the service of the federal government, but it may stop all who are not thus constitutionally protected by the superior power of the Union.

This reading of the constitution is in conformity with all the rules of construction, but that it is right, can be shown from the language of the instrument itself. In article 1st, section 9th, clause 3d, we find this provision—"No bill of attainder, or *ex post facto* law, shall be passed." In article 1st, section 10th, clause 1st, which section is composed entirely of restraints on the power of the states, we find this provision—"No *state* shall pass any bill of attainder, *ex post facto* law, &c. &c." Had the provision of the clause 3d, sect. 9th, been intended to limit the powers of the states, clause 1st, sect. 10th, would clearly have been unnecessary. The latter provision therefore, is one of the few instances, in which the power of the states themselves, is positively restrained by the constitution of the United States.

Although the several states have conceded to the United States most of the higher attributes of sovereignty, they have reserved to themselves nearly all of the functions that render governments free, or otherwise. In declaring war, regulating commerce, keeping armies and navies, coining money, which are all high acts of sovereignty, despotisms and democracies are alike; all forms of governments equally controlling these interests, and usually in the same manner.

The characters of institutions depend on the

repositories of power, in the last resort. In despotisms the monarch is this repository; in aristocracies,
the few; in democracies, the many. By the constitution of the United States, its government is composed of different representations, which are
chosen, more or less directly, by the constituencies of
the several states. As there is no common rule for the
construction of these constituencies, their narrow-
ness, or width, must depend on the fundamental
laws of the states, themselves. It follows that the
federal government has no fixed character, so far as
the nature of its constituency is concerned, but one
that may constantly vary, and which has materially
varied since the commencement of the government,
though, as yet, its changes have always been in the
direction of popular rights.

The only distinctive restriction imposed by the
constitution of the United States on the character of
the state governments, is that contained in article
4th, section 4th, clause 1st, which guarantees to each
state a republican form of government. No monarchy, therefore, can exist in this country, as existed
formerly, and now exists, in the confederation of
Germany. But a republican form of government is
not necessarily a free government. Aristocracies are
oftener republicks than any thing else, and they
have been among the most oppressive governments
the world has ever known.

No state can grant any title of nobility; but titles of
nobility are oftener the consequence than the cause
of narrow governments. Neither Venice, Poland,
Genoa, Berne, (a canton of Switzerland,) nor most of
the other narrow aristocracies of Europe, had any
titular nobles, though some of these countries were

afflicted by governments of great oppression. Any state of this Union, by altering its own constitution, may place the power of its own government, and, by consequence, its representation in the government of the United States, in any dozen families, making it perpetual and hereditary. The only guarantee against such an act is to be found in the discretion of the people of the several states, none of whom would probably part with power for such a purpose, and the check which the other states might hold over any one of their body, by amending the constitution. As this instrument now exists, however, there can be no reasonable doubts of the power of any one, or of all the states, so to alter their polities.

By considering these facts, we learn the true nature of the government, which may be said to have both a theoretical character, and one in fact. In theory, this character is vague, and, with the immaterial exception of the exclusion of a monarchy and the maintenance of the representative form, one altogether dependent on the policy of the states, by which it may be made a representative aristocracy, a representative democracy, or a union of the two. The government, in fact, is a near approach to that of a representative democracy, though it is not without a slight infusion from a few mild aristocracies. So long as slavery exists in the country, or, it were better to say, so long as the African race exists, some portion of this aristocratic infusion will probably remain.

Stress is laid on the foregoing distinctions, because the government of the Union is a compact between separate communities, and popular misconceptions on the nature of the institutions, in a nation so much controlled by popular opinion, not only lead to injustice, but may lead to dissension. It is the duty of every citizen to acquire just notions of the terms of the bargain before he pretends to a right to enforce them.

JAMES FENIMORE COOPER

On Property

As property is the base of all civilization, its existence and security are indispensable to social improvement. Were it possible to have a community of property, it would soon be found that no one would toil, but that men would be disposed to be satisfied with barely enough for the supply of their physical wants, since none would exert themselves to obtain advantages solely for the use of others. The failure of all attempts to form communities, even on a small scale, with a common interest, goes to prove this. Where there is a rigid equality of condition, as well as of rights, that condition must necessarily be one of a low scale of mediocrity, since it is impossible to elevate those who do not possess the requisite qualities any higher. Thus we see that the societies, or religious sects, in which a community of property prevails, are content with merely supplying the wants of life, knowing little or nothing of its elegancies, refinements, or mental pleasures. These communities, moreover, possess an outlet for their idle and dissolute, by resorting to expulsion, a remedy that society itself cannot apply. . . .

In nations where the mass have no political rights, means have been found to accumulate power by the aid of wealth. The pretence has been that none but the rich have a stake in society. Every man who has wants, feelings, affections and character, has a stake in society. Of the two, perhaps, the necessities of men are a greater corrective of political abuses, than their surplus means. Both may lead to evil, beyond a doubt, but, as laws which are framed by all, must be tolerably impartial and general in their operation, less danger arises from the rule of the former, than from the rule of the latter. When property rules, it rules alone; but when the poor are admitted to have a voice in government, the rich are never excluded. Such is the nature of man, that all exclusive power is uniformly directed to exclusive purposes. Property always carries with it a portion of indirect political influence, and it is unwise, and even dangerous, to strengthen this influence by adding to it constitutional privileges; the result always being to make the strong stronger, and the weak weaker.

On the other hand, all who love equal justice, and, indeed, the safety of free institutions, should understand that property has its rights, and the necessity of rigidly respecting them. It is the right of the possessor of property to be placed on an equal footing with all his fellow citizens, in every respect. If he is not to be exalted on account of his wealth, neither is he to be denounced. In this country, it is the intention of the institutions, that money should neither increase nor lessen political influence.

There are habits that belong to every condition of life. The man of hereditary wealth, is usually a man of leisure, and he little understands the true spirit of democracy, who supposes that such a man is not to enjoy the tastes and inclinations, which are the fruits of leisure and cultivation, without let or hindrance. Democracy leaves every man the master of his acts and time, his tastes and habits, so long as he discharges his duty to the publick, and respects the laws. He who declaims against another for holding himself aloof from general association, arrogates to himself a power of censure that he does not rightly possess, and betrays his own consciousness of inferiority. Men of really high social station never make this complaint, for they are above jealousy; and they who do, only discover a feeling that is every way removed from the manliness and spirit of true inde-. pendence.

One may certainly be purse-proud, and of all the sources of human pride, mere wealth is the basest and most vulgar minded. Real gentlemen are almost invariably above this low feeling, and they who attribute habits, that have their rise in sentiment, tastes, knowledge and refinement, to such a cause, usually make the mistake of letting their own ignorance of the existence of motives so elevated, be known. In a word, if the man of property has no more personal legal immunities, than the man who has none, neither has he fewer. He is privileged to use his own means, under the general regulations of society, in the pursuit of his own happiness, and they who would interfere with him, so far from appreciating liberty, are ignorant of its vital principles.

If left to itself, unsupported by factitious political aid, but sufficiently protected against the designs and rapacity of the dishonest, property is an instrument of working most of the good that society enjoys. It elevates a national character, by affording the means of cultivating knowledge and the tastes; it introduces all above barbarism into society; and it encourages and sustains laudable and useful efforts in individuals. Like every other great good, its abuses are in proportion to its benefits.

The possessor of property is not, half the time, as much the object of envy as the needy imagine, for its corrupting influence endangers eternal peace. Great estates are generally of more benefit to the community than to their owners. They bring with them anxiety, cares, demands, and, usually, exaggerated notions, on the part of the publick, of the duties of the rich. So far from being objects of envy, their possessors are oftener the subjects of commiseration; he who has enough for his rational wants, agreeably to his habits and education, always proving the happier man.

The possessions of new families are commonly exaggerated in the publick mind, while those of long established families are as commonly diminished.

A people that deems the possession of riches its highest source of distinction, admits one of the most degrading of all influences to preside over its opinions. At no time, should money be ever ranked as more than a means, and he who lives as if the acquisition of property were the sole end of his existence, betrays the dominion of the most sordid, base, and grovelling motive, that life offers.

Property is desirable as the ground work of moral independence, as a means of improving the faculties, and of doing good to others, and as the agent in all that distinguishes the civilized man from the savage.

Property has been made the test of political rights, in two distinct forms. It has been *represented,* and it has been established as a *qualification.* The *representation* of property is effected in two modes; first, by giving the proprietor more votes than one, according to the number and situation of his freeholds; and, secondly, by raising the test of qualification so high, as to exclude all but the affluent from the franchise. The first was the English system, previously to the recent changes; the last, is the actual system of France.

A government founded on the representation of property, however direct or indirect, is radically vicious, since it is a union of two of the most corrupting influences to which man is subject. It is the proper business of government to resist the corruptions of money, and not to depend on them.

To a qualification of property, if placed so low as to embrace the great majority of the people, there is no very serious objection, though better tests might, perhaps, be devised. Residence, character, information, and fixed relations with society, ought to be added to this qualification; and it might be better, even, could they be made entirely to supersede it. In local governments, or those of towns and villages, which do little more than control property, a low property qualification is the true test of the franchise, though even in these cases, it might be well to add information and character.